Viaja por avión.
(He travels by airplane.)

BARRON'S E-Z SPANISH GRAMMAR

Boris Corredor, Ph.D.

BARRON'S

Second Edition

Illustrations: Dre Design
Illustrations on pages 17, 19, 25, 26, 29, 32, 35, 37, 173: Alfredo Garzón

ISBN-13: 978-0-7641-4249-9
ISBN-10: 0-7641-4249-6
Library of Congress Control Number 2009031371

All inquiries should be addressed to:
Barron's Educational Series, Inc.
250 Wireless Boulevard
Hauppauge, New York 11788
www.barronseduc.com

Library of Congress Cataloging-in-Publication Data
Corredor, Boris
E-Z Spanish grammar / Boris Corredor. — 2nd ed.
p. cm.
Prev. ed. cataloged under the title: Spanish grammar the easy way.
ISBN-13: 978-0-7641-4249-9
ISBN-10: 0-7641-4249-6
1. Spanish language—Grammar. I. Corredor, Boris Spanish grammar the easy way.
II. Title. III. Title: Easy Spanish grammar.
PC4105.C66 2010
468.2'421—dc22 2009031371

Printed in the United States of America
9 8 7 6 5 4 3 2 1

CONTENTS

INTRODUCTION

E-Z Spanish Grammar is intended for individual learners who need essential information on the structure of the Spanish language or for students enrolled in a formal language course. It will also be useful to anybody who is planning a trip to Latin America or Spain and wishes to go beyond a basic level.

This book is designed to give students a clear picture of the form and function of Spanish, and to help them develop comprehension and vocabulary skills in a user-friendly and interesting way.

E-Z Spanish Grammar is organized into 18 chapters that cover pronunciation, parts of speech, and specific features of Spanish grammar that students often find daunting or, at the very least, confusing. In order to further assist the learner, contrasts are made between English and Spanish so as to highlight similarities and differences in grammatical concepts, syntax, and vocabulary. Every topic is immediately followed by practice exercises designed to increase comprehension and to develop vocabulary. After completing these exercises, students should check their answers using the Answer Keys found in Appendix A.

All questions and answers should be read aloud in order to practice pronunciation and to improve comprehension. The glossary at the end of the text (Appendix B) offers the meaning of each word as well as its grammatical function; it should be consulted often. Throughout the book, students will encounter "Tip Boxes" that clarify aspects of grammar that often are confusing or difficult.

The organization of the book by grammar topics allows for flexible use. The learner may go through it sequentially or choose to focus on a particular area where he or she needs more reinforcement.

Boris Corredor
Boston, December 2009

1

Pronunciation

This chapter focuses on Spanish pronunciation. We will compare the "sounds" in Spanish and English as well as compare their written forms related to pronunciation (i.e. accent marks).

TIP BOX

Speech sounds are called *phonemes*; these phoneme symbols are written in slant brackets.

TIP BOX

American Spanish has eighteen consonant phonemes and ten vowel phonemes; Castilian Spanish, which is mainly spoken in Northern Spain, has two more consonant phonemes. These regional distinctions, however, will not be treated in this book.

I. Vowels

A. VOWEL SOUNDS

The phoneme **/a/** in Spanish is represented by the letter <a> and it is pronounced like the English <a> in the words "f**a**r," "f**a**ther," "p**a**lm." The phoneme **/a/** is also pronounced in Spanish as the letter <o> in English, as in the words "l**o**ck," "h**o**t," "r**o**t," "c**o**t," "t**o**p."

Example

<m**a**-s**a**> *(dough)*

The phoneme **/e/** in Spanish is represented by the letter <e>. The closest pronunciation is the English <e> in the word "**e**gg" or the <a> in the word "l**a**te." In Spanish, this sound is shorter and crisper than the sound in English.

Example

<b**e**-b**é**> *(baby)*

The phoneme **/i/** in Spanish is represented by the letter <i>. The Spanish <i> is pronounced like the <ea> in the word "l**ea**k" or the <e> in the word "b**e**" or <ee> in the word "b**ee**," or <ea> in the word "b**ea**t." In Spanish, the sound is shorter than the sound in English.

Example

<s**í**> *(yes)*

The phoneme **/o/** in Spanish is represented by the letter <o>. The Spanish <o> is pronounced like the <o> in the words "l**o**cation," "b**o**w," or "b**o**at," except that the sound is shorter.

Example

<b**o**-b**o**> *(dumb)*

The phoneme **/u/** in Spanish is represented by the letter <u>. The Spanish <u> is pronounced like the <u> in the word "L**u**ke" or the <oo> in the word "l**oo**k." Again, the difference is that in Spanish the sound is shorter.

Example

<b**u**s> *(bus)*

B. SEMIVOWEL DIPHTHONG SOUNDS

The phoneme **/aw/** in Spanish is represented by the combination letters <au>. This phoneme is composed of the phonemes /a/ and /u/ and it is pronounced as one syllable. The closest like pronunciation is the English <o> in the words "c**o**w," "h**o**w." In Spanish, however, the final /u/ sound is longer.

Example

<**au**-la> *(classroom)*

The phoneme **/ay/** in Spanish is represented by the combination letters <ai> and <ay>. This phoneme is composed of the phonemes /a/ and /i/ and it is pronounced as one syllable. The closest pronunciation is the <i> in the word "h**i**gh." In Spanish, the final /i/ sound is longer.

Example

<**ai**-re> *(air)*
<h**ay**> *(there is)*

The phoneme **/ew/** in Spanish is represented by the combination letters <eu>. This phoneme is composed of the phonemes /e/ and /u/ and it is pronounced as one syllable. There is no close pronunciation in English.

Example

<**Eu**-ro-pa> *(Europe)*

The phoneme **/ey/** in Spanish is represented by the combination letters <ei> and <ey>. This phoneme is composed of the phonemes /e/ and /i/ and it is pronounced as one syllable. The closest pronunciation is the <ay> in the words "b**ay**" and "l**ay**." In Spanish, the final /i/ sound is longer.

Example

<r**ei**-na> *(queen)*
<r**ey**> *(king)*

The phoneme **/oy/** in Spanish is represented by the combination letters <oi> and <oy>. This phoneme is composed of the phonemes /o/ and /i/ and it is pronounced as one syllable. The closest pronunciation is the <oy> in the word "b**oy**." The difference is that in Spanish the final /i/ sound is longer.

Example

<b**oi**-na> *(beret)*
<h**oy**> *(today)*

II. Consonants

A. CONSONANT SOUNDS

The phoneme **/b/** in Spanish is represented by the letters <b> and <v>. If either is at the beginning of a word or follows a consonant, it is pronounced like an English <b>. Otherwise, they have a sound that falls somewhere in between the <b> and the <v>.

Example

<**b**ar-co>	(*boat*)	<á-**ba**-co>	(*abacus*)
<**v**a-ca>	(*cow*)	<a-**ve**>	(*bird*)
<a**b**-so-lu-to>	(*absolute*)		

The phoneme **/č/** in Spanish is represented by the letter <ch> and it is pronounced like the <ch> in "**ch**ocolate."

Example

<**chi**-**cha**>	(South American indigenous drink made from corn)

The phoneme **/d/** in Spanish is represented by the letter <d> and it is pronounced like the <d> in English. However, when it falls between vowels and follows <l> or <n>, it is pronounced like the <th> in "**th**e."

Example

<**d**os>	(*two*)	<cal-**d**o>	(*broth*)
<ha-**d**a>	(*fairy*)	<ven-**d**er>	(*to sell*)

The phoneme **/f/** in Spanish is represented by the letter <f> and it is pronounced like <f> in the word "**f**ather."

Example

<**f**a-mi-lia>	(*family*)
<**f**a-ma>	(*fame*)

The phoneme **/g/** in Spanish is represented by the letter <g>. It is pronounced /g/ only when followed by <a, o, u>, like the letter <g> in the word "**g**et."

Example

<**ga**-to>	(*cat*)	<**gu**-sa-no>	(*worm*)
<**go**-rra>	(*cap*)		

The phoneme **/h/** in Spanish is represented by the letter <j>, and by <g> when the latter is followed by <e, i>. It is pronounced like the English <h>, but stronger.

Example

<**j**i-ra-fa>	(*giraffe*)	<**g**i-rar>	(*to spin*)
<**G**e-rar-do>	(*Gerard*)		

The phoneme **/k/** in Spanish is represented by the letter <c> when it is followed by <a, o, u>. Similarly, the letter <q>, when followed by <ue, ui>, is pronounced /ke/ and /ki/. The letter <k>, as in the example "*kilogramo*," is pronounced like the <c> in the word "**c**at."

Example

<**c**a-sa>	(*house*)	<bu-**q**ue>	(*ship*)
<**c**o-mi-da>	(*food*)	<**q**uin-to>	(*fifth*)
<**c**u-ra>	(*priest*)	<**k**i-lo>	(*kilogram*)

The phoneme **/l/** in Spanish is represented by the letter <l> and it is pronounced like an English <l>.

Example

<**l**o-bo> (*wolf*)

The phoneme **/m/** in Spanish is represented by the letter <m> and it is pronounced like an English <m>.

Example

<**m**a-**m**á> (*mother*)

The phoneme **/n/** in Spanish is represented by the letter <n> and it is pronounced like an English <n>.

Example

<**n**o> (*no*)

The phoneme **/ñ/** in Spanish is represented by the letter <ñ> and it is pronounced like the <n> in the word "ca**ny**on."

Example

<ca-**ñ**ón> (*cannon*)

The phoneme **/p/** in Spanish is represented by the letter <p> and it is pronounced like an English <p>.

Example

<**p**e-lo> (*hair*)

The phoneme **/r/** in Spanish is represented by the letter <r>. When a word does **not** begin with an initial <r> or is preceded by <l, n, s>, the <r> is pronounced like the English <r> in "**r**ain."

Example

<a-**r**o> *(hoop)*

The phoneme **/rr/** in Spanish is represented by the letter <r> when a word begins with <r> or the letter <r> is preceded by <l, n, s> or by the letters <rr> in the middle of a word. The /rr/ phoneme is pronounced as an English <r> but stronger, which in Spanish is done by trilling the tongue.

Example

<**r**a-tón>	*(mouse)*	<son-**r**i-sa>	*(smile)*
<al-**r**e-de-dor>	*(around)*	<Is-**r**a-el>	*(Israel)*

The phoneme **/s/** in Latin American Spanish is represented by the letter <s>, the letter <c> when followed by <e, i>, or the letter <z>. It is pronounced like the English <s> in the word "**s**un."

Example

<ab-**s**ur-do>	*(absurd)*	<**c**in-co>	*(five)*
<**c**e-los>	*(jealousy)*	<**z**a-pa-to>	*(shoe)*

The phoneme **/t/** in Spanish is represented by the letter <t> and it is pronounced like an English <t>.

Example

<**t**an-go> *(tango)*

B. SEMICONSONANT SOUNDS

The phoneme **/y/** in Latin American Spanish is represented by the letter <y>, by the letter <i> when the latter is followed by <a, e, o, u>, and by the letter <ll> when the latter is followed by <a, e, i, o, u>. It is pronounced like the English <y> in "**y**ou."

Example

<**y**a>	*(already)*	<v**i**o>	*(saw)*
<ha-c**i**a>	*(towards)*	<v**i**u-da>	*(widow)*
<h**i**e-lo>	*(ice)*	<ca-**ll**e>	*(street)*

The phoneme **/w/** in Spanish is represented by the letter <u> when it is followed by <a, e, i, o>. It is pronounced like the English <w> in "**w**ell."

Example

<**cu**an-do>	(*when*)	<**cu**o-ta>	(*quota*)
<h**ue**-vo>	(*egg*)	<**cu**i-dar>	(*to take care of*)

Exercise 1. Match the syllables that have a similar sound. A few answers will involve two syllables.

1. ca	a. ke	1. ________
2. bo	b. va	2. ________
3. co	c. gi	3. ________
4. ji	d. lla	4. ________
5. sa	e. ka	5. ________
6. bu	f. ce	6. ________
7. yi	g. za	7. ________
8. ya	h. ko	8. ________
9. ba	i. zu	9. ________
10. que	j. ki	10. ________
11. je	k. zi	11. ________
12. qui	l. ze	12. ________
13. so	m. vi	13. ________
14. se	n. llu	14. ________
15. bi	o. llo	15. ________
16. yo	p. vo	16. ________
17. si	q. ci	17. ________
18. be	r. ku	18. ________
19. ye	s. lle	19. ________
20. cu	t. lli	20. ________
21. su	u. zo	21. ________
22. yu	v. ge	22. ________
	w. ve	
	x. vu	

Exercise 2. Mark with ✔ the words that contain the sound /r/ and with ✗ those that have the sound /rr/.

1. furia _____	7. muerto _____	13. roto _____
2. verde _____	8. Ramón _____	14. riñón _____
3. río _____	9. ratón _____	15. rama _____
4. aro _____	10. mar _____	16. avaro _____
5. Israel _____	11. cura _____	17. mujer _____
6. carro _____	12. barril _____	18. alrededor _____

Exercise 3. Read the following words aloud and divide them into syllables.

1.	furia	________	muerto	________	rabia	________
2.	huevo	________	Diana	________	cuidado	________
3.	tiempo	________	verde	________	Juan	________
4.	juego	________	agua	________	viuda	________
5.	viaja	________	carroña	________	guarida	________
6.	ciudad	________	tregua	________	lengua	________
7.	puente	________	recuerdo	________	abuelo	________
8.	nieve	________	tiempo	________	reumatismo	________
9.	viuda	________	Luisa	________	viruela	________
10.	pañuelo	________	azalea	________	Europa	________
11.	antiguo	________	cuanto	________	cuadro	________

Exercise 4. Pronounce and memorize the following tongue twisters.

1. Erre con erre cigarro,
   erre con erre barril,
   rápido corren los carros,
   cargados de azúcar al ferrocarril.

Translation:
R with an R, cigar.
R with an R, barrel.
Rapid travel the cars (of the train)
carrying the railroad's sugar.

2. Tres tristes tigres comían trigo,
   en tres tristes trastos repletos de trigo.

Translation:
Three sad tigers ate wheat.
From three sad pots full of wheat.

3. Compadre, cómprame un coco.
   Compadre, coco no compro,
   que el que poco coco come,
   poco coco compra.

Translation:
"Friend, buy me a coconut."
"Friend, I don't buy coconuts,
because he who eats few coconuts,
few coconuts buys."

4. Pablito clavó un clavito,
   ¿qué clavito clavó Pablito?

Translation:
Pablito nailed a nail.
Which nail nailed Pablito?

5. El amor es una locura
   que sólo el cura lo cura,
   pero el cura que lo cura
   comete una gran locura.

Translation:
Love is a crazy thing
that only a priest can cure,
but the priest who cures it
commits a crazy act.

III. Intonation

TIP BOX

Words are built by a process of combining consonants and vowels in characteristic patterns that are unique for each language that uses the alphabetic system. Once you understand the sound system in Spanish, the next step is to understand the rules for intonation.

Intonation means the stress you put on a specific syllable in a word as well as the pitch you apply on syllables when you pronounce a whole sentence. In Spanish, words are built by stressed (tonal) and non-stressed (atonal) syllables. In contrast with English, words in Spanish have only one stressed syllable.

TIP BOX

In Spanish, stress placement may have a grammatical function, that is, changing the stress to another syllable can change the part of speech and the meaning of the word.

Example

pa-pá (father)	*pa-pa (potato)*
lás-ti-ma (pity)	*las-ti-ma (hurt)*

Exercise 5. Read the following verses to practice intonation in Spanish.

Nuestras vidas son los ríos
que van a dar en la mar,
que es el morir.
Jorge Manrique (1440–1479)

Translation:
Our lives are rivers
that flow into the sea,
which is death.

Verde que te quiero verde.
Verde viento. Verdes ramas.
El barco sobre la mar
y el caballo en la montaña.
Federico García Lorca (1898–1936)

Translation:
Green, how I want you green.
Green wind. Green branches.
The ship out on the sea
and the horse on the mountain.

¡Juventud, divino tesoro,
ya te vas para no volver!
Cuando quiero llorar, no lloro
y a veces lloro sin querer...
Rubén Darío (1867–1916)

Translation:
Youth, divine treasure,
you leave never to return!
When I want to cry, I cannot
and sometimes I cry without wanting to...

La más bella niña de nuestro lugar,
hoy viuda y sola, y ayer por casar,
viendo que sus ojos a la guerra van,
a su madre dice, que escucha su mal:
"Dejadme llorar a orillas del mar".
Luis de Góngora (1561–1627)

Translation:
The loveliest girl in all our countryside,
today forsaken, yesterday a bride,
Seeing her love ride forth to join the wars,
to her mother says,
"Let me cry at the seashore."

IV. The Spanish Accentuation System

A. WORDS ENDING IN *VOWEL* OR CONSONANT *N* OR *S*

The accentuation system in Spanish is very simple. When words end in a **vowel** or the consonant **n** or **s**, the next to last syllable is stressed.

Example

ca-lle (*street*), es-tu-**dian**-te (*student*), **be**-llo (*beautiful*), es-tu-**dian**-tes (*students*), **can**-tan (*they sing*)

B. WORDS ENDING IN *CONSONANTS* OTHER THAN *N* OR *S*

For words ending in a consonant other than **n** or **s,** the stress falls on the last syllable.

Example

co-**lor** (*color*)
a-**rroz** (*rice*)
fe-**liz** (*happy*)

Exceptions for the rules above are words marked with an accent showing which syllable is stressed.

Example

lá-*piz* (*pencil*)
a-***vión*** (*airplane*)

C. DIPHTHONGS

When two vowels are side by side (example: viuda: *widow*), it is important to distinguish if both vowels are part of the same syllable or are divided into different syllables. To understand how this is done, remember that the combination of a strong vowel (a, e, o) with a weak vowel (i, u) or the combination of two weak vowels (i, u) together form **one** unique sound.

In these cases, however, when the stress is on the syllable that contains the combination of the two vowels, the stress is placed on the strong vowel (a, e, o) or on the second vowel when two weak vowels are combined.

In the following examples, the stressed syllable is marked in bold; the combination of two vowels together is underlined; and the strong vowel or the second vowel when the combination is formed by two weak vowels is marked in italics.

Example

Strong + Weak Vowel	Weak + Strong Vowel	Weak + Weak Vowel
***a*i**-re (*air*)	**Di*a***-na (*Diana*)	ci*u*-**dad** (*city*)
***a*u**-llar (*howl*)	re-na-**cu*a***-jo (*toad*)	**ru*i***-do (*noise*)
r*e*i-na (*queen*)	**vi*e*n**-to (*wind*)	
*e*u-ca-**lip**-to (*eucalyptus*)	**tru*e***-no (*thunder*)	
*o*i-**dor** (*hearer*)	a-**vi*ó*n** (*airplane*)	
S*o*u-sa (*Souza*)	in-di-**vi**-du*o* (*individual*)	
r*e*u-**nir** (*to gather*)	**du*e***-lo (*sorrow*)	

All other words that **do not** follow the preceding rules have a marked accent on the weak vowel (i, u), or on the second weak vowel when the combination is formed by two weak vowels. The accent mark indicates that the stress must be applied there.

Example

Strong + Weak Vowel	Weak + Strong Vowel	Weak + Weak Vowel
ra-**íz** (*root*)	**dí**-a (*day*)	í-u (*there are no words*)
ma-**ú**-llo (*meow*)	**grú**-a (*tow truck*)	ú-i (*there are no words*)
pro-te-**í**-na (*protein*)	son-**rí**-e (*smile*)	
re-**í** (*I laughed*)	a-cen-**tú**-e (*stress*)	
o-**í**-do (*ear*)	**rí**-o (*river*)	
no-**ú**-me-no (*neumenon*)	**dú**-o (*duet*)	
re-**ú**-na (*gather*)		

Two strong vowels, however, are always divided in two different syllables.

Example

Strong + Strong Vowel
tra-**er** (*to bring*)
ba-ca-**la**-o (*codfish*)
al-**de**-a (*village*)
a-**é**-re-o (*by air*)
an-**cho**-a (*anchovy*)
ro-e-**dor** (*rodent*)

TIP BOX

Adverbs ending in "-mente" have an accent mark only if the adjectives from which they derive have an accent mark.

Example

fácil → fácilmente (*easy* → *easily*)
cortés → cortésmente (*courteous* → *courteously*)

Exercise 6. Divide the following words into syllables and underline the diphthongs.

accionista __________
aceituna __________
adverbio __________
aire __________
aplaudir __________
astronauta __________
atribuir __________
autor __________
baile __________
béisbol __________
bueno __________
buitre __________
canción __________
causa __________
ciento __________
construir __________
continuo __________
cuidar __________
deuda __________
eucalipto __________
Europa __________
idioma __________
influencia __________
ingenuo __________
italiano __________
Liliana __________
Luisa __________
majestuoso __________
muerto __________
naipes __________
paisaje __________
peine __________
piano __________
piedra __________
reina __________
reunir __________
siempre __________
suela __________
superfluo __________
tienda __________
trueno __________

D. ACCENTS DISTINGUISH A WORD WITH DIFFERENT MEANINGS

In Spanish, some words with the same spelling may or may not have an accent depending on their meaning or grammatical function.

a. Demonstrative adjectives and demonstrative pronouns (este/a/os/as, ese/a/os/as, aquel, aquella/as/os) are written similarly, but they are distinguished by the context. However, in cases of ambiguity (the cases of actual ambiguity are rare), demonstrative pronouns take an accent mark.

Example

Esta habla del pueblo.
This talk (as a dialect) of the town.

Ésta habla del pueblo.
This (woman) talks about the town.

b. The following possessive adjectives and personal pronouns are distinguished by an accent mark.

Possessive Adjectives	**Personal Pronouns**
mi (*my*)	mí (*me*)
tu (*your*)	tú (*you*)

Example

Julia me regaló el libro a mí y no a ti.
Julia gave the book to me, not to you.

Mi perro Tobías ladra muy fuerte.
My dog, Tobías, barks very loud.

c. All interrogative words have a written accent that distinguishes them from other pronouns; these interrogatives are accented when used to introduce an interrogative sentence.

¿Cómo?	*How?*
¿Cuál(es)?	*Which (which ones)?*
¿Cuándo?	*When?*
¿Cuánto(o), (a)?	*How much?*
¿Cuánto(os), (as)?	*How many?*
¿Dónde?	*Where?*
¿Qué?	*What?*
¿Quién(es)?	*Who, whom?*

Example

¿<u>Cuándo</u> vamos a cine?
"*When are we going to go to the movies?*"

<u>Cuando</u> tenga tiempo.
"*When I have time.*"

d. Other words.

- **aún** (*still, yet*) **aun** (*even*)

Example

Que pasará con María que <u>aún</u> no llega.
What happened to María that she's not here yet.

<u>Aun</u> después de comer Jorge seguía con hambre.
Even after eating Jorge continued to be hungry.

- **cómo** (*how*) **como** (*as, like*)

Example

¿<u>Cómo</u> te llamas?
What's your name?

María es tan alta <u>como</u> José.
María is as tall as José.

- **más** (*more*) **mas** (*but*)

Example

Quiero <u>más</u> helado, por favor.
I want more ice cream, please.

Te busqué <u>mas</u> no te encontré.
I looked for but I did not find you.

- **sí** (*yes*) **si** (*if*)

Example

María vendrá <u>si</u> quiere.
María will come if she wants to.

—¿Estás contento?
"Are you happy?"

—Sí, estoy muy contento.
"Yes, I am very happy."

- **sólo** (*only*) **solo** (*alone*)

cinco.
'clock.

la de Almodóvar.
ast film.

ıto syllables and underline the stressed syllable.

	toalla	cuerda	maestro	ciudad
	durazno	abstracto	completo	destruir
o	septiembre	peligro	resplandor	lápiz
	baúl	frío	alcohol	lección
	desplazar	influir	león	cereal
er	feliz	película	título	gramática

Exercise 8. The following words have the stressed syllable in bold. Put an accent on the words that require it.

1.	**jo**ven	re**loj**	**la**piz	**an**gel	**de**bil	ho**tel**	se**gun**
2.	a**mor**	**ce**lebre	ol**vi**do	pe**li**cula	musul**man**	**jo**venes	**an**geles
3.	direc**tor**	**or**denes	**ti**tulo	**cre**dito	**ter**mino	ter**mi**no	**vic**tima
4.	infe**liz**	fe**liz**	ani**mal**	**u**nico	mu**jer**	se**ñor**	sim**pa**tico
5.	**vir**genes	inte**res**	es**ta**	**es**ta	gra**ma**tica	pe**li**gro	ameri**ca**nos
6.	chimen**e**a	**sa**la	e**xa**men	e**xa**menes	ra**zon**	ra**zo**nes	**ar**bol
7.	azal**e**a	tar**e**a	mu**jer**	hipo**po**tamo	pa**pa**	an**ti**guo	**pa**pa

Exercise 9. The following sentences are missing accent marks or have unnecessary accent marks. Put an accent on the words that require it or remove the unnecessary accent mark.

1. Julio está sólo con su mascota.
2. El te es una bebida.
3. Te invito a cine.
4. Lola y Josefa quieren más te.
5. ¿Cuanto cuesta aquél sombrero?
6. Cómo no he cumplido 21 años, aun no puedo ir a la discoteca contigo.
7. Todos creímos que el sabía que estabas casada.
8. Solo iremos sí nos invitas.
9. Tu no querrás ir, pero yo si.
10. Queremos ir, más no tenemos tiempo.

2

The Noun and the Articles

What is a noun?

In Spanish (as in English) a **noun** refers to a person (*padre*—father), an animal (*el gato*—the cat), a place (*el barrio*—the neighborhood), a thing (*el libro*—the book), an event (*la fiesta*—the party) or an abstract concept (*la justicia*—justice). However, nouns in Spanish are characterized by gender with a corresponding article. The definite article **el** accompanies a masculine noun and the definite article **la** accompanies a feminine noun. Nouns are usually classified as either common or proper.

Yo soy un sustantivo.
(I am a noun.)

TIP BOX

Common nouns name concrete things that are tangible and nonspecific including persons, animals, places, things, and events. Examples are *mujer* (woman), *gato* (cat), *casa* (house), *manzana* (apple), *agua* (water), *hada* (fairy), *árbol* (tree), *mesa* (table), and *dragón* (dragon). Common nouns also name abstract concepts such as *la justicia* (justice), *la inteligencia* (intelligence), *la pobreza* (poverty), or *la vida* (life).

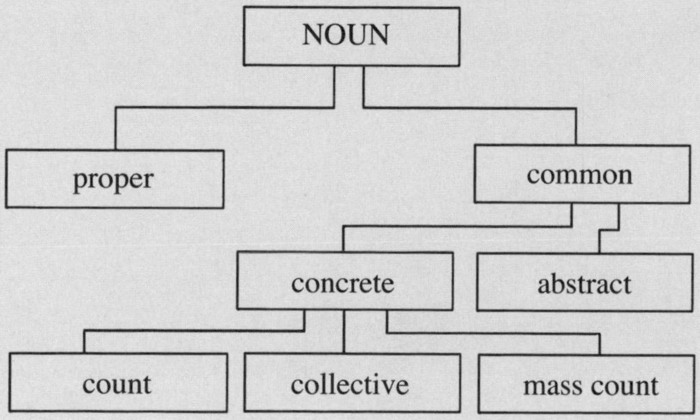

I. The Gender of Nouns

A. NOUNS THAT REFER TO HUMAN BEINGS OR ANIMALS

Nouns that refer to human beings or animals show their gender by their inherent meaning.

In order to deduce the masculine or feminine form of a noun, the following rules apply.

GENDER RULES

a. Nouns that end in **-o** (masculine), change to feminine by replacing the final **-o** with an **a**.

Masculine	Feminine	English Translation
el abuel**o**	**la** abuel**a**	*grandfather/grandmother*
el amig**o**	**la** amig**a**	*male friend/ female friend*
el compañer**o**	**la** compañer**a**	*classmate/female classmate*
el cuñad**o**	**la** cuñad**a**	*brother-in-law/sister-in-law*
el espos**o**	**la** espos**a**	*husband / wife*
el gat**o**	**la** gat**a**	*male cat / female cat*
el herman**o**	**la** herman**a**	*brother/sister*
el muchach**o**	**la** muchach**a**	*boy/girl*
el perr**o**	**la** perr**a**	*dog / bitch*
el prim**o**	**la** prim**a**	*cousin/female cousin*
el sobrin**o**	**la** sobrin**a**	*nephew/niece*
el suegr**o**	**la** suegr**a**	*father-in-law/mother-in-law*
el tí**o**	**la** tí**a**	*uncle/aunt*
el vecin**o**	**la** vecin**a**	*neighbor/female neighbor*

Exercise 1. Complete the following sentences using the genealogical tree above.

1. Liliana es ___ ______ preferida de ___ _______ Rosario.
2. ___ ______ de María Sol es Andrés.
3. Felipe es ___ ______ de Gabriela.
4. María es ___ _______ de Julián.
5. Margarita es ___ _______ de Andrés.
6. Tobías es ___ _______ de la familia.
7. Rosario es ___ _______ de Gabriela.
8. Julián es ___ _______ de María Sol.
9. Laura es ___ _______ de Alfonso y Gabriela.
10. Gabriela es ___ _______ de Margarita.

Exercise 2. Change the underlined nouns either to masculine or feminine.

Example

El amigo de tu hermana tiene sueño.
***La amiga** de tu hermana tiene sueño.*

1. El hermano de José tiene hambre.
   ______ de José tiene hambre.
2. El vecino de mi tía tiene treinta años.
   ______ de mi tía tiene treinta años.
3. La amiga de mi prima baila bien.
   ______ de mi prima baila bien.
4. El sobrino de María estudia en Boston.
   ______ de María estudia en Boston.
5. La abuela cumple ochenta años.
   ______ cumple ochenta años.
6. El sicólogo trabaja en el consultorio.
   ______ trabaja en el consultorio.
7. El gato toma leche.
   ______ toma leche.
8. La perra juega con los niños.
   ______ juega con los niños.
9. La tía llega del trabajo temprano.
   ______ llega del trabajo temprano.
10. El primo de Cecilia tiene doce años.
    ______ de Cecilia tiene doce años.

b. Nouns that end in the consonants **-n**, **-r**, **-l**, **-s** (masculine) change to the feminine by adding an **-a**.

Masculine	Feminine	English Translation
el leó**n**	**la** leon**a**	*lion*
el peató**n**	**la** peaton**a**	*pedestrian*
el auto**r**	**la** autor**a**	*author*
el docto**r**	**la** doctor**a**	*doctor*
el españo**l**	**la** español**a**	*Spaniard*
el colegia**l**	**la** colegial**a**	*schoolboy / schoolgirl*
el francé**s**	**la** frances**a**	*Frenchman / Frenchwoman*
el burgué**s**	**la** burgues**a**	*bourgeois / bourgeoise*

Exercise 3. Complete the following sentences using the appropriate definite article **el** or **la**.

1. __ doctor trabaja en el hospital.
2. __ escritor escribe una novela.
3. __ leona cuida sus crías.
4. __ peatón cruza la calle.
5. __ profesora escribe en el tablero.
6. María, __ española, es de Madrid.
7. __ profesor de español es simpático.
8. __ escritora Gabriela Mistral ganó el premio Nobel de literatura.
9. __ león atrapó una cebra.
10. __ doctora examina al paciente.

Exercise 4. Change the underlined nouns and articles either to masculine or feminine.

Example

El fundador del instituto nos invitó a la fiesta de fin de año.

***La fundadora** del instituto nos invitó a la fiesta de fin de año.*

1. La patrona paga muy bien a sus empleados.
   ____ paga muy bien a sus empleados.
2. El señor Mendoza trabaja mucho.
   ______ Mendoza trabaja mucho.
3. La doctora examina al paciente.
   ______ examina al paciente.
4. El rector del colegio renunció.
   ______ del colegio renunció.
5. La directora anunció un aumento de salarios.
   _______ anunció un aumento de salarios.
6. El embajador renunció a su cargo.
   ______ renunció a su cargo.
7. La vendedora promociona su nuevo producto.
   ______ promociona su nuevo producto.
8. El conductor de la escuela conduce despacio.
   ______ de la escuela conduce despacio.
9. El explorador llegó al Polo Norte.
   ______ llegó al Polo Norte.
10. El administrador de la compañía llegó tarde esta mañana.
    ______ de la compañía llegó tarde esta mañana.

c. Some nouns are identical in both masculine and feminine forms, and the only way to determine their gender is by the adjacent word (an article or an adjective) or by the word's context.

Masculine	Feminine	English Translation
el adolescente	**la** adolescente	*adolescent*
el agente	**la** agente	*agent*
el artista	**la** artista	*artist*
el astronauta	**la** astronauta	*astronaut*
el atleta	**la** atleta	*athlete*
el camarada	**la** camarada	*comrade*
el cantante	**la** cantante	*singer*
el cliente	**la** cliente	*client*
el espía	**la** espía	*spy*
el estudiante	**la** estudiante	*student*
el joven	**la** joven	*youth*
el testigo	**la** testigo	*witness*
el visitante	**la** visitante	*visitor*

Exercise 5. According to the context, complete the following sentences using the appropriate definite article ***el*** or ***la***.

1. María, ____ estudiante, está content**a**.
   José, ____ estudiante, está content**o**.
2. Juan es ____ testigo del crimen.
   Marta es ____ testigo del crimen.
3. El señor Rodríguez es ____ visitante más importante.
   La señora Rodríguez es ____ visitante más importante.
4. ____ cliente es amig**a** de mi padre.
   ____ cliente es amig**o** de mi padre.
5. ____ agente es amig**o** de mi madre.
   ____ agente es amig**a** de mi madre.
6. ____ novelista es muy famos**a**.
   ____ novelista es muy famos**o**.
7. ____ astronauta Julia se prepara para viajar a Marte.
   ____ astronauta Carlos se prepara para viajar a Marte.
8. Teresa, ____ adolescente, juega para el equipo de fútbol de su escuela.
   Jorge, ____ adolescente, juega para el equipo de fútbol de su escuela.
9. ____ cantante Isabel recibió muchos aplausos anoche en el concierto.
   ____ cantante Romeo recibió muchos aplausos anoche en el concierto.

Exercise 6. According to the context, complete the following sentences using the appropriate definite article ***la, el, las,*** or ***los***.

1. ___ joven Sofía estudia biología en la Universidad Autónoma de México.
2. ___ mejor atleta de la universidad está enferma.
3. Juliana, ___ astronauta, hace experimentos en el transbordador espacial.
4. ___ agentes secretos descubrieron el crimen.
5. ___ cantantes del grupo de música Las Bandidas llegaron a Nueva York.
6. Todos ___ estudiantes de la universidad protestaron en contra de la guerra.
7. Aquellas mujeres son ___ clientes del salón de belleza de tu madre.
8. Ella es ___ artista de que te hablé el otro día.
9. ___ espías fueron sorprendidos por el Servicio Secreto.

d. Some nouns have special masculine and feminine forms.

Masculine	Feminine	English Translation
el actor	**la** actriz	*actor/actress*
el barón	**la** baronesa	*baron/baroness*
el caballero	**la** dama	*gentleman / lady*
el caballo	**la** yegua	*horse / mare*
el carnero	**la** oveja	*sheep / ewe*
el hombre	**la** mujer	*man / woman*
el macho	**la** hembra	*male / female*
el padre	**la** madre	*father / mother*
el príncipe	**la** princesa	*prince / princess*
el rey	**la** reina	*king / queen*
el toro	**la** vaca	*bull / cow*
el yerno	**la** nuera	*son-in-law / daughter-in-law*

Exercise 7. Complete the following crossword puzzle using the opposite or inverse masculine or feminine corresponding noun.

Across:
1 princesa
4 reina
7 yegua
9 hembra
10 padre
11 mujer
15 carnero
20 yerno
21 madre
22 rey
23 vaca

Down:
2 dama
3 príncipe
5 caballo
6 caballero
8 actriz
10 hombre
12 barón
13 oveja
14 toro
16 macho
17 actor
18 nuera
19 baronesa

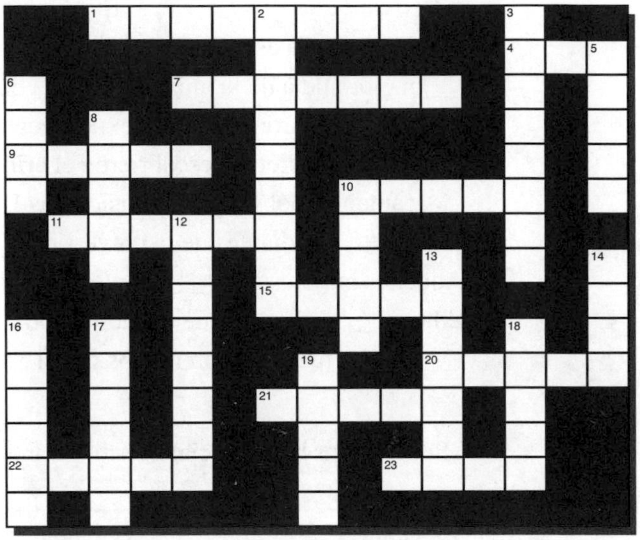

B. GENDER OF NOUNS WITH AN ARBITRARY REFERENT

To determine the gender of a noun that has an arbitrary referent, the following rules apply:

a. Nouns are feminine if they end in **-a, -d, -is, -sión, -ción,** and **-z.**

la vid**a** (*life*)
la realida**d** (*reality*)
la síntes**is** (*synthesis*)
la deci**sión** (*decision*)
la can**ción** (*song*)
la lu**z** (*light*)

b. All others nouns are masculine if they end in **-o, -e, an accented vowel**, consonants that are neither **-d** or **-z**, and nouns ending in **-is**, **-sión**, and **-ción**.

el abanic**o** (*fan*)
el perfum**e** (*perfume*)
el coli**brí** (*hummingbird*)
el ár**bol** (*tree*)
el co**jín** (*cushion*)
el mot**or** (*engine*)

Vocabulary

El cuarto

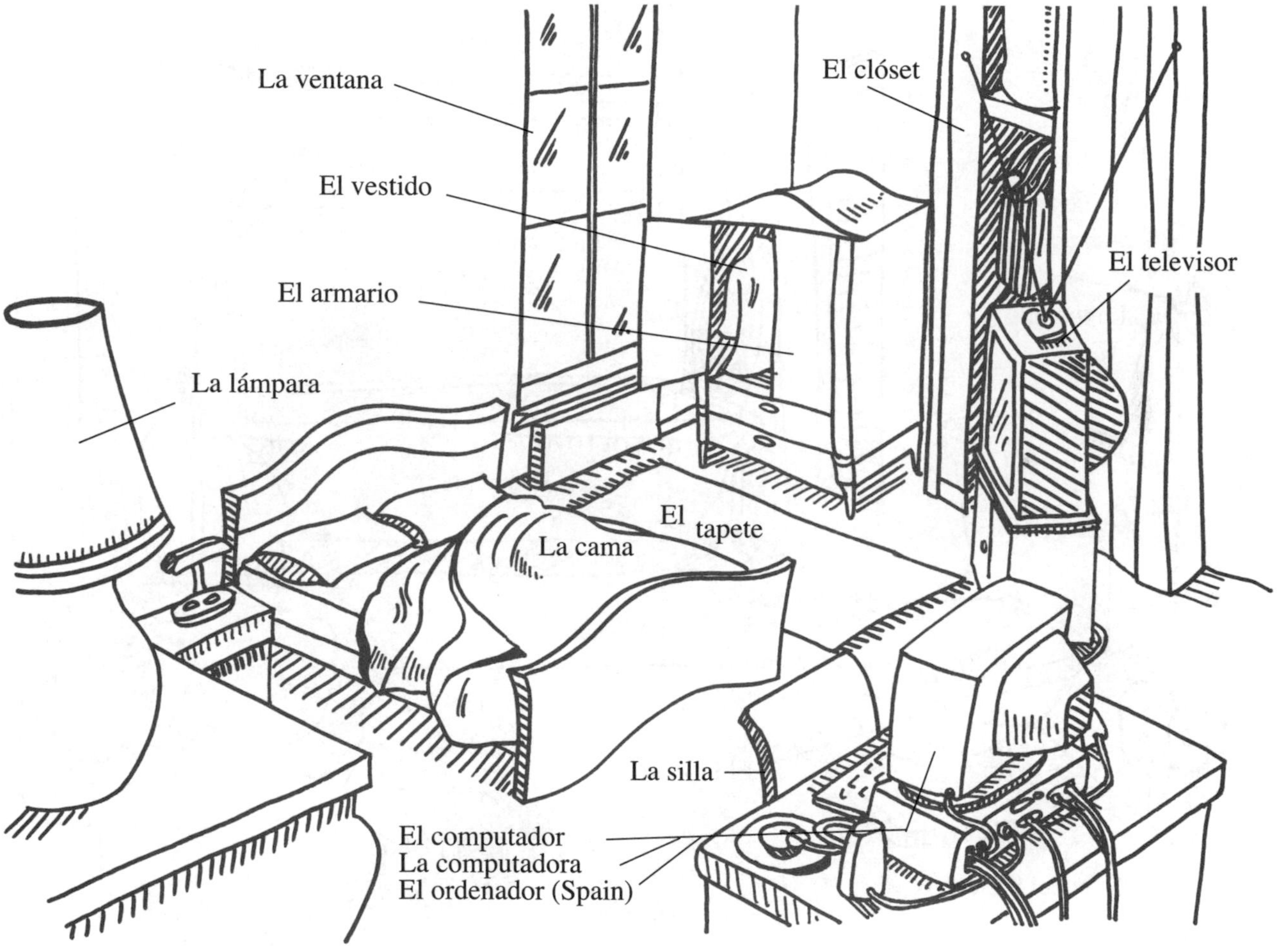

Exercise 8. Complete the following sentences using the appropriate definite article ***el*** or ***la.***

1. ___ señora olvidó hacer ___ cama está mañana.
2. En ___ habitación está ___ computador, ___ silla, ___televisor, ___ cama y ___ lámpara.
3. ___ ventana está cerrada y ___ clóset está abierto.
4. María compró ___ vestido en ___ almacén.
5. ___ tapete de la sala está sucio.
6. Mi abrigo negro está en ___ armario.

Vocabulary

El baño

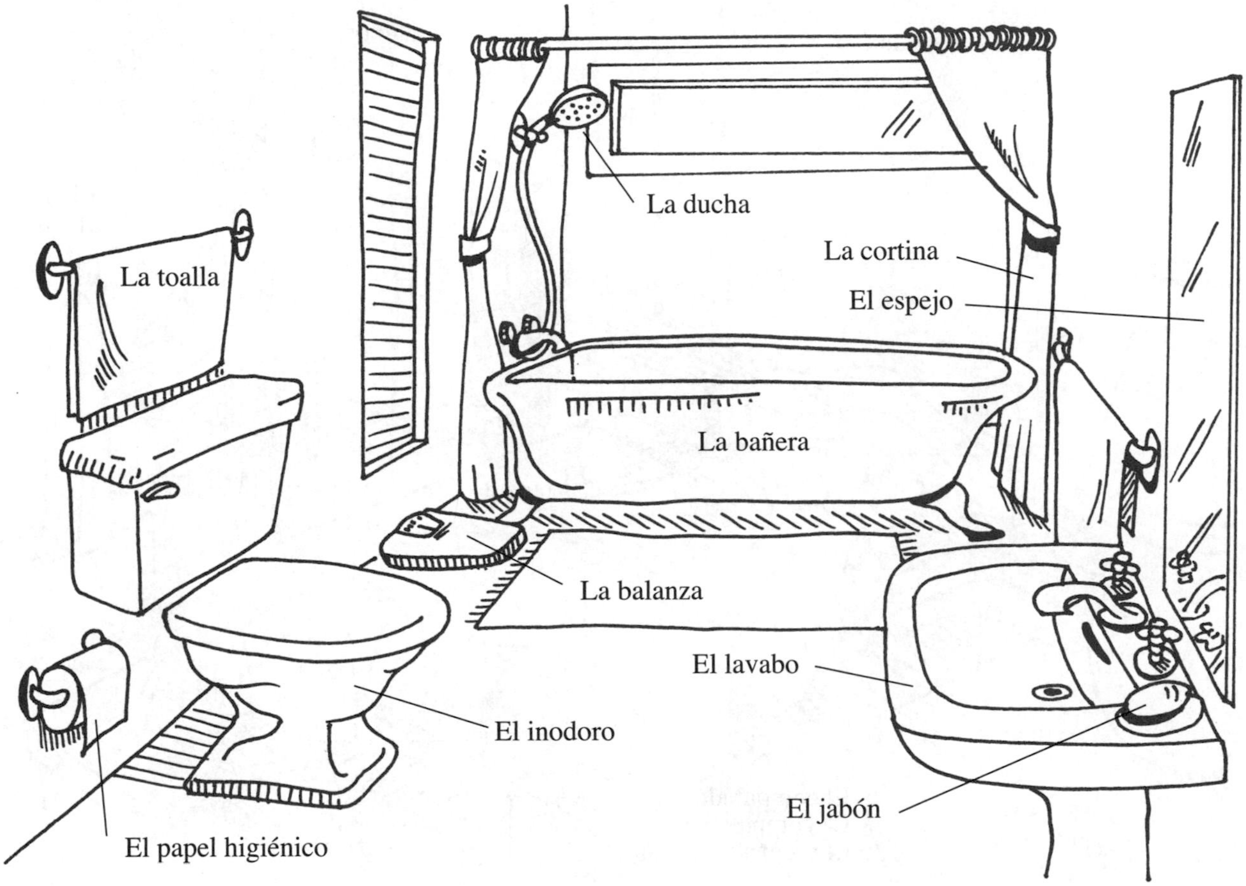

Exercise 9. Complete the following sentences using the appropriate definite article ***el*** or ***la***.

1. El señor se resbaló en ___ bañera de su casa.
2. Las manos se lavan en ___ lavabo.
3. Laura se pesa en ___ balanza.
4. Rosario se lava las manos con ___ jabón y se seca con ___ toalla.
5. Gabriela se peina mirándose en ___ espejo.
6. Margarita olvida siempre cerrar ___ cortina de baño cuando está en ___ ducha.

Exercise 10. Put the appropriate definite article ***el*** or ***la*** for the following nouns.

___ acné *the acne*
___ actividad *the activity*
___ admiración *the admiration*
___ afiche *the poster*
___ agresividad *the aggressiveness*
___ aljibe *the cistern*
___ amabilidad *the amiability*
___ ambición *the ambition*
___ amplificador *the amplifier*
___ ansiedad *the anxiety*
___ antibiótico *the antibiotic*
___ aptitud *the aptitude*
___ arco *the arch*
___ atracción *the attraction*
___ baile *the dance*
___ banco *the bank*
___ barco *the ship*
___ bondad *the kindness*
___ cable *the cable*
___ cacao *the cocoa*
___ café *the coffee*
___ calefacción *the heating*
___ cantidad *the quantity*
___ capacidad *the capacity*
___ circulación *the traffic*
___ ciudad *the city*
___ claridad *the clarity*
___ coalición *the coalition*
___ coco *the coconut*
___ composición *the composition*
___ cruce *the intersection*
___ cruz *the cross*
___ decisión *the decision*
___ declaración *the declaration*
___ depresión *the depression*
___ destornillador *the screwdriver*
___ dirección *the direction*
___ domingo *the Sunday*
___ dulce *the sweet*
___ educación *the education*
___ electrodoméstico *the appliance*
___ embarcación *the vessel*
___ equipaje *the baggage*
___ escasez *the shortage*
___ estupidez *the stupidity*
___ evaluación *the evaluation*
___ habilidad *the skill*
___ humidificador *the humidifier*
___ infección *the infection*
___ liberación *the liberation*
___ libertad *the freedom*
___ luz *the light*
___ madurez *the maturity*
___ meteoro *the meteor*
___ monitor *the monitor*
___ nación *the nation*
___ nariz *the nose*
___ niñez *the childhood*
___ operación *the operation*
___ pared *the wall*
___ pasión *the passion*
___ piedad *the piety*
___ prisión *the prison*
___ profesión *the profession*
___ propiedad *the property*
___ publicidad *the advertising*
___ reflector *the reflector*
___ retrovisor *the rearview mirror*
___ revolución *the revolution*
___ salud *the health*
___ sed *the thirst*
___ selección *the selection*
___ sencillez *the simplicity*
___ superstición *the superstition*
___ tabaco *the tobacco*
___ televisión *the television*
___ televisor *the television*
___ tempestad *the tempest*
___ tensión *the tension*
___ timidez *the shyness*
___ tóxico *the toxic*
___ tronco *the trunk*
___ vapor *the steam*
___ vegetación *the vegetation*
___ versión *the version*
___ virtud *the virtue*
___ voz *the voice*

c. Feminine exceptions.

- Nouns that are Greek in origin generally end in **-ma** and are masculine.

Example

el aroma *(the aroma)*	**el** arma *(the weapon)*
el asma *(the asthma)*	**el** axioma *(the axiom)*
el clima (*the weather*)	**el** dilema (*the dilemma*)
el esquema (*the scheme*)	**el** idioma (*the language*)
el problema (*the problem*)	**el** sistema (*the system*)
el telegrama *(the telegram)*	**el** diploma *(the diploma)*
el tema (*the theme*)	**el** drama (*the drama*)
el teorema (*the theorem*)	**el** enigma (*the enigma*)

- The following nouns that end in **-a**, **-d**, **-is,** and **-z** are **NOT** feminine.

-a	-d	-is	-z
el día (*day*)	**el** césped (*lawn*)	**el** análisis (*analysis*)	**el** aprendiz (*apprentice*)
el mapa (*map*)	**el** huésped (*host*)		**el** avestruz (*ostrich*)
el planeta (*the planet*)	**el** ataúd (*coffin*)		**el** cáliz (*goblet*)
el tranvía (*street car*)			**el** arroz (*rice*)
			el pez (*fish*)
			el lápiz (*pencil*)
			el ajedrez (*chess*)
			el antifaz (*mask*)
			el altavoz (*speaker*)
			el maíz (*maize*)

Exercise 11. Complete the following paragraph, using the following words and their corresponding articles: **el problema**, **el esquema**, **el teorema**, **el clima**, **el dilema**, **el idioma**, **el tema**.

María Sol utilizó ___ _______ de Pitágoras para resolver ___ _______ de matemáticas. Ahora tiene que terminar la tarea de español. ___ _______ español es muy fácil. La tarea de ciencias es más difícil. María Sol debe escribir un ensayo. ________ del ensayo es sobre ___ _______ tropical. ___ _______ de María es escribir directamente el ensayo o hacer primero ___ _______.

Exercise 12. Give the appropriate noun for each picture and remember to give it its corresponding article.

1. ____________

2. ____________

3. ____________

4. ____________

5. ____________

6. ____________

7. ____________

8. ____________

9. ____________

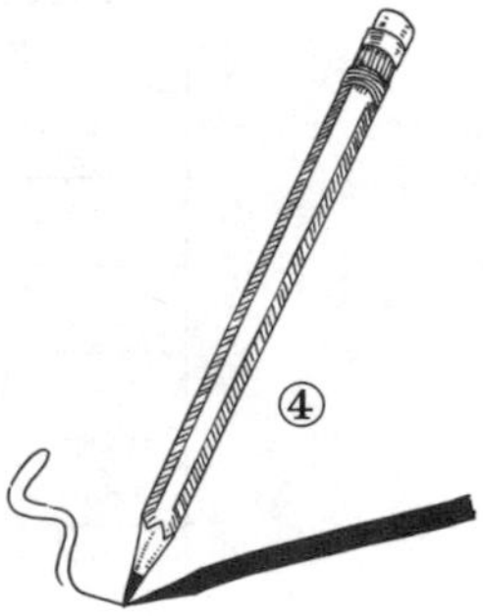
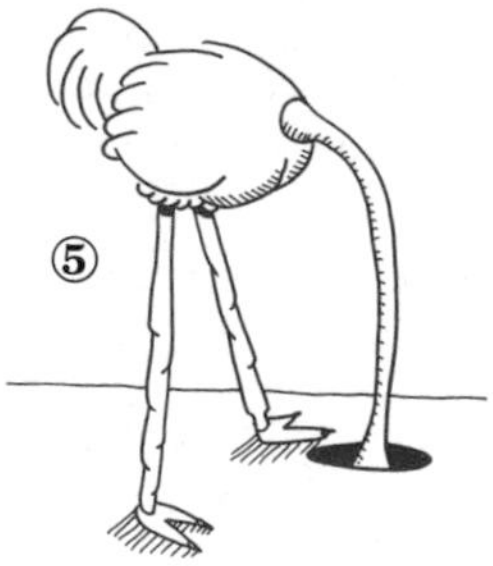

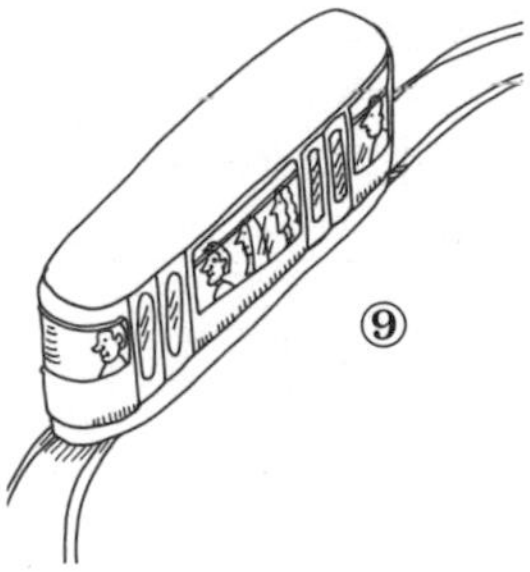

d. Masculine exceptions.

-o	**-e**	**-stress vowel**	Consonants That Are Neither **-d** nor **z**
la foto (*photo*)	**la** llave (*key*)	**la** fe (*faith*)	**la** miel (*honey*)
la mano (*hand*)	**la** calle (*street*)		**la** sal (*salt*)
la moto (*motorcycle*)	**la** fiebre (*fever*)		**la** hiel (*bile*)
	la carne (*meat*)		**la** piel (*skin*)
	la frase (*sentence*)		
	la gente (*people*)		
	la nieve (*snow*)		
	la noche (*night*)		
	la nube (*cloud*)		
	la sangre (*blood*)		
	la suerte (*luck*)		
	la tarde (*afternoon*)		
	la muerte (*death*)		

Exercise 13. Solve the following riddles.

1. Cinco hijos tiene cada una
   y dan golpes como ninguna.

   ____

   Five children has each one
   and they give blows as no one.

2. Pequeña como un ratón
   y guarda la casa como un león.

   ____

   Small as a mouse,
   but as a lion
   she guards the house.

3. Todos pasan por mí
   y yo no paso por nadie;
   todos preguntan por mí,
   yo no pregunto por nadie.

   ____

   Everybody steps on me,
   and I do not step on anybody;
   everybody asks for me,
   I do not ask for anybody.

4. Cuando no estoy cocida roja soy,
cuando me cocinan me pongo marrón,
y soy alimento del león.

When I am raw, red I am;
when I am cooked, brown I get,
and the food of the lion I am.

____

5. Blanca, muy blanca eres;
pero cuando calienta el sol,
rápido desapareces.

White, very white you are,
but when the sun heats,
quickly you disappear.

____

6. Soy enemiga del sol y en mí
brillan los soles
y a pesar de tantas luces
me iluminan con faroles.

I am an enemy of the sun, in me
the suns shine, and
in spite of so many lights
with lanterns they illuminate me.

____

7. Una señora
que se deshace
llora que llora.
¿Quién es?

A lady that dissolves
while crying and crying.
Who is she?

____

8. Rojo ha sido siempre mi vivir,
pero algunos de azul
me quieren vestir.

All my life I have been red,
but some in blue
want me to dress.

____

9. Blanca soy,
nací en el mar;
y en tu bautizo
tuve que estar.

White I am,
I was born in the sea;
and in your baptism
I had to be.

____

Exercise 14. Give each picture the appropriate noun and corresponding definite article.

1. ____________

2. ____________

3. ____________

4. ____________

5. ____________

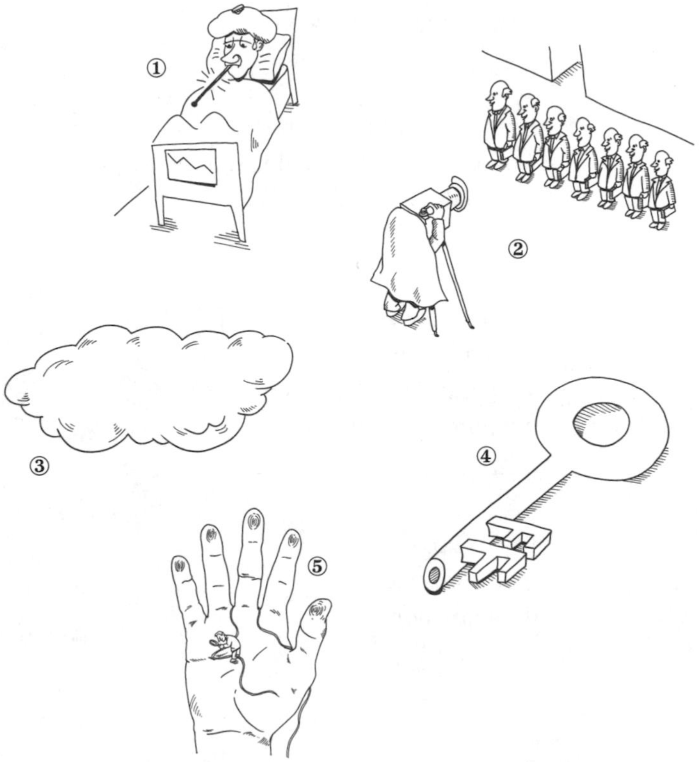

C. NOUNS WITH DIFFERENT MEANINGS

The meanings of some nouns depend on how the article is used.

Spanish		English Translation	
Masculine	**Feminine**	**Masculine**	**Feminine**
el capital	la capital	*capital (money)*	*capital (city)*
el corte	la corte	*cut*	*court*
el cura	la cura	*priest*	*healing*
el guía	la guía	*guide (person)*	*guidebook*
el modelo	la modelo	*model (example)*	*fashion model*
el orden	la orden	*order (arrangement)*	*order (command)*
el papa	la papa	*pope*	*potato*
el policía	la policía	*policeman*	*police*

Exercise 15. Using the list on your left, choose the appropriate noun and its corresponding article.

1. ___ __________ de ojos negros ganó el concurso de moda.
2. ___ __________ en el salón de clase era perfecto.
3. ___ __________ vive en el Vaticano.
4. ___ __________ del museo del Prado que compramos en la librería es excelente.
5. ___ __________ para tu enfermedad es el reposo.
6. ___ __________ de España es Madrid.
7. ___ __________ determinó que la ley era inconstitucional.
8. ___ __________ de coche que compraste me gusta mucho.
9. ___ __________ recibió ____ ________ de captura.
10. ___ __________ de la carne argentina es especial.
11. ___ __________ es una raíz comestible.
12. ___ __________ nos mostró todos los lugares turísticos.

Exercise 16. Give each picture the appropriate noun and corresponding definite article.

1.

____

2.

____

3.

____

4.

____

5.
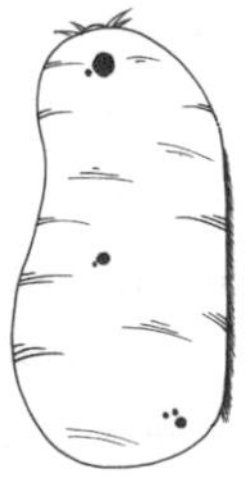

____

6.

____

II. The Plural Forms of Nouns

In Spanish, plural nouns are formed in three ways:

a. When the noun ends in an unstressed vowel, an **-s** is added.

Example

el libro	los libro**s**	*book/books*
la casa	las casa**s**	*house/houses*
la madre	las madre**s**	*mother/mothers*

Exercise 17. Rewrite the following sentences in the plural.

Example

El libro está en la estantería.
Los libros están en la estantería.

1. El chocolate está sobre la mesa.
____
2. La cama está sin tender.
____
3. La casa está al norte de la ciudad.
____
4. El tigre está en la jaula.
____
5. El problema está en los gobernantes.
____
6. La tienda está en el barrio.
____

Exercise 18. Rewrite the following words to the singular form.

1. los hermanos ______________
2. las amigas ______________
3. las almendras ______________
4. los edificios ______________
5. los coches ______________
6. las candidatas ______________
7. los sindicatos ______________
8. las modelos ______________
9. los curas ______________
10. las máquinas ______________
11. las noches ______________
12. las calles ______________

Exercise 19. Use the correct definite articles ***el***, ***la***, ***el***, ***los*** with the following nouns.

1. _______ casas _______ perros _______ gatas
2. _______ dormitorios _______ problemas _______ manos
3. _______ teorema _______ días _______ motos

4. _______ noches _______ luna _______ Tierra
5. _______ sistemas _______ viaje _______ planetas
6. _______ mapas _______ poemas _______ programas

Vocabulary

La cocina

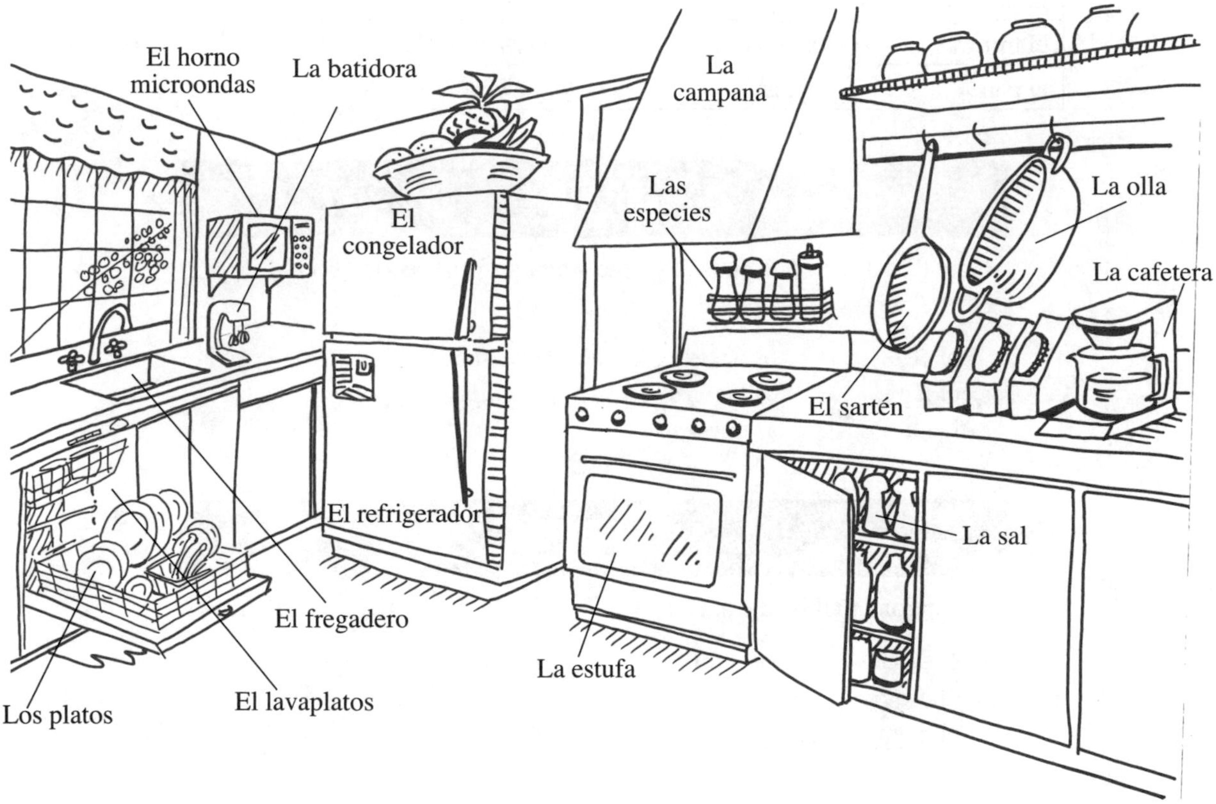

Exercise 20. Rewrite the following sentences in the plural.

Example

La ventana es transparente.
***Las** ventanas **son** transparentes.*

1. El horno microondas es negro.

____

2. La batidora es verde.

____

3. El fregadero es metálico.

____

4. La olla es grande.

____

5. La cafetera es eléctrica.

____

6. La estufa es blanca.

____

b. When the noun ends in a consonant, a stressed vowel, or a *-y*, **-es** is added.

el árbol	los árbol**es**	*tree/trees*
el actor	los actor**es**	*actor/actors*
el maniquí	los maniquí**es**	*mannequin/mannequins*
la ley	las ley**es**	*law/laws*
el tren	los tren**es**	*train/trains*
el pan	los pan**es**	*loaf/loaves*

TIP BOX

Note that if the noun ends in **-z**, the singular form becomes a **-c-** before the **-es** in the plural.

el pez	los pe**ces**	*fish/fishes*
el lápiz	los lápi**ces**	*pencil/pencils*
la nuez	las nue**ces**	*nut/nuts*

TIP BOX

Exceptions to this rule are:

el café	los cafés	*coffee/coffees*
el esquí	los esquís	*ski/skies*
el menú	los menús	*menu/menus*
el papá	los papás	*daddy/daddies*
el pie	los pies	*foot/feet*

Exercise 21. Rewrite the following sentences in the plural.

Example

El señor es alt**o**.
***Los** señor**es son** alto**s**.*

1. El refrigerador del hotel es blanco.
____

2. El congelador de mi casa es eficiente.
____

3. El tren es lento.
____

4. La ley es obsoleta.
____

5. El ataúd es de madera.
____

6. El sartén es de hierro.
____

Exercise 22. Rewrite the following sentences in their singular form.

Example

Los señores están animados.
El señor está animado.

1. Los empleados están cansados.
____
2. Los motores están encendidos.
____
3. Los reyes están presos.
____
4. Los actores están desesperados.
____
5. Los maniquíes están en la vitrina.
____
6. Los panes están crujientes.
____

Vocabulary

La sala

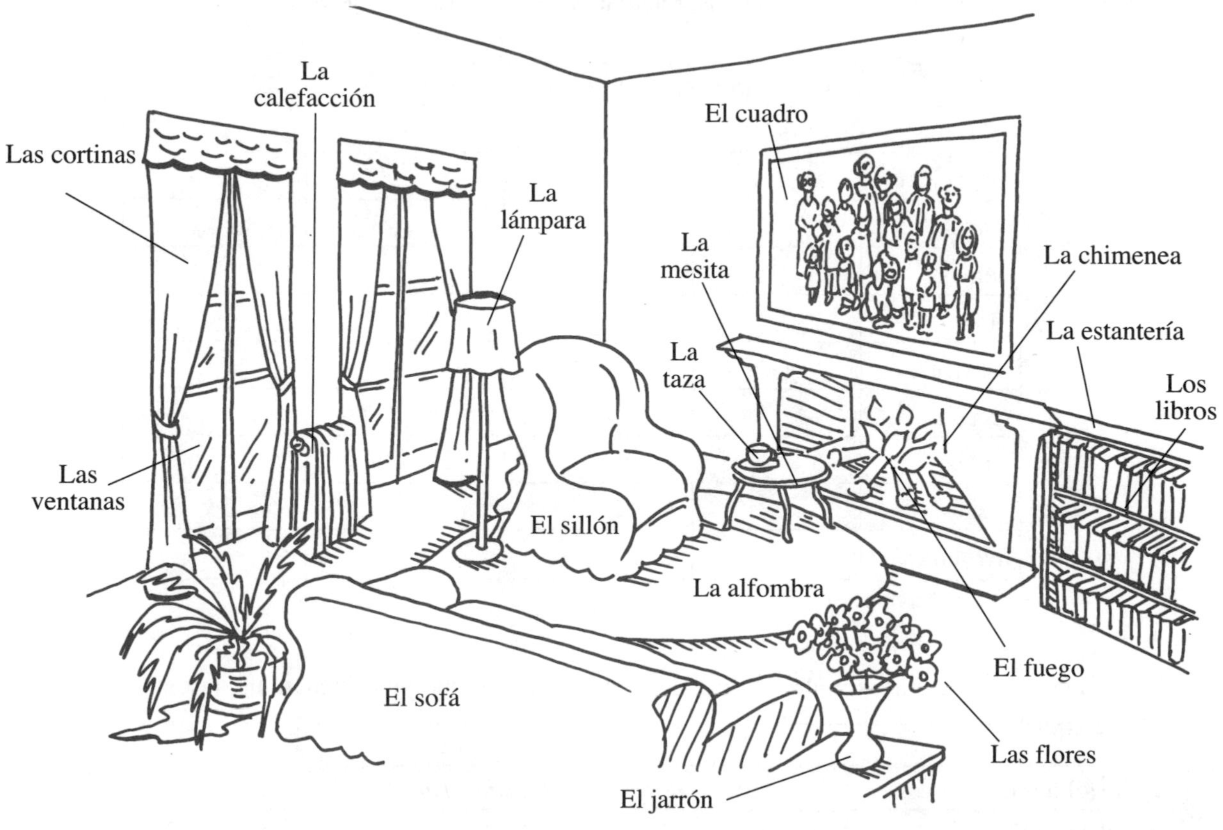

Exercise 23. Use the preceding vocabulary to write the appropriate definite article and corresponding noun, in plural or singular form.

Todos los días la abuela Rosario entra a ____________ y mira ____________ pintado por su hijo. Luego toma uno de _________ que están en ____________ al lado de la mesita y se sienta en _______________ cerca de la ventana. Cuando hace frío, enciende _______________ o prende ____________ en ____________. En __________ coloca ____________ de té. A la abuela Rosario le encantan ____________ frescas.

Exercise 24. Rewrite the following words in the plural.

1. la nuez
____
2. el lápiz
____
3. el pez
____
4. el pie
____
5. el café
____
6. el papá
____

Exercise 25. Indicate with a ✔ the gender and number of the following words.

	Masculine	Feminine	Singular	Plural
planetas	✔			✔
leyes				
jarrones				
temas				
dilemas				
actrices				
perdiz				
cafés				
peces				
teoremas				

c. Nouns ending in **-s** in the singular remain the same in the plural unless the last syllable is stressed.

el martes	los martes	*Tuesday/Tuesdays*
la crisis	las crisis	*crisis/crises*
el análisis	los análisis	*analysis/analyses*

TIP BOX

Exceptions to this rule are:

el bus	los bus**es**	*bus/buses*
el ciprés	los cipres**es**	*cypress/cypresses*
el burgués	los burgues**es**	*bourgeois*

Exercise 26. Use the correct definite articles ***el, la, los, las*** according to the meaning.

1. Todos _____ martes voy a clase de español.
2. _____ crisis económica es mundial.
3. El doctor tiene todos _____ análisis de sangre.
4. _____ miércoles de la próxima semana iremos a bailar.
5. _____ diabetes es una enfermedad.
6. _____ tesis sobre el calentamiento global son muchas.

Exercise 27. Underline the stressed syllable, then rewrite the words in the plural.
Model: finland<u>és</u>—*finlandeses*

1. el microbús _______________
2. el compás _______________
3. el gas _______________
4. el mes _______________
5. el entremés _______________
6. el burgués _______________

Exercise 28. Rewrite the following words in the singular.

Example

irlandeses–*irlandés*

1. apendicitis _______________
2. artritis _______________
3. caries _______________
4. escoceses _______________
5. fotosíntesis _______________
6. franceses _______________
7. ingleses _______________
8. jueves _______________
9. lunes _______________
10. miércoles _______________
11. oasis _______________
12. viernes _______________
13. virus _______________
14. tenis _______________

TIP BOX

Note that some nouns are only used in their plural form.

las esposas	*handcuffs*
las gafas	*glasses*
las tijeras	*scissors*
los calzoncillos	*underwear*
los celos	*jealousy*
los prismáticos	*binoculars*
las vacaciones	*vacation*

Variation in the Plural

Note also that plural variation usually causes changes in the syllables of the word. Since the stressed syllable vowel is maintained in the singular, an accent may be dropped or added.

Example

el jo-ven/los jó-ve-nes (*the young one/the young ones*)
el in-te-rés/los in-te-re-ses (*interest/interests*)

III. Articles

An article is a word placed before a noun or an adjective. As in English, in Spanish there are two types of articles, **definite** and **indefinite**.

The **definite** articles are those that speak of something well-known and that you can identify.

The **indefinite** articles are those that do not speak of something well-known or that you cannot identify.

	Spanish				English			
	Masculine		Feminine		Masculine		Feminine	
	Singular	Plural	Singular	Plural	Singular	Plural	Singular	Plural
Indefinite	un	unos	una	unas	a/an	some	a/an	some
Definite	el	los	la	las	the	the	the	the

A. DEFINITE AGREEMENT PATTERNS

Definite articles agree with nouns according to the following pattern.

a. The singular article ***el*** agrees with singular masculine words.

Example

el hij**o**, **el** gat**o**, **el** libr**o**, **el** Año Nuev**o** (*son, cat, book, New Year*)

b. The plural article ***los*** agrees with plural masculine words.

Example

los hij**os**, **los** gat**os**, **los** libr**os**, **los** añ**os** nuev**os** (*sons, cats, books, New Years*)

c. The singular article ***la*** agrees with singular feminine words.

Example

la hij**a**, **la** gat**a**, **la** cam**a**, **la** Navida**d** (*daughter, cat, bed, Christmas*)

d. The plural article ***las*** agrees with plural feminine words.

Example

las hij**as**, **las** gat**as**, **las** cam**as**, **las** navida**des** (*daughters, cats, beds, Christmas*)

TIP BOX

1. When the article ***el*** is preceded by the preposition ***a*** or ***de***, a contraction occurs as follows:

a) **a + el = al**

Example

Todos los días, voy ***al*** **(a + el)** restaurante.
Every day I go to the restaurant.

b) **de + el = del**

Example

Mis amigos ***del*** **(de + el)** colegio me invitaron a cenar.
My friends from school invited me to dinner.

This rule does NOT apply to formal nouns, such as the names of countries.

Example

Acabo de llegar de El Salvador.
I just arrived from El Salvador.

2. When the noun that qualifies the definite article is singular and feminine and begins with a stressed **a-** or **ha-**, the article **el** (not **la**) is used.

Example

el **a**gua negra	las agu**as** negr**as**	*wastewater*
el **á**guila blanca	las águil**as** blanc**as**	*the white eagle, the white eagles*
el h**a**cha afilada	las hach**as** afilad**as**	*the sharp ax, the sharpaxes*
el **a**lma perdida	las alm**as** perdid**as**	*the lost soul, the lost souls*

Exercise 29. Underline the stressed syllable of the words in boldface, then write the definite articles that correspond to the following nouns.

Example

el **ánima** bendita. *las* **ánimas** benditas.
la **alcoba** grande. *las* **alcobas** grandes.

1. ______ **abeja** africana
   ______ **abejas** africanas
2. ______ **agua** mineral
   ______ **aguas** minerales
3. ______ **águila** calva
   ______ **águilas** calvas
4. ______ **ala** del avión
   ______ **alas** del avión
5. ______ **alcaparra** en vinagre
   ______ **alcaparras** en vinagre
6. ______ **alma** muerta
   ______**almas** muertas
7. ______ **almendra** tostada
   ______ **almendras** tostadas
8. ______ **almohada** de plumas
   ______ **almohadas** de plumas
9. ______ **arma** de fuego
   ______ **armas** de fuego
10. ______ **azalea** es una flor
    ______ **azaleas** son unas flores
11. ______ **hacha** de piedra
    ______ **hachas** de piedra
12. ______ **hambruna**
    ______ **hambrunas**

Exercise 30. Complete the following sentences; use contractions when necessary.

1. La familia va de vacaciones a______ playa.
2. Federico escribe una carta a______ presidente.
3. Gabriela es hermana de______ señor Alfonso Naranjo.
4. Margarita y Federico van todos los días a jugar a______ parque.
5. Laura llega de______ trabajo a______ seis de la tarde.
6. Tobías le ladra a______ cartero.
7. Mario va a______ fiesta esta noche.
8. Salimos de______ casa temprano.

Exercise 31. Rewrite the underlined part of the following sentences to the singular.

1. Qué interesante es esa mujer de los guantes rojos. ________________________
2. Me gusta ver el gracioso ir y venir de las mariposas. ________________________
3. Vete a los infiernos. ________________________
4. No es buena idea contaminar las aguas de los ríos. ________________________
5. El castillo de los Duques de Aranjuez es muy bonito. ________________________
6. El padre de las hermanas Ortiz está enfermo. ________________________

B. INDEFINITE AGREEMENT PATTERNS

Indefinite articles agree with nouns in the following pattern:

a. The article ***un*** agrees with singular masculine words.

Example

un hijo, **un** gato, **un** libro, **un** Año Nuevo (*a son, a cat, a book, a New Year*)

b. The article ***unos*** agrees with plural masculine words.

Example

unos hijos, **unos** gatos, **unos** libros, **unos** años nuevos (*some sons, some cats, some books, some New Years*)

c. The article ***una*** agrees with singular feminine words.

Example

una hija, **una** gata, **una** cama, **una** Navidad (*a daughter, a cat, a bed, a Christmas*)

d. The article ***unas*** agrees with plural feminine words.

Example

unas hijas, **unas** gatas, **unas** camas, **unas** Navidades *(some daughters, some cats, some beds, some Christmases)*

Exercise 32. Rewrite the following nouns with an indefinite article.

Example

el libro — ***un** libro*

1.	los problemas	____________	7.	el idioma	____________
2.	la balanza	____________	8.	la toalla	____________
3.	la decisión	____________	9.	las canciones	____________
4.	el perfume	____________	10.	el príncipe	____________
5.	el hombre	____________	11.	las yeguas	____________
6.	el escritor	____________	12.	los leones	____________

Exercise 33. Complete the following sentences using the correct indefinite article ***un***, ***una***, ***uno***, ***unas***, ***unos***.

1. Hay ______ museo de historia natural en la ciudad.
2. Todos los años, Gabriela visita a ______ amiga de la familia en Madrid.
3. Rosario prepara ______ delicioso plato con mariscos.
4. Federico enseña en ______ universidad del estado.
5. Los niños juegan en ______ parque al norte de la ciudad.
6. El arqueólogo estudia ______ huesos de mamut.

C. USES OF THE DEFINITE AND INDEFINITE ARTICLES

a. If the noun refers to an entity that is considered a generic whole or an abstract concept, a definite article is used.

Example

El vino es bueno para la salud.
Wine is healthy.

El vino (wine) in this sentence is considered a generic whole; therefore a definite article is used.

Exercise 34. Complete the following sentences using the correct definite article ***la***, ***el***, ***las***, ***los***.

1. ______ vino es bueno para ______ salud.
2. ______ leche es un buen alimento.
3. ______ azúcar tiene muchas calorías.
4. ______ justicia y ______ paz son inseparables.
5. ______ tiempo es un concepto abstracto.
6. ______ matemáticas y ______ física son ciencias exactas.

b. If the noun refers to an entity that is specific or is considered unique among others, a definite article is used.

Example

El vino de California es excelente.
The wine from California is excellent.

In this sentence *vino* (wine) is considered a specific entity.

Exercise 35. Complete the following sentences using the correct singular or plural definite articles ***la***, ***el***, ***las***, ***los***.

1. ______ vino de Francia es delicioso.
2. ______ leche de vaca es un buen alimento.
3. ______ azúcar de caña sabe igual que ______ azúcar de remolacha.
4. ______ justicia no existe en algunos países.
5. ______ tiempo para mañana es nublado con posibilidad de lluvia.
6. ______ matemáticas y ______ física en tu universidad son fáciles de aprender.

c. If the noun is located after the verb and refers to an entity that is singular and non-countable, no article is used.

Example

Quiero beber vino.
I want to drink wine.

Exercise 36. Determine which of the following sentences needs an article. Then decide if it needs a definite or indefinite article.

1. Quiero beber ______ vino de California.
2. Hay ______ leche en el supermercado.
3. Rosario compra ______ azúcar de caña.
4. No hay ______ justicia en algunos países.
5. Sin tiempo, no podré terminar ______ ensayo de español.
6. Estudia ______ matemáticas y ______ física en la universidad.
7. Nosotros hablamos ______ inglés.

d. If the noun refers to an entity that is a part of a whole or, in other words, that is countable (one in some), an indefinite article is used.

Example

Quiero beber una copa de vino.
I want to drink a glass of wine.

Exercise 37. Complete the following sentences using the correct indefinite article.

1. ______ **copa** de vino va muy bien con la comida.
2. ______ **vaso** de leche de vaca es un buen alimento.
3. ______ **cucharadita** de azúcar de caña sabe igual que ______ **cucharadita** de azúcar de remolacha.
4. En algunos países hace falta ______ **poco** de justicia.
5. Quiero dejar de fumar por ______ tiempo.
6. ______ **poco** de matemáticas y ______ **poco** de física son muy útiles.

Exercise 38. Complete the following sentences using the correct definite or indefinite article.

1. ___ domingo pasado vimos ___ globos en ___ parque del barrio.
2. ___ niño encontró ___ guante en ___ puerta del teatro.
3. Necesitamos ___ libra de azúcar y ___ par de huevos para preparar ___ postre preferido de papá.
4. Juan tuvo que esperar ___ minutos antes de entrar a ___ oficina de su jefe.
5. En ___ zoológico de la ciudad vimos ___ jirafa, ___ león, ___ elefante, ___ tigre y ___ tortugas.
6. ___ animal preferido de todos fue ___ gorila.

Exercise 39. Complete the following paragraph using the correct definite or indefinite article.

___ joven Javier, todos ___ días se levanta a ___ seis de ___ mañana. Se baña, se viste y bebe ___ taza de café con ___ galleta. Luego, se cepilla ___ dientes y toma ___ bus para ir a ___ universidad. ___ martes a ___ ocho de ___ mañana tiene clase de estadística. Javier es ___ mejor estudiante de la clase. ___ vez a la semana juega fútbol con ___ amigos que conoció en la universidad.

REVIEW

Exercise 40. Complete according to the model.

Example

Un amigo ecuatoriano y *una amiga ecuatoriana*.

1. Un señor triste y _____________.
2. Un hombre fiel y _____________.
3. Un marido feliz y _____________.
4. Un oficial capaz y _____________.
5. Un policía valiente y _____________.
6. Un gato angora y _____________.
7. Un rey déspota y _____________.
8. Un gobernador popular y _____________.

Exercise 41. Complete the following sentences according to the model.

Example

Gabriel es un muchacho adorado. Liliana *es una muchacha adorada*.

1. El señor Gutiérrez es un artista famoso. La señora Gómez _____________.
2. Julio es un actor famoso. Lucía _____________.
3. Pedro es un campeón de tenis. Martina _____________.
4. Roberto es un cantante excepcional. María _____________.

Exercise 42. Rewrite the following text to the feminine.

1. Tengo un perro valiente, _________________________,
2. un caballo inteligente, _________________________,
3. un gato paciente, _________________________,
4. un ratón inocente, _________________________,
5. y un marido desesperante. _________________________.

Exercise 43. Put the following sentences in the plural according to the model.

Example

Gabriela Mistral es una poeta conocida.
Gabriela Mistral *y César Vallejo son unos poetas conocidos.*

1. John Glenn es un astronauta intrépido.
   John Glenn y Neil Armstrong ______________________________.
2. Nicole Kidman es una actriz famosa.
   Nicole Kidman y Tom Cruise ______________________________.
3. Lance Armstrong es un ciclista veloz.
   Lance Armstrong y Robbie McEwen ______________________________.
4. Batistuta es un futbolista estupendo.
   Batistuta y Romario ______________________________.

Exercise 44. Complete the following sentences using the correct (plural or singular) definite or indefinite article.

1. ____ casa de Julia está en ____ centro de ____ ciudad.
2. ____ hermanos de José viven en ____ apartamento pequeño.
3. ____ filosofía es ____ ciencia olvidada.
4. ____ verano es ____ estación maravillosa.
5. ____ vacas y ____ caballos son mamíferos.
6. ____ actriz Morella y ____ papa viven en Roma.

3

Adjectives

An adjective is a word that qualifies a noun or a pronoun. Depending on how the adjective qualifies the noun or the pronoun, an adjective is classified as **descriptive**, **possessive**, **interrogative** or **demonstrative**.

A. DESCRIPTIVE ADJECTIVES

As its name indicates, a descriptive adjective describes the noun or pronoun it qualifies.

Example

El coche **rojo**
The red car

a. THE GENDER OF THE ADJECTIVE

In terms of gender, **two** types of adjectives exist: those with four possible endings and those with two possible endings.

TIP BOX

Adjectives agree in number and gender with the noun or pronoun they modify:

Four possible endings

la casa amarill**a**	(*the yellow house*)
el coche amarill**o**	(*the yellow car*)
las casas amarill**as**	(*the yellow houses*)
los coches amarill**os**	(*the yellow cars*)

Two possible endings

la mujer **elegante**	(*the elegant woman*)
las mujeres **elegantes**	(*the elegant women*)
el hombre **elegante**	(*the elegant man*)
los hombres **elegantes**	(*the elegant men*)

TIP BOX

The Number of the Adjective

The plural for adjectives is formed by adding **-es** if the adjective ends in a stress vowel or consonant. In other cases, only an **-s** is added. (In general, the same number rules that apply to nouns, apply to adjectives.)

Singular	**Plural**	**English**
grande	grande**s**	*big*
rico	rico**s**	*rich*
blanco	blanco**s**	*white*
iraní	iraní**es**	*Iranian*
atroz*	atro<u>c</u>**es**	*awful*
azul	azul**es**	*blue*

*Note that if the noun ends in **–z**, the singular form becomes a **–c** before the **–es** in the plural.

1. Adjectives that are characterized as having four endings always end with an unstressed **-o**, or with a **consonant** when referring to nationalities.

	Masculine	**Feminine**	**English**
Singular	alto	alta	*tall*
Plural	altos	altas	*tall*
Singular	alemán	alemana	*German*
Plural	alemanes	alemanas	*Germans*

- Adjectives that end in **-o:**

bajo
alto

bonita
fea

bueno
malo

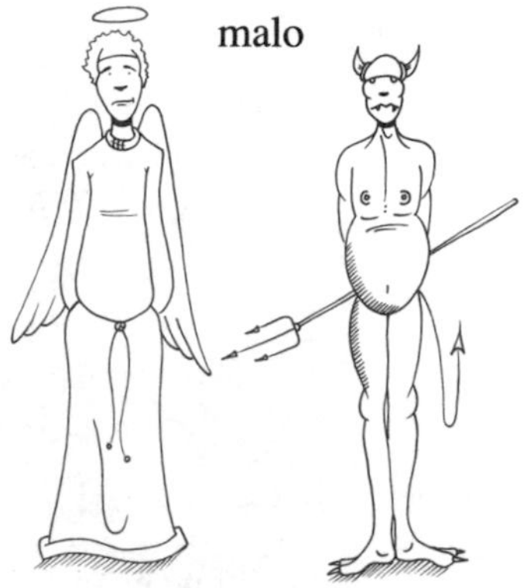

barato
caro

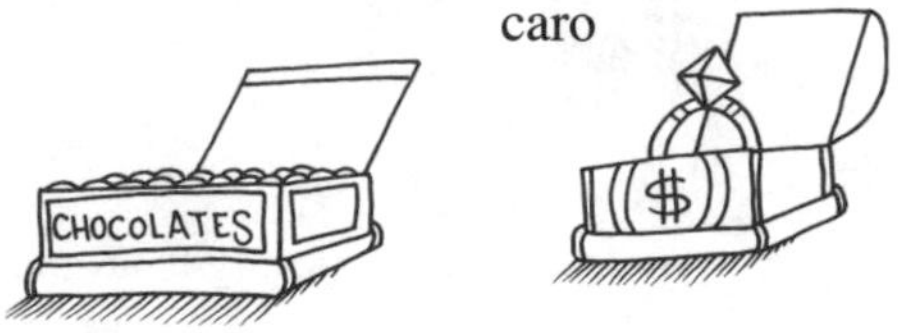

corto
largo

delgada
gordo

sucio
limpio

loco
cuerdo

simpático
antipático

Other adjectives of this type include amarillo *(yellow),* blanco *(white),* negro *(black),* rojo *(red).*

Exercise 1. Choose the appropriate adjective from the list below and fill in the blanks. Use the pictures as clues.

alto/a/os/as	sucio/a/os/as
delgado/a/os/as	caro/a/os/as
hermoso/a/os/as	largo/a/os/as

1. Jaime es un muchacho  ; no come mucho.

2. La camisa de Carlos está  ; acaba de jugar un partido de fútbol.

3. La familia Sandoval vive en una casa  ; costó mucho dinero.

4. El avestruz tiene piernas  ; es muy veloz.

5. Los plátanos de la tienda son muy 

; no puedo creer cómo han subido los precios.

6. La torre de la iglesia es muy  ; allí viven muchas palomas.

Exercise 2. Draw a line from the noun on the left to the appropriate adjective on the right.

1. hombres	a. sucios
2. salud	b. gordo
3. aguas	c. asquerosas
4. platos	d. simpáticos
5. dedo	e. negras
6. basuras	f. buena

- Adjectives ending in a consonant that refer to nationalities:

Masculine	Feminine	English
alemán	alemana	*(German)*
danés	danesa	*(Danish)*
español	española	*(Spaniard)*
finlandés	finlandesa	*(Finnish)*
francés	francesa	*(French)*
irlandés	irlandesa	*(Irish)*
japonés	japonesa	*(Japanese)*
libanés	libanesa	*(Lebanese)*
tailandés	tailandesa	*(Thai)*

Example

Un estudiante danés	Una estudiante danes**a**	*(A Danish student)*
Unos estudiantes danes**es**	Unas estudiantes danes**as**	*(Some Danish students)*

TIP BOX

Note that nationalities are not capitalized in Spanish.

Exercise 3. Complete the following sentences with the appropriate form of the adjective (remember that number and gender must agree).

1. Federico es _______________ (español)
2. María es _______________ (ecuatoriano)
3. El coche de tu padre es _______________ (americano)
4. Los aviones del ejército son _______________ (sueco)
5. Los camiones de la empresa son _______________ (japonés)
6. Las compañeras de Gabriela son _______________ (suizo)
7. La compañía donde trabaja tu padre es _______________ (inglés)
8. Los quesos que compraste son _______________ (francés)
9. La madre de Federico es _______________ (portugués)
10. La suegra de Pedro _______________ (boliviano)
11. Los marineros que están en el puerto son _______________ (alemán)
12. Las señoritas Delgado son _______________ (panameño)
13. Tu amiga es _______________ (salvadoreño)
14. Ximena y Carmen son _______________ (argentino)

2. Adjectives that are characterized as having two possible endings always end in **-e** or a **consonant**.

- Two-form adjectives ending in **-e**:

La niña está triste. (*The girl is sad.*)	Las niñas están tristes. (*The girls are sad.*)
El niño está triste. (*The boy is sad.*)	Los niños están tristes. (*The boys are sad.*)

agradable (*pleasant*)
alegre (*happy*)
brillante (*brilliant*)
desconcertante (*disconcerting*)
excelente (*excellent*)
firme (*firm*)
fuerte (*strong*)
grande (*big*)
importante (*important*)
insignificante (*insignificant*)
inteligente (*intelligent*)
interesante (*interesting*)
miserable (*miserable*)
rebelde (*rebellious*)
reconfortante (*comforting*)
torpe (*clumsy*)
triste (*sad*)
verde (*green*)

Exercise 4. Fill in the blank with the adjective that best completes each sentence.

interesante
importante
grande
rebelde
alegre
verde

1. El ejercicio es_______________ para la salud; dicen que prolonga la vida.
2. Vimos una película ___________ y nos reímos mucho.
3. La casa ___________ de la esquina es de mis tíos.
4. Este es un libro _______________de ciencia ficción; es muy entretenido.
5. Julián es un niño desobediente y ___________; su mamá lo castiga mucho.
6. Gloria perdió su bolso __________; lo olvidó en el parque.

TIP BOX

These two adjectives have **only** two forms, singular and plural.

Singular	**Plural**
La mujer hipócrita *(The hypocritical woman)*	Las mujeres hipócritas *(The hypocritical women)*
El hombre hipócrita *(The hypocritical man)*	Los hombres hipócritas *(The hypocritical men)*
El hombre homicida *(The homicidal man)*	Los hombres homicidas *(The homicidal men)*
La mujer homicida *(The homicidal woman)*	Las mujeres homicidas *(The homicidal women)*

The **-a** ending remains the same regardless of the noun gender.

Exercise 5. Choose the adjective in parentheses that best completes each sentence.

1. José no pudo contener sus impulsos ____________ (hipócritas, homicidas) y mató a su rival.
2. ¿Escuchas ese sonido ____________ en el sótano? (chocante, fuerte) ¿Será la tubería?
3. Revisé mis ejercicios y sólo encontré errores ____________. (insignificantes, miserables)
4. Admiro a las personas ____________. (desconcertantes, inteligentes)
5. El café te quedó ____________; (excelente, firme) va muy bien con el postre de manzana.
6. José le dio a su amigo un abrazo ____________ (excelente, reconfortante) después de la pérdida de su abuelo.

- Adjectives taking only two endings that end in a consonant:

La casa **azul** (*The blue house*)	Las casas **azules** (*The blue houses*)
El coche **azul** (*The blue car*)	Los coches **azules** (*The blue cars*)

atroz (*atrocious*)
azul (*blue*)
cortés (*polite*)
cruel (*cruel*)
difícil (*difficult*)
especial (*special*)
fácil (*easy*)
feliz (*happy*)
gris (*grey*)
joven (*young*)
mejor (*best*)
peor (*worst*)
pertinaz (*persistent*)
sutil (*subtle*)
útil (*useful*)
virgen (*virgin*)

TIP BOX

Adjectives ending in *-án*, *-ón*, *-or*, and *-in*, have **four** endings when referring to a person.

holgazán	holgazana	*(lazy)*
charlatán	charlatana	*(charlatan)*
trabajador	trabajadora	*(worker)*
creador	creadora	*(creative)*

Exercise 6. Claudia talks with her sister Ana while she gets ready to go to a party. Use the following adjectives below to fill in the blanks.

cortés	atroz	joven	peor	feliz
fácil	especial	cruel	gris	

1. Ana:—Te ves ____________ con ese vestido; te hace ver gorda.
2. Claudia:—No seas tan ____________. Es el mejor que tengo.
3. Ana:—Puedes ponerte mi vestido ____________, es perfecto para un baile.
4. Claudia:—¿Estás loca? Ese vestido es ____________.
5. Ana:—No es verdad. Eres ____________ y todo te luce bien.
6. Claudia:—Gracias, Ana. Si eso te hace ____________, me pondré tu vestido.

Exercise 7. Match the noun on the left with one of the adjectives on the right.

1. selva (*jungle*)	a. sutil
2. caballero (*knight*)	b. difícil
3. ejercicio (*exercise*)	c. virgen
4. asunto (*issue*)	d. fácil
5. lluvia (*rain*)	e. pertinaz
6. maquillaje (*makeup*)	f. cortés

Exercise 8. Complete each sentence with the appropriate adjective. Remember that adjectives must agree in gender and number with the noun they qualify.

azul especial joven mejor trabajador útil

1. Mis tíos son muy ____________ pero debido a la recesión económica perdieron su trabajo.
2. ¡Qué árboles tan altos! Y lo más increíble de todo es que son muy ____________; los sembramos tan sólo hace 3 años.
3. Juntos caminamos bajo el cielo ____________ oscuro.

4. ¡Qué navaja tan ___________! Trae hasta lupa.
5. Mis abuelitos son ___________. Siempre que los visito me cuentan unas anécdotas interesantísimas.
6. Las hamburguesas del restaurante de la esquina, definitivamente son las ___________.

TIP BOX

An adjective that refers to two or more nouns takes the plural form. If the nouns are masculine, the adjectives also will be in the masculine form. Adjectives accompanying feminine nouns will be in the feminine form.

Example

El coche y el vestido de José son roj**os**.
José's car and suit are red.

Tanto la planta como la flor son blanc**as**.
This plant and flower are both white.

When the nouns are from both genders, the masculine adjective form is used.

Example

María, Liliana, Josefina y José son tímid**os**.
María, Liliana, Josefina, and José are timid.

b. SHORT-FORM ADJECTIVES

Some adjectives have a shortened form; they lose their last vowel or syllable when they precede a masculine singular noun. An exception occurs when the adjective is preceded by the adverb **más** (*more*) or **menos** (*less*).

Adjectives that drop their last syllable are **bueno**, **malo**, and **grande** (*good, bad,* and *big*).

Example

Un **buen** hombre *A good man*	Un **mal** comienzo *A bad beginning*
Una **buena** mujer *A good woman*	Una **mala** persona *A bad person*

TIP BOX

Note that the adjective **grande** loses its last syllable when it precedes either a masculine or feminine singular noun.

Un **gran** hombre *A great man*	Una **gran** mujer *A great woman*

TIP BOX

Note that Catholic saints in Spanish drop the last syllable of the word **santo** when it precedes a masculine proper noun in the case of *San Juan, San Andrés, San Francisco, San Ignacio.*

Exceptions: *Santo Tomás* and *Santo Domingo.*

Exercise 9. Complete the following sentences with the appropriate form of the adjective.

1. La isla de ______ Juan de Puerto Rico está en el mar Caribe. (San *or* Santo)
2. Federico es un ______ amigo. (grande *or* gran)
3. Liliana es la más ______ de todas nuestras amigas. (grande *or* gran)
4. ______ Teresa de Jesús es famosa por sus poemas. (San or Santa)
5. Todos tenemos a veces un ______ día. (malo *or* mal)
6. No es bueno estar rodeado de ______ compañías. (mal *or* malas)

TIP BOX

Descriptive adjectives exist in two categories, depending how they are connected to the noun or pronoun they modify.

Predicative adjectives are connected by a linking verb such as *estar* (to be), *ser* (to be), *sentirse* (to feel), *resultar* (to result), *parecer* (to seem), *semejar* (to look like), *continuar* (to continue), *seguir* (to follow) to the noun or pronoun they modify.

Example

La señora está aburrida. *The woman is bored.*	El señor es mexicano. *The man is Mexican.*

El señor parece argentino.
The man seems to be Argentinean.

Attributive adjectives follow or precede the noun or pronoun they qualify. In Spanish, however, attributive adjectives commonly **follow** the noun they modify and, in doing so, make the noun more specific.

Example

Las chicas chilenas están en la biblioteca.
The Chilean girls are in the library.

El coche rojo de Juan es nuevo.
Juan's red car is new.

When the adjective **precedes** the noun, it qualifies from an emotional standpoint, while the adjective that follows the noun characterizes the object logically.

Example

Los dorados cabellos de María.
Maria's golden hair.

Las hermosas playas del Caribe.
The beautiful Caribbean beaches.

TIP BOX

Many adjectives have different meanings depending on if they precede or follow the noun or pronoun they qualify.

Example

Pobre hombre (pobre = miserable, desgraciado)
Poor man!, He is lonely.

Hombre pobre (pobre = sin dinero)
That man is poor; he has no money.

Mi casa nueva (nueva = reciente, construida hace poco)
My house was recently built.

Mi nueva casa (vivía en otra hace poco)
My new house is near to the old address I had.

Exercise 10. Complete each sentence with the appropriate adjective.

blanca delicado excelente feliz pobre triste

1. Todos se burlaron del ___________ viejo.
2. De repente apareció el caballero de la ___________ luna.
3. Con un ___________ paso avanzó hacia adelante y desenfundó su espada.
4. Nos dieron de comer una ___________ carne asada.
5. Qué ___________ vida la del pobre Lara.
6. Los padres de Esther nos desearon un___________ año nuevo.

c. ADJECTIVES AS NOUNS

An adjective may have the function of a noun.

Example

Los pobres no tienen que comer.
The poor do not have anything to eat.

El rojo es mi color preferido.
Red is my favorite color.

Exercise 11. Change the following sentences by transforming the adjectives into nouns.

Example

La mujer rubia está trabajando.
La rubia está trabajando.

1. El pobre hombre está sin trabajo. ______________________________.
2. La señorita joven ganó el concurso de belleza. ______________________________.
3. Los empleados trabajadores pidieron un aumento de salario. ____________________.
4. El chico alemán viajó por Sudamérica. ______________________________.
5. Las mujeres argentinas son muy simpáticas. ______________________________.
6. El coche negro es mi preferido. ______________________________.

B. DEMONSTRATIVE ADJECTIVES

A demonstrative adjective is a word used to signal or emphasize a noun.

Example

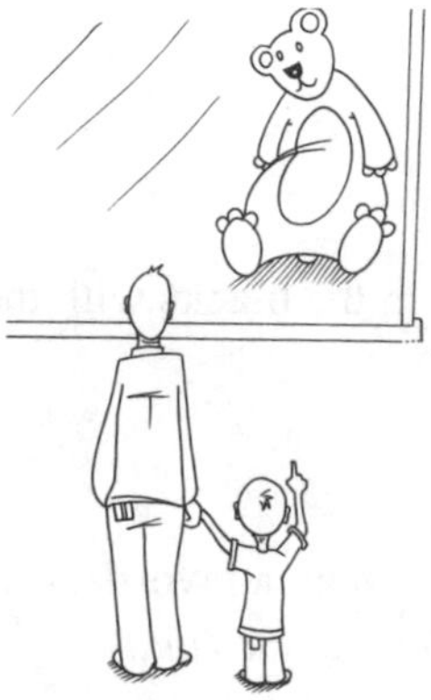

Este oso nos está mirando.
This *bear is looking at us.*

Ese león está dormido.
That *lion is sleeping.*

Aquellos monos están jugando.
Those *other monkeys are playing.*

FORMS OF THE DEMONSTRATIVE ADJECTIVES

Masculine		Feminine	
Singular	**Plural**	**Singular**	**Plural**
este *this*	estos *these*	esta *this*	estas *these*
ese *that*	esos *those*	esa *that*	esas *those*
aquel *that over there*	aquellos *those over there*	aquella *that over there*	aquellas *those over there*

Exercise 12. Write the correct form of the adjective on the line provided.

1. Me gustan _____________ flores. (este)
2. _____________ restaurante es el mejor de la ciudad. (aquel)
3. Te traje _____________ pasteles para la cena. (este)
4. Ten cuidado con _____________ copas. Son muy delicadas. (ese)
5. _____________ periódico dice que hará frío hoy. (este)
6. ¿Por qué tienes _____________ libros en el suelo? (este)

Exercise 13. Gabriela and her mother are at the supermarket. Fill in the blanks with the demonstrative adjective that corresponds to the one in parentheses.

—Mamá, compremos _____________ jabón. *(this)*
—Vamos a comprar _____________ jabón rosado, Gabriela. Es mi marca favorita. *(that over there)*
—Pero no me gusta el perfume de _____________ marca de jabón, mamá. *(that)*
—¿Qué te parece _____________ jabón cremoso? *(this)*
—Me gusta mucho más. ¿Ves _____________ flores? *(these)*
—¡Qué lindas! Quedan perfectas en _____________ jarrón que te regaló papá. *(that over there)*

C. POSSESSIVE ADJECTIVES

Spanish has two forms of possessive adjectives, a short form that is used before nouns, and a long form that is used after nouns.

a. SHORT-FORM POSSESSIVE ADJECTIVES

Singular	Plural	Translation
mi	mis	*my*
tu	tus	*your (informal)*
su	sus	*your (formal), its, his, her, their*
nuestro(a)	nuestros(as)	*our*
vuestro(a)	vuestros(as)	*your*

Short-form possessive adjectives precede the noun they modify and agree with that noun in number and, in the case of **nuestro** and **vuestro**, also in gender.

Example

¿Dónde están **mis** llaves?
Where are my keys?

Nuestra casa es blanca.
Our house is white.

TIP BOX

Possessive adjectives are not used when possession is evident. For example:

Me puse la camisa. Me lavo la cara.
I put my shirt on. *I wash my face.*

Vuestro is only used in Spain, as it refers to the **vosotros** pronoun.

Exercise 14. Fill in the blanks in the paragraph with the correct adjective.

mis su mi tu nuestra mis

Estoy buscando ____________ mochila. Me voy de viaje con ____________ primos Arturo y Gonzalo. ____________ tía Carmen y ____________ esposo tienen una casa en el campo y vamos a visitarlos. Préstame ____________ auto y devuélveme ____________ maletas. Las voy a necesitar.

Exercise 15. Somebody switched the adjectives in this exercise. Write the correct adjective in the parentheses at the end of each sentence.

1. Así son, <u>tu</u> amigos. Esa es la pura verdad. (_____)
2. Dame <u>vuestras</u> teléfono. Te llamo mañana. (_____)
3. Lucía y Marta dejaron <u>tus</u> maletas en el hotel. (_____)
4. El panadero comienza <u>su</u> trabajo muy temprano. (_____)
5. Mi hermana y yo donamos <u>sus</u> ropa vieja a los pobres. (_____)
6. Pensad en la felicidad de <u>nuestra</u> familias. (_____)

b. LONG-FORM POSSESSIVE ADJECTIVES

Long-form possessive adjectives follow the noun they modify and agree with that noun in number and in gender.

Singular		Plural		Translation
Masculine	**Feminine**	**Masculine**	**Feminine**	
mío	mía	míos	mías	*my, of mine*
tuyo	tuya	tuyos	tuyas	*your (singular informal)*
suyo	suya	suyos	suyas	*your (singular or plural formal), its, his, her, their, of yours, of theirs*
nuestro	nuestra	nuestros	nuestras	*our, of ours*
vuestro	vuestra	vuestros	vuestras	*your (plural informal), of yours*

Example

¿Dónde están las llaves **mías**?
Where are my keys?

La casa **nuestra** es blanca.
Our house is white.

TIP BOX

In Spanish, short-term possessive adjectives are more commonly used than long-term possessive adjectives. Both forms are interchangeable. However, when using the long-term possessive adjective, a definite or an indefinite article is usually used to determine the noun.

Example

Miré los muros de **mi** patria.
Miré los muros de **la** patria **mía**.
(Francisco de Quevedo, 1580–1645)
I looked upon my native country's walls.

Also note that long-term possessive adjectives are identical to possessive pronouns.*

* See Chapter 8, Pronouns.

Exercise 16. Replace in the following sentences the short-form possessive adjectives with the corresponding long-form possessive adjectives.

Example

Tu camisa está sucia.
La camisa **tuya** está sucia.

1. Francisco me invitó a **su** finca el fin de semana.

   ____

2. Pero, yo prefiero quedarme en **mi** casa.

   ____

3. Felipe, **mi** novio, llega de Chile mañana.

   ____

4. Iremos a un bar el viernes en la noche con **nuestras** amigas de la universidad.

   ____

5. El sábado en la tarde iremos con **tus** hijos a la playa.

____

6. Santiago perdió **tus** libros.

____

7. Lola no puede abrir **su** coche porque perdió **sus** llaves.

____

8. El futuro de **vuestro** país no es muy prometedor.

____

D. CARDINAL AND ORDINAL NUMBERS

Cardinal numbers are used to refer to nouns that are of a specific quantity, and ordinal numbers refer to the order or position of a noun.

a. CARDINAL NUMBERS

TIP BOX

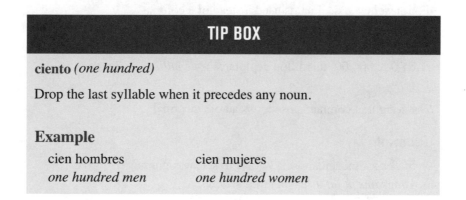

ciento *(one hundred)*

Drop the last syllable when it precedes any noun.

Example

cien hombres — cien mujeres
one hundred men — *one hundred women*

Cardinal numbers are formed by combining a series of basic numbers to form all possible numbers.

Cardinal Numbers			
0	cero	12	doce
1	uno (un)/ una	13	trece
2	dos	14	catorce
3	tres	15	quince
4	cuatro	16–19	(diez y seis or dieciséis, diez y siete or diecisiete, etc.)
5	cinco		
6	seis	20	veinte
7	siete	21–29	(veintiuno, veintidós, etc.)
8	ocho	30	treinta
9	nueve	31–100	(treinta y uno, treinta y dos, etc., except numbers that are multiples of 10)
10	diez		
11	once		

40	cuarenta	200	doscientos/as* (hay doscient**as** mujeres, hay doscient**os** hombres, same pattern from 200 to 900)
50	cincuenta		
60	sesenta		
70	setenta	500	quinientos/as
80	ochenta	900	novecientos/as
90	noventa	1000	mil
100	cien	1,000,000	un millón
101–199	(ciento uno/a, ciento dos, etc.)		

* Any number that has in one of its parts the ending **-tos**, if qualifying a feminine noun, changes to **-tas**.

TIP BOX

Notation of Cardinal Numbers

In Spanish, notation numbering is as follows:

For currency, a decimal is used instead of a comma.

Example

$1.000.000,00: un millón de dólares (*one million dollars*)

For weight, a comma is used instead of a decimal.

Example

56,3 kg: cincuenta y seis kilos y trescientos gramos (*fifty-six kilograms point three hundred grams*)*

* 1 kilogram = 1000 grams

Exercise 17. Write out the following numbers.

1. 245 ________________ coches
2. 45 ________________ televisores
3. 1282 ________________ manzanas
4. 145.765 ________________ personas
5. 554.898 ________________ trabajadores
6. 1.289.908 ________________ naranjas
7. 209 ________________ muchachos
8. 229.000 ________________ mujeres
9. 101 ________________ niñas
10. 590 ________________ naranjas
11. 21 ________________ balones
12. 33 ________________ almacenes

Exercise 18. Rewrite the following sentences using numbers.

1. Aquel pescado pesa siete kilos y medio. ______________________________.
2. Tengo tres mil quinientos dólares en el banco. ______________________________.
3. El préstamo es de un millón trescientas mil euros. ______________________________.
4. El bebé pesó seis kilos y treinta gramos. ______________________________.
5. La deuda externa de Argentina es de ciento cuarenta mil millones de dólares.
______________________________.

TIP BOX

To say the time in Spanish we use the following pattern.

Example

¿Qué hora es?
What time is it?

Son las doce.

Son las doce y 5.

Son las doce y cuarto.

Son las doce y veinticinco.

Son las doce y media.

Es la una menos veinticinco.

Es la una menos cuarto.

Es la una.

Exercise 19. ¿Qué hora es?

1. 

2. 

3. 

4. 

5. 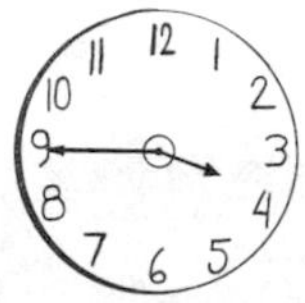

6. 

7. 

8. 

b. ORDINAL NUMBERS

Ordinal numbers are adjectives that agree in gender and number with the noun they qualify. They refer to the order or position of a noun in a series.

Ordinal numbers *primero* (first) and *tercero* (third) drop the vowel **-o** when qualifying a masculine singular noun. For example:

El **primer** hombre *(the first man).* El **tercer** piso *(the third floor).*

Ordinal Numbers					
1°	*primero / primer*	first	12°	*duodécimo*	twelfth
2°	*segundo*	second	13°	*decimotercero/ decimotercer*	thirteenth
3°	*tercero / tercer*	third	14°	*decimocuarto*	fourteenth
4°	*cuarto*	fourth	15°	*decimoquinto*	fifteenth
5°	*quinto*	fifth	16°	*decimosexto*	sixteenth
6°	*sexto*	sixth	17°	*decimoséptimo*	seventeenth
7°	*séptimo*	seventh	18°	*decimoctavo*	eighteenth
8°	*octavo*	eighth	19°	*decimonoveno*	nineteenth
9°	*noveno*	ninth	20°	*vigésimo*	twentieth
10°	*décimo*	tenth			
11°	*undécimo*	eleventh			

TIP BOX

Ordinal numbers are also used to designate kings, queens, and popes.

Example

Alfonso **VI** (Alfonso **sexto**)
Alfonso the sixth

Cardinal numbers are used for dates. The sole exception is the first of the month.

Example

Hoy es **primero** de julio.
Today is the first of July.

Mañana es **dos** de julio.
Tomorrow is July second.

Exercise 20. Complete the following sentences with the corresponding ordinal number.

1. Neil Armstrong fue el ___________ (1°) hombre en pisar la Luna.
2. La ___________ (3°) semana de marzo iremos a Madrid.
3. Juan fue el ___________ (1°) en llegar, pero Alberto fue el ___________ (1°) niño en cruzar la meta.
4. El apartamento de Rosario está en el ___________ (3°) piso y el de Gabriela en el ___________ (4°) piso.
5. María y José fueron los ___________ (1°) invitados que llegaron a la fiesta.
6. En la competencia de ciclismo, Federico fue el ___________ (13°) ciclista en cruzar la meta.

Exercise 21. According to the picture, answer the following sentences.

1. El hombre soltero baila solo en el __________ piso.

2. Los viejitos del __________ piso están comiendo.

3. La pastelería está en el __________ piso.

4. Los jóvenes se divierten en el __________ piso.

5. La señorita está pasando la aspiradora en el __________ piso.

6. La madre del __________ piso está dándole de comer a su hijo.

REVIEW

Exercise 22. Put the adjective in the feminine according to the model.

Example

José es boliviano. Lucía *es boliviana*.

1. Julio es colombiano.
   Marta __________________.
2. Mi tío es español.
   Mi tía es __________________.
3. Mi hermano es guapo.
   Mi hermana __________________.
4. Mi amigo está contento.
   Mi amiga__________________.
5. Pablo es inteligente.
   Liliana es __________________.
6. Mi tío es simpático.
   Mi tía es __________________.
7. Tu abuelo es amable.
   Tu abuela es __________________.
8. La gata está enferma.
   El perro está __________________.
9. Tu profesor es alemán.
   Tu profesora es __________________.
10. Raúl es hipócrita.
    Lucía es __________________.

Exercise 23. Put the adjective in the feminine according to the model.

Example

Un coche amarillo y una casa *amarilla*.

1. Un helicóptero eficiente y un avión ___________.
2. Un jugo refrescante y una fruta ___________.
3. Un amigo fiel y una compañera ___________.
4. Un actor famoso y una actriz ___________.
5. Un empleado perezoso y una empleada ___________.
6. Un profesor exigente y una profesora ___________.
7. Un niño inteligente y una niña ______________.
8. Un país interesante y una ciudad ______________.
9. Unos animales inmensos y unos árboles ______________.
10. Un coche rojo y una moto ______________.

Exercise 24. Rewrite the following sentences by spelling the numbers.

1. Hay 68.000 soldados en Afganistán. ______________________________.
2. Tenemos 3.673 francos suizos. ______________________________.
3. José ganó 578.000.000 de pesos. ______________________________.
4. Ese toro pesa 787 Kg. ______________________________.
5. El premio mayor de la lotería es 231.537.000 dólares. ______________________________.
6. Ese anillo de oro pesa 18 onzas. ______________________.
7. Al concierto asistieron más de 200 personas. ______________________.
8. La Luna se encuentra a 384.400 kilómetros de la Tierra. ______________________.
9. Entre todos reunimos más de 22.250 pesos. ______________________.
10. Colón viajó a América en 1492. ______________________.

Exercise 25. Complete the following sentences with the appropriate demonstrative adjective.

1. ¿Cuánto cuesta (that) __________ coche?
2. Me gusta (this) __________ casa.
3. (These) __________ niños me tienen desesperado.
4. (That) __________ lavadora de platos no sirve para nada.
5. Javier, ¿sabes quién es (that) __________ muchacha?
6. (This) _______ marca de chocolates es la mejor.
7. (These) _______ aguacates están muy caros.
8. ¡Díme por favor quién es (that over there) _______ mujer!
9. ¿Qué es (that) _______ luz que se ve a lo lejos?
10. Sí, (that over there) _______ perro fue el que me mordió.

Exercise 26. Complete the following sentences with the appropriate possessive or demonstrative adjective.

1. (These)___ pantalones son ____ (de mí) pantalones. ____ (de ti) pantalones están sobre la cama.
2. (Those over there) ____ muchachos están compitiendo con ____ (de ellos) bicicletas.
3. (That) ____ señora tiene ____ (de ti) libros de español.
4. ¿(That over there) ____ muchacho tiene ____ (de él) perro?
5. (This) ____ es ____ (de nosotros) amigo Marco.
6. (This) ____ es ____ (de vosotros) casa, ¿verdad?
7. La emoción de (those over there) _______ recuerdos le humedecieron _______ (de él) ojos.
8. Para salir de (this) _______ crisis económica lo mejor es consumir poco.
9. ¿Recuerdas (that over there) _______ noche, _______ (de mí) perros ladrando?
10. ¿No te acuerdas? (That) _______ tarde _______ (de ti) hermana se desmayó.

Exercise 27. Complete the following sentences with the corresponding ordinal number.

1. Fernando y Gabriel fueron los ____________ (1º) en llegar a casa.
2. José, es la ____________ (3º) vez que te lo digo. ¡Vete de aquí!
3. Jorge fue el ____________ (1º) novio de Teresa.
4. ¡Este es el ____________ (5º) día que paso sin comer!
5. De todas las sinfonías de Beethoven, la _______ (6º) es la mejor.
6. La familia Pérez vive en _______ (3º) piso.
7. Carlos _______ (5º) fue rey de España durante el siglo XVI.
8. Hoy es el _______ (1º) día del mes.
9. ¡Es el colmo! ¡Esta es la _______ (15º) vez que llegas tarde a clase!

4

Verbs: Simple Tenses of the Indicative

miro	miras	mira
hablo	hablas	habla
trabajo	trabajas	trabaja
busco	buscas	busca
compro	compras	compra
viajo	viajas	viaja

I. The Present Indicative

There are three different verb classes in Spanish—those ending in **-ar**, **-er**, and **-ir**. Some verbs are **regular** whereas others are **irregular**.

A. REGULAR VERBS

The **regular conjugation** in the present indicative is formed by adding the following endings to the stem of the verbs.

Subject Pronoun	Verb Endings in the Present Indicative		
	-ar	**-er**	**-ir**
yo	-o	-o	-o
tú	-as	-es	-es
él, ella, usted	-a	-e	-e
nosotros/as	-amos	-emos	-imos
vosotros/as	-áis	-éis	-ís
ellos, ellas, ustedes	-an	-en	-en

TIP BOX

Example

To conjugate the verb *hablar* (to speak) in the present indicative, add to the stem **habl-** the corresponding verb ending for the verbs that end in **-ar**: **-o**, **-as**, **-a**, **-amos**, **-áis**, **-an**.

yo habl**o** (*I speak*)
tú habl**as** (*you speak*)
él, ella, usted habl**a** (*he, she speaks, you (sing.) speak*)
nosotros/as habl**amos** (*we speak*)
vosotros/as habl**áis** (*you (pl.) speak*)
ellos, ellas, ustedes habl**an** (*they speak*)

The following common verbs are regular in the present indicative.

-ar class verbs	*-er* class verbs	*-ir* class verbs
alistar *(to make ready)*	aprender (*to learn*)	abrir *(to open)*
amar *(to love)*	beber (*to drink*)	admitir *(to admit)*
bailar *(to dance)*	ceder *(to yield)*	aplaudir *(to applaud)*
buscar *(to look for)*	comer (*to eat*)	asistir *(to assist)*
caminar *(to walk)*	comprender (*to understand*)	decidir *(to decide)*
comprar *(to buy)*	correr (*to run*)	escribir *(to write)*
ducharse* *(to take a shower)*	creer (*to believe*)	existir *(to exist)*
enviar *(to send)*	deber *(to must)*	exprimir *(to squeeze)*
hablar *(to speak)*	emprender (*to start*)	insistir *(to insist)*
llegar *(to arrive)*	leer (*to read*)	omitir *(to omit)*
mirar *(to look)*	meter *(to put)*	oprimir *(to oppress, to press)*
necesitar *(to need)*	prometer *(to promise)*	partir *(to divide, to leave)*
retirar *(to withdraw)*	responder (*to answer*)	permitir *(to allow)*
trabajar *(to work)*	retroceder *(to move back)*	pulir *(to polish)*
viajar *(to travel)*	romper *(to break)*	recibir *(to receive)*
dibujar *(to draw)*	socorrer (*to help*)	regalar *(to give a present)*
saltar *(to jump)*	sorprender *(to surprise)*	resumir *(to summarize)*
casarse* *(to get married)*	suspender *(to suspend)*	reunirse* *(to meet)*
graduarse* *(to graduate)*	temer (*to fear*)	subir *(to go up)*
ganar *(to win)*	vender (*to sell*)	vivir *(to live)*

*See Chapter 7, Pronominal Verbs.

Exercise 1. Complete the following sentences using the present tense.

1. Yo ________(llegar) siempre tarde.
2. Nosotros ________ (temer) que tu te extravíes si vas solo.
3. Ellos________ (creer) ciegamente en sus dirigentes.
4. Mis padres ________ (vivir) en Cartagena.
5. Tú nunca me ________ (responder) lo que te pregunto.
6. Ustedes ________ (mirar) de una manera extraña.
7. Marcelo ________ (insistir) en comprarme mi vaca.
8. Mi madre no me ________ (comprender).
9. León y Lucía ________ (necesitar) un lápiz, ¿les puedes prestar el tuyo?
10. Los perros no ________ (hablar).

11. ¿Cómo hacéis? ¿Primero ___________ (saltar) y luego nadáis?
12. ¡Qué bonito es ver cómo las olas se ___________ (romper) sobre el acantilado!
13. Los espectadores ___________ (aplaudir) después de la función.
14. Santiago ___________ (dibujar) muy bien.
15. ¡Tú siempre ___________ (prometer) pero nunca cumples!
16. Es increíble esta máquina. Sólo (tú) ___________ (oprimir) un botón e inmediatamente tienes un delicioso café.
17. ¡Ese tipo *(guy)* siempre ___________ (ganar)! ¡Seguro que hace trampa!
18. Todavía muchas hijas ___________ (ceder) sus derechos legales de poder heredar de sus padres.
19. En abril mi novio y yo ___________ (partir) para Lisboa, ¡y no pensamos volver a esta ciudad nunca jamás!
20. Los ríos no ___________ (retroceder); siempre corren hacia el mar.

B. VERBS WITH SPELLING CHANGES

This group of verbs are regular as they do not change in form. They only change their spelling to reflect their pronunciation. Such verbs are all those ending in **-cer**, **-cir**; **-ger**, **-gir**; **-guir**; **-uir**; and **-iar**, **-uar**.

a. Verbs that end in **-cer** and **-cir** change ONLY in the first person singular (*yo*) of the present indicative in two ways:

SPELLING RULES

When the stem of the verb ends in consonant (**n** or **r**) the -**c**- from the ending **-cer** or **-cir** changes to **z**		When the stem of the verb ends in vowel a **z** is added before the **c**	
conven**cer** (*to convince*)	espar**cir** (*to scatter*)	cono**cer** (*to know*)	condu**cir** (*to drive*)
yo conven**z**o	yo espar**z**o	yo cono**z**co	yo condu**z**co

Other verbs ending in **-cer** and **-cir** preceded by a consonant are:

ejer**cer** (*to exert*)
espar**cir** (*to disperse*)
frun**cir** (*to frown*)
ven**cer** (*to vanquish*)
zur**cir** (*to darn*)

Other verbs ending in **-cer**, **cir** preceded by a vowel are:

aborre**cer** (*to detest*)
agrade**cer** (*to thank*)
apete**cer** (*to feel an urge for*)
dedu**cir** (*to deduce*)
desapare**cer** (*to disappear*)
indu**cir** (*to induce*)
introdu**cir** (*to introduce*)
na**cer** (*to be born*)
recono**cer** (*to recognize*)
redu**cir** (*to reduce*)

Exercise 2. Complete the following sentences using the present tense.

1. Yo __________ (zurcir) el vestido y tú __________ (zurcir) los calcetines. ¿Vale?
2. Yo __________ (ejercer) mi profesión y tú __________ (ejercer) la tuya. ¿De acuerdo?
3. Juan me __________ (aborrecer) y yo le __________ (aborrecer).
4. ¡Yo le __________ (apetecer) y tú le __________ (apetecer)!
5. Yo __________ (reducir) la comida y ustedes __________ (reducir) la bebida. ¿De acuerdo?
6. María __________ (fruncir) las cejas y yo __________ (fruncir) el ceño.

Exercise 3. Complete the following sentences using the present tense.

1. Él no________(reconocer) pero yo sí ________(reconocer) que todo ha cambiado.
2. (yo) ________(vencer) a mis rivales si cometen errores.
3. (yo) ________ (esparcir) el grano de trigo sobre la tierra húmeda.
4. En cuanto veo a mis deudores, (yo) ________ (desaparecer).
5. Si (yo) me________ (introducir) en la caverna paso desapercibido.
6. Todas las mañanas (yo) ________ (agradecer) al Señor por el nuevo día.
7. (yo) ________ (aborrecer) las tardes lluviosas.
8. Cada día me (yo) ________ (convencer) más de que estás loco.
9. (yo) ________ (conducir) siempre que Juan se emborracha.

b. Verbs that end in **-ger**, **-gir** change ONLY in the first person singular (*yo*) of the present indicative.

SPELLING RULES

Verbs ending in **-ger, gir** change from **g** to **j** in the first person singular (*yo*)	
prote**ger** (*to protect*)	exi**gir** (*to demand*)
yo prote**j**o	yo exi**j**o

Other verbs ending in **-ger**, **gir** that change **g** to **j** in the first person singular *(yo)* are:

aco**ger** (*to greet*)
afli**gir** (*to afflict*)
co**ger** (*to grab*)
corre**gir** (*to correct*)
diri**gir** (*to direct*)
ele**gir** (*to elect*)
emer**ger** (*to emerge*)
enco**ger** (*to shrink*)
esco**ger** (*to choose*)
exi**gir** (*to demand*)
fin**gir** (*to simulate*)
infrin**gir** (*to infringe*)
prote**ger** (*to protect*)
reco**ger** (*to pick up*)
restrin**gir** (*to restrain*)
resur**gir** (*to re-emerge*)
ru**gir** (*to roar*)
sumer**gir** (*to submerge, to drown*)
sur**gir** (*to emerge*)
ur**gir** (*to urge*)

Exercise 4. Complete the following sentences using the present tense.

1. Yo __________ (recoger) las naranjas y tú __________ (recoger) las fresas.
2. Tú __________ (elegir) al presidente y yo __________ (elegir) a los senadores.
3. Yo siempre __________ (emerger) limpio y cristalino pero vosotros __________ (emerger) sucios y deshonestos.
4. Tú me __________ (corregir) el inglés y yo te __________ (corregir) el español.
5. ¡No es justo! Tú me __________ (exigir) mucho y yo no te __________ (exigir) nada.
6. Tú te __________ (encoger) de hombros ante mis problemas y yo me __________ (encoger) por dentro de rabia.
7. Es verdad que a veces yo __________ (infringir) la ley, ¡pero no te hagas el inocente! tú también la __________ (infringir).
8. Ellos se __________ (afligir) de mí pero yo no me __________ (afligir) por ellos.
9. De mi ceniza, siempre (yo)__________ (resurgir) como el fénix, pero tú siempre __________ (resurgir) para destruirme.
10. Yo__________ (escoger) tu traje y tú __________ (escoger) mi vestido. ¿De acuerdo?

Exercise 5. Complete the following paragraphs using the present tense.

1. Si quieres yo________(recoger) el desorden de la fiesta. Pero a cambio te________ (exigir) que no traigas más amigos. Así, además te ________(proteger) el bolsillo. Porque si yo ________ (acoger) bien esa gente es porque siempre me ________ (restringir) de decir lo que pienso y ________ (fingir) ser un cálido huésped.
2. Porque como bien lo sabes, yo no ________ (escoger) a quien traer y más bien siempre me________ (dirigir) a mi habitación y me ________ (sumergir) en mis divagaciones. Pues con ellos no tengo nada de que hablar.

c. Verbs that end in **-guir** change ONLY in the first person singular (*yo*) in the present indicative.

SPELLING RULES

Verbs ending in ***-guir*** change **gu** to **g** in the first person singular (*yo*)
distin**guir** (*to distinguish*)
yo distin**go**

Other verbs ending in **-guir** that change **gu** to **g** in the first person singular *(yo)* are:

conse**guir*** (*to come by; to get*)
prose**guir*** (*to proceed*)
extin**guir** (*to extinguish*)
se**guir*** (*to follow*)
perse**guir*** (*to go after*)
er**guir*** (*to build*)

Note: *The stem of these verbs also changes from **e** to **i** (cons**i**go, pros**i**go, etc.). Because the verb **erguir** starts with the vowel **e,** the beginning of the stem (**ie**) changes to **y** (yo yergo, tú yergues, él yergue, nosotros erguimos, vosotros erguís, ellos yerguen).

Exercise 6. Complete the following sentences using the present tense.

1. Yo __________ (conseguir) la bebida y ustedes __________ (conseguir) la música.
2. Yo __________ (seguir) contigo pero tú ya no__________ (seguir) con él.
3. Yo __________ (erguir) mi cabeza ante la ignominia, mientras que vosotros no __________ (erguir) la vuestra.
4. Yo __________ (perseguir) un ideal y tú __________ (perseguir) los honores vanos.

Exercise 7. Complete the following sentences using the present tense.

1. (yo) No ________(distinguir) un sapo de una rana.
2. Al llegar al cerro siempre tomo un pequeño descanso y ________ (proseguir) mi camino.
3. Ve adelante que yo te ________ (seguir).
4. Este es el último incendio que (yo) ________ (extinguir). ¡En un mes me pensiono de bombero y voy a ser carpintero!
5. Él construye imperios financieros, yo en cambio sólo________ (erguir) castillos de arena.
6. Nunca ________ (conseguir) terminar a tiempo mis deberes.
7. Cuando ________ (perseguir) la liebre durante una jornada de caza vuelvo animado a la casa.

d. Verbs that end in **-uir** change from **i** to **y** before **o** and **e** in all persons except in the first (*nosotros)* and second plural (*vosotros)* persons.

SPELLING RULES

Verbs ending in **-uir** change **i** to **y** before **o** and **e**	
*concl**uir*** (to conclude)	
yo concluyo	nosotros/as concluimos
tú concluyes	vosotros/as concluís
él, ella, usted concluye	ellos, ellas, ustedes concluyen

Other verbs ending in **-uir** that change **i** to **y** before **o** and **e** are:

arg**üir** (*to argue*)
distrib**uir** (*to distribute*)
atrib**uir** (*to attribute to, to confer*)
h**uir** (*to run away*)
constit**uir** (*to constitute*)
incl**uir** (*to include*)
constr**uir** (*to construct*)
infl**uir** (*to influence*)
contrib**uir** (*to contribute*)
int**uir** (*to intuit*)
destit**uir** (*to dismiss*)
obstr**uir** (*to obstruct*)
destr**uir** (*to destroy*)
recl**uir** (*to confine*)
dil**uir** (*to dilute*)
reconstr**uir** (*to reconstruct*)
dismin**uir** (*to diminish*)
sustit**uir** (*to substitute*)

Exercise 8. Complete the following sentences using the present tense.

1. ¿Tú le __________ (atribuir) ese escrito a Jim? ¡Yo se lo __________ (atribuir) a Platón!
2. Nosotros __________ (huir) del huracán y ellos __________ (huir) de los acreedores.
3. ¿(yo) __________ (incluir) en el informe la tasa de crecimiento y luego (nosotros) __________ (incluir) la tasa de desempleo?
4. Los problemas económicos __________ (influir) en mi vida y yo __________ (influir) en tu vida.
5. Los economistas __________ (argüir) que la recesión económica se debe al problema de las hipotecas; yo __________ (argüir) que se debe a una disminución del poder adquisitivo de la población.
6. Tú __________ (constituir) tu empresa y yo __________ (constituir) la mía. ¿Vale?

Exercise 9. Complete the following sentences using the present tense.

1. Como Robin Hood, todo lo que robas (tú) lo ________(distribuir).
2. Te dejo este ejercicio y así (tú) lo ________ (concluir).
3. Dicen que ellos ________ (diluir) la gasolina para ganar más dinero.
4. Mis tíos ________ (destruir) toda la herencia en baratijas.
5. Me pagarán más si (nosotros) ________ (reconstruir) la casa.
6. El río ________ (obstruir) el paso.
7. Vosotros________ (disminuir) la gravedad de los hechos.
8. La policía ________ (recluir) al ladrón en la cárcel.
9. ¿Quién ________ (sustituir) a un buen padre?
10. Los monopolios ________ (contribuir) al deterioro en la calidad de los productos y servicios.

e. Some verbs that end in **-iar** and **-uar** stress the **i** and **u** (in all persons except *nosotros* and *vosotros*) in the stem by splitting the semiconsonant group **-io-** and **-ia-** into two syllables: **í-o** and **í-a**. The semi-consonant group **-ua-** is also split in two: **ú-a**.*

SPELLING RULES

Some verbs ending in **-iar** and **-uar** change **i** to **í** and **u** to **ú** in all forms except *nosotros* and *vosotros*	
env**iar** (to send)	act**uar** (to act)
yo en-v**í-**o tú en-v**í-**as él, ella, usted en-v**í-**a nosotros/as en-via-mos vosotros/as en-viá-is ellos, ellas, ustedes en-v**í-**an	yo ac-t**ú-**o tú ac-t**ú-**as él, ella, usted ac-t**ú-**a nosotros/as ac-tua-mos vosotros/as ac-tuá-is ellos, ellas, ustedes ac-t**ú-**an

* See Chapter 1, IV. C, Diphthongs.

Other verbs ending in **-iar** and **-uar** that change the **i** to **í** and the **u** to **ú** are:

acent**uar** (*to accent, to emphasize*)
ampl**iar** (*to enlarge*)
ans**iar** (*to wish*)
conf**iar** (*to trust*)
contin**uar** (*to continue*)
deval**uar** (*to devalue*)
efect**uar** (*to carry out*)
enfr**iar** (*to cool, to chill*)
evac**uar** (*to evacuate, to vacate*)
eval**uar** (*to evaluate*)
grad**uar**se *(to graduate)*
gu**iar** (*to guide*)
insin**uar** (*to insinuate*)
perpet**uar** (*to perpetuate*)
sit**uar** (*to locate, to situate*)
var**iar** (*to vary*)

Exercise 10. Complete the following sentences using the present tense.

1. Ellos ________(evaluar) sus propios ejercicios.
2. Si (vosotros) ________ (ampliar) vuestro apartamento, tendréis más espacio.
3. Él ________ (enfriar) su café antes de tomarlo.
4. ¡Tú siempre te ________ (situar) en el lugar más inoportuno!
5. El Señor ________ (guiar) mis pasos.
6. ¡Ese trabajo ________ (perpetuar) sus penas!
7. ¿Vosotros ________ (insinuar) que yo miento?
8. En tu país todos los días ________ (devaluar) la moneda.
9. Ellos ________ (efectuar) cambios que son fundamentales para nuestra compañía.
10. Ella ________ (continuar) trabajando en su proyecto de grado.

Exercise 11. Complete the following sentences using the present tense.

1. ¡Tú siempre __________ (acentuar) las palabras mal! Nosotros, en cambio sí las __________ (acentuar) bien.
2. ¡Nosotros __________ (ansiar) la paz y el sosiego! Ellos en cambio__________ (ansiar) vengarse de nosotros.
3. Yo __________ (confiar) en ti, pero tú no __________ (confiar) en mí.
4. Los paramédicos __________ (evacuar) a los heridos y la policía __________ (evacuar) a los curiosos.
5. Si nosotros__________ (variar) nuestra posición tú __________ (variar) la tuya. ¿De acuerdo?
6. ¿Vosotros __________ (insinuar) que el calentamiento global no es verdad? Nosotros __________ (insinuar) lo contrario.

C. VERBS WITH STEM CHANGES

Some verbs from any of the three conjugations (**-ar**, **-er**, **-ir**) have some systematic changes in the vowel (**e**, **i**, **o**, **u**) of their stem in all persons EXCEPT the first and second formal persons plural (*nosotros*, *vosotros*). These changes occur in the vowel of the stem in six different ways (**e** to **ie**, **e** to **i**, **i** to **ie**, **o** to **ue**, **o** to **hue**, **u** to **ue**).

a. Stem vowel change from **e** to **ie**.

cerrar (*to close*)	
yo cierro	nosotros/as cerramos
tú cierras	vosotros/as cerráis
él, ella, usted cierra	ellos, ellas, ustedes cierran

Other verbs with stems changing from **e** to **ie** are:

atender (*to attend to*)
atravesar (*to cross, to pierce*)
calentar (*to warm*)
comenzar (*to begin*)
confesar (*to confess*)
consentir (*to consent, to agree*)
defender (*to defend*)
descender (*to descend*)
despertar (*to wake up*)
divertir (*to have fun, to enjoy*)
empezar (*to begin*)
encender (*to switch on, to ignite, to light*)
encerrar (*to confine, to enclose*)
entender (*to understand*)
gobernar (*to govern*)
mentir (*to lie*)
negar (*to deny*)
pensar (*to think*)
perder (*to lose*)
preferir (*to prefer*)
querer (*to want*)
recomendar (*to recommend*)
sentar (*to sit*)
sentir (*to feel*)
sugerir (*to suggest*)

Exercise 12. Complete the following sentences using the present tense.

1. Yo __________ (encender) el fuego y vosotros __________ (calentar) la comida.
2. Eladio __________ (confesar) sus pecados al cura, pero nosotros le __________ (mentir).
3. ¡No te das cuenta! Adela no te __________ (querer) y tú la __________ (defender).
4. Yo __________ (atender) a los cachorros y vosotros __________ (encerrar) a la perra.
5. Ellos__________ (gobernar) sin tenernos en cuenta y nosotros __________ (consentir) en todo.
6. Nosotros __________ (descender) de los primates, pero tú lo __________ (negar).
7. María __________ (comenzar) a trabajar a las 8 a.m. Nosotros __________ (empezar) a las 8 p.m.
8. Susana se__________ (divertir) y nosotros nos __________ (sentar) a esperarla sin decir nada.
9. Iván nos __________ (sugerir) comprar una casa. Yo __________ (entender) que es muy mal negocio.

Exercise 13. Complete the following dialogue using the present tense:

Visita al psiquiatra

—Doctor, siempre temo cuando él ________(atravesar) la calle y (yo) ________ (pensar) que algo le va a pasar.
—¿Qué es lo que (tú) ________ (sentir)?
—No sé Dr. Algo ________ (gobernar) mis sentidos y (yo) ________ (preferir) alzarlo en mis brazos. Mis amigos me ________ (recomendar) comprar un cargador para bebés y (ellos) se ________ (divertir) burlándose de mí. Y me preguntan con quién me ________ (despertar) en las mañanas... Pero yo soy normal y sólo temo cuando (nosotros) ________ (atravesar) la calle...
—Por favor empieza de nuevo, es que (yo) ________ (perder) el hilo con mucha facilidad. ¿Qué raza es tu perro?

b. Stem vowel change from **e** to **i**.

pedir (*to ask*)	
yo p**i**do	nosotros/as pedimos
tú p**i**des	vosotros/as pedís
él, ella, usted p**i**de	ellos, ellas, ustedes p**i**den

Other verbs with stems changing from **e** to **i** are:

cons**e**guir (*to get*)
corr**e**gir (*to correct*)
desp**e**dir (*to fire*)
el**e**gir (*to elect*)
imp**e**dir (*to impede*)
m**e**dir (*to measure*)
pers**e**guir (*to follow*)
r**e**ír (*to laugh*)
rep**e**tir (*to repeat*)
s**e**guir (*to follow*)
sonr**e**ír (*to smile*)
v**e**stirse* (*to get dressed*)

Exercise 14. Complete the following sentences using the present tense.

1. Ella sólo ________(vestir) diseños exclusivos.
2. Pilar ________ (repetir) las canciones y no ________ (conseguir) aprenderlas.
3. Mi profesor ________ (corregir) el libro de ejercicios todas las mañanas.
4. Él ________ (medir) más de un metro con ochenta centímetros, pero no es tan guapo.
5. Si tú no ________ (elegir) a alguien ahora te vas a quedar soltera.
6. ¡Vosotros os ________ (despedir) pero no os vais!
7. Nosotros ________ (impedir) que robaran la otra sucursal del banco.
8. Si (tú) ________ (seguir) estudiando vas a aprender español pronto.
9. La policía ________ (perseguir) al sospechoso.

*See Chapter 7, Pronominal Verbs.

Exercise 15. Complete the following crossword.

Across:

1. "to correct" conjugated in the "yo" form
2. "to measure" conjugated in the "yo" form
4. "to repeat" conjugated in the "nosotros" form
7. "to elect" conjugated in the "nosotros" form
8. "to impede" conjugated in the "ellos" form

Down:

1. "to get" conjugated in the "tú" form
3. "to chase" conjugated in the "él" form
5. "to fire" conjugated in the "él" form
6. "to follow" conjugated in the "vosotros" form

c. Stem vowel change from **i** to **ie**. Only two common verbs are affected: **adquirir** (*to acquire*) and **inquirir** (*to inquire*).

adquirir (*to acquire*)	
yo adqu**ie**ro	nosotros/as adquirimos
tú adqu**ie**res	vosotros/as adquirís
él, ella, usted adqu**ie**re	ellos, ellas, ustedes adqu**ie**ren

Exercise 16. Complete the following sentences using the present tense.

1. Ellos _________(adquirir) prestigio con tu compañía.
2. Lucía _________ (adquirir) una mansión con el dinero de su herencia.
3. El juez _________ (inquirir) sobre lo ocurrido la noche del crimen.
4. Vosotros _________ (adquirir) conocimientos útiles.

d. Stem vowel change from **o** to **ue**.

recordar (*to remember*)	
yo rec**ue**rdo	nosotros/as recordamos
tú rec**ue**rdas	vosotros/as recordáis
él, ella, usted rec**ue**rda	ellos, ellas, ustedes rec**ue**rdan

Other verbs with stems changing from **o** to **ue** are:

abs**o**lver (*to absolve*)
ac**o**rdar *(to agree) –*se *(to remember)*
ac**o**star *(to put to bed) –*se *(to go to bed)*
alm**o**rzar (*to eat lunch*)
c**o**cer (*to boil, to bake*)
c**o**lgar *(to hang)*
c**o**ntar (*to count*)
c**o**star (*to cost*)
dem**o**ler (*to demolish*)
dev**o**lver (*to return*)
dis**o**lver (*to dissolve*)
d**o**ler *(to hurt)*
d**o**rmir (*to sleep*)
enc**o**ntrar (*to find*)
env**o**lver (*to wrap*)
ll**o**ver (*to rain*)
m**o**ler (*to grind*)
m**o**rder *(to bite)*
m**o**rir (*to die*)
m**o**strar (*to show*)
m**o**ver (*to move*)
oler* (*to smell*)
p**o**der (*to be able to*)
pr**o**bar (*to taste, to prove*)
prom**o**ver (*to promote*)
rec**o**rdar (*to remember*)
rem**o**ver (*to remove*)
res**o**lver (*to resolve*)
ret**o**rcer (*to twist*)
rev**o**lver (*to mix*)
r**o**gar *(to request)*
s**o**ñar (*to dream*)
s**o**nar (*to sound*)
t**o**rcer (*to twist*)
v**o**lar *(to fly)*
v**o**lver *(to return)*

*Note: The verb **oler** changes the stem vowel from an **o** to **hue** (yo huelo, tú hueles, él huele...).

Exercise 17. Complete the following crossword.

Across:

1. "to count" conjugated in the "él" form.
3. "to twist" conjugated in the "tú" form.
5. "to put to bed" conjugated in the "yo" form.
8. "to move" conjugated in the "ellos" form.
9. "to absolve" conjugated in the "yo" form.
11. "to find" conjugated in the "nosotros" form.
12. "to fly" conjugated in the "nosotros" form.
16. "to promote" conjugated in the "nosotros" form.
19. "to demolish" conjugated in the "él" form.
20. "to dream" conjugated in the "tú" form.
21. "to bite" conjugated in the "vosotros" form.
22. "to agree" conjugated in the "nosotros" form.

Down:

1. "to cost" conjugated in the "ellos" form.
2. "to remove" conjugated in the "tú" form.
4. "to dissolve" conjugated in the "ustedes" form.
6. "to boil, to bake" conjugated in the "tú" form.
7. "to beg" conjugated in the "ellas" form.
10. "to wrap" conjugated in the "él" form.
13. "to hurt" conjugated in the "vosotros" form.
14. "to grind" conjugated in the "vosotros" form.
15. "to mix" conjugated in the "yo" form.
17. "to twist" conjugated in the "yo" form.
18. "to hang" conjugated in the "yo" form.

Exercise 18. Complete the following sentences using the present tense.

1. Ellos se ___________ (encontrarse) en España y nosotros nos ___________ (encontrarse) en Madagascar.
2. ¿Tú te ___________ (acordarse) de lo que siempre nos dice el profesor? Porque yo no me ___________ (acordarse) de nada.
3. ___________ (llover) a cántaros. ¡Resguardémonos en aquella iglesia!
4. Ellos ___________ (almorzar) todos los días mientras que nosotros sólo ___________ (almorzar) los fines de semana.
5. Yo ___________ (recordar) muy bien donde está el restaurante. ¿Pero ustedes ___________ (recordar) el nombre?
6. Julio siempre ___________ (devolver) los libros que le presto pero vosotros nunca los ___________ (devolver).
7. Nosotros nos ___________ (moverse) en un mundo de realidades, pero tú te ___________ (moverse) en un mundo de ilusiones.
8. Nosotros siempre ___________ (volver) a casa después de comer, tú en cambio nunca ___________ (volver).
9. Este compuesto se ___________ (disolver) en agua pero estos otros sólo se ___________ (disolver) en alcohol.
10. Nosotros siempre te ___________ (mostrar) nuestra ciudad; en cambio, tú no nos ___________ (mostrar) la tuya.

Exercise 19. Complete the following sentences using the present tense.

1. Si (tú) _________(volver) a preguntarle, él seguro que te lo va a decir.
2. ¡Él_________ (morir) por ti!
3. La guerra no _________ (resolver) nada, más bien complica todo.
4. Lo bueno de esa sinfonía es que todos los instrumentos _________ (sonar) de manera caótica.
5. Tomás y yo _________ (almorzar) todos los días donde mi mamá.
6. Vosotros _________ (dormir) como osos en invierno.
7. Ella _________ (poder) decir lo que quiera. Igual no le voy a hacer caso.
8. Como los perros, yo _________ (oler) todo antes de probar.
9. Ellos _________ (recordar) muy bien lo que el gobierno hizo con sus propiedades.
10. Nunca vamos a ver el final pues (tú) siempre __________ (devolver) la película en el mismo punto.

e. Stem vowel change from **u** to **ue**. Only one verb is affected: **jugar** (*to play*).

jugar (*to play*)	
yo **jue**go	nosotros/as jugamos
tú **jue**gas	vosotros/as jugáis
él, ella, usted **jue**ga	ellos, ellas, ustedes **jue**gan

Exercise 20. Complete the following sentences using the present tense.

1. ¡Tú ________(jugar) con lo más sagrado!
2. La verdad, yo a eso no ________ (jugar).
3. Yo no entiendo. Gabriel y su amigos siempre practican mucho y ________ (jugar) muy mal.
4. Todos los niños ________ (jugar) con todo menos con sus juguetes.
5. A mí me parece que Lola ________ (jugar) muy bien tenis.

D. VERBS WITH IRREGULAR FORMS

Verbs with irregular forms are mostly irregular in the present indicative, but only in the first person. A few others are irregular in all persons.

a. The following are irregular verbs in the present indicative in the first person.

	caber (*to fit*)	**dar** (*to give*)	**saber** (*to know*)	**ver** (*to see*)
yo	**quep**o	do**y**	**sé**	v**e**o
tú	cabes	das	sabes	ves
él, ella, usted	cabe	da	sabe	ve
nosotros/as	cabemos	damos	sabemos	vemos
vosotros/as	cabéis	dais	sabéis	veis
ellos, ellas, ustedes	caben	dan	saben	ven

	decir (*to say*) + **e** to **i**	**hacer** (*to do*)	**oír** (*to hear*) + **i** to **y**	**poner** (*to put*)	**salir** (*to go out*)	**tener** (*to have*) + **e** to **ie**	**traer** (*to bring*)	**venir** (*to come*) + **e** to **ie**	**valer** (*to value, to cost*)
yo	**dig**o	**hag**o	**oig**o	**pong**o	**salg**o	**teng**o	**traig**o	**veng**o	**valg**o
tú	**di**ces	haces	**oy**es	pones	sales	**tie**nes	traes	**vie**nes	vales
él, ella, usted	**di**ce	hace	**oy**e	pone	sale	**tie**ne	trae	**vie**ne	vale
nosotros/as	decimos	hacemos	oímos	ponemos	salimos	tenemos	traemos	venimos	valemos
vosotros/as	decís	hacéis	oís	ponéis	salís	tenéis	traéis	venís	valéis
ellos, ellas, ustedes	**di**cen	hacen	**oy**en	ponen	salen	**tie**nen	traen	**vie**nen	valen

Exercise 21. Complete the following sentences using the present tense.

1. La casa se llena de vida cuando él ________(traer) los niños, yo en cambio no ________ (traer) los míos nunca.
2. Vosotros ________ (dar) más de lo que tenéis, yo en cambio no ________ (dar) nada.

3. No sé qué pasa, siempre (tú)________ (decir) una cosa y ________ (hacer) otra! Yo en cambio ________ (decir) y ________ (hacer) al mismo tiempo.
4. Selma ________ (venir) de estudiar, yo en cambio ________ (venir) de hacer ejercicio.
5. Ese sofá no ________ (caber) en la sala, y yo tampoco ________ (caber) en él; mejor lo tiro a la basura.
6. Vosotros siempre ________ (poner) orden en vuestra casa, yo en cambio nunca ________ (poner) orden.
7. Sólo una vez al año Lola ________ (venir) a visitarme, en cambio yo voy y ________ (venir) tres veces al año.
8. Casandra es la única que no________ (ver) lo que yo ________ (ver) y todos los demás ________ (ver).
9. Todo lo que yo ________ (tener) es esta casa, en cambio tú ________ (tener) muchas propiedades.
10. Los esquimales ________ (saber) cazar focas, yo en cambio no ________ (saber).
11. Tulia y Francisco ________ (decir) que tú no ________ (saber) nada, yo en cambio ________ (decir) que eres un genio.
12. (Yo) ________ (oír) un ruido extraño. ¿Lo ________ (oír) tú?
13. En este juego (yo) siempre ________ (salir) perdiendo y tú ________ (salir) ganando.
14. Tú ________ (valer) mucho, yo en cambio no ________ (valer) nada.

b. The following are irregular verbs in the present indicative in all persons.

	estar *(to be)*	**ser** *(to be)*	**haber*** *(to have)*	**ir** *(to go)*
yo	estoy	soy	he	voy
tú	estás	eres	has	vas
él, ella, usted	está	es	ha	va
nosotros/as	estamos	somos	hemos	vamos
vosotros/as	estáis	sois	habéis	vais
ellos, ellas, ustedes	están	son	han	van

Exercise 22. Use the following words to make sentences in the present tense.

1. La niña / **estar** / triste
____
2. Los niños / **ir** / a la escuela
____
3. Yo / **ir** / contigo
____
4. Nosotros no / **haber** / hecho las tareas
____
5. Julio y María / **estar** / cansados
____

*Note: The verb **haber** is used as an auxiliary verb. See Chapter 6, The Perfect Tenses of the Indicative.

Exercise 23. Complete the following paragraph using the present tense.

Me gustan los libros de caballerías porque ________(ser) entretenidos. Por el contrario, los libros de gramática que (yo) ________ (haber) estudiado me aburren. Un libro de aventuras ________ (ser) siempre más divertido, y aún más, cuando ________ (estar) escrito con humor. Porque si vosotros ________ (estar) leyendo algo aburrido, ________ (ir) directo a dormir. De todas maneras, recuerda que con voluntad y entusiasmo ________ (ser) más fácil aprender cualquier idioma.

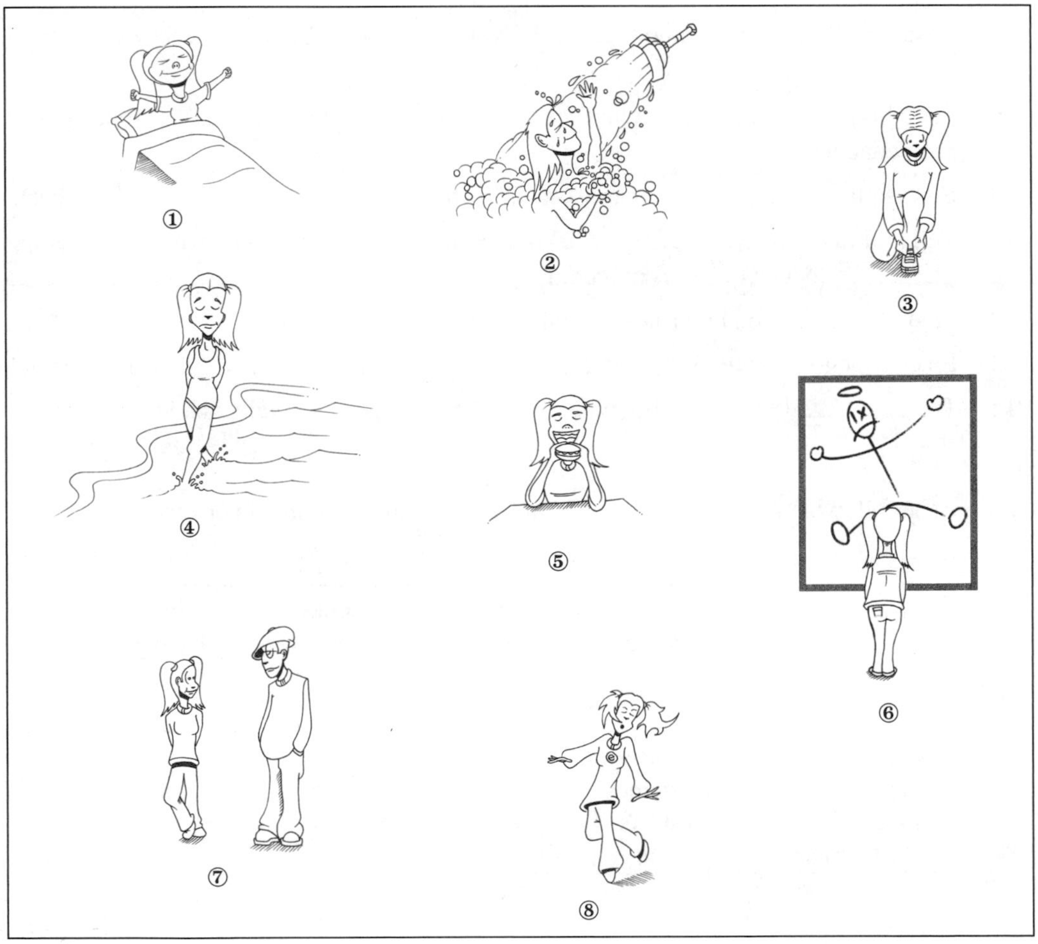

Exercise 24. Look at the pictures above and, using the following words, make sentences in the present tense. Order the sentences according to one day in Sonia's vacation.

Sonia / ponerse / los zapatos	1. ________________
Sonia / levantarse	2. ________________
Sonia / comer / en un restaurante	3. ________________
Sonia / caminar / por la playa	4. ________________

Sonia / bailar / en una discoteca 5. ______________________
Sonia / ducharse 6. ______________________
7. ______________________
8. ______________________

E. USES OF THE PRESENT TENSE

The present indicative refers to events which, in terms of order, are simultaneous with the event of speaking. The present indicative may represent one single event or express an habitual action. This distinction is always characterized by context. English, however, uses the simple present to express a single event and the present progressive for an habitual action.

Habitual action (Spanish) (Simple Present)	**Habitual action (English)** (Simple Present)
—¿Qué estudias? —Estudio [illegible]	*"What do you study?"* *"I study economics."*
Single event (Spanish) (Simple Present)	**Single event (English)** (Present Progressive)
—¿Qué estudias? —Estudio para el examen de economía.	*"What are you studying?"* *"I am studying for the economics exam."*

Other uses of the Spanish present indicative are similar to English. The present indicative describes timeless events and is also commonly used to express **future** events.

Timeless event (Spanish) (Simple Present)	**Timeless event (English)** (Simple Present)
[illegible]s.	*All men **are** mortal.*
Future event (Spanish) (Simple Present ir + a + infinitive)	**Future event (English)** (Present Progressive)
[illegible]	*Tomorrow we **are going to** the beach.*

TIP BOX

The Spanish present progressive is used more frequently to emphasize a single event.

—¿Qué **estás estudiando**?	*"What are you studying?"*
—**Estoy estudiando** para el examen de economía.	*"I am studying for the economics exam."*

Exercise 25. Complete the following dialogue in the present tense using the following verbs: **llamarse, hacer, trabajar, estudiar, ir, querer, verse**

Paco: —Hola, ¿Cómo te ________?
Pilar: —Me ________ Pilar.
Paco: —Yo me ________ Paco. ¿Qué ________? ¿ ________ o ________?
Pilar: —________ en una librería. ¿Y tú, qué ________?
Paco: —________ administración de empresas. ¿Quieres una cerveza?
Pilar: —¡Vale!
Paco: —Esta noche __________ a ir con unos amigos a un concierto de música de Senegal. ¿ ________ venir?
Pilar: —¡Estupendo!
Paco: —Entonces, nos ________ en el Teatro Real a las ocho en punto.
Pilar: —De acuerdo. Hasta entonces.
Paco: —Hasta luego.

REVIEW

Exercise 26. Complete the following paragraph using the present tense.

Marta y Carlos __________ (ser) novios. Ambos __________ (asistir) a la Universidad Nacional y __________ (estudiar) Biología. En un mes __________ (ir) a graduarse, y por eso Marta __________ (buscar) un trabajo urgentemente. __________ (vivir) juntos porque no __________ (poder) estar separados un minuto. Los viernes __________ (jugar) tenis por la tarde y por la noche __________ (bailar) salsa. Los sábados, Marta __________ (dormir) hasta las ocho de la mañana, se __________ (vestir) y __________ (correr) siete kilómetros. Cuando Carlos __________ (decidir) ir con ella, siempre le dice: "Marta, esta vez sí te __________ (vencer)", pero la verdad es que nunca la __________ (vencer). Cuando ella lo __________ (socorrer), Carlos le __________ (contestar): "Mi amor te lo __________ (agradecer)". Yo les __________ (confesar) algo: "Carlos __________ (ser) un flojo" y Marta siempre lo __________ (proteger). Yo lo __________ (conocer) desde hace dos años. A Marta le __________ (reconocer) su ternura. Pero, también le __________ (exigir) prudencia. Ese hombre __________ (ser) un vividor. __________ (perseguir) a las muchachas dulces y las __________ (hacer) sentir diosas. Pero luego, cuando __________ (adquirir) confianza, se __________ (mudarse) a su apartamento. Allí, __________ (almorzar), __________ (comer) y __________ (dormir) y no __________ (traer) nada, sólo __________ (distribuir) sonrisas y palabras bonitas, y una las __________ (oír) como venidas del cielo. Luego que una se __________ (haber) ilusionado, __________ (tener) la desfachatez de decir que algo extraño le __________ (suceder) y dice: "Mi pasión se __________ (enfriarse), lo __________ (sentir) corazón pero me __________" (irse). Cuando __________ (decir) aquello, no __________ (caber) la menor duda que __________ (ser) porque __________ (haber) visto otra mujer. Lo __________ (decir) yo, que lo __________ (haber) vivido en carne propia.

II. The Preterit

In Spanish two simple tenses are used to talk about the past: the **preterit** and the **imperfect.** The preterit is used **to narrate** in the past, and the imperfect is used **to describe** something in the past.

A. REGULAR VERBS

The **regular conjugation** in the preterit is formed by adding the following endings to the stem of the verbs:

	Verb Endings in the Preterit	
	-ar	**-er, -ir**
yo	-é	-í
tú	-aste	-iste
él, ella, usted	-ó	-ió
nosotros/as*	-amos	-imos
vosotros/as	-asteis	-isteis
ellos, ellas, ustedes	-aron	-ieron

TIP BOX

*Note that in the **first person of the plural** there is no difference between the present and the preterit. Therefore, the distinction is made by the context of the sentence.

Example

Ayer trabajamos toda la noche.
Yesterday we worked all night.

Nosotros trabajamos generalmente en las tardes.
We usually work every afternoon.

Exercise 27. Complete the following sentences using the appropriate form of the preterit tense.

1. Dicen que el Libertador Simón Bolívar ________ (amar) a Manuelita Sáenz.
2. Yo ________ (aprender) un poco de español en la escuela.
3. Fernando ________ (abrir) la puerta y ________ (encontrar) algo terrible.
4. Amalia y Joaquín ________ (bailar) toda la noche.

5. No la pude alcanzar a pesar de que ________ (correr) a gran velocidad.
6. ¿Cómo se llama la obra de teatro a la que (tú) ________ (asistir) anoche?
7. Yo ________ (socorrer) a mi gato cuando se cayó en la alberca.
8. Lo siento, (vosotros) ________ (decidir) muy tarde. La casa está vendida.
9. ¿Cuántas horas (usted) ________ (caminar) para atravesar la montaña?
10. Bolívar ________ (emprender) la campaña libertadora siendo muy joven.
11. ¿Quiénes ________ (escribir) la Biblia?
12. Te estoy diciendo que la linterna está en la maleta, porque (yo) ________ (alistar) todo antes de empacar.
13. Ella________ (insistir) en comprar zapatos rojos.
14. Se quemó la tienda donde (tú) ________ (comprar) la mesa.
15. Ximena ________ (comer) grillos cuando estuvo en la China.
16. Anoche por fin (yo) ________ (hablar) con mis padres acerca de mi matrimonio.

Exercise 28. Rewrite the following sentences putting the underlined verb in the preterit tense.

1. La verdad es que nosotros no <u>comprendemos</u> nada.

   ____.

2. Carlos Sastre <u>sube</u> los Pirineos en el Tour de Francia en primer lugar.

   ____.

3. Otra vez Andrew <u>llega</u> tarde a clase.

   ____.

4. Martín Lutero <u>vive</u> entre 1483 y 1546.

   ____.

5. ¡La última semana de clase mi profesor <u>mira</u> los ejercicios de todo el curso!

   ____.

6. Andrea le <u>responde</u> muy mal al jefe.

   ____.

7. Yo siempre le estoy agradecido, porque cuando <u>necesito</u> dinero, ella me lo <u>presta</u>.

   ____.

8. Todos <u>tememos</u> el terremoto.

   ____.

9. Exactamente un año después del exilio en Elba, Napoleón <u>retorna</u> a Francia en febrero de 1815.

   ____.

10. Ellos <u>venden</u> todo antes de partir.

    ____.

11. Darwin y Wallace <u>trabajan</u> independiente y simultáneamente para elaborar la teoría de la evolución.

    ____.

12. Pedro y su esposa viajan en avión a Bruselas.

____.

13. Los padres de mis primos les permiten muchas cosas a sus hijos.

____.

14. Lucho envía sus cartas por correo rápido.

____.

15. Sócrates bebe una infusión de cicuta antes de morir.

____.

16. Los estudiantes reciben sus calificaciones el lunes.

____.

B. VERBS WITH SPELLING CHANGES

This group of verbs changes their spelling to reflect their pronunciation.

a. Verbs ending in **-car**, **-gar**, **-guar**, **-zar** are affected only in the first conjugation of the singular (*yo*).

SPELLING RULES

	-car	**-gar**	**-guar**	**-zar**
	c to **qu**	**g** to **gu**	**u** to **ü**	**z** to **c**
	colocar (*to place*)	**cargar** (*to carry*)	**averiguar** (*to find out*)	**alcanzar** (*to reach*)
yo	colo**qué**	car**gué**	averig**üé**	alcan**cé**
tú	colocaste	cargaste	averiguaste	alcanzaste
él, ella, usted	colocó	cargó	averiguó	alcanzó
nosotros/as	colocamos	cargamos	averiguamos	alcanzamos
vosotros/as	colocasteis	cargasteis	averiguasteis	alcanzasteis
ellos, ellas, ustedes	colocaron	cargaron	averiguaron	alcanzaron

Other verbs ending in **-car**, **-gar**, **-guar**, and **-zar** are:

-car		
acercar *(to bring closer)*	diagnosticar *(to diagnose)*	marcar *(to mark)*
ahorcar *(to hang)*	duplicar *(to duplicate)*	modificar *(to modify)*
aparcar *(to park)*	edificar *(to build)*	pecar *(to sin)*
arrancar *(to start* [a machine,	educar *(to educate)*	pescar *(to fish)*
a car], *to pull out)*	embarcar *(to embark)*	practicar *(to practice)*
atacar *(to attack)*	empacar *(to pack)*	provocar *(to cause)*
buscar *(to look for)*	enfocar *(to focus)*	publicar *(to publish)*
calificar *(to grade)*	enmarcar *(to frame)*	roncar *(to snore)*
cercar *(to surround, to fence)*	equivocar *(to mistake)*	sacar *(to remove)*
clasificar *(to classify)*	especificar *(to specify)*	secar *(to dry)*
colocar *(to put)*	explicar *(to explain)*	simplificar *(to simplify)*
comunicar *(to communicate)*	fabricar *(to manufacture)*	suplicar *(to entreat)*
criticar *(to criticize)*	falsificar *(to falsify)*	tocar *(to touch)*
dedicar *(to consagrate)*	identificar *(to identify)*	ubicar *(to locate)*
desempacar *(to unpack)*	indicar *(to indicate)*	
destacar *(to emphasize)*	justificar *(to justify)*	

-gar		
abrigar *(to shelter)*	descolgar *(to take down)*	madrugar *(to rise early)*
agregar *(to add)*	despegar *(to separate)*	navegar *(to sail)*
ahogar *(to drown)*	devengar *(to yield)*	negar *(to deny)*
alargar *(to extend)*	dialogar *(to talk)*	obligar *(to oblige)*
albergar *(to harbor)*	divulgar *(to divulge)*	otorgar *(to offer)*
amargar *(to make bitter)*	embriagar *(to intoxicate)*	pagar *(to pay)*
apagar *(to turn off)*	encargar *(to entrust)*	pegar *(to hit)*
arriesgar *(to risk)*	enjuagar *(to rinse)*	postergar *(to defer)*
cabalgar *(to ride)*	entregar *(to deliver)*	prolongar *(to prolong)*
cargar *(to charge)*	fumigar *(to fumigate)*	rasgar *(to rip)*
castigar *(to punish)*	halagar *(to flatter)*	regar *(to water)*
colgar *(to hang)*	interrogar *(to interrogate)*	restregar *(to rub)*
conjugar *(to conjugate)*	investigar *(to investigate)*	rogar *(to beg)*
desahogar *(to relieve)*	jugar *(to play)*	sosegar *(to calm)*
descargar *(to discharge)*	llegar *(to arrive)*	subyugar *(to subjugate)*

-guar		
amortiguar *(to muffle)*	averiguar *(to ascertain)*	menguar *(to decrease)*
apaciguar *(to appease)*	desaguar *(to drain)*	santiguar *(to bless)*
atestiguar *(to testify)*	fraguar *(to forge)*	

-zar		
abrazar *(to embrace)*	cruzar *(to cross)*	localizar *(to locate)*
adelgazar *(to make thin)*	deslizar *(to slide)*	memorizar *(to memorize)*
alcanzar *(to reach)*	danzar *(to dance)*	modernizar *(to modernize)*
almorzar *(to have lunch)*	desplazar *(to displace)*	organizar *(to organize)*
alzar *(to raise)*	destrozar *(to destroy)*	privatizar *(to privatize)*
analizar *(to analyze)*	disfrazar *(to disguise)*	rechazar *(to reject)*
aplazar *(to postpone)*	economizar *(to save)*	reemplazar *(to replace)*
aterrizar *(to land)*	empezar *(to begin)*	responsabilizar *(to blame)*
aterrorizar *(to terrify)*	estabilizar *(to stabilize)*	rezar *(to pray)*
autorizar *(to authorize)*	esterilizar *(to sterilize)*	tranquilizar *(to calm down)*
avanzar *(to advance)*	generalizar *(to generalize)*	tropezar *(to trip)*
bautizar *(to baptize)*	gozar *(to enjoy)*	visualizar *(to visualize)*
bostezar *(to yawn)*	idealizar *(to idealize)*	
cazar *(to hunt)*	indemnizar *(to compensate)*	
comenzar *(to begin)*	inmortalizar *(to immortalize)*	
comercializar *(to market)*	lanzar *(to launch)*	

Exercise 29. Complete the following sentences with the appropriate form of the preterit tense.

1. Ellos ________ (ubicar) sus campamentos lejos de la ciudad.
2. Con ese poema creo que (yo) ________ (tocar) tu corazón.
3. A pesar de que yo ________ (suplicar) clemencia. El jurado lo condenó.
4. Los pinos ________ (secar) la tierra a su alrededor.
5. En la última película me dormí cuando Clint Eastwood ________ (sacar) el revólver.
6. *El País* de España ________ (publicar) un reportaje sobre toreras hace dos semanas.
7. En la última temporada yo ________ (pescar) con esa misma clase de anzuelos.
8. Vosotros ________ (fabricar) ese engaño para quedaros con mi herencia.
9. La profesora ________ (explicar) el ejercicio dos veces; sin embargo, sigo sin entender.
10. Adelaida dijo que ellos ________ (empacar) todo lo necesario.
11. El invierno ________ (duplicar) la energía que consumo regularmente.
12. Sus problemas radican en que yo les ________ (dedicar) demasiado tiempo.
13. Lo que yo ________ (buscar) no fue la fama ni el oro. Ellos llegaron por añadidura.
14. Yo la ________ (atacar) por estar en contra de mí.
15. Todos ________ (calificar) de excelente la última película de Almodóvar.
16. (Yo) ________ (colocar) la mesa en medio del patio. ¿Estás de acuerdo?
17. (yo) ___________ (aparcar) la camioneta debajo del almendro.
18. (yo) ___________ (clasificar) las canciones de acuerdo a mi gusto.
19. Ellos nos ___________ (criticar) toda la noche y por eso no volvimos.
20. El banquero ___________ (falsificar) los documentos para cometer la estafa.

Exercise 30. Complete the following sentences with the appropriate form of the preterit tense.

1. Sólo me pude dormir cuando el conductor ________ (apagar) el radio.
2. Vosotros siempre ________ (arriesgar) sus intereses.
3. Cuando llegó la mañana (yo) ________ (cargar) mi carro y desaparecí.
4. (yo) ________ (colgar) mi ropa en el patio.
5. ¡Buenos días señor! Me da por favor los víveres que mi mamá le ________ (encargar) hace un momento por teléfono.
6. No sé cómo siguen creciendo estas matas si (yo) ________ (fumigar) todo el terreno dos veces.
7. Nosotros ________ (jugar) como nunca y perdimos como siempre.
8. La razón por la cual no conseguimos boletos es porque tú ________ (llegar) tarde.
9. Afortunadamente el jefe ________ (pagar) toda la cuenta anoche.
10. A pesar del intenso verano, el jardín está muy lindo gracias a que (yo) lo ________ (regar) dos veces por semana.
11. (yo) __________ (amargar) mi vida para siempre al venderle mi alma al diablo.
12. Primero (él) los __________ (halagar) y luego les pidió dinero prestado.
13. Lloré por un rato y luego me __________ (sosegar).
14. Primero (ellos) __________ (devengar) intereses muy altos y luego los estafaron.
15. Como no pudo pagar su casa, el banco la __________ (embargar).

Exercise 31. Complete the following sentences with the appropriate form of the preterit tense.

1. En cuanto vio a su madre el niño ________ (apaciguar) su llanto.
2. Ellos lo asesinaron; supongo que (él) ________ (atestiguar) contra la mafia.
3. No sé cómo, pero (yo) ________ (averiguar) su escondite.
4. Vino el plomero y ________ (desaguar) la bañera.
5. Todos saben que (yo) ________ (fraguar) el complot con astucia.
6. Juan Pablo II ________ (santiguar) a la multitud al final de la ceremonia.
7. En la corte, (yo) __________ (atestiguar) en su contra.
8. Las bolsas de aire del coche__________ (amortiguar) el golpe en el accidente.
9. Con la crisis económica, el gobierno __________ (menguar) los gastos.
10. Después de muchas pesquisas, (yo) __________ (averiguar) el verdadero nombre de Pancho Villa.

Exercise 32. Complete the following sentences with the appropriate form of the preterit tense.

1. Él ________ (abrazar) a su hija y sin decir nada partió.
2. Creo que Lucila y Juan ________ (adelgazar) porque tomaron esta nueva droga.
3. (yo) ________ (alcanzar) todo lo que quería.
4. No gracias. Nosotros ________ (almorzar) hace un ratito.
5. Nosotros ________ (alzar) los niños y pararon de llorar.
6. Yo ________ (analizar) toda la situación y creo que lo mejor es construir un nuevo parqueadero.

7. Los cazadores ________ (cazar) tantos elefantes, que los exterminaron.
8. Los hombres que poblaron América ________ (cruzar) el estrecho de Bering.
9. ¡Tú y tu pelota ________ (destrozar) mi jarrón de cristal!
10. Si confías en mí, continúo la obra que (tú) ________ (empezar).
11. Antonio ________ (encabezar) la marcha por la paz.
12. En cuanto recibí el balón (yo) ________ (lanzar) a la canasta y anoté dos puntos en contra de mi propio equipo.
13. Debes hacerte cargo de la fiesta que tu ________ (organizar).
14. El presidente Obama ________ (reemplazar) al presidente Bush.
15. Ellos ________ (memorizar) todas las formas de los verbos en español.
16. Cuando vosotros ________ (localizar) el avión ya era demasiado tarde.
17. Sólo cuando Julia ________ (tranquilizar) a mi gato, pude ver que estaba herido.
18. El gato ________ (tropezar) cuando saltaba el balcón y se lastimó.
19. Baryshnikov __________ (danzar) para el ballet del Teatro Bolshoi.
20. Ayer (yo) __________ (analizar) los datos, pero no encontré nada interesante.

b. Verbs ending in **-caer**, **-eer**, **-oer**, **-oír**, and **-uir** are affected in the third conjugation of the singular *(él, ella, usted)* and in the third conjugation of the plural *(él, ellos, ellas, ustedes)*.

caer *(to fall)*	**leer** *(to read)*	**roer** *(to gnaw)*	**oír** *(to listen)*	**huir** *(to escape)*
yo caí	leí	roí	oí	huí
tu caíste	leíste	roíste	oíste	huiste
el, ella, usted cayó	leyó	royó	oyó	huyó
nosotros/as caímos	leímos	roímos	oímos	huimos
vosotros/as caísteis	leísteis	roísteis	oísteis	huisteis
ellos, ellas, ustedes cayeron	leyeron	royeron	oyeron	huyeron

Other verbs ending in **-caer**, **-eer**, **-oer**, **-óir**, and **-uir** are:

-caer	
decaer *(to decay)*	recaer *(to fall again)*

-eer	
creer *(to believe)*	proveer *(to provide)*
poseer *(to possess)*	releer *(to reread)*

-oer
corroer *(to corrode)*

-oír	
entreoír *(to half-hear)*	desoír (*to ignore*)

-uir		
atribuir *(to attribute)*	destruir *(to destroy)*	intuir *(to sense)*
concluir *(to conclude)*	diluir *(to dilute)*	obstruir *(to block)*
constituir *(to constitute)*	disminuir *(to diminish)*	recluir *(to imprison)*
construir *(to build)*	distribuir *(to distribute)*	sustituir *(to substitute)*
contribuir *(to contribute)*	incluir *(to include)*	
destituir *(to dismiss)*	influir *(to influence)*	

Exercise 33. Complete the following sentences with the appropriate form of the preterit tense.

1. El ácido de la batería _________ (corroer) parte de las latas de mi coche.
2. Durante la segunda guerra mundial, ¿exactamente en qué año_________ (caer) Kiev en manos de los alemanes?
3. El _________ (poseer) tierras y ganados y hoy todo lo ha perdido.
4. Los ratones _________ (roer) el queso de la alacena.
5. A la muerte de su madre las responsabilidades de la casa _________ (recaer) sobre sus hombros.
6. Yo no _________ (creer) lo que dijiste. Lo siento mucho.
7. Ese mismo manantial_________ (proveer) de agua a toda la región por muchos años.
8. Con la recesión económica, las exportaciones ___________ (decaer) a su nivel más bajo en muchos años.
9. Para el examen los estudiantes ___________ (releer) la novela.
10. Los ratones ___________ (roer) la alacena.

Exercise 34. Complete the following sentences with the appropriate form of the preterit tense.

1. Traté de advertírselo pero Laura no_________ (oír).
2. La policía _________ (atribuir) el crimen al novio de la víctima.
3. El juez _________ (concluir) que la policía estaba equivocada.
4. Todos ellos _________ (reconstruir) los hechos con evidencia falsa.
5. Así fue como los abogados _________ (destruir) los argumentos del fiscal durante el juicio.
6. El nivel del agua _________ (disminuir) 1,3% en todos los lagos de la cordillera de los Andes.
7. Ese almacén no_________ (distribuir) buena mercancía; sólo baratijas.
8. Quiero saber, ¿por qué (tú) no me _________ (incluir) en la lista de tus invitados?
9. Vosotros _________ (influir) en la decisión que él tomó.
10. Angelita _________ (sustituir) a Ana en la vicepresidencia de las Hermanas de la Caridad.

11. La niña ___________ (desoír) los consejos de su papá.
12. Los incas___________ (construir) la ciudad de Machu-Picchu.
13. El derrumbe ___________ (obstruir) la carretera.
14. ¿(tú) ___________ (diluir) el reactivo?
15. Después de apresarlos, (a ellos) los ___________ (recluir) en la cárcel.

C. STEM-CHANGING *-IR* VERBS ONLY

a. Stem-changing ***–ir*** verbs (**e** to **ie**, **e** to **i**, **o** to **ue**) in the present tense* change their corresponding vowel of the stem in the preterit in the third conjugation singular *(él, ella, usted)* and plural *(ellos, ellas, ustedes)* in two different ways: **e** to **i** and **o** to **u**.

STEM-CHANGING RULES

e to **ie** → **e** to **i**	**e** to **i** → **e** to **i**	**o** to **ue** → **o** to **u**
sentir *(to feel)*	**pedir** *(to ask)*	**morir** *(to die)*
yo sentí tú sentiste él, ella, usted s**i**ntió nosotros/as sentimos vosotros/as sentisteis ellos, ellas, ustedes s**i**ntieron	pedí pediste p**i**dió pedimos pedisteis p**i**dieron	morí moriste m**u**rió morimos moristeis m**u**rieron

Other such stem-changing verbs are:

e to **ie** → **e** to **i**	**e** to **i** → **e** to **i**	**o** to **ue** → **o** to **u**
as**e**ntir *(to agree)* cons**e**ntir *(to agree)* conv**e**rtir *(to convert)* div**e**rtir *(to amuse)* inv**e**rtir *(to invest)* m**e**ntir *(to lie)* pref**e**rir *(to prefer)* res**e**ntir *(to suffer)* s**e**ntir *(to feel)* sug**e**rir *(to suggest)*	consegu**i**r *(to get)* corr**e**gir *(to correct)* desp**e**dir *(to fire)* el**e**gir *(to elect)* imp**e**dir *(to impede)* m**e**dir *(to measure)* pers**e**guir *(to follow)* r**e**ír *(to laugh)* rep**e**tir *(to repeat)* s**e**guir *(to follow)* sonr**e**ír *(to smile)* v**e**stir(se) *(to get dressed)*	d**o**rmir *(to sleep)* m**o**rir *(to die)*

*For a list of stem-changing **–ir** verbs (**e** to **ie**, **e** to **i**, **o** to **ue**) see the present tense section in this chapter.

Exercise 35. Complete the following sentences with the appropriate form of the preterit tense.

1. Los padres de mi abuela ________ (consentir) en su matrimonio.
2. Él ________ (divertir) al público con su humor exquisito.
3. Cuando llegaron mis padres nosotros ________ (mentir) para evitar un terrible castigo.
4. Carlos ________ (preferir) vivir en París y no en Honolulu.
5. He mejorado desde que hice lo que el Dr. me ________ (sugerir).
6. Andrés y Daniel ________ (sentir) mucha alegría al saber sus notas de geografía.
7. (yo) ___________ (asentir) con la cabeza.
8. Los campesinos ___________ (resentir) mucho la recesión económica.
9. Las grandes corporaciones ___________ (invertir) en Asia.
10. Tú te ___________ (convertir) en mi razón de ser.

Exercise 36. Complete the following sentences with the appropriate form of the preterit tense.

1. La familia Rojas ________ (conseguir) casa nueva.
2. El profesor no ________ (corregir) los ejercicios.
3. Andrés ________ (despedir) a todos los empleados y ahora tiene problemas.
4. Sara________ (elegir) este vestido rojo para su boda.
5. La lluvia ________ (impedir) zarpar la noche acordada.
6. Esto sucedió porque el piloto no ________ (medir) las consecuencias de salir tan tarde.
7. Pero la policía británica nunca ________ (perseguir) a Jack el destripador.
8. Todos ________ (reír) de todo lo que el presidente dijo por la televisión esta mañana.
9. Ana y Mary________ (repetir) todos los ejercicios hasta comprender el pretérito.
10. Él ________ (seguir) el mismo camino que su padre.
11. Vosotros ________ (sonreír) cuando hice mi presentación.
12. El año pasado nosotros ________ (vestir) a la virgen para la procesión.
13. Los niños ___________ (despedir) a su papá en el aeropuerto.
14. Al presidente (ellos) lo ___________ (elegir) democráticamente.
15. Jorge ___________ (conseguir) trabajo en la Universidad Bolivariana.

Exercise 37. Complete the following sentences with the appropriate form of the preterit tense.

1. En su primera noche en casa, el bebé ________ (dormir) sin interrupciones.
2. El presidente McKinley y el Presidente Kennedy ________ (morir) en actos públicos.
3. En su viaje al Amazonas mis padres ________ (dormir) en un bohío indígena.
4. No recuerdo bien a mis abuelos pues yo era muy niño cuando ellos ________ (morir).
5. Tú ___________ (dormir) muy mal anoche. ¿Estás preocupada?

D. VERBS WITH IRREGULAR FORMS

a. The verbs **ir** (to go) and **ser** (to be) are both irregular, but note that they also share the same conjugation form.

ir/ser	
yo fu**i**	nosotros/as fu**imos**
tú fu**iste**	vosotros/as fu**isteis**
él, ella, usted f**ue**	ellos, ellas, ustedes f**ueron**

b. The verb **dar** (to give) is conjugated with the endings of the **-er** and **-ir** verbs but without accents.

dar	
yo d**i**	nosotros/as d**imos**
tú d**iste**	vosotros/as d**isteis**
él, ella, usted d**io**	ellos, ellas, ustedes d**ieron**

Exercise 38. Rewrite the following sentences in the preterit.

1. Carlos le da las gracias al taxista.

   ____.

2. María y José le dan un regalo de cumpleaños a su hijo.

   ____.

3. Tú das dinero para proteger el medio ambiente.

   ____.

4. Nosotros le damos la bienvenida al astronauta.

   ____.

5. Yo doy lo mejor de mí.

   ____.

c. The following verbs are irregular. Memorize the first conjugation form and then add to the irregular stem the corresponding preterit endings.

-ar	-er	-ir
andar yo **anduv**e	tener yo **tuv**e	venir yo **vin**e
estar yo **estuv**e	caber yo **cup**e	decir yo **dij**e
	haber yo **hub**e	producir (plus verbs ending in **-cir**) yo **produj**e
	poder yo **pud**e	traer (plus verbs ending in **-traer**) yo **traj**e
	poner yo **pus**e	
	saber yo **sup**e	
	hacer* yo **hic**e	
	querer yo **quis**e	

* The verb **hacer** changes the **c** to **z** in the third conjugation of the singular *(él, ella, usted hizo)*.

TIP BOX

The following rule may be used for these irregular verbs.

For example, to conjugate the verb **andar** (to go, to walk):

1. Memorize its first-person conjugation (**Yo anduve**)
2. Take the irregular stem (**anduv**)
3. Add the corresponding ending (**-e, iste, -o, -imos, -isteis, -ieron**)

andar	
yo anduv**e**	nosotros/as anduv**imos**
tú anduv**iste**	vosotros/as anduv**isteis**
él, ella, usted anduv**o**	ellos, ellas, ustedes anduv**ieron**

Exercise 39. Complete the following sentences with the appropriate form of the preterit tense.

1. Ayer, nosotros ________ (andar) por el parque.
2. La liebre ________ (estar) en su guarida toda la mañana.
3. Javier y sus amigos________ (tener) unas veladas muy amenas.
4. Todo era gris hasta que (tú)________ (venir) a mi vida.
5. La verdad es que tú nunca ________ (caber) en esta familia.
6. Los periódicos________ (decir) esta mañana que el agua escasea en la Tierra.
7. ________ (haber) una tormenta terrible anoche y ahora no hay energía.
8. Los hindúes fueron los primeros que ________ (producir) arroz, y sólo en el medioevo se expandió su consumo al sur de Europa.
9. Las labores de asistencia social ________ (reducir) la cifra de muerte de niños recién nacidos en un 30%.
10. Los romanos ________ (poder) conquistar un vasto territorio.
11. Yo ________ (traer) mis pinturas para mostrártelas.
12. Él se ________ (retraer) mucho después de la muerte de su esposa.
13. Los niños ________ (poner) la mesa.
14. Nosotros ________ (saber) sólo después que era prohibido traer el perro a la iglesia.
15. La torta de queso está deliciosa, la (yo) ________ (hacer) anoche.
16. He oído que ________ (querer) más a tu primer esposo que a mí. ¿Es verdad?

Exercise 40. Rewrite the following sentences in the preterit.

1. El Sr. Urrutia viene de compras a Miami.

   ____.
2. Yo hago la tarea por la mañana.

   ____.
3. El presidente no puede convencer a los congresistas.

   ____.
4. Los niños andan en bicicleta por la mañana.

   ____.
5. La herida le produce mucho dolor.

   ____.
6. Los niños traen sus mochilas a clase, pero vacías.

   ____.
7. Antes de salir, hacemos la comida.

   ____.
8. Yo no le digo la verdad.

   ____.
9. No sé adonde va.

   ____.
10. Ana no viene a clase el lunes.

    ____.

E. USES OF THE PRETERIT

As previously mentioned, the preterit is used to narrate in the past; in other words, it expresses an action accomplished and completed in the past and not connected with the present.

Example

Ayer estuve en la biblioteca hasta las once de la noche.
Yesterday, I was in the library until eleven p.m.

José me acompañó luego a casa.
Afterwards, José accompanied me home.

Exercise 41. Complete the following sentences with the appropriate form of the preterit tense.

1. Brasil no ________ (incluir) a Romario en la lista de su seleccionado nacional para las próximas eliminatorias al mundial.
2. Nos quedamos sólo un par de horas tomándonos unos vinos después que te ________ (retirar) a tu cuarto.
3. Yo ________ (repetir) estos ejercicios hasta que me quedaron bien.
4. Cuando llegamos a esta ciudad nosotros ________ (pagar) por adelantado el alquiler de la casa.
5. La cultura romana________ (influir) grandemente sobre todo el mundo occidental.
6. Ellos te ________ (explicar) que es importante usar protector solar para no contraer cáncer.
7. Yo ________ (destrozar) todas tus cartas, para no recordarte.
8. En el viaje nosotros________ (caminar) dos días antes de encontrar un ser humano.
9. Yo ________ (temer) no verte nunca más.
10. El niño se ________ (reír) cuando su padre se resbaló.
11. Aboné 100.000 dólares a la deuda y de esta manera (yo) ________ (reducir) las cuotas mensuales a sólo 500 dólares.
12. Todo era tranquilo en este pueblo hasta que ellos ________ (llegar) con sus dos mil jaulas de pericos.
13. Todavía seguimos utilizando el mismo vidrio que los fenicios________ (fabricar).
14. Nosotros ________ (decidir) aprender español porque nos gusta la música latina.
15. ¿Ustedes ________ (cruzar) la cordillera por el lado menos inclinado?

Exercise 42. Complete the following sentences with the appropriate form of the preterit tense.

1. Todo salió bien cuando hice lo que mi madre me ________ (sugerir).
2. Los bandidos ________ (socorrer) a los periodistas perdidos en la noche.
3. Jorge era un necio hasta que Dios le ________ (proveer) sabiduría.
4. Fue en las costas de Jamaica donde nosotros ________ (pescar) un mero por primera vez.
5. Ella lo ________ (perseguir) hasta que logró casarse con él.
6. Mi amiga siempre estuvo ahí cuando yo la ________ (necesitar).
7. Nosotros ________ (jugar) bien pero nuestros contrincantes lo hicieron mejor.
8. ________ (haber) aguaceros torrenciales en Europa el mes pasado.
9. Los misioneros ________ (distribuir) los alimentos entre los damnificados del terremoto.
10. Mira este conejito que Lucas ________ (cazar) para la cena de esta noche.
11. Todos nosotros________ (sentir) mucho la muerte de tu padre.
12. Esta mañana Lola ________ (responder) toda su correspondencia acumulada de una semana.
13. La primera novela que Faulkner ________ (publicar) fue *La paga de los soldados*.
14. La torta quedó dura porque Berta no ________ (medir) bien la harina.
15. Ayer (yo) ________ (fumigar) esta casa y todavía hay hormigas por todas partes.
16. Los computadores ________ (disminuir) el mercado de máquinas de escribir pero no de calculadoras.

Exercise 43. Complete the following sentences with the appropriate form of the preterit tense.

1. La madre chimpancé ________ (abrazar) a su hijo y lo protegió de la mirada de los curiosos.
2. Finalmente los argentinos ________ (poder) estabilizar el valor de su divisa.
3. Te felicito por la ambiciosa carrera que (tú) ________ (emprender).
4. Tu abuelita ________ (empezar) a sufrir de sonambulismo desde que perdió su osito de felpa.
5. La linterna debe estar en alguna de las cajas pues recuerdo bien que nosotros la ________ (empacar).
6. Después de que yo ________ (andar) por la ciudad de Granada me salieron callos.
7. Perdiste la partida porque desde el principio ________ (ubicar) mal a tu dama.
8. Es extraño, pero ellos aseguran que ________ (oír) lobos anoche.
9. Susana y Mario________ (dormir) en una cabaña en lo alto de la montaña.
10. Por su buena actuación Charlotte ________ (conseguir) un óscar como mejor actriz de reparto.
11. Mi problema fue que mis padres nunca me ________ (comprender).
12. El incendio se ________ (apagar) dejando un gran sector del bosque destruido.
13. No es cierto cuando dicen que Beethoven ________ (amar) a muchas mujeres.

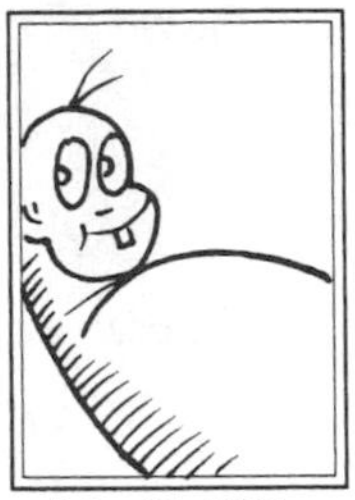

May 21, 1920

June 5, 1941

March 7, 1942

July 23, 1945

May 3, 1950

August 3, 1955

May 5, 1969

April 3, 1970

Exercise 44. Based on the pictures above, tell some souvenirs about the life of abuelo Marco. Use the following verbs: tener un hijo, casarse, arrestar a su hijo, graduarse, accidentarse, ganar un concurso, ir al matrimonio de su hijo.

1. *El abuelo Marco nació el 21 de mayo de 1920.*
2. ____
3. ____
4. ____
5. ____
6. ____
7. ____
8. ____

III. The Imperfect

The **imperfect,** as stated before, is mostly used **to describe** something in the past.

A. REGULAR VERBS

The **regular conjugation** in the imperfect indicative is formed by adding the following endings to the stem of the verbs.

	Verb Endings of the Imperfect	
	-ar	**-er /-ir**
yo	-aba	-ía
tú	-abas	-ías
él, ella, usted	-aba	-ía
nosotros/as	-ábamos	-íamos
vosotros/as	-abais	-íais
ellos, ellas, ustedes	-aban	-ían

TIP BOX

There are no stem-changing verbs in the imperfect.

Exercise 45. Complete the following sentences using the appropriate form of the imperfect tense.

1. Cuando niño, todos los días, ________ (recoger) piedritas.
2. Cuando Arnoldo era joven________ (hacer) cien abdominales diarias.
3. Era mejor cuando tú ________ (almorzar) fuera de la casa.
4. Los árboles que derrumbaron ________ (proteger) los nacimientos de agua.
5. Nosotros fuimos a casa a hacer una fiesta, mientras vosotros ________ (insistir) en ir a la fiesta del club.
6. Dicen que Antonio ________ (escribir) su último libro cuando sufrió el infarto.
7. Él advirtió que nosotros perderíamos el dinero si________ (decidir) no tomar el apartamento.
8. Mis padres________ (asistir) todos los años a la celebración de año nuevo en casa de la familia Torres, mientras ellos estuvieron vivos.
9. Cuando era estudiante Tonino ________ (vender) emparedados en la universidad.
10. Todos los inversionistas ________ (temer) una nueva caída de los precios en la bolsa de Nueva York.
11. Liliana, cuando era adolescente, ________ (responder) mal con sus deberes escolares.

12. Los fenicios ________ (creer) en un solo dios.
13. Cuando era joven no ________ (comprender) a los adultos y ahora tampoco.
14. Mientras Sara ________ (buscar) un sitio de reposo, sus hijos gritaban sin parar.
15. A esta misma hora hace dos años, Teresa ________ (bailar) con Joaquín Sabina en un bar de Madrid.
16. En el año 2001 mis primos________ (tener) la misma novia y no sabían.
17. Cuando Susana era joven, ________ (dormir) profundamente; ahora sufre de insomnio.

B. VERBS WITH IRREGULAR FORMS

Only three verbs are irregular in the imperfect: **ir**, **ser**, and **ver**.

	ir	**ser**	**ver**
yo	iba	era	veía
tú	ibas	eras	veías
él, ella, usted	iba	era	veía
nosotros/as	íbamos	éramos	veíamos
vosotros/as	ibais	erais	veíais
ellos, ellas, ustedes	iban	eran	veían

Exercise 46. Complete the following sentences using the appropriate form of the imperfect tense.

1. A los seis años Diego pensaba que ________ (ir) a ser bombero.
2. Cuando mi abuela vivía, nosotras ________ (ir) en la tardes a caminar por el campo.
3. Vosotros ________ (ser) más divertidos antes de tener tanto dinero.
4. Orlando ________ (ser) mas feliz cuando vivía en Bolivia.
5. Mis amigos y yo ____________ (ver) cine mudo todos los viernes en la tarde cuando salíamos de la escuela.
6. Los López ________ (ser) sus mejores amigos antes de su divorcio.
7. ¿Adónde ________ (ir) ustedes de vacaciones cuando vivían con sus padres?
8. ¡Sí, ya recuerdo ese grupo! Pero mis amigos ________ (ser) Javier y Tomás, a los otros chicos realmente no los conocí bien.
9. ¿Por qué David no ________ (ir) a la escuela con los otros niños del barrio cuando vivía en Lima?
10. Cuando llegaba del colegio todas las tardes, Germán ________ (ver) Plaza Sésamo en la tele.
11. Antes, Jaime ________ (ser) más amable con las visitas.
12. ¿Cómo se llamaba esa muchacha que (tú) ________ (ver) con frecuencia mientras vivimos en Buenos Aires?
13. La vida cotidiana__________ (ser) muy distinta antes de la popularización de los computadores.

C. USES OF THE IMPERFECT TENSE

The imperfect is used to describe the past in the following ways.

a. To describe a routine or an habitual action that used to occur in the past.

Example

Cuando era niño, todos los días jugaba con mi vecino.
When I was a child, I used to play with my neighbor every day.

Los domingos íbamos a comer en un restaurante.
Every Sunday, we would go to a restaurant for dinner.

Durante las vacaciones viajábamos a la costa Atlántica para disfrutar de la playa.
During our vacations, we would travel to the Atlantic Coast to enjoy the beach.

Exercise 47. Complete the following text using the appropriate form of the imperfect tense of the following verbs.

beber, caminar, comer, divertirse, esconderse, estar, enviar, ir, jugar, organizar, venir

Ahora, recuerdo que cuando ____________ en la escuela secundaria, para poder ir de paseo ____________ rifas. En los paseos muchos de mis compañeros ____________ aguardiente a escondidas y les ____________ serenatas a sus prometidas sin el consentimiento de sus padres. En casa, nuestros padres eran muy estrictos. Todos los días ____________ en una mesa diferente a la de los adultos. Allí, en esa mesa exclusiva para nosotros los niños, nos ____________ monstruosamente, especialmente con mis primos que todos los años ____________ en las vacaciones a visitarnos. Después de comer, durante el verano todas las tardes ____________ a la playa y ____________ voleibol. A veces, ____________ por la montaña y nos ____________ de mi hermano menor.

b. To describe a situation that occurred in the past.

Example

En aquel tiempo, vivíamos en el campo.
In those days, we lived in the countryside.

Yo tenía ocho años y ayudaba a mi padre ordeñando las vacas.
I was eight years old and I used to help my father milk the cows.

Exercise 48. Complete the following exercise as shown in the example below.

Example

Actualmente, mi hermana es la mejor estudiante, *pero antes era la peor.*

1. Ricardo tiene dos novias, ____________________. (sólo una)
2. Adriana canta rock, ____________________. (tango)
3. Alberto y Daniel escriben para el diario más importante del país, ____________________. (para el diario local)
4. Mi madre sonríe sólo de vez en cuando, ____________________. (todo el tiempo)
5. Lucrecia no duerme mucho, ____________________. (muchas horas)
6. Ahora nunca miento, ____________________. (todo el tiempo)
7. Rosa corre tres kilómetros, ____________________. (diez kilómetros)
8. Mi padre no tiene mucho dinero, ____________________. (mucho)
9. Hoy, mi madre no posee nada, ____________________. (una fortuna)

c. To describe a person in the past either physically or morally.

Example

Mi profesora tenía los ojos negros y era muy amable.
My teacher had dark eyes and she was very charming.

Exercise 49. Following the example below, put the following sentences in the past, using the imperfect tense.

Example

Mi abuelo tiene los ojos azules. *Mi abuelo tenía los ojos azules.*

1. Mi perra es grande y blanca y es muy juguetona.

   ____

2. Mi profesora tiene el cabello negro y es muy estricta.

   ____

3. Los niños son muy inquietos y tienen mucha energía.

   ____

4. María y Josefa son altas y bondadosas, y además tienen mucha paciencia.

   ____

5. Rosa es muy simpática y se viste muy elegante.

   ____

6. Fernando es guapo, tiene los ojos negros y el cabello oscuro. Además es inteligente.

   ____

d. To describe either a condition affecting the psyche or a mood in the past.

Example

Se sentía triste y abandonada.
She felt sad and abandoned.

Estaba enferma y tenía fiebre.
She was sick and had a fever.

Exercise 50. Complete the following text using the appropriate form of the imperfect tense of the following verbs.

aburrir, creer, decir, entrar, estar, gustar, ir, llorar, mirar, pensar, reprender, sentir, sentirse, tener

Julia ____________ agobiada cuando nuestra madre la ____________. A ninguno nos ____________ estudiar. La escuela nos ____________ y (nosotros) ____________ desconsoladamente todos los lunes cuando ____________ camino a la escuela. (nosotros) ____________ a los pescadores y al mar con nostalgia. (nosotros) ____________ que la libertad era lanzar piedras desde el acantilado. Julia además siempre ____________ miedo cuando ____________ a la clase de latín. Muchas veces para no ir a la escuela ____________ que ____________ enferma y que ____________ náuseas. Pero mamá nunca le ____________.

e. To describe attitudes and convictions in the past.

Example

Todos creían que el chamán tenía el poder de la curación.
All of them believed the shaman had healing power.

Pensábamos que iba a morir.
We thought he would die.

Exercise 51. Following the example below, put the following sentences in the past using the imperfect tense.

Example

Todos estamos convencidos de tu inocencia. *Todos estábamos convencidos de tu inocencia.*

1. Mis padres piensan que soy un perezoso.

   ____

2. Yo creo que tengo una enfermedad grave.

   ____

3. Mi hermana está segura de mi lealtad.

   ____

4. Raúl nos asegura que tiene un secreto.

   ____

5. Andrea piensa que yo nunca tengo la razón, y es cierto.

____

6. Yo no reconozco que me equivoco.

____

7. Clemente insinúa que yo pierdo todo.

____

8. Yo insisto en ser astronauta.

____

9. Ellas siempre averiguan dónde es la fiesta.

____

f. To describe an action in process in a specific moment of the past.

Example

—¿Qué hacías cuando oíste la explosión?
—Compraba el periódico en el kiosco.

"What were you doing when you heard the explosion?"
"I was buying a newspaper in the kiosk."

Exercise 52. Complete the following sentences using the appropriate form of the imperfect tense.

1. Él ________ (hacer) sus maletas cuando se inundó la casa.
2. Lola y María ________ (mirar) al cielo cuando cayó una estrella fugaz.
3. Nosotros ________ (vivir) en Santiago cuando ocurrió el golpe de estado.
4. Yo________ (trabajar) en el segundo piso cuando escuché unos pasos en el corredor.
5. Mi abuelo________ (recoger) los tomates en la huerta cuando sufrió el infarto.
6. Ellos________ (encender) las luces de Navidad en el momento que todo Chicago sufrió el apagón.
7. Yo ________ (aparcar) dando marcha atrás y no vi el poste que estaba a mi izquierda. Por eso lo choqué.
8. ¿Exactamente qué oración ________ (rezar) cuando dices que la imagen apareció?
9. Yo ________ (leer) a Byron cuando decidí ser escritor.
10. Ellos ________ (vender) las joyas de su familia cuando su madre entró y los descubrió.

g. To describe the setting of a story that happened in the past.

Example

Era una mañana de junio; alegre, tibia y sonrosada.
It was a joyful, warm, and reddish June morning.

El sol anunciaba sus rayos en los colores vivos de las nubes de Oriente.
The sun announced its lively colored rays on the eastern clouds.

TIP BOX

Most of the time, the Spanish imperfect corresponds to the English expression *used to + infinitive* or to the progressive past form *was/were + present participle (-ing)*.

Exercise 53. Complete the following text using the imperfect tense.

1. Todo _________ (ser) armonía en la casa de mis padres.
2. El riachuelo _________ (hacer) un ruido tenue sobre el silencio de la montaña.
3. _________ (llover) torrencialmente y no había lugar dónde guarecerse.
4. La música _________ (seguir) sonando en el salón mientras afuera _________ (nevar).
5. _________ (hacer) un claro día de invierno.
6. La mar_________ (estar) en calma, no _________ (hacer) viento.
7. _________ (ser) un terreno pantanoso y difícil de transitar.
8. El sol _________ (haber) caído y se acercaba una tormenta.
9. La tarde _________ (correr) lentamente en el sopor del trópico.

Exercise 54. Describe what Mom saw when she came back from the party. Use the following verbs: dibujar, beber, mirar, destruir

1. ____
2. ____
3. ____
4. ____

D. THE IMPERFECT VERSUS THE PRETERIT

a. As previously stated, the imperfect is used to evoke memories or remembrances.

Example

Cuando era niño, tenía un labrador.
When I was a child, I had a golden retriever.

b. The preterit is used to narrate or recount events.

Example

Un día perdí mi labrador.
One day, I lost my golden retriever.

In a past narrative, both past tenses are used: the preterit to recount events and the imperfect for descriptions and situations.

Example

Aquel día en que perdí mi labrador, estaba en el parque. Jugaba con mis amigos. En aquella época tenía doce años y lloré inconsolablemente la pérdida de mi perro.

The day I lost my golden retriever, I was in the park. I was playing with my friends. I was twelve years old at that time and I cried inconsolably for the loss of my dog.

A good metaphor for the imperfect is a photograph that describes the setting of a situation, whereas for the preterit it is the plot of a film that shows a sucession of events.

Hacía sol, todos disfrutábamos del hermoso día. De repente, escuchamos una fuerte explosión. Corrimos al lugar y encontramos un cráter de por lo menos 10 metros de diámetro. Un meteorito había caído a tan sólo un kilómetro de donde estábamos.

It was sunny and we were enjoying the beautiful day. Suddenly, we heard a strong explosion. We ran to the place and we found a crater which was at least 10 meters in diameter. A meteorite had fallen only one kilometer from where we had been.

c. The preterite is used when we talk about periods of time that are well defined (with a beginning and a precise end). The imperfect, on the contrary, is used when talking about indefinite periods of time.

Definite period of time
Entre 1989 y 1999, toqué el harpa. *Between 1989 and 1999, I played the harp.*
Durante 10 años, toqué el harpa. *For 10 years, I played the harp.*
Desde que tenía ocho años hasta cumplir 18 años, toqué el harpa. *Between the ages of eight and 18, I played the harp.*

Indefinite period of time
Antes, tocaba el harpa con frecuencia. *Before, I played the harp regularly.*
Cuando era joven, tocaba el harpa con frecuencia. *When I was young, I played the harp regularly.*
En aquella época, tocaba el harpa con frecuencia. *During that time, I played the harp regularly.*

d. The preterit indicates a change in relation to a common habit or a change in relation to a given situation.

Imperfect (common habit)
Antes pasábamos las vacaciones en la finca de mi abuelo. *We used to spend our vacation on my grandfather's farm.*

Preterit (change in relation to a common habit)
Pero un día mi abuelo murió y no volvimos nunca más. *But, one day my grandfather died and we never returned.*

Imperfect (given situation)
Ayer hacía un día hermoso. *Yesterday, it was a beautiful day.*

Preterit (change in the given situation)
De repente se nubló y cayó un agacuero torrencial. *Suddenly, it became cloudy and a strong rain fell.*

Exercise 55. Divide the following text into one column with the phrases in the imperfect doing the same for the other column in the preterit.

Era alrededor de las ocho de la mañana cuando oímos gritos en la calle. Marta y yo nos levantamos y nos asomamos a la ventana. Afuera había miles de personas gritando. Era un día de verano y el cielo estaba completamente azul. Todos en la calle iban vestidos con disfraces de variados colores y cantaban y bailaban como locos.

—Ya comenzó el Carnaval—, le dije a Marta. Nos vestimos rápidamente, tomamos la cámara y salimos a la calle. Todos nos miraban de manera extraña. No había duda que éramos un par de idiotas turistas.

Imperfect	**Preterit**
Era alrededor de las ocho de la mañana	*oímos gritos en la calle.*
____________________	____________________
____________________	____________________
____________________	____________________
____________________	____________________
____________________	____________________
____________________	____________________

Exercise 56. Put the following text in the past, using either the imperfect or the preterit.

El Bogotazo

El señor Torres es un hombre maduro, casado con una mujer que trabaja en la oficina de correos. El 9 de abril de 1948, se encuentra bebiendo una cerveza en el Café Royal, sobre la calle Séptima. De repente, escucha una multitud de hombres armados que vienen enfurecidos de todas partes, con palos y machetes. Como no tiene tiempo suficiente para levantarse y salir corriendo, decide refugiarse en el bar. Desde la ventana ve cómo hombres enfurecidos destruyen y saquean todo lo que está a su alrededor. Todo el centro de la ciudad de Bogotá está en llamas. El señor Torres pasa la noche en el bar y sólo al día siguiente logra salir. Se dirige a su casa, preocupado por su mujer. No sabe si está viva. Aunque hay muertos por todas partes, el señor Torres encuentra a su mujer sana y salva.

Exercise 57. Answer the following questions, using the preterit or the imperfect.

1. ¿Por qué apagaste la calefacción?

   ____

2. ¿Por qué vendiste tu auto?

   ____

3. ¿Por qué no me invitaste a la fiesta?

   ____

4. ¿Por qué te quedaste en casa ayer?

____

5. ¿Por qué no fuiste a trabajar?

____

Exercise 58. Complete the following text using the preterit or imperfect tense.

El barbero se ____________ (quedar) mirando a Evaristo, no ____________ (dar) crédito al cuento, y ____________ (pensar) que más bien ____________ (tener) delante a uno de esos temibles bandidos, quizá cómplice o el mismo asesino de Tules, pues ya ____________ (haber) leído en los periódicos el suceso; pero ____________ (tener) miedo; ____________ (hacer) sentar al cliente en la silla, le ____________ (atar) una toalla en el cuello y ____________ (comenzar) a cortar aquellas greñas espesas, pegadas con la sangre que ____________ (haber) brotado de la herida que le ____________ (hacer) Juan con el serrote. Después lo ____________ (rasurar) y le ____________ (presentar) un espejito. Evaristo mismo no se ____________ (reconocer) ...

Extracto
Manuel Payno. *Los bandidos de Riofrío*.

IV. Progressive Tenses

A. FORMS OF THE PROGRESSIVE TENSES

The progressive tenses are formed with the auxiliary verb **estar** (in any tense) plus the gerund (or present participle).*

	Progressive Tenses		
	Present	**Preterit**	**Imperfect**
	cantar	correr	abrir
yo	estoy cantando	estuve corriendo	estaba corriendo
tú	estás cantando	estuviste corriendo	estabas corriendo
él, ella, usted	está cantando	estuvo corriendo	estaba corriendo
nosotros/as	estamos cantando	estuvimos corriendo	estábamos corriendo
vosotros/as	estáis cantando	estuvisteis corriendo	estabais corriendo
ellos, ellas, ustedes	están cantando	estuvieron corriendo	estaban corriendo

* See Chapter 5, II. The Gerund.

B. USES OF THE PROGRESSIVE TENSES

Progressive tenses are used to emphasize an action or to express that which is specific or exceptional.

Example

¡Silencio! Estoy estudiando.
Silence! I am studying!

Ayer estuve corriendo toda la tarde.
Yesterday, I ran all afternoon.

Ayer estaba paseando y me encontré un anillo de oro.
Yesterday, I was walking and I found a gold ring.

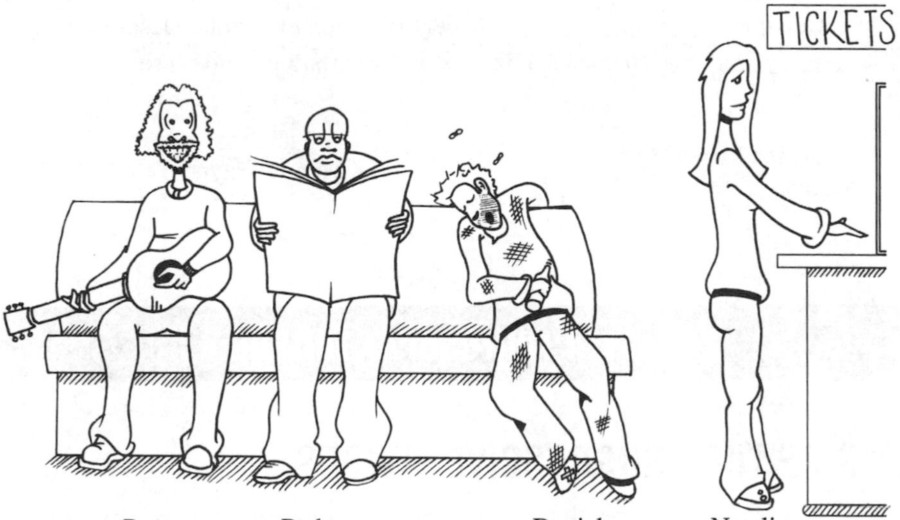

Paco Pedro Daniel Natalia

Exercise 59. Describe what people at the airport are doing. Use the following verbs: **tocar**, **leer**, **dormir**, **comprar**

1. ______________________________
2. ______________________________
3. ______________________________
4. ______________________________

Exercise 60. Complete the following sentences using the appropriate form of the present progressive tense.

1. Debes esperar porque apenas _____ _________ (encender) el horno.
2. No llores, si aún no nos _____ _________(despedirse).
3. En esta región de Colombia siempre _____ _________ (llover).
4. ¡Tan pronto (tú) _____ _________ (alistar) tus maletas para el viaje!
5. No lo saques del revelador todavía, que la imagen apenas _____ _________(aparecer).
6. No me gusta este libro que (tú) _____ _________(escribir).
7. (yo) _____ _________(leer) la vida espiritual de sor Juana Inés.
8. El padre _____ _________(asistir) a una ceremonia en otra población. Ahora no va a poder atenderte.
9. (yo) _____ _________ (comprar) una nueva casa y por eso no debo excederme en gastos.
10. Te he dicho que no hables mientras (tú) _____ _________ (comer).

Exercise 61. Form sentences using the appropriate form of the preterit progressive tense.

1. Durante el otoño las hojas / caer / sobre el jardín.
2. El año pasado / Tomás /escribir/ sus memorias.
3. Anoche / Nicolás / alistar / todo su equipaje.
4. Ayer / nosotros / mirar / su última obra de teatro pero no nos gustó.
5. Ayer en la tarde / el profesor /corregir / las partes mal escritas de las composiciones.
6. ¿Por qué ayer (ustedes) / recoger / las uvas si aún no estaban maduras?
7. ¡Durante toda la comida (tú) / sonreír / con el esposo de tu amiga!
8. Nos duelen las piernas porque / caminar / ayer toda la tarde.
9. ¿Cómo se llamaba esa muchacha con la que (tú) / vivir / en Bruselas?
10. Los niños están cansados/ toda la tarde / subir / los muros de los vecinos.

Exercise 62. Complete the following sentences using the appropriate form of the imperfect progressive tense.

1. Cuando la madre de Joselito entró en la casa, su hermano y sus amigos _________ (beber) el whisky de su papá.
2. Lo detuvo la policía porque al parecer lo encontraron cuando _________ (vender) narcóticos.
3. Mi perro cayó al hueco porque _________ (buscar) huesos.
4. La señora se enojó porque cuando llegó, su esposo y la secretaria _________ (bailar) encima del escritorio.
5. Mis padres _________ (viajar) cuando mi abuela murió.

6. Yo _________ (oír) a mi madre cuando él entró.
7. Tú _________ (leer) una revista de autos la tarde en que te vi por primera vez.
8. Nosotros _________ (asistir) al matrimonio de mis primos cuando nuestro perro se enfermó.
9. Ellos _________ (construir) el ferrocarril cuando descubrieron las minas de oro.
10. Cuando papá llamó mi hermana y yo ___________ (jugar) con mi hermano menor.

V. The Future Tense

A. REGULAR VERBS

The **regular conjugation** in the future indicative is formed by adding the following endings to the infinitive of the verb.

	Verb Endings of the Future Indicative	**amar (to love)**
yo	-é	amar**é**
tú	-ás	amar**ás**
él, ella, usted	-á	amar**á**
nosotros/as	-emos	amar**emos**
vosotros/as	-éis	amar**éis**
ellos, ellas, ustedes	-án	amar**án**

TIP BOX

Note that the endings correspond to the endings of the irregular verb **haber** in the present indicative.

haber (to have)	
yo	**he**
tú	**has**
él, ella, usted	**ha**
nosotros/as	**hemos**
vosotros/as	**habéis**
ellos, ellas, ustedes	**han**

Exercise 63. Complete the following sentences using the appropriate form of the future tense.

1. Roberto ________(escribir) sus memorias.
2. Hoy estoy cansada. Mañana (yo) ________ (alistar) lo del viaje.
3. Nosotros ________ (leer) su libro.
4. No sé que decir porque de todas manera él________ (insistir) en que tengo que ir.
5. El próximo invierno Rosalba ________ (comprar) una piel de jabalí.
6. El sábado la familia Aznar________ (comer) con vosotros.
7. Mis primos me________ (permitir) usar su computador esta noche.
8. Él ________ (enviar) el dinero mañana en la tarde.
9. Mañana no estaré, ¿te ________ (beber) el remedio antes de dormir?
10. Hoy estamos muy ocupados pero mañana (tú) ________ (recibir) una sorpresa.

B. IRREGULAR VERBS

The irregular verbs in the future either drop the vowel of their infinitive ending or they replace it with the consonant **d**.

a. The **-er** verbs **caber**, **haber**, **saber**, **poder**, **querer** drop the vowel **e**.

	Future (irregular verbs that drop the **e**)				
	caber	**haber**	**saber**	**poder**	**querer**
yo	cabré	habré	sabré	podré	querré
tú	cabrás	habrás	sabrás	podrás	querrás
él, ella, usted	cabrá	habrá	sabrá	podrá	querrá
nosotros/as	cabremos	habremos	sabremos	podremos	querremos
vosotros/as	cabréis	habréis	sabréis	podréis	querréis
ellos, ellas, ustedes	cabrán	habrán	sabrán	podrán	querrán

Exercise 64. Complete the following sentences using the appropriate form of the future tense.

1. No te preocupes el coche es grande y ________(caber) tus maletas y las mías.
2. Para cuando llegues yo ya me ________ (haber) ido.
3. Si insistes en molestarme________ (saber) de lo que soy capaz.
4. Este paquete es muy chico, seguro que ________ (caber) en tu maleta de mano.
5. Con esfuerzo, nosotros________ (poder) ir a conocer la biblioteca de Alejandría el próximo verano.

6. Mariela está hoy muy triste pero mañana ya lo ________ (haber) olvidado todo.
7. Los extraterrestres no ________ (querer) irse de nuestro planeta después de que conozcan Acapulco.
8. No pensemos que es difícil y mañana ya lo ________ (haber) hecho.
9. Los científicos creen que en unos años ________ (saber) cómo funciona el cerebro humano.

b. The verbs **poner**, **salir**, **tener**, **valer**, **venir** replace the ending vowel by **d**.

	Future (irregular verbs that replace the ending vowel by **d**)*				
	poner	**salir**	**tener**	**valer**	**venir**
yo	pon**d**ré	sal**d**ré	ten**d**ré	val**d**ré	ven**d**ré
tú	pon**d**rás	sal**d**rás	ten**d**rás	val**d**rás	ven**d**rás
él, ella, usted	pon**d**rá	sal**d**rá	ten**d**rá	val**d**rá	ven**d**rá
nosotros/as	pon**d**remos	sal**d**remos	ten**d**remos	val**d**remos	ven**d**remos
vosotros/as	pon**d**réis	sal**d**réis	ten**d**réis	val**d**réis	ven**d**réis
ellos, ellas, ustedes	pon**d**rán	sal**d**rán	ten**d**rán	val**d**rán	ven**d**rán

Exercise 65. Complete the following sentences using the appropriate form of the future tense.

1. Dejaré la televisión en tus manos y para mañana sé que tú la ________(componer).
2. Si trabajamos más duro, en un año ________ (tener) ahorrado suficiente para comprar una granja.
3. Cuando deje de llover las ardillas ________ (salir) de sus madrigueras.
4. Él________ (poner) el capital y nosotros la fuerza de trabajo.
5. Para el año 2020 un galón de agua ________ (valer) lo mismo que uno de petróleo.
6. Vosotros________ (sobresalir) en la competencia porque sois los mejores.
7. Tú, sal por la puerta de atrás que nosotros lo ________ (entretener).
8. Rocío ________ (venir) más temprano para ir al cine en la tarde.
9. Un yen en los próximos diez años ________ (equivaler) a lo mismo que dos hoy.
10. Mis padres ________ (intervenir) en las decisiones de mis hermanos, pero en las mías no.

* Related verbs that follow the same pattern are **componer** (to compose), **deponer** (to depose), **descomponer** (to break down), **disponer** (to arrange), **imponer** (to impose), **oponer** (to oppose), **presuponer** (to assume), **proponer** (to propose) **suponer** (to suppose), **sobresalir** (to excel), **abstener** (to abstain), **contener** (to contain), **detener** (to stop), **entretener** (to entertain), **mantener** (to maintain), **obtener** (to obtain), **retener** (to retain, to maintain), **sostener** (to equal), **equivaler**, **contravenir** (to contravene), **convenir** (to agree), **intervenir** (to intervene), **prevenir** (to prevent), **sobrevenir** (to happen unexpectedly).

c. The verbs **decir** and **hacer** and related verbs* are also irregular, because they drop the **-ec-** or the **-ce-**.

	Future (irregular verbs that drop **-ec-** or **-ce-**)	
	decir (*to say*)	**hacer** (*to do*)
yo	diré	haré
tú	dirás	harás
él, ella, usted	dirá	hará
nosotros/as	diremos	haremos
vosotros/as	diréis	haréis
ellos, ellas, ustedes	dirán	harán

Exercise 66. Complete the following sentences using the appropriate form of the future tense.

1. Mis hijos _________(decir) mañana que yo los eduqué con disciplina.
2. Tú _________ (hacer) lo que yo diga.
3. Si le cuentas a todos (yo) _________ (contradecir) tus palabras y nada podrás probar.
4. Tú_________ (decir) y yo obedeceré.
5. Algunos de nuestros descendientes_________ (deshacer) lo que hemos construido.
6. Nosotros _________ (decir) exactamente lo que pasó.
7. Con esfuerzo (ellos) _________ (rehacer) la casa destruida.
8. Francisca esta cansada, (ella) _________ (hacer) sus deberes mañana.
9. Él _________ (satisfacer) todos sus caprichos.
10. Julián _________ (rehacer) el documento.

*Related verbs that follow the same pattern are **contradecir** (to contradict), **deshacer** (to untie, to undo), **rehacer** (to do again, to redo), **satisfacer** (to satisfy).

Exercise 67. Write about what the kids will do after school. Use the following verbs: **hacer**, **jugar**, **comer**, **ver**.

1. ______________________________

2. ______________________________

3. ______________________________

4. ______________________________

C. USES OF THE FUTURE TENSE

a. The future tense refers to future actions by imagining the future or by planning future projects.

Example

Mañana compraremos el coche.
Tomorrow we will buy the car.

Iremos de vacaciones a España el próximo año.
Next year we will go on vacation to Spain.

En cinco años, tendremos nuestro primer hijo.
In five years, we will have our first child.

Exercise 68. Following the example below, put the following sentences in the future tense.

Example

Ahora vivo en Boston, *pero el próximo año viviré en Madrid.*

1. Ahora no tengo bastante dinero, ________________________________.
2. Ahora no hablo muy bien español, ________________________________.
3. Ahora trabajo en Estados Unidos, ________________________________.
4. Ahora no hago mucho ejercicio, ________________________________.
5. Ahora te obedezco en todo, ________________________________.
6. Ahora soy muy responsable, ________________________________.

Exercise 69. Complete the following mini-dialogues using the appropriate form of the future tense.

—Todos las Nochebuenas vamos a la Misa de Gallo. ¿ _________(ir, tú) este año?
—No lo sé porque el párroco está enfermo y no sabemos si la _________ (celebrar).

—He oído que ganaste la lotería. ¿Qué _________ (hacer) con todo ese dinero?
—Me voy a Ibiza, _________ (comprar) un carro nuevo y el resto se lo _______(regalar) a los pobres.

—¿Cuándo_________(ir) al odontólogo?
—La semana entrante y también _________(visitar) a mi psicólogo.

—Son la cinco de la tarde y el bus no pasa. ¿Crees que_________ (pasar) pronto?
—No lo sé, pero de seguro que _________ (dejar) la estación a las 5:30 así que _________ (estar) acá a las 5:35 a más tardar.

—Vete ahora, que en un momento_________ (llegar) mi padre y nos _________(sorprender).
—Espero que pronto me _________ (presentar) a tu familia como tu novio oficial.

—Nosotros _________ (organizar) la venta de las boletas y tú _________ (prestar) tu casa para la rifa. ¿Qué dices?
—Esta bien, ¿pero yo cuánto _________ (ganar)?

Exercise 70. Complete the following sentences using the appropriate form of the future tense.

—¿Quién crees que _________ (ganar) las elecciones para el cargo de alcalde?
—No sé, pero dicen que Guerra de seguro _________ (tratar) de hacer trampa.

—En el futuro cercano todo lo que haces y dices lo _________ (saber) el gobierno.
—¿Dijiste lo _________ (saber)? Hace tiempo ya lo saben.

—Ayer un virus atacó el internet a nivel mundial. ¿Cómo sabremos que esto no se _________ (producir) de nuevo?
—Creo que eso nadie lo _________ (garantizar).

Exercise 71. Complete using the future tense.

levantarse tomar el bus ir a trabajar hablar con los clientes
hacer ejercicio comer bailar

Mañana viernes, como de costumbre, Ana se levantará, ...

____________________________________,
____________________________________,
____________________________________,
____________________________________,
____________________________________,
y ____________________________________.

b. The future tense expresses probability and conjecture in the present.

Example

—¿Qué pasa con Javier que aún no llega?
"What happened to Javier that he's not here yet?"

—Estará retrasado su avión.
"His airplane is probably late."

—Estará durmiendo.
"He's probably sleeping."

—Estará discutiendo con su novia.
"He's probably arguing with his girfriend."

Exercise 72. We do not know why Jorge is not in class at this time. We will try to guess what he is most probably doing at this very instant.

Rewrite the following sentences using the future as shown.

Example

Probablemente Jorge está durmiendo. *Estará durmiendo.*

1. Probablemente Jorge está enfermo. ________________________
2. Probablemente Jorge y Juan están jugando fútbol. ________________________
3. Probablemente Jorge y Liliana están viendo televisión. ________________________
4. Probablemente Jorge está en la corte. ________________________
5. Probablemente Jorge está en un embotellamiento de tráfico. ________________________
6. Probablemente Jorge está hablando con sus amigos. ________________________
7. Probablemente Jorge está escuchando música. ________________________

Exercise 73. Susana is a jealous girl. Her boyfriend, Ollie, went to Cali on vacation. She is thinking about his life without her over there.

Example

pensar / en mi
¿Pensará en mí?

1. salir / a bailar todas las noches

 ____

2. tener /nuevas amigas

 ____

3. querer / volver

 ____

4. ir / a muchos bares

 ____

5. nadar / en el río con amigas

 ____

TIP BOX

The future tense can be expressed by using the verb **ir** in the present indicative + the preposition **a + an infinitive**.

Example

Mañana <u>**voy a bailar**</u> en una discoteca.
Tomorrow I <u>am going to dance</u> in a discotheque.

Exercise 74. Change the following sentences in the future tense to the present tense form that expresses future action.

Example

Pasado mañana iremos al cine.
Pasado mañana vamos a ir al cine.

1. Las golondrinas saldrán con el sol.

 ____

2. El precio de la carne aumentará.

 ____

3. Las computadoras serán más baratas en unos años.

____

4. Tendré una entrevista para un nuevo empleo el próximo mes.

____

5. Tú emprenderás un largo viaje.

____

6. Tus planes serán exitosos.

____

7. Esta historia tomará un rumbo impredecible.

____

8. Dos grandes editoriales españolas se fusionarán en el transcurso de este año.

____

9. Si todo sale bien compraremos un yate en abril.

____

10. La crisis económica afectará especialmente a los pobres.

____

VI. The Conditional Tense

A. REGULAR VERBS

The **regular conjugation** of the conditional is formed by adding the following endings to the infinitive of the verb.

	Verb Endings in the Conditional Tense	**amar (*to love*)**
yo	-ía	amar**ía**
tú	-ías	amar**ías**
él, ella, usted	-ía	amar**ía**
nosotros/as	-íamos	amar**íamos**
vosotros/as	-íais	amar**íais**
ellos, ellas, ustedes	-ían	amar**ían**

TIP BOX

Note that the conditional is formed by adding the imperfect endings from the **-er**, **-ir** verbs to the infinitive form of the verb.

B. IRREGULAR VERBS

Irregular verbs in the conditional have the same stem change as irregular future tense verbs. (See Section V of this Chapter.)

Conditional (irregular verbs)		
caber: yo cabría	poner: yo pondría	decir: yo diría
haber: yo habría	salir: yo saldría	hacer: yo haría
saber: yo sabría	tener: yo tendría	
poder: yo podría	valer: yo valdría	
querer: yo querría	venir: yo vendría	

C. USES OF THE CONDITIONAL TENSE

The conditional expresses either a future or possible action. It is used to express advice, desire, or wishes as well as politeness. It is also used to express a future event in relation to another event that is in the past, and to express probability or conjecture in the past.

a. To express advice, desire, and/or politeness.

- Advice

Example

En tu lugar, no gastaría tanto dinero en ese coche.
If I were in your shoes, I would not spend so much money on that car.

Antes de irte deberías terminar tus deberes.
Before leaving you should finish your homework.

–¿Invitamos a José a la fiesta?
–Should we invite José to the party?

–Yo que tú, no lo invitaría.
–If I were you, I wouldn't (invite him).

Exercise 75. Following the example, write correct sentences.

Example

presentar el examen/Francisca/estudiar más
***Antes de presentar** el examen, Francisca **debería** estudiar más.*

1. gritar/Julio/razonar ____________________________
2. salir a jugar/(ellos)/comer ____________________________
3. comenzar un nuevo proyecto/(nosotros)/terminar este ____________________________
4. precipitarte/(tú)/calmarte ____________________________
5. regalarle dinero a los bancos/el presidente/reflexionar un poco más ____________________
6. subir la montaña/(vosotros)/preparar el equipo ____________________________
7. comprar una casa/(usted)/comprar un coche ____________________________
8. comer/(tú)/lavarte las manos ____________________________

Exercise 76. Following the example, answer the questions with an expression of advice.

Example

—¿Compramos la casa?
—Yo que ustedes, no la compraría. (or) *—Yo que vosotros, no la compraría.*

1. —¿Voy a Colombia?
   —____.
2. —¿Invertimos en la bolsa?
   —____.
3. —¿Me retiro de la universidad?
   —____.
4. —¿Me salgo del equipo de fútbol?
   —____.
5. —¿Nos ponemos estos disfraces?
   —____.
6. —¿Salgo con Jorge?
   —____.

- Desire or wishes

Example

Me gustaría* verte otra vez.
I would like to see you again.

*See Chapter 15, Special Constructions With Indirect Objects.

Exercise 77. Following the example below, make sentences that express desire or wishfulness.

Example

hablar español (a mí)
Me gustaría hablar español.

1. tener más tiempo libre (a nosotros) ____________________________
2. conocer más gente (a él) ____________________________
3. vivir en Granada (a mí) ____________________________
4. salir más a menudo por la noche (a ellos) ____________________________
5. ir con más frecuencia a cine (a vosotros) ____________________________
6. tener más libertad (a nosotros) ____________________________

- Politeness

Example

¿Me podría traer un vaso de agua?
Could you bring me a glass of water?

Exercise 78. Following the example below, create sentences using the form that expresses politeness or courtesy.

Example

el menú
¿Me podría usted traer el menu, por favor?

1. pan

   ____________________________________.

2. un vaso de agua

   ____________________________________.

3. una garrafa de vino

   ____________________________________.

4. una paella

   ____________________________________.

5. flan de postre

   ____________________________________.

6. la cuenta, por favor

   ____________________________________.

RESTAURANTE *EL VASCO*
MENÚ

Entradas
Plato de jamón y lomo ibérico
Ensalada natural
Pimientos rellenos de bacalao en su propia salsa

Carnes
Solomillo al oporto con setas
Delicias de solomillo rellenas de *foie* con salsa *roquefort*

Pescados
Merluza en salsa verde con almejas y gambas
Chipirones rellenos en su tinta con flan de arroz

Postres
Cuajada de leche de oveja con miel
Queso con membrillo y nueces
Helados variados

Bebidas
Botella de vino
Caña de cerveza

Exercise 79. Order from the menu above expressing politeness.

1. ____.
2. ____.
3. ____.
4. ____.
5. ____.

Exercise 80. Following the example, answer the questions expressing politeness.

Example

—¿Quiere usted una taza de chocolate o una taza de café?
—*Quisiera una taza de café.*

1. —¿Quiere usted azúcar o miel?
   —______________________________________

2. —¿Quiere una tostada o un panecillo?
   —______________________________________

3. —¿Quieren agua o jugo de naranja?
   —______________________________________

4. —¿Quiere huevos fritos o huevos revueltos?
—____

5. —¿Quieren fruta o helado?
—____

6. —¿Quieren pagar en efectivo o con tarjeta de crédito?
—____

b. In subordinated clauses, the conditional expresses a future event in relation to another event that is in the past.

Example

El profesor nos dijo que tendríamos el examen la próxima semana.
The teacher told us that we would have the exam next week.

Exercise 81. Following the example, answer the questions expressing desire.

Example

María

—¿Qué dijo María? (enviar las cartas en una hora)
—Dijo que enviaría las cartas en una hora.

1. —¿Qué dijeron Julia y Luis? (recoger el niño en la guardería) ____________________
2. —¿Qué dijo el abogado? (retirar la demanda) ____________________
3. —¿Qué dijeron los senadores? (aprobar la ley) ____________________
4. —¿Qué dijo el presidente? (terminar la guerra) ____________________
5. —¿Qué dijeron los manifestantes? (protestar hasta el final) ____________________
6. —¿Qué dijo la policía? (meter a la cárcel a los ladrones) ____________________

c. To express probability or conjecture in the past.

Example

—¿Qué pasó con Lucía que no vino?
—What happened to Lucía that she did not come?

—Perdería su avión.
—Probably she missed her flight.

—No se despertaría a tiempo.
—She probably did not wake up on time.

—Preferiría no venir.
—She probably preferred not to come.

Exercise 82. We do not know why María was not at work yesterday. We will try to guess what she was probably doing yesterday. Rewrite the following sentences using the conditional as shown in the example below.

Example

Probablemente María estaba durmiendo. *Estaría durmiendo.*

1. Probablemente María estaba enferma.

   ____

2. Probablemente María estaba discutiendo de política.

   ____

3. Probablemente María estaba escuchando un concierto.

   ____

4. Probablemente María estaba hablando por teléfono.

   ____

5. Probablemente María estaba en una reunión muy importante.

   ____

6. Probablemente María estaba redactando la composición.

   ____

7. Probablemente María estaba visitando a su médico.

   ____

Exercise 83. Susana is a jealous girl. Her boyfriend Ollie went to Cali on vacation and he should be home by now, but he has not arrived yet. Susana is worried.

Example

perder / el avión
¿Perdería el avión?

1. encontrar / a otra mujer

   ______________________________.

2. tener / un problema en el aeropuerto

   ______________________________.

3. comprar / una finca

   ______________________________.

4. despilfarrar / el dinero

   ______________________________.

5. extraviar / su pasaporte

   ______________________________.

5

Verbs: The Infinitive and Participle Forms

¡Atender y entender para aprender!

I. The Infinitive

As stated previously, Spanish verbs are grouped in three categories according to the ending of the infinitive form: **-ar**, **-er**, **-ir**. The infinitive is the verb form that Spanish uses as a noun.

A. FORMS OF THE INFINITIVE

The infinitive has two forms: The simple infinitive and the perfect infinitive.

	Verb Endings		
	-ar	**-er**	**-ir**
Simple Infinitive	cant**ar** *(to sing)*	com**er** *(to eat)*	viv**ir** *(to live)*
Perfect Infinitive	hab**er** cant**ado**	hab**er** com**ido**	hab**er** viv**ido**

TIP BOX

In Spanish, the infinitive is used when the verb is preceded by a preposition* or by another conjugated verb. The infinitive is also used after the expression "Tengo que."+

Hay que estudiar mucho **para sacar** buenas notas.
It's necessary to study a lot to obtain good grades.

Quiero comprar un abrigo.
I want to buy a coat.

Tengo que ir de compras.
I have to go shopping.

*See Chapter 18 "Prepositions"
+See Chapter 16 "Special Verbs and Verb Expressions"

B. USES OF THE INFINITIVE

In Spanish, the infinitive is the noun form of the verb. Like all nouns, the infinitive may function as a subject, an object of the verb, or an object of the preposition.

a. The infinitive as a subject.

Example

Aprender español es divertido.
Learning Spanish is fun.

Exercise 1. Using the infinitive, complete the following sentences with the verb that best describes the action.

1. ____________ es interesante.

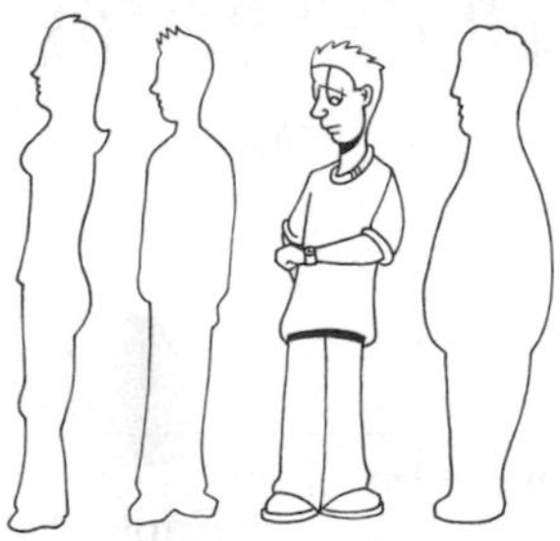

2. ____________ fila es aburrido.

3.

____________ es divertido.

4.

____________ cerveza es refrescante.

5.

____________ al cine es divertido.

6.

____________ es buen ejercicio.

7.

____________ sano es muy importante.

8.

____________ distraído es peligroso.

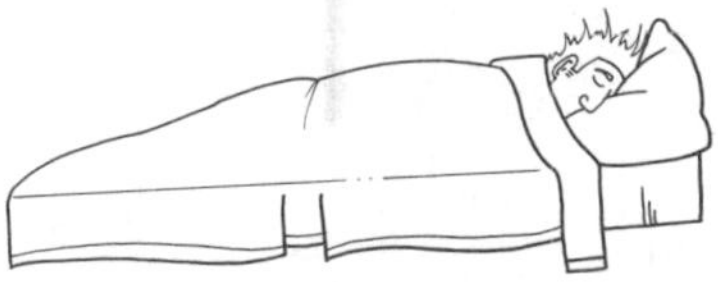

9.

____________ bien es importante.

10.

____________ rápido es peligroso.

b. The infinitive as an object of the verb.

Example

Quiero **viajar** a España este año.
I want to travel to Spain this year.

Necesito **comprar** el boleto de avión pronto.
I need to buy the airplane ticket soon.

Escuché **llorar** a tu bebé.
I heard your baby crying.

Es importante **ahorrar** dinero.
It's important to save money.

Exercise 2. Change the following sentences using the infinitive as shown in the example.

Example

Como langosta en la playa.
***Quiero comer** langosta en la playa.*

1. Paseo en el parque.
 ________________________________.
2. Nado con frecuencia para sentirme bien.
 ________________________________.
3. Corto el césped del jardín durante el fin de semana.
 ________________________________.
4. Voy al cine porque estrenan una película interesante.
 ________________________________.
5. Leo una novela antes de dormirme.
 ________________________________.
6. Voy a un concierto de jazz con mis amigos.
 ________________________________.

Exercise 3. Transform the following sentences using the infinitive as shown.

Example

Ayer vimos cómo volaban los gansos.
Ayer vimos volar los gansos.

1. Observé cómo mi abuela preparaba la tarta.*
 ____.
2. Escuché cómo la orquesta ensayaba para el concierto.
 ____.

* Note that the personal **a** is needed in these sentences.

3. Oí a un chico que pedía auxilio en la calle.
_______________________________________.

4. ¿Ves cómo sale el sol desde tu habitación?
_______________________________________.

5. Miramos cómo los niños patinaban sobre el hielo.*
_______________________________________.

6. ¿Escuchaste cómo el guitarrista daba un concierto?*
_______________________________________.

7. Sentiste que tu hermano cerraba la puerta.*
_______________________________________.

8. Contemplaremos cómo Óscar hace una escultura.*
_______________________________________.

9. Vi cómo Patricia entraba en correos.*
_______________________________________.

10. Oyes cómo suena el teléfono.
_______________________________________.

c. The infinitive as an object of the preposition.
In Spanish the infinitive is always used after a preposition in the following ways.

- Use as a prepositional phrase.

Example

Al **llegar** a casa, me acosté en la hamaca.
Upon arriving home, I lay down in the hammock.

TIP BOX

In Spanish the contraction **al** (a + el) followed by the infinitive is equivalent in English to *upon, when,* or *as*.

Exercise 4. Change the following sentences using the infinitive as shown in the example.

Example

Mientras subía las escaleras, me caí.
Al subir las escaleras, me caí.

1. Cuando me gradué, viajé a Chile.
_______________________________________.

* Note that the personal **a** is needed in these sentences.

2. Mientras abría la puerta, escuché a alguien hablar dentro de la casa.

   ____.

3. Cuando leí el libro, aprendí mucho sobre la cultura azteca.

   ____.

4. Cuando vimos las noticias, nos enteramos de que nevaría mañana.

   ____.

5. Cuando hablé con Laura por teléfono, me dijo que no estabas.

   ____.

6. Mientras salíamos del museo, nos encontramos a Pepe.

   ____.

7. Mientras hacías la compra, descubriste que habías olvidado el dinero.

   ____.

8. Cuando abrí el mapa, supe dónde estaba.

   ____.

9. Mientras tomaba un café, me quemé la lengua.

   ____.

10. Mientras manejaba al trabajo, escuchaba las noticias por la radio.

    ____.

- Use as a modifier of an adjective.

Example

Estoy ansioso de **verte.**
I am anxious to see you.

Exercise 5. Write sentences in the present using the following words.

Example

(yo) tener / ganas / de / ver / a Juan.
Tengo ganas de ver a Juan.

1. Lisa / estar / feliz / de / no / tener / clase

   ____.

2. Santiago /estar / interesado / en / leer / *El siglo de la luces.*

   ____.

3. Marta / estar / empeñada / en / visitar / el museo del Prado.

   ____.

4. Nunca / (yo) ir / a vivir / pobre / para / morir / rico.

   ____.

5. ¿Todavía / Sonia / estar / con deseos / de / terminar con su novio?

   ____.

- Use as a modifier of a noun.

Example

La torta para **regalar** está lista.
The cake that we are bringing is ready.

Exercise 6. Write sentences in the preterit using the following words.

Example

A Lucía / dar / cien dólares / para / comprar / regalos.
A Lucía le dieron cien dólares para comprar regalos.

1. El / municipio / nos / dar / el permiso / para / construir
   ______________________________________.
2. El / congreso / aprobar / el dinero / para / reconstruir / las escuelas
   ______________________________________.
3. Los estudiantes / leer / el libro / para / comentar / en clase
   ______________________________________.
4. María / traer / cerveza / para / dar / y / convidar
   ______________________________________.
5. Zoraida / comprar / un vino / delicioso / para / beber
   ______________________________________.

- Use as a modifier of an adverb.

Example

Yo lo abracé antes de **partir**.
I hugged him before leaving.

Exercise 7. Write sentences in the preterit using the following words.

Example

Juan / salir / después / de comer
Juan salió después de comer.

1. Jorge y Ana / hacer / ejercicio / después / de / nadar
   ______________________________________.
2. Julia / comprar / palomitas / antes / de / comenzar / la función
   ______________________________________.
3. esa lámpara / además / de / iluminar / sirve / para / calentar
   ______________________________________.

4. luego / de / llegar / a / un / acuerdo / (ellos) firmar / el / contrato

_______________________________________.

5. Jorge /con tal / de / ganar / dinero / engañar / a / sus / conciudadanos

_______________________________________.

II. The Gerund (or Present Participle)

A. FORMS OF THE GERUND

The gerund is formed in regular verbs by adding the ending **-ando** to the stem of the **-ar** verbs and **-iendo** to the stem of **-er** and **-ir** verbs.

-ar	**-er**	**-ir**
cant**ar**	ten**er**	decid**ir**
cant**ando**	ten**iendo**	decid**iendo**

TIP BOX

Stem-change verbs ending in **-ir*** have an irregular stem in the gerund. They change as follows:

- The **e** of the stem changes to **i**.

Example

herir (ie) changes to h**i**riendo.

- The **o** of the stem changes to **u**.

Example

dormir (ue) changes to d**u**rmiendo.

When the stem of the verbs **-er** and **-ir** ends in a vowel, as in verbs such as **caer**, **creer**, **leer**, **construir**, **ir**, **oír**, the gerund is **–yendo**.

Example

La nieve está ca**yendo**. *(The snow is falling.)*
María está le**yendo**. *(Maria is reading.)*

* See Chapter 4 for a list of stem-change **-ir** verbs.

B. USES OF THE GERUND

a. The gerund (or present participle) is used with the progressive tenses.* Progressive tenses are formed with the verb **estar** and the gerund.

Example

No entres que me estoy **bañando**.
Do not enter; I am taking a bath.

Exercise 8. Complete the following sentences using the gerund of the verb in the parentheses.

Example

Camilo se está _________ (bañar) en el lago.
Camilo se está bañando en el lago.

1. Isabel está ________ (plantar) un árbol en su jardín.
2. Eva está ________ (comer) un helado.
3. Pedro y Andrés están _______ (dar) un paseo en bicicleta.
4. En nuestra ciudad están _______ (construir) más edificios porque ahora hay más habitantes.
5. Miguel todavía está _______ (dormir) porque anoche trabajó hasta muy tarde.
6. Estoy _______ (leer) mi correo electrónico.

b. The gerund is used with an adverbial function that may indicate manner, cause, reason, time, or condition.

Example

María salió de la casa **gritando**.
María left the house screaming.

Ayer, **bailando** en la discoteca, vi a tu novia.
Yesterday, dancing in a discotheque, I saw your girlfriend.

Exercise 9. Transform the following sentences using the present participle, as shown.

Example

Mientras escribía me acordé de ti.
Escribiendo me acordé de ti.

1. Mientras vivía en Madrid conocí a Pepe.

____

*See Chapter 4, IV. "Progressive Tenses."

2. Si haces ejercicio, te sentirás mejor.

____

3. Mientras viajaba a Guatemala aprendí a cocinar tamales.

____

4. Mientras veía el partido de tenis, me tomé una cerveza.

____

5. Si lees el periódico, estarás informado.

____

6. Mientras entraba a la oficina, me dijeron que había una reunión importante.

____

Exercise 10. Answer the following questions using the gerund. Base your answer on the picture.

Example

¿Cómo llegó Pepito a la escuela?
Pepito llegó a la escuela llorando.

1. ¿De qué manera llegó Benito a ser presidente?

____

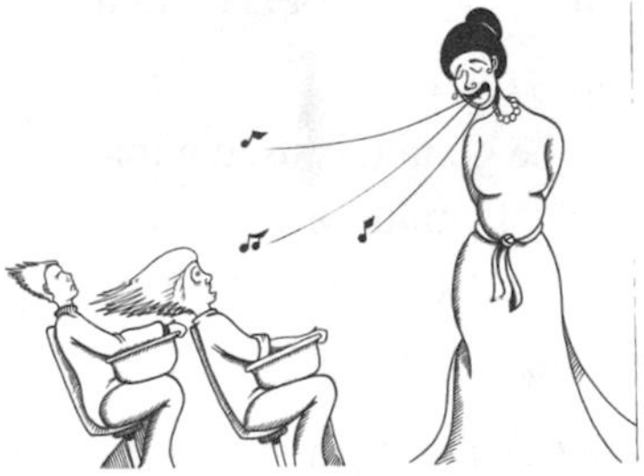

2. ¿Cómo enseña la profesora a los niños?

____

3. ¿Cómo salieron los niños de la escuela?

____

4. ¿Cómo atravesó Juan el Canal de la Mancha?

____

TIP BOX

The gerund (**-ando**, **-iendo**) is the equivalent of the English gerund (**-ing**). The Spanish gerund or present participle, however, cannot be used as a noun as it is used in English. In Spanish the infinitive is used instead.

Example

<u>Correr</u> es buen ejercicio.
Running is good exercise.

Another important difference is that the Spanish gerund cannot be used as an adjective to directly modify a noun, as can the English **-ing** form. In Spanish, a relative clause is used instead.

Example

El niño <u>que llora</u> es mi hijo.
The crying baby is my son.

III. The Past Participle

A. FORMS OF THE PAST PARTICIPLE

a. The past participle is formed in regular verbs by adding the ending **-ado** to the stem of the **-ar** verbs and **-ido** to the stem of the **-er** and **-ir** verbs.

-ar	**-er**	**-ir**
cantar *(to sing)*	**tener** *(to have)*	**venir** *(to come)*
cant**ado**	ten**ido**	ven**ido**

b. There are, however, exceptions in which the past participle is irregular.

Infinitive	Irregular Past Participle
abrir (*to open*)	abierto (*opened*)
absolver (*to absolve*)	absuelto (*absolved*)
cubrir (*to cover*)	cubierto (*covered*)
decir (*to say*)	dicho (*said*)
descubrir (*to discover*)	descubierto (*discovered*)
encubrir (*to cover up*)	encubierto (*covered up*)
escribir (*to write*)	escrito (*written*)
hacer (*to do*)	hecho (*done*)
morir (*to die*)	muerto (*died*)
poner (*to put*)	puesto (*put*)
resolver (*to solve*)	resuelto (*solved*)
romper (*to break*)	roto (*broken*)
satisfacer (*to satisfy*)	satisfecho (*satisfied*)
ver (*to see*)	visto (*seen*)
volver (*to come back*)	vuelto (*come back*)

B. USES OF THE PAST PARTICIPLE

a. The past participle, used together with the verb **haber** (to have), forms the perfect tense.* Note that in this case there is NO concordance between the past participle and the subject of the sentence. The past participle does not vary.

Example

La joven **ha encontrado** la felicidad.
The young girl has found happiness.

Los muchachos **han nadado** en el río.
The boys have swum in the river.

*Refer to Chapters 6 and 7 about the perfect tenses.

b. The past participle, used with a linking verb (**estar**—*to be*, **ser**—*to be*, **parecer**—*to seem*), has the aspect of a predicative adjective. In this case it agrees with the subject of the verb.

Example

La novela *El Quijote* **fue escrita** por Miguel de Cervantes Saavedra.
The novel El Quijote *was written by Miguel de Cervantes Saavedra.*

Los niños **están encerrados** en el cuarto.
The kids are locked in the room.

María **parece cansada**.
María seems tired.

c. The past participle, when it has the aspect of an adjective, agrees with the noun it modifies.

Example

Cuando llegamos a la casa encontramos la puerta **abierta**.
When we arrived home we found the door opened.

Los arqueólogos encontraron las momias bien **preservadas**.
Archeologists found the mummies well preserved.

Exercise 11. Complete the following sentences using the appropriate past participle (Perfect Tenses).

1. Ya habíamos _________ (salir) cuando nos llamó.
2. Eduardo se ha _________ (entrenar) mucho durante este año.
3. Siempre habías _________ (llevar) una vida sana hasta hace un año.
4. ¿No fuiste al espectáculo? Te habrías _________ (divertir).
5. He ________ (trabajar) cuarenta horas durante esta semana.
6. Para cuando te llame, ¿habrás ________ (decidir) qué quieres hacer?
7. Paula ha ________ (abrir) la ventana porque hacía calor.
8. Jaime habría ________ (preferir) descansar, pero Amalia quería salir a pasear.
9. Víctor ha ________ (decir) la verdad.
10. Para el lunes habré _________ (mandar) la solicitud.

Exercise 12. Complete the following sentences using the appropriate past participle.

1. En el metro hay letreros ________ (escribir) en español.
2. El cheque ya está _________ (firmar).
3. Tenemos la mesa _________ (poner) y la cena _________ (preparar).
4. Tras una larga investigación, las joyas fueron _________ (encontrar).
5. Esta casa fue _________ (construir) hace más de un siglo.

6. El presidente fue _________ (elegir) la semana pasada.
7. Encontré la puerta _________ (cerrar).
8. Los marineros fueron _________ (rescatar) del naufragio.
9. Esta foto fue _________ (tomar) desde el balcón de mi casa.
10. No te preocupes, ese problema ya está _________ (resolver).

Exercise 13. Complete the following sentences using the appropriate past participle.

1. No puedo escuchar su mensaje porque lo he ________ (borrar) accidentalmente.
2. El cuadro *Guernica* fue ________ (pintar) por Pablo Picasso.
3. Los libros ________ (usar) son más baratos.
4. Durante este año hemos _________ (tener) éxito en nuestro trabajo.
5. Cuando fui a su casa, él ya se había _______ (ir).
6. ¿No estás _________ (preocupar) por el medio ambiente?
7. Maite se ha _________ (hacer) socia de un gimnasio que hay cerca de su casa.
8. Javier Bardem es un actor muy _________ (conocer).
9. Machu Pichu fue _________ (construir) por los incas.
10. Antes del 2009 no había _______ (correr) en un maratón.

Exercise 14. Give the past participle and gerund form of the following verbs as shown below.

Example

cantar	*cantado*	*cantando*
1. abrir	______________	______________
2. absolver	______________	______________
3. amar	______________	______________
4. beber	______________	______________
5. comer	______________	______________
6. cubrir	______________	______________
7. decir	______________	______________
8. descubrir	______________	______________
9. encubrir	______________	______________
10. escribir	______________	______________
11. estar	______________	______________
12. hablar	______________	______________
13. hacer	______________	______________
14. jugar	______________	______________
15. leer	______________	______________
16. morir	______________	______________
17. pedir	______________	______________
18. podrir	______________	______________

6

The Perfect Tenses of the Indicative

I. Forms of the Perfect Tenses

The perfect tenses of the indicative are formed with the verb *haber* in the corresponding tense (present, imperfect, future, or conditional) + the past participle.*

Yo he atrapado un pescado.
(I have caught a fish.)

	Perfect Tenses			
	amar (*to love*)			
	Present Perfect	**Past Perfect**	**Future Perfect**	**Conditional Perfect**
yo	**he** amado	**había** amado	**habré** amado	**habría** amado
tú	**has** amado	**habías** amado	**habrás** amado	**habrías** amado
él, ella, usted	**ha** amado	**había** amado	**habrá** amado	**habría** amado
nosotros/as	**hemos** amado	**habíamos** amado	**habremos** amado	**habríamos** amado
vosotros/as	**habéis** amado	**habíais** amado	**habréis** amado	**habríais** amado
ellos, ellas, ustedes	**han** amado	**habían** amado	**habrán** amado	**habrían** amado

*See Chapter 5 to learn more about the past participle.

TIP BOX

Remember, the past participle in the perfect tenses does NOT agree with the subject.

Example

José y Julián han viajado a Bolivia tres veces.
José and Julián have traveled three times to Bolivia.

María ha viajado a Bolivia tres veces.
María has traveled three times to Bolivia.

Note also that no word falls between the verb *haber* and the participle.

Example

Marta no **ha viajado** a Bolivia.
Marta has not traveled to Bolivia.

Marta ya **ha regresado** de Bolivia.
Marta has already returned from Bolivia.

II. Uses of the Perfect Tenses

Perfect Tenses in Spanish (as in English) are used when the speaker wants to emphasize the fact that the action performed by the verb (in past participle) has begun or has ended before a particular point of reference. The use of perfect tenses is very similar in both the English and Spanish languages.

A. PRESENT PERFECT

	cantar (***to sing***)	**oler** (***to smell***)	**partir** (***to leave***)
yo	he cantado	he olido	he partido
tú	has cantado	has olido	has partido
él, ella, usted	ha cantado	ha olido	ha partido
nosotros/as	hemos cantado	hemos olido	hemos partido
vosotros/as	habéis cantado	habéis olido	habéis partido
ellos, ellas, ustedes	han cantado	han olido	han partido

In the present perfect the action referred to by the verb is located prior to the point of reference.

Example

Lina ya **ha llegado;** ya podemos servir la comida.
Lina has arrived; we may now serve the meal.

In the previous example, the fact of arriving occurs before the reference point, which in this case is in the present tense.

When there is no obvious point of reference, the reference point is usually the moment of the act of speaking.

Los niños **han comido** muy bien.
The children have eaten very well.

TIP BOX

The present tense is usually used with the adverb **ya**.

Example

—¿**Ya han llegado** los niños? —*Have the children already arrived?*	or	–¿**Ya llegaron** los niños? –*Did the children already arrive?*
—No, **todavía no han** llegado. —*No, they have not arrived yet.*		–Sí, **ya llegaron**. –*Yes, they already arrived.*

Exercise 1. Complete the following sentences using the appropriate form of the present perfect tense.

1. (yo) _______ _________ (caminar) diez kilómetros y no veo un alma.
2. Él _______ _________(escribir) muchos libros sin publicar ni uno.
3. Ella _______ _________(leer) todo lo que escribió Agatha Christie.
4. Nosotros _______ _________(comprar) esta casa en muy mal estado.
5. Los invitados se _______ _________(comer) todo lo que había.
6. No _______ _________(permitir, nosotros) invitarlos a casa.
7. (vosotros) _______ _________(beber) todo el vino de su cava.
8. (yo) _______ _________(insistir) en verte para decirte algo muy importante.
9. A pesar de tus intrigas no (tú) _______ _________(conseguir) separarnos.
10. El gobierno me _______ _________(enviar) a cumplir una misión fuera del país.

Exercise 2. Complete the following sentences using the appropriate form of the present perfect tense.

1. Yo_______ _________(escribir) mil versos.
2. Tú no_______ _________ (decir) nada esta noche.
3. Yo_______ _________ (volver) sólo para verte.
4. Nosotros no _______ _________ (morir) por una suerte loca.
5. Las cocineras no _______ _________ (freír) el pescado.
6. Sus amigos_______ _________ (leer) todos sus libros por pura cortesía.
7. Tú no _______ _________ (ver) nada. Eres demasiado joven.
8. Los chinos _______ _________ (descubrir) un dinosaurio volador con cuatro alas entre otras muchas cosas maravillosas.
9. Los arqueólogos_______ _________ (abrir) las tumbas sin establecer aún la fecha exacta del entierro.
10. Mis hermanos me _______ _________ (cubrir) el rostro con crema de afeitar.

Exercise 3. Answer the following sentences using the present perfect or the preterit tense.

Example

—¿Ya llevaste a los niños al colegio?
—No, todavía no he llevado a los niños al colegio. (or) *—Sí, ya llevé a los niños al colegio.*

1. —¿Ya fuiste al banco?
   —No, _______________
2. —¿Ya limpiaste la loza de la comida?
   —Si, _______________
3. —¿Ya comiste?
   —Sí, _______________
4. —¿Ya conoces el nuevo teatro?
   —No, _______________
5. —¿Ya hiciste tus ejercicios de español?
   —No, _______________
6. —¿Ya terminaste de leer el libro?
   —No, _______________
7. —¿Ya grabaste tus archivos en otro disco?
   —Sí, _______________
8. —¿Sabes si Andrés ya hizo sus deberes?
   —Sí, _______________
9. —¿Anita y Milena ya terminaron el bordado?
   —No, _______________
10. —¿La compañía de teatro ya se fue del pueblo?
    —No, _______________

B. PAST PERFECT

	cantar	oler	partir
yo	había cantado	había olido	había partido
tú	habías cantado	habías olido	habías partido
él, ella, usted	había cantado	había olido	había partido
nosotros/as	habíamos cantado	habíamos olido	habíamos partido
vosotros/as	habíais cantado	habíais olido	habíais partido
ellos, ellas, ustedes	habían cantado	habían olido	habían partido

In the past perfect, the action referred to by the verb is also located before the point of reference.

Example

Lina ya **había llegado** cuando servimos la comida.
Lina had already arrived when we served the meal.

The fact of arriving occurs before the reference point (serving the meal), but in this case, the reference point is located in the past. Therefore, the past perfect is used in Spanish as it is used in English: to express a past action completed prior to another past action.

Exercise 4. Complete the following sentences using the appropriate form of the present perfect tense.

1. Yo no ______ _________(abrir) la puerta cuando el ladrón me atacó.
2. Tú ya ______ _________(bailar) con ella cuando decidiste hacerlo conmigo.
3. Antes de estudiar medicina el ______ _________(estudiar) biología
4. No le creí cuando dijo que nunca antes ______ _________ (venir) a Málaga.
5. No era su primera experiencia en Europa, antes ellos_____ _______ (vivir) en Austria.
6. Mi mamá fue la última en enterarse que nosotros _____ _________ (romper) el jarrón.
7. Dijeron que ya _____ _________ (comer).
8. No, nunca antes Jorge _________ _________ (visitar) Estocolmo.
9. A pesar de que Mónica no _____ _________ (llegar) decidimos iniciar la reunión.
10. Mis padres ya ______ _________ (morir) cuando decidimos destruir la antigua casa.

Exercise 5. Complete the following dialogue using the past perfect or the simple preterit.

1. —¿Ya (tú) _________(ver) la última película de Penélope?
   —¿Cuál? ¿Una en que _________ (hacer) el papel de monja?
   —¡No! Esa ya la _________ (hacer) antes de venir a Hollywood.

2. —Cuando Martín _________ (entrar) a la casa, ya Andrea____ _____(hacer) sus maletas y se disponía a partir.
—¿Y él qué ______ (hacer)?
—Le pidió la llave del buzón del correo, pero ella le dijo que ya la _________ (dejar) encima de la nevera con una carta para él.

3. —¡La última vez que te vi aún no _________ (dejar) los pantalones cortos! ¡Y mira ya hasta te _________ (salir) bigote!
—Sí es verdad, la última vez que te _________ (ver), fue cuando _________ (venir) a visitar a mi padre. Ud. recientemente ___________(publicar) su primer libro, ¿verdad?

C. FUTURE PERFECT

	cantar	oler	partir
yo	habré cantado	habré olido	habré partido
tú	habrás cantado	habrás olido	habrás partido
él, ella, usted	habrá cantado	habrá olido	habrá partido
nosotros/as	habremos cantado	habremos olido	habremos partido
vosotros/as	habréis cantado	habréis olido	habréis partido
ellos, ellas, ustedes	habrán cantado	habrán olido	habrán partido

a. The future perfect is used to express a future action finished before another future action.

Example

Para la próxima semana ya se **habrá reanudado** la producción de petróleo en Venezuela.
By next week, Venezuela's oil production will have resumed.

No te preocupes. Para cuando llegues ya **habré terminado** el trabajo.*
Don't worry. When you arrive I will have already finished all the work.

Exercise 6. Complete the following sentences using the appropriate form of the future perfect.

1. Para mañana, ya _______ _________(terminar/yo) de leer el libro.
2. En diez años ya te _______ _________(casarse/tú) y _______ _________ (tener) dos hijos.
3. Te aseguro que cuando cumpla 25 años Germán ya _____ __________ (despilfarrar) toda su fortuna.
4. Cuando te decidas por ella, ella ya _____ __________ (conseguir) un novio.
5. En un año ya _______ _________ (hacer/nosotros) nuestra casa de campo.

*For an explanation regarding the use of the subjunctive in this sentence, see The Present Subjunctive in Adverbial Clauses, Chapter 10.

6. Sé que es duro el divorcio, pero antes de que me dé cuenta ya _______ _________ (comenzar/yo) de nuevo mi vida.
7. Para cuando yo me pensione tú ya _______ _________(ir) a la universidad y serás independiente.
8. Antes de que regreses ya_______ _________(oír) muy buenas noticias de nuestro proyecto.
9. No te preocupes, para entonces yo ya_______ _________(llegar).
10. Cuando llegue el aburrido de Juan, nosotros ya _______ _________(partir).

b. The future perfect is also used to express probability in the past, when the action is seen as finished. (This is very similar to the use of the conditional when expressing probability.)

Example

—¿Por qué no vino?
"Why did he not come?"

—Se **habrá ido a otra parte.**
"He probably went to another place."

—¿Dónde está Liliana? Aún no llega.
"Where is Liliana? She has not arrived yet."

—**Habrá perdido** el avión.
"Maybe she missed her plane."

Exercise 7. Rewrite the following sentences using the future perfect as shown.

Example

El detenido probablemente habló.
¿El detenido habrá hablado?

1. Los asesinos probablemente se llevaron el cadáver.

____

2. La policía probablemente perdió la pista de los delincuentes.

____

3. Un testigo probablemente estuvo en el lugar del crimen.

____

4. El testigo probablemente lo vio todo.

____

5. La policía probablemente entrevistó al testigo.

____

6. El testigo probablemente es uno de los asesinos.

____

Exercise 8. Make conjectures about what a lonely dog could do. Follow the example and key words.

Example

dormir/calle
Probablemente el perro habrá dormido en la calle.

1. comer/basura
____
2. recorrer/la ciudad con otros perros
____
3. entrar/a un restarante a comer
____
4. morder/un policía
____
5. jugar/con niños en el parque
____
6. correr/entre los coches
____

D. CONDITIONAL PERFECT

	cantar	**oler**	**partir**
yo	habría cantado	habría olido	habría partido
tú	habrías cantado	habrías olido	habrías partido
él, ella, usted	habría cantado	habría olido	habría partido
nosotros/as	habríamos cantado	habríamos olido	habríamos partido
vosotros/as	habríais cantado	habríais olido	habríais partido
ellos, ellas, ustedes	habrían cantado	habrían olido	habrían partido

USES OF THE CONDITIONAL PERFECT

a. The conditional perfect is used to indicate a future action related to a moment in the past, but previous to another moment existent in the sentence.

Example

Te dije que cuando llegaran,* ya **habrían comido**.
I told you that by the time they arrived, they would have already eaten.

Ese día te **habría invitado** pero no tenía dinero.
That day I would have invited you, but I didn't have money.

Exercise 9. Rewrite the following sentences using the conditional perfect as shown.

Aquella tarde/(yo)/salir/contigo/no tener dinero.
Aquella tarde habría salido contigo pero no tenía dinero.

1. Aquel día/nosotros/comer/no tener hambre
____
2. Esa noche/(yo)/ir/al cine con ustedes/no tener tiempo
____
3. Aquella mañana/María/lo/besar/no lo/conocer/lo suficiente
____
4. Esa tarde/(yo)/jugar/contigo al fútbol/no tener el balón
____
5. Aquel año/(yo)/estudiar/no tener dinero para pagar la matrícula
____
6. Aquella noche/(yo) decirte/ la verdad/no tener la valentía de decírtelo
____
7. Ese día/nosotros nos/quedar/en casa viendo películas/tener/que trabajar
____
8. Jorge y Tomás/ ir/a la fiesta/tener que estudiar para un examen
____
9. Ellos/construir/la casa/no tener los medios
____
10. Aquel día, el presidente/nos/atender/estar/muy ocupado
____

b. The second use of the conditional perfect is to express probability of an action that has already been completed.

Example

—¿Por qué no vino?	—Se **habría ido** a otra parte.
"Why did he not come?"	*"He probably went to another place."*

*For an explanation regarding the use of the subjunctive in this sentence, see The Present Subjunctive in Adverbial Clauses, Chapter 10.

TIP BOX

Other uses are related with conditional clauses.*

Example

De tener tiempo te **habríamos visitado**.
If we had had time, we would have visited you.

Si hubiéramos tenido tiempo, te **habríamos visitado**.
If we had had time, we would have visited you.

*See Chapter 11, Conditional Clauses.

Exercise 10. Rewrite the following sentences using the conditional perfect as shown.

Example

La cantante probablemente ya había terminado de cantar cuando llegamos al teatro.
La cantante ya habría terminado de cantar cuando llegamos al teatro.

1. Marcela probablemente ya había probado las albóndigas en casa de su abuela.
   ________________________________.
2. El señor Rodríguez probablemente ya había muerto cuando llegó al hospital.
   ________________________________.
3. Mi madre probablemente ya había llamado cuando yo llegué a casa.
   ________________________________.
4. Roberto probablemente ya había salido del trabajo cuando yo lo llamé.
   ________________________________.
5. Filomena y su hija probablemente ya habían hecho las maletas cuando llegó el taxi.
   ________________________________.
6. El presidente probablemente ya había tomado la decisión de ir a la guerra cuando asumió la presidencia.
   ________________________________.
7. Lucía probablemente ya había pensado abandonar a su esposo cuando se marchó.
   ________________________________.

7

Pronominal Verbs

Pronominal verbs have the pronoun **se** as part of their infinitive, e.g. *vestir***se**, *besar***se**, *morder***se**, *alegrar***se**, *jactar***se**, which is how they are listed. They have different uses according to their grammatical function. They are expressed by the following pronouns.

me	*myself*
te	*yourself (informal)*
se	*himself, herself, itself, yourself (formal)*
nos	*ourselves*
os	*yourselves (informal)*
se	*themselves, yourselves (formal)*

Yo <u>me</u> peino.
(I comb myself.)

These pronouns vary according to the personal pronouns.

Yo	**me**	levant**o**	
Tú	**te**	levant**as**	
Él / Ella / Usted	**se**	levant**a**	temprano
Nosotros	**nos**	levant**amos**	
Vosotros	**os**	levant**áis**	
Ellos / Ellas / Ustedes	**se**	levant**an**	

I. Reflexive Construction

A pronominal verb in a reflexive construction indicates that the subject of the sentence has performed an action on itself. This means that the subject and direct object should be the same, and this is why reflexive constructions always need a transitive verb.

A transitive verb is a verb capable of taking a direct object. In theory, any transitive verb may perform as reflexive when the subject of the verb and the object of the sentence are the same.

Example

María cortó la carne.
María cut the meat.

María se cortó.
María cut herself.

María vistió al niño.
María dressed the child.

María se vistió.
María got dressed.

The example shows that the person who dresses (María, the subject) and the person cut or dressed (María, the direct object) are the same.

The following verbs are commonly used in this kind of construction.

agacharse *(to bend over)*
bañarse *(to take a bath)*
ducharse *(to take a shower)*
hundirse *(to collapse, to sink)*
limpiarse *(to clean oneself)*
presentarse *(to show up)*
arrodillarse *(to kneel down)*
levantarse *(to get up)*
ahogarse *(to drown)*
castigarse *(to be punished)*
emborracharse *(to get drunk)*
lastimarse *(to injure oneself)*
matarse *(to be killed)*
maquillarse *(to put on makeup)*
cortarse *(to cut oneself)*
ocultarse *(to hide)*
apoyarse *(to lean on)*
congelarse *(to freeze oneself)*
esconderse *(to hide)*
lavarse *(to wash oneself)*
mezclarse *(to get mixed)*
vestirse *(to get dressed)*
gobernarse *(to be governed)*
ensuciarse *(to get dirty)*

TIP BOX

Reflexive pronouns are similar to direct and indirect object pronouns, in terms of positioning.* They usually precede a conjugated verb, but in the presence of an *infinitive verb, a present participle, or an affirmative direct command*, they are usually attached at the end. A reflexive pronoun precedes an object pronoun when they occur in the same sentence.

Example

—Esta mañana **me** levanté temprano y **me** bañé.
"This morning, I woke up early and I took a shower."
—Y, ¿**te** lavaste el cabello?
"And, did you wash your hair?"

—Sí, **me** lo lavé.
"Yes, I washed it."
—Yo hace un mes que no **me** lo lavo.
"I haven't washed mine in a month."
—**Lávatelo**, no seas sucio.
"Wash it, don't be gross."
—Mi peluquero me dijo que **lavarse** el cabello a menudo no es bueno.
"My stylist told me that washing one's hair too often is not good."

*See Chapter 8, III. Object Pronouns.

Exercise 1. Write a reflexive sentence based on the given words. You may choose the verb tense.

Example

Jorge/acostarse/temprano
Jorge se acuesta temprano.

1. Lucía/maquillarse/todas las mañanas ____________________
2. El buzo/ahogarse/en el mar ____________________
3. Tú siempre/emborracharse/en las fiestas ____________________
4. El bebé/levantarse/muy temprano todos los días ____________________
5. Lucía/presentarse/al jefe como una buena empleada ____________________
6. Fernando/mezclarse/entre los invitados ____________________
7. Julia/ducharse/con agua caliente ____________________
8. María/mirarse/en el espejo ____________________
9. Pablito/esconderse/en el clóset ____________________
10. Liliana/vestirse/elegantemente para la fiesta ____________________

Exercise 2. Translate the following sentences from Spanish to English.

1. Julio se agachó.
____
2. Gabriel se cortó y se quejó.
____
3. Marta se apoyó sobre la mesa.
____
4. Lucía se arrodilló durante la misa.
____
5. La niña se baña en la tina.
____

6. El cura se castigó.

____

7. Nos congelamos afuera.

____

8. Los países pobres se gobiernan solos.

____

9. El barco se hundió.

____

10. Yo me lastimé.

____

II. Reciprocal Construction

A pronominal verb in a reciprocal construction is conjugated always in plural form (**ellos**, **ellas**, **ustedes**, **nosotros**). Two or more persons or things perform an action to each other.

Example

María y Juan se casaron.
María and Juan got married.

María y Juan se besaron.
María and Juan kissed each other.

The following verbs are commonly used in this kind of construction.

atacarse	detestarse	hablarse
felicitarse	matarse	aborrecerse
mirarse	besarse	pelearse
abrazarse	despedirse	escribirse
saludarse	ayudarse	

Exercise 3. Complete the following sentences using the verbs in parentheses in the appropriate tense.

1. Gonzalo y Marcos ____________ (turnarse) para lavar el auto.
2. Los amigos ____________ (reunirse) para jugar fútbol el domingo.
3. Rosario y Juan ____________ (besarse) con pasión.
4. Julia y su hija ____________ (abrazarse) antes de despedirse.
5. Los novios ____________ (mirarse) a los ojos con dulzura.
6. Marta y José ____________ (pelearse) ayer.
7. Adela y yo __________ (conocerse) el año pasado.
8. Roberto y Ana recién __________ (separarse).
9. Santiago y Sabrine __________ (mirarse) tiernamente.
10. Todos vosotros __________ (reunirse) en el centro de convenciones.

Exercise 4. Translate the following sentences from Spanish to English.

1. Juan y Pedro se detestan.

   ____

2. Luis y Felipe se felicitaron.

   ____

3. Luna y Liliana se despidieron.

   ____

5. El novio y la novia se besaron.

   ____

5. Madre e hija se escribieron.

   ____

III. Semi-Reflexive Construction

A. WITH TRANSITIVE VERBS

A pronominal verb in a semi-reflexive construction occurs when the subject is acting upon a part of the body or a possession of the subject. Consequently, in these types of construction the direct object of the sentence is different from the subject.

María se cortó. (Reflexive)
María cut herself.

María se cortó el dedo. (Semi-reflexive)
María cut her finger.

TIP BOX

In Spanish, the part of the body or possession of the subject is modified by the definite or indefinite article (**el, la, los, las; un, una, unos, unas**), whereas in English it requires a possessive adjective.

Example

María **se** cortó **la** mano.
*María cut **her** hand.*

María **se** ensució **la** blusa.
*María got **her** blouse dirty.*

Exercise 5. Fill in the blanks with an appropriate verb chosen from the list. Don't forget to conjugate the verbs.

pintarse abrocharse ponerse lavarse frotarse fracturarse

Después de una larga siesta, Juana __________ los ojos, __________ la cara, __________ los labios, __________ los pantalones y __________ un cinturón nuevo para ir a la fiesta. Al salir, tuvo un accidente y __________ la pierna.

Exercise 6. Translate the following sentences from Spanish into English.

1. Felipe se ensució la camisa.
 ____
2. Los niños se lavaron las manos.
 ____
3. Yo me limpié los zapatos.
 ____
4. Tú te lavaste el cabello.
 ____
5. Laura y José se rompieron el pie.
 ____

B. WITH INTRANSITIVE VERBS

A pronominal verb in a semi-reflexive construction may also be an intransitive verb. An intransitive verb is a verb that does not take a direct object, such as *caminar, ir*.

- Some of these verbs only exist in the pronominal form in Spanish, and are usually followed by a preposition, such as:

abstenerse de (*to abstain*)
arrepentirse de (*to repent*)
atreverse a (*to dare*)
dignarse a (*to deign*)
jactarse de (*to boast*)
rebelarse contra (*to revolt against*)
quejarse de (*to complain about*)

Example

Jorge siempre se queja de su esposa.
Jorge always complains about his wife.

Exercise 7. Fill in the blanks with an appropriate verb chosen from the list. Don't forget to conjugate the verbs.

rebelarse jactarse arrepentirse abstenerse quejarse

Muy a menudo, los adolescentes ___________ contra sus padres. Muchas veces ___________ de saberlo todo y ___________ de que nadie los comprende. Los padres a veces ___________ de darles dinero y entonces los adolescentes ___________ de ser rebeldes.

- Some others change their meaning in the pronominal form, such as:

Non-pronominal	Pronominal
abonar *(to fertilize; to pay)*	abonarse a *(to subscribe to something)*
acordar *(to agree)*	acordarse de *(to remember)*
burlar *(to evade)*	burlarse de *(to make fun of)*
encontrar *(to find)*	encontrarse en *(to be)*
fijar *(to fix)*	fijarse en *(to notice)*
ir *(to go)*	irse a *(to leave)*
marchar *(to march)*	marcharse a/de *(to go away)*
ocupar *(to occupy a space)*	ocuparse de *(to look after)*
parar *(to stop)*	pararse a/en *(to stand up)*
conducir *(to drive)*	conducirse *(to behave)*
fiar (*to sell on credit*)	fiarse de (*to trust*)
negar (*to deny*)	negarse a (*to refuse*)

Example

María **acordó** devolver el dinero.
María agreed to return the money.

María no **se acordó** de devolver el dinero.
María forgot to return the money.

Los estudiantes **marcharon** durante la manifestación.
The students marched during the rally.

Nos marchamos apenas llegó tu papá.
We left as soon as your dad arrived.

TIP BOX

The difference in meaning between the non-pronominal and the pronominal forms of certain verbs is very small, for instance:

caer / caerse (*to fall*)
morir / morirse (*to die*)
comer / comerse (*to eat*)

The non-pronominal form tends to be more formal, whereas the pronominal form is more colloquial and emphatic.

Example

Santiago se comió toda la paella.
Santiago ate up the whole paella.

Exercise 8. Complete the following sentences using the verbs in parentheses in the appropriate form (pronominal or non-pronominal) according to the meaning of the sentence. Use the preterit tense.

1. ¿(tú) __________ (fijar/se) en la noticia que apareció en el periódico?
2. Lucía __________ (abonar/se) a la revista *Espacio*.
3. Jorge __________ (encontrar/se) un anillo en la calle.
4. Después de la crisis económica muchas industrias __________ (marchar/se) del país.
5. En la escuela, todos __________ (burlar/se) de Demetrio.
6. Los niños no __________ (conducir/se) bien en la escuela.
7. Los abuelos de Luz tenían más de 90 años cuando murieron. Luz __________ (ocupar/se) de ellos durante sus últimos años.
8. ¡María __________ (comer/se) todos los espaguetis que quedaban!
9. Los ciudadanos ya no __________ (fiar/se) de los bancos.
10. Los agricultores __________ (abonar/se) sus terrenos antes de cultivar.

- Certain verbs are used in the pronominal form to express a change of mood, attitude or behavior. In English, such changes are commonly (but not exclusively) expressed by:

***get* or *become* + adjective**

enojarse (*to get mad*)
enfermarse (*to get sick*)
dormirse (*to fall asleep*)
alegrarse (*to get happy*)
abochornarse (*to become ashamed*)
acostumbrarse (*to get used to*)
cansarse (*to get tired*)
fastidiarse (*to get bored*)
mejorarse (*to get better*)
interesarse (*to become interested*)
callarse (*to get quiet*)

Example

Me cansé de verte.
I got tired of seeing you.

Exercise 9. Complete the following sentences using the verbs in parentheses in the preterit.

1. Los niños ___________ (enfermarse) de comer tanto.
2. Yo ___________ (perderse) entre la multitud.
3. Julio ___________ (alegrarse) de ver a sus hermanos.
4. Lola no ___________ (animarse) a ir al paseo.
5. Todos nosotros ___________ (sorprenderse) de verte tan delgada.
6. Pilar ___________ (quedarse) asombrada de tanto despilfarro.
7. La sociedad ___________ (acostumbrarse) a consumir productos inútiles.
8. Después de la debacle económica los trabajadores ___________ (desilusionarse) de sus gobernantes.
9. Los estudiantes ___________ (fastidiarse) del profesor.
10. Los ciudadanos ___________ (enojarse) contra los ejecutivos de las instituciones financieras.

IV. The Use of *Se* to Express English Passive and Impersonal Sentences

In Spanish, constructions with Se + verb are used to render an idea impersonal and objective. Such ideas are expressed in English by the passive voice.

Example

Mi papá vendió el apartamento. (Sentence with a specific subject)
My father sold the apartment.

Se vendió el apartamento. (Impersonal sentence)
The apartment was sold.

a. The impersonal Se + verb agrees with the object of the sentence when the object is a thing.

Example

Se venden cuadros.
Paintings are sold.

Se habla inglés.
English is spoken.

Exercise 10. Transform the following active and personal sentences with the impersonal Se.

Example

Juan construyó un edificio.
Se construyó un edificio.

1. Rafael y Julia saben la verdad.
____
2. Todos dicen mentiras en tu casa.
____
3. El fotógrafo tomará las fotos.
____
4. Los congresistas firmaron la ley.
____
5. La niña compró muchos dulces.
____

Exercise 11. Rewrite the following passive sentences using the impersonal Se.

Example

El puente fue construido sobre el río Usumacinta.
Se contruyó el puente sobre el río Usumacinta.

1. Ese producto fue retirado del mercado.
____
2. Los animales fueron encerrados en el corral.
____
3. Las abejas fueron sacadas de la colmena.
____
4. El dinero fue retirado de los bancos.
____
5. Los coches fueron llevados al taller.
____

Exercise 12. Put the following instructions in the correct order and conjugate the verb in the present indicative accordingly.

Receta de tortilla española

1. Se _________ (servir) la tortilla en un plato y se come. _____
2. A fuego alto en una sartén y con una gota de aceite se _________ (colocar) las papas y los huevos. _____

3. Se _________ (cortar) las papas y la cebolla en rodajas. __1___
4. Se les _________ (añadir) un poco de sal a las papas. _____
5. Se _________ (sofreír) en aceite a fuego lento. _____
6. Una vez cocinadas, se _________ (sacar) las papas del aceite _____
7. Aparte en un recipiente, se _________ (batir) los huevos. _____
8. Se _________ (añadir) las papas a lo huevos. _____
9. Se le _________ (dar) la vuelta a la tortilla y se _________ (cocinar) a fuego bajo por cuatro minutos. _____

b. The impersonal Se + verb remains in the third personal singular when the object of the sentence is a person. In this case the object has to be preceded by the preposition **a** (personal a).

Example

Se golpeó **al** prisionero.
The prisoner was hit.

Se insultó **a** los estudiantes.
The students were insulted.

Exercise 13. Transform the following sentences to an impersonal sentence using the pronominal verb given.

Example

Los invitados esperan a los delegados.
***Se espera** a los delegados.*

1. Los soldados encierran a los presos.

____

2. El profesor castiga a los niños.

____

3. La hacienda necesita inmigrantes para recoger fresas.

____

4. Lo senadores elogiaron a los ejecutivos.

____

5. El chofer recogió a los invitados en el aeropuerto.

____

c. The impersonal Se + verb remains in the third personal singular when it refers to verbs that have no object (intransitive verbs).

Example

Se va a la escuela en bus.
One goes to the school by bus.

Se come muy bien en este restaurante.
One eats well in this restaurant.

Exercise 14. Complete the following sentences in the present tense using the verbs in parentheses.

1. (correrse) ___________ por el parque.
2. (caminarse) ___________ por los pasillos.
3. (preocuparse) ___________ de sus hijos.
4. (ocuparse) ___________ de la ciudad.
5. (hablarse) ___________ de las elecciones presidenciales por todo el país.
6. (nadarse) ___________ muy bien en esa piscina del club.
7. (llegarse) ___________ únicamente por coche o autobús.
8. (viajarse) ___________ por tierra.
9. (comerse) ___________ a las tres de la tarde en España.
10. (dedicarse) ___________ a sus hijos todo el tiempo.

REVIEW

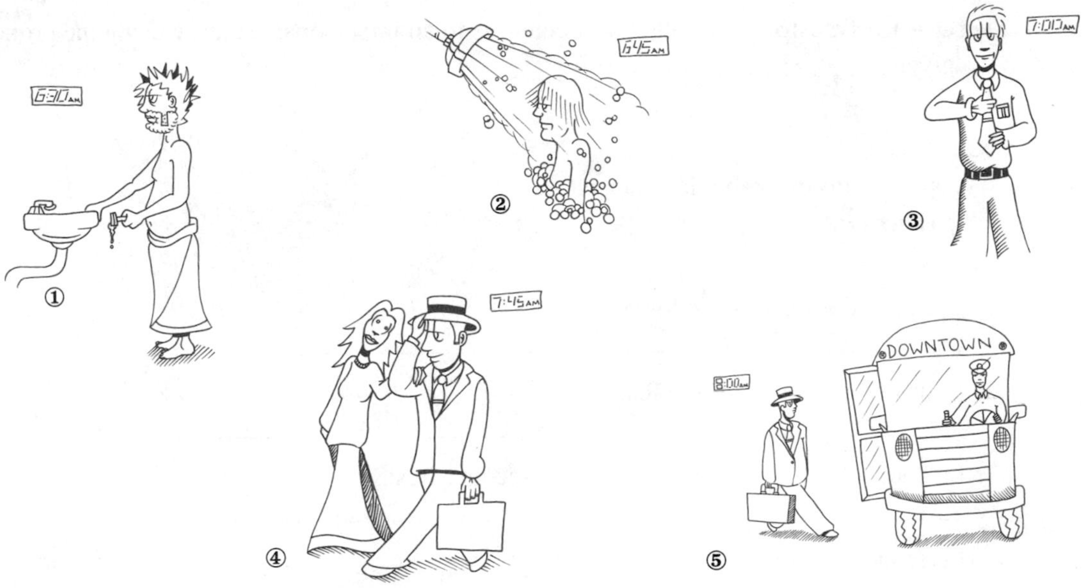

Exercise 15. Write five sentences describing one day in Jorge's life.

Example

Jorge se levanta a las seis y treinta de la mañana.

1. (afeitarse) ______________________________________.
2. (bañarse) ______________________________________.
3. (vestirse) ______________________________________.
4. (ponerse; despedirse) ______________________________________.
5. (subirse) ______________________________________.

8

Pronouns

I. Personal Pronouns

A. SUBJECT PRONOUNS

Subject pronouns are words that replace a subject noun. They can be classified according to number, person, gender (male or female), and formality (formal or informal).

Tú y yo jugamos.
(You and I play.)

	Spanish		English	
	Singular	**Plural**	**Singular**	**Plural**
First person	yo	nosotros	*I*	*we*
Second person	tú *(informal)* usted *(formal)*	vosotros *(informal)* ustedes *(formal)*	*you*	*you*
Third person	él, ella	ellos, ellas	*he, she, it*	*they*

The main difference between English and Spanish is that, in Spanish, subject pronouns may be omitted once the speaker knows who the subject is.

TIP BOX

The pronouns **nosotros**, **vosotros**, and **ellos** have feminine forms: **nosotras**, **vosotras**, and **ellas**. When referring to a mixed male and female group of people the **-os** form is used.

TIP BOX

Vosotros, the plural form for **tú**, is mainly used in Spain. In other Spanish-speaking countries the form **ustedes** is used.

There is also another second person singular form, **vos**, which is used in some Latin American countries, especially in the Southern Cone (Argentina, Chile, Paraguay, and Uruguay), and it is sometimes used in Costa Rica and Nicaragua.

Exercise 1. Change the noun in bold with a subject pronoun.

1. **Juan** (____) está cansado porque trabaja mucho en la oficina.
2. **Marta y Consuelo** (____) viven en un apartamento muy bonito.
3. **Julio y yo** (____) queremos ir al concierto de Shakira.
4. **¡Arturo,** (____) estás loco! *(you informal)*
5. **Los niños** (____) juegan en el parque a ladrones y policías.

Exercise 2. Match the sentence with the corresponding personal pronoun.

1.	Ayer, **Gabriel, María y yo** fuimos a la playa.	yo
2.	—**¡Jorge!** ¡Tienes la camisa sucia! *(you informal)*	él
3.	Quiero conocer a tus vecinos. *(I)*	nosotros
4.	**Lucía y Rosa** llegaron muy cansadas después del partido.	ellos
5.	**Luis** sale de viaje esta noche.	ella
6.	**Marta** siempre está dedicada a su trabajo.	tú
7.	**Lola y Juan** están dispuestos a ayudarnos.	vosotros
8.	—**¡Marta y José!** ¿Salisteis por la puerta principal? *(you informal)*	ellas

Exercise 3. Fill in the blank with the appropriate subject pronoun.

1. Helena tiene más hambre que ____. *(you formal)*
2. Cuando ____ llegó a la estación, el tren ya había salido. *(Susana)*
3. A ____ no les gusta ayudar en las labores de jardinería. *(the boys)*
4. El portero dijo que ____ viniste anoche. *(you informal)*
5. ____ no sé qué hora es. *(I)*
6. Cuando ____ oímos la noticia, nos preocupamos mucho. *(Simón and I)*
7. Catalina quiere que ____ compre los boletos para el concierto. *(Julio)*
8. Quiero que ____ vengan a la fiesta del sábado. *(Clara and Irene)*

B. OBJECT PRONOUNS

a. Forms of direct object pronouns. **Direct object pronouns** are used to avoid repetition. They may replace **a person** or **a thing.**

Direct Object Pronouns: Singular		**Direct Object Pronouns: Plural**	
me	*me*	nos	*us*
te	*you (informal)*	os	*you (informal)*
lo	*you (formal masculine), him, it*	los	*you (formal, masculine), them (masculine)*
la	*you (formal feminine), her, it*	las	*you (formal, feminine), them (feminine)*

TIP BOX

In some regions of Spain and Latin America, **le** and **les** are used as direct object pronouns instead of **lo** and **los** when referring to people. This practice is called "**leísmo.**"

Direct object pronouns vary according to the person or thing they substitute.

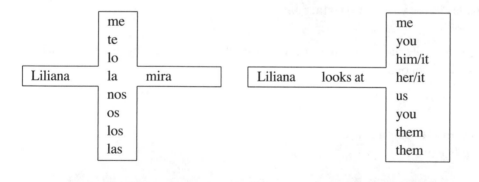

	me	
	te	
	lo	
Liliana	la	mira
	nos	
	os	
	los	
	las	

		me
		you
		him/it
Liliana	looks at	her/it
		us
		you
		them
		them

TIP BOX

A direct object pronoun exists only in the presence of a transitive verb. A transitive verb is a verb that requires a direct object to complete its meaning.

Example

—¿Compraste las bebidas para la fiesta?	*"Did you buy the drinks for the party?"*
—No, no **las** compré.	*"No, I did not buy them."*
—Entonces, **¡cómpralas!**	*"So, buy them!"*
—Y no te olvides de **ponerlas** en la nevera.	*"And don't forget to put them in the refrigerator."*

TIP BOX

A direct object pronoun usually precedes a conjugated verb; however, in the presence of an **infinitive verb**, a **gerund** or an **affirmative direct command**,* a direct object pronoun usually is attached.

Exercise 4. Complete the following sentences with the appropriate direct object pronoun.

1. Victoria abraza a **Nicolás** todos los días. Victoria ___ abraza todos los días.
2. Recibimos a **la entrenadora** con un aplauso. ___ recibimos con un aplauso.
3. Compré estas **flores** en la calle. ___ compré en la calle.
4. El jugador lanzó **la pelota** con desgano. ___ lanzó con desgano.
5. Tengo que comprar **amortiguadores** para el auto. Tengo que comprar___.
6. Jorge y Mario vieron **la película** anoche. Jorge y Mario ___ vieron anoche.
7. Toma las llaves y abre **la puerta**. Ábre___.

Exercise 5. Rewrite the following sentence substituting the direct object (in bold) with the corresponding pronoun.

Example

Marta envió **el paquete** ayer.
*Marta **lo** envió ayer.*

1. En la reunión el presidente discutió **el problema**.
   ____.
2. La multitud aprobó **los cambios**.
   ____.
3. Leí **las obras completas de Cervantes**.
   ____.
4. Estoy buscando **los apuntes que tomé en clase**.
   ____.

*See Chapter 12, "Commands."

5. No conozco a **la nueva profesora de español**.

____.

6. Los científicos encontraron **la solución del experimento**.

____.

7. Gabriela vende **flores** en la feria.

____.

b. Forms of indirect object pronouns. **Indirect object pronouns** are used to avoid repetition. They replace **personal nouns.**

Indirect Object Pronouns: Singular		**Indirect Object Pronouns: Plural**	
me	*me*	nos	*us*
te	*you (informal)*	os	*you (informal)*
le, se	*you (formal), him, her*	les, se	*you (formal), them*

Indirect object pronouns vary according to the person they substitute.

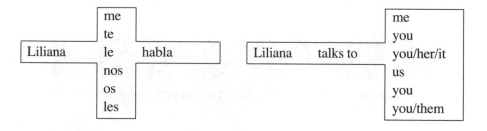

Liliana me / te / le / nos / os / les habla

Liliana talks to me / you / you/her/it / us / you / you/them

TIP BOX

What is an indirect object noun?

In a sentence, an indirect object noun is to whom or for whom the action of the verb is done and who is receiving the direct object. In a sentence it must be a direct object to have an indirect object.

Example

Laura le envía una carta a su madre.
DO IO

Laura sent a letter to her mother.

Note that the indirect objects are frequently expressed twice in the same sentence. Notice that indirect and direct object pronouns are the same except for ***le*** and ***les***. Since ***le*** and ***les*** may replace ***él*** or ***ella*** or ***ellos*** or ***ellas***, a prepositional phrase is added to avoid ambiguity.

Example

Ayer les compré unos juguetes a tus hijos.
Yesterday I bought some toys to your kids.

Indirect object pronouns follow the same pattern as do direct object pronouns. They usually precede a conjugated verb; however, in the presence of an **infinitive verb**, a **gerund**, or an **affirmative direct command**, indirect object pronouns are usually attached at the end.

Example

—Estamos aburridos. **Cuéntanos** algo divertido.
—Vale, voy a **contarles** un chiste.

—We are bored. Tell us an amusing story.
—OK, I am going to tell you a joke.

TIP BOX

Indirect object pronouns precede the direct object pronoun when the two are used together.

Example

—¿Pero, quién te contó esa mentira?
—Me la contó Liliana.

"But, who told you that lie?"
"Liliana told it to me."

Exercise 6. Complete the following sentences using the appropriate indirect object pronoun.

1. Marta ___ compra zapatos **a su hija**.
2. ¿Por qué ___ diste un golpe **a la puerta**?
3. ___ dicen que vayamos primero a la oficina del director. *(a nosotros)*
4. Esta es la persona que ___ regaló tus botas nuevas. *(a ti)*
5. ¡___ advertí que no llegarais tarde! *(a vosotros)*
6. **Las ruedas** no suenan cuando ___ pongo aceite.
7. ¡Eres muy dulce! Siempre ___ traes las cosas que prefiero. *(a mí)*

Exercise 7. Match the indirect object to each indirect object pronoun.

1. El cartero **me** entregó las cartas.	a él
2. **Te** trajimos una bicicleta nueva.	a nosotros
3. Arturo se emocionó cuando **le** dimos el regalo.	a ustedes
4. Si **les** contara lo que me pasó, no me creerían.	a mí
5. Antes de salir, píde**les** a tus padres las llaves.	a ella
6. **Nos** dieron otra semana de plazo para presentar el examen.	a ellos
7. No creo que a Juana **le** parezca buena la idea.	a ti

c. Double object pronouns. The indirect object pronoun **se** is used instead of **le** and **les** before the direct object pronouns **lo**, **la**, **los**, and **las**.

Example

Margarita: —¡Federico! ¿**Le** devolviste el libro a Liliana?
Margarita: "Federico! Did you return the book to Liliana?"

Federico: —Sí, **se lo** devolví ayer.
Federico: "Yes, I returned it to her yesterday."

TIP BOX

Remember: when there are two third person object pronouns, the indirect object pronoun changes to **se**.

le + lo = se lo
le + la = se la
le + los = se los
le + las = se las

Exercise 8. In a new, short sentence replace the words underlined with the appropriate object pronouns. Indirect object pronouns are in bold.

Example

Mi padre **me** envió un regalo.
*Mi padre **me lo** envió.*

1. Roberto **le** entregó una carta a Sonia.

 ______________________________________.

2. No olvides de entregar**le** este mensaje a Carlos.

 ______________________________________.

3. Luis **le** regaló flores a su novia.

   ____.

4. Mi madre **me** lavó la ropa.

   ____.

5. Tu hermano **te** compró tu auto.

   ____.

6. Desafortunadamente no **nos** dieron la beca.

   ____.

7. El profesor **le** explicó la lección muy bien a Felipe.

   ____.

8. Finalmente el banco **nos** devolvió el dinero.

   ____.

9. Raúl **le** dibujó un cuadro muy bonito a su esposa.

   ____.

10. Rita **les** pidió dinero a sus padres.

    ____.

Exercise 9. Complete the following dialogue with an appropriate direct or indirect object pronoun.

—¡Qué desorden hay en este cuarto! ¿Has visto mis **zapatos**?
—No ____ he visto. ¿Dónde los dejaste?
—Dentro de **una caja blanca**. ¿ ____ viste por aquí?
—Sí. ____ dejé sobre el escritorio.
—No veo **el escritorio**. ¿Dónde ____ pusiste?
—____ saqué a la calle para que alguien se lo lleve.
—¡No puede ser! ¿Desocupaste **los cajones**?
—Ni ____ miré. ¿Tenías algo dentro?
—Mi colección de **postales**. ¿Cómo voy a recuperar ____?
—Estaba bromeando. Aquí están tus **postales**. ____ guardé en este sobre.
—Casi ____ matas del susto (a mí). Me alegro de que no ____ hayas perdido.

II. Possessive Pronouns

A possessive pronoun replaces a noun that is qualified by a possessive adjective.*

Example

possessive adjective	possessive pronoun
↓	↓
Me gusta <u>mi</u> casa.	**Me gusta la <u>mía</u>.**
I like my house.	*I like mine.*

Possessive pronouns have four forms and they agree in number and gender **with the noun they replace**.

Singular		Plural		Translation
Masculine	**Feminine**	**Masculine**	**Feminine**	
mí**o**	mí**a**	mí**os**	mí**as**	*mine*
tuy**o**	tuy**a**	tuy**os**	tuy**as**	*yours (informal)*
suy**o**	suy**a**	suy**os**	suy**as**	*his/hers/its*
nuestr**o**	nuestr**a**	nuestr**os**	nuestr**as**	*ours*
vuestr**o**	vuestr**a**	vuestr**os**	vuestr**as**	*yours (informal)*

Exercise 10. Answer the following questions using a possessive pronoun.

Example

¿Es tuya aquella chaqueta?
Sí, es mía or *No, no es mía.*

¿Son tuyas aquellas flores?
Sí, son mías or *No, no son mías.*

1. ¿Es de tu hermano aquel coche negro?
   ______________________________.
2. ¿Son de vosotros las chaquetas que están sobre la silla?
   ______________________________.
3. ¿Son de ellos los perros que ladraban anoche?
   ______________________________.
4. ¿Es tuya esta botella de agua?
   ______________________________.
5. ¿Son vuestros aquellos autos?
   ______________________________.

*See Chapter 3, Adjectives.

6. ¿Es de ella esa libreta marrón?
   ________________________________.
7. ¿Es de ellas esa mesa de madera?
   ________________________________.
8. ¿Me pertenece el paraguas negro?
   ________________________________.

Exercise 11. Complete the mini-dialogues using the appropriate possessive pronoun.

1. —Este es mi libro.
   —No, es el ___. *(mine)*
2. —¿Cómo está tu familia?
   —Muy bien, gracias. ¿Y la ____? *(yours)*
3. —El equipo visitante ganó el campeonato de tenis.
   —¿De veras? Pensé que el ___ había ganado. *(ours)*
4. —Me parece que Ricardo tiene la chaqueta de Manuel.
   —¿Sí? Entonces, Ricardo olvidó la ___ en el restaurante. *(his)*
5. —¿Recordáis la cámara que os presté?
   —¿Era ___? No lo sabíamos. *(yours informal)*
6. —Quisiera tener el cabello tan negro como el ___. (yours)
   —¡Qué gracioso! Yo quisiera que el ___ fuera rubio. *(mine)*
7. —Esta es la mejor computadora que tenemos.
   —¡Es la que necesitamos! La ___ no tiene suficiente memoria. *(ours)*
8. —¿De quién son estos zapatos?
   —Son de José. Los ___ están en mi cuarto. *(mine)*
9. —Marcela compró sus flores en el supermercado.
   —¿Ah, sí? Juliana cultivó las ___. *(hers)*
10. —Aquí está el dinero de Aníbal.
    —Lo pondré en mi gaveta. Aníbal tiene la ___ completamente llena. *(his)*

Exercise 12. Write the appropriate possessive pronoun under each picture.

1.
—¡Este planeta es _______!
–¡No! ¡Este planeta es _______!

2.
—¿Esta casa es de sus padres?
No, esta casa es ______________.

3. 

—¿Ese computador es ______________?
—Sí, es ______________.

4. 

¿Esos caballos son ______________?
Sí, son ______________.

5. 

¡No puedo creerlo! ¿Doctor, ese coche es ______________?
—Sí, es ______________. Las apariencias engañan.

III. Demonstrative Pronouns

Singular Demonstrative Pronouns		
Masculine	**Feminine**	**Translation**
éste	ésta	*this one (here)*
ése	ésa	*that one (there)*
aquél	aquélla	*that one (over there)*

Plural Demonstrative Pronouns		
Masculine	**Feminine**	**Translation**
éstos	éstas	*these (here)*
ésos	ésas	*those (there)*
aquéllos	aquéllas	*those (over there)*

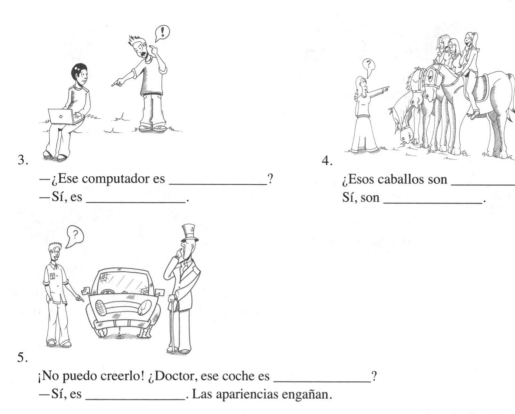

TIP BOX

Although demonstrative adjectives and demonstrative pronouns look identical, they are distinguished by the context. However, in cases of ambiguity, the demonstrative pronouns take an accent mark.

Neuter Demonstrative Pronouns	
esto	*this (here)*
eso	*that (there)*
aquello	*that (over there)*

Neuter demonstrative pronouns never bear an accent mark because they are always pronouns and therefore no ambiguity is possible. They are used to refer to nonspecific things, ideas, or situations in a general way.

Example

—¿Qué es **eso?**
"What's that?"

—**¿Esto?** ¿Mis gafas?
"This? My glasses?"

—No, **¡aquello!**
"No, that!"

—¡Ah! un encendedor.
"Ha! A lighter"

Exercise 13. Complete the following sentences with the appropriate demonstrative pronoun.

1. Estas flores están más frescas que ____________ que están allí. (those, over there)
2. _____ me parece imposible. (this)
3. Tráeme la copa. No, _____ que está sobre el piano. (that)
4. De todos mis amigos, _____ es el más simpático. (this)
5. Ya leí estos libros. Ahora voy a leer _____. (those)
6. ¿Qué vestido prefieres? ¿ _____? (this)
7. Me gusta más _____ (that) que está sobre la silla.
8. ¿ _____? (that, over there) Tienes muy buen gusto.
9. La historia es verídica. _____ pasó hace mucho tiempo. (that)
10. Esta es mi sobrina Olga y _____ es su hermanita Liliana. (that, over there)

Exercise 14. Complete the following sentences choosing the correct demonstrative pronoun.

1. –¿Dónde están los camellos?
   –¿Cuáles?
   –______________________ (aquel / aquellos).
2. –¿Qué silla es más grande __________ (este / esta) o __________ (ese / esa)?
3. ¿Qué te gusta más __________ (aquella / este) cuadro o __________ (aquel / esa) otro?
4. ¿Qué prefieres __________ (aquel / estos) duraznos o __________ (aquellos / esas) que están allá?
5. ¿Me puedes alcanzar __________ (aquel / esas) manzanas y __________ (esas / aquella) peras?
6. Señor, quiero comprar __________ (este / esta) pescado y __________ (esos / esas) calamares.
7. ¡__________ (esta / este) teléfono no sirve y __________ (aquel / aquella) tampoco!

IV. Relative Pronouns

Relative pronouns connect a *dependent clause* to a *main clause*. They refer back to a noun in the main clause, called the antecedent. In contrast to English, the relative pronoun can never be omitted in Spanish.

TIP BOX

There are two types of *dependent clauses*: restrictive clauses, which can not be omitted, and unrestricted or parenthetical clauses, which provide additional information and may be omitted without affecting the meaning of the main sentence.

A. THE RELATIVE PRONOUNS *QUE, QUIEN, EL QUE, EL CUAL*

Masculine		**Feminine**	
Singular	**Plural**	**Singular**	**Plural**
que (*that, which, who, whom*)	que	que	que
quien (*who or whom after a preposition*)	quienes	quien	quienes
el que (*that, which, who, whom*)	los que	la que	las que
el cual (*that, which, who, whom*)	los cuales	la cual	las cuales

In a dependent clause, the relative pronoun can function as:

a. SUBJECT

Example

(Restrictive Clause)
Es una <u>mujer</u> **que** está sentada debajo del árbol. (person)
It's a woman who is sitting under the tree.

Es un <u>coche rojo</u> **que** está estacionado afuera. (thing)
It's a red car that's parked outside.

(Unrestricted or Parenthetical Clause)
<u>Esa mujer</u>, **que (quien, la que, la cual)** está sentada debajo del árbol, es mi esposa. (person)
That woman, who is sitting under the tree, is my wife.

<u>Ese coche</u>, **que (el que, el cual)** está estacionado afuera, es mío. (thing)
That car, which is parked outside, is mine.

TIP BOX

The pronoun **el cual** is more formal than **que;** therefore, when there is no ambiguity in everyday conversation, **que** is preferred.

Example

Conocí al abuelo de tu madre, el cual (el que) acaba de morir.
I met your mother's grandfather, who has just died.

Conocí al abuelo de tu madre, que acaba de morir.
(There is an ambiguity in this sentence; we don't know who dies the mother or the grandfather.)
I met your mother's grandfather who has just died.

Exercise 15. In the following sentences, underline the antecedent of the relative pronoun and conjugate the verb in the present tense according to the antecedent.

Example

Compré un libro que ________________ (traer) unas ilustraciones muy bonitas.
Compré <u>un libro</u> que **trae** unas ilustraciones muy bonitas.

1. Perdí un collar que _______________ (tener) unas cuentas de marfil.
2. Me invitó un amigo que _______________ (ser) arquitecto.
3. Ese perro, el que _______________ (estar) allá junto al árbol, es el mío.
4. La única recesión que _______________ (parecerse) a ésta es la de 1929.
5. Los perros que _______________ (ladrar) en la noche son de Julia.
6. La profesora, la que _______________ (dictar) francés, es muy amable.
7. Es un amigo de tu hermana, el cual _______________ (hablar) alemán, francés y español.
8. Las personas, que _______________ (esperar) en la fila, tiritan de frío.
9. Los amigos de Sol, quienes _______________ (estar) enfermos, no pueden venir.
10. Siento una pena que me _______________ (oprimir) la garganta.

Exercise 16. Combine the following sentences according to the example.

Example

El parque está en el centro de la ciudad. El parque es hermoso.
El parque que está en el centro de la ciudad es hermoso.

1. Las flores están en el jarrón. Las flores son de muchos colores.
   ____.
2. El collar de perlas costó mucho dinero. El collar de perlas es de Julián.
   ____.
3. Presentamos el examen de química. El examen fue muy fácil.
   ____.
4. Es un pasaje de avión. El pasaje costó 300 dólares.
   ____.
5. Vivo en un apartamento. El apartamento tiene cinco alcobas.
   ____.
6. Vimos una película de horror. La película se llama "La pesadilla".
   ____.
7. Juan vende una computadora. La computadora tiene un disco duro de 1T.
   ____.
8. Silvia tiene una casa en la playa. La casa es muy valiosa.
   ____.
9. Encontré unos libros en el parque. Los libros eran de Gustavo.
   ____.
10. El camino lleva a la laguna. El camino está lleno de baches.
    ____.

b. OBJECT

Example

Invité a salir a la mujer **que (a quien)** me presentaste anoche. (person)
I invited the woman you introduced me to last night, on a date.

Compré el coche **que** me aconsejaste. (thing)
I bought the car you told me to.

TIP BOX

A relative pronoun is sometimes omitted in English, but never in Spanish.

Example

La mujer **que (a quien)** amas es mi hermana.
The woman (whom) you love is my sister.

El coche **que** compré.
The car (that) I bought.

Exercise 17. In the following sentences, circle the relative pronoun and underline its antecedent. Write the subject pronoun that matches the verb.

Example

Perdí el anillo que _____ me regalaste.
Perdí el anillo **que** (tú) me regalaste.

1. Nos robaron el coche que _____ nos vendiste.
2. No crean los rumores que _____ escuchan en la calle.
3. Encontraste a la mujer que _____ buscabas por el internet.
4. Les compramos el café que _____ nos pidieron.
5. ¡Encontraste el gato que _____ nos regalaron!
6. Roberto trajo unos dulces horribles que _____ compró en el aeropuerto.
7. Finalmente compramos la casa que _____ nos aconsejaron.
8. Llevamos a reparar la máquina de café que _____ me obsequiaste.
9. Mi madre envió el paquete que _____ le diste.
10. ¿Hallaste a la señora a quien _____ buscábamos?

Exercise 18. Combine the following sentences according to the example.

Example

Mis / amigos / hablan / de temas / conozco / muy bien.
Mis amigos hablan de temas ***que*** *conozco muy bien.*

1. Lucía /vendió / la casa / compró / en abril.
   ____.
2. Juan / no / quiso / el regalo / tú / le / obsequiaste / ayer.
   ____.
3. Visitamos / los países / Juan / nos / sugirió.
   ____.
4. Pedimos / una cita / con el médico / tu padre / nos sugirió.
   ____.
5. ¿Hablasteis / con el agente / te dije?
   ____.

c. OBJECT OF A PREPOSITION

Example

Este es <u>mi amigo</u> <u>con</u> **quien (el que**, **el cual)** fuimos a la fiesta el año pasado. (person)
This is my friend with whom I went to the party last year.

Este es <u>el coche</u> <u>en</u> **el que (que**, **el cual)** me estrellé el año pasado. (thing)
This is the car in which I crashed last year.

TIP BOX

A relative pronoun agrees in gender and number with its antecedent, with the exception of the invariable pronoun **que**.

Example

<u>Estos libros</u>, por **los que** pagué mucho dinero, me gustan mucho.
These books, for which I paid a lot of money, are very pleasing to me.

<u>Este libro</u>, por **el que** pagué mucho dinero, me gusta mucho.
This book, for which I paid a lot of money, is very pleasing to me.

Exercise 19. Choose the appropriate relative pronoun for each sentence.

1. Esta es Lola, la amiga con __________ (quien / que) visité Madrid.
2. Este es el banco en __________ (quien / el que) deposité todo mi dinero.
3. Este es mi jefe para __________ (el cual / que) trabajo.
4. Los libros sobre __________ (quienes / los que) te hablé ya están a la venta.
5. Los enemigos contra __________ (quienes / que) luchamos son muy peligrosos.
6. ¡El coche en __________ (la que / que) me trajiste está buenísimo!
7. Los chicos, para __________ (los cuales / que) hemos preparado la bienvenida, llegarán mañana.
8. Llegamos al hotel en __________ (la que / el que) nos alojamos.
9. La crisis económica, por __________ (la que / quien) estamos viviendo, no se sabe cuando va a terminar.
10. Tu hijos, por __________ (quienes / que) das tu vida, son unos malcriados.

Exercise 20. Choose the appropriate relative pronoun for each sentence.

1. El barco ___________ (quien / que) había zarpado minutos antes se esfumó entre la niebla.
2. Los amigos ___________ (que / las que) invitamos a la fiesta no pudieron venir.
3. No conozco a la chica con __________ (la que / que) bailabas.
4. Mi familia ___________ (que / el que) vive en Panamá es muy hospitalaria.
5. El dueño de la tienda, ___________ (a quién / el cual) le pedimos señas de cómo llegar, nos dio todos los datos.
6. Tú eres la persona con ___________ (quien / el que) me siento más a gusto.
7. José es el abogado con ___________ (el que / que) trabaja mi novia.
8. Los saltamontes, ___________ (que / quienes) se habían escondido entre la hierba, formaron una nube sobre la granja.
9. Manolo se acercó a su madre, ___________ (quien / el cual) lo abrazó con gran ternura.
10. El hidrógeno y el oxígeno, ___________ (quienes / los cuales) tienen un peso molecular de 16, son los dos componentes del agua.
11. El médico, ___________ (el cual / a quién) acudimos de inmediato, nos examinó minuciosamente.
12. Los gerentes, ___________ (que / los que) se habían reunido para discutir la reunión, tomaron una decisión importante.
13. Las muchachas de ___________ (los cuales / las que) me hablaste acaban de llegar.
14. El cielo ___________ (que / la que) se veía desde mi ventana se estaba tornando gris.
15. Los niños, ___________ (los cuales / a quienes) no se les han aplicado vacunas, pueden contraer enfermedades contagiosas.
16. Mi abuela es la persona ___________ (el que / que) más admiro.
17. La joven ___________ (el cual / que) ves allí es mi hermana.
18. La portera del edificio, ___________ (la cual / el que) no ve muy bien, no reconoció a los recién llegados.
19. El presidente ___________ (que, la cual) acaba de posesionarse se encargó de la situación.

TIP BOX

The pronoun **el cual** is more formal than **que**; therefore, when there is no ambiguity in every day conversation, **que** is preferred.

B. THE RELATIVE PRONOUNS *LO QUE* AND *LO CUAL*

The neuter relative pronouns **lo que** and **lo cual** are only used to refer to a concept or a preceding idea.

The pronoun **lo que** is mainly used in restrictive clauses.

Neuter Relative Pronouns
lo que *(which, what)* lo cual *(which, what)*

Example

Lo que quiero es que vuelvas.
What I want is you to come back.

No se hace todo **lo que** uno quiere sino **lo que** uno puede.
We do not do all we can but what we are able.

In a nonrestrictive clause, either **lo cual** or **lo que** is used, and may be preceded by a preposition.

Example

Estaba enfermo, **lo cual** (**lo que**) me entristeció enormemente.
He was sick, which makes me extremely sad.

Tenía miedo a la guerra, **por lo cual** (**por lo que**) deduje que era un hombre sensible.
He was scared of the war, by which I deduced that he was a sensible man.

Exercise 21. Write a new sentence using **lo que**, according to the example.

Example

Quiero que me acompañes al centro.
Lo que *quiero* ***es*** *que me acompañes al centro.*

1. Quiero salir con él.

   ______________________________.
2. Quiero viajar a caballo y no a pie.

   ______________________________.

3. Quiero salir temprano para no perder el tren.

 ____.

4. Quiero apagar la televisión para no distraerme.

 ____.

5. Quiero verte pronto.

 ____.

6. Quiero casarme contigo.

 ____.

7. Quiero un buen trabajo.

 ____.

8. Quiero descansar.

 ____.

9. Quiero besarte.

 ____.

10. Quiero decirte la verdad.

 ____.

Exercise 22. Complete the following sentences using the correct relative pronoun.

1. No es posible; _________ (el que / los cuales) te lo dijo te mintió.
2. _________ (Los que / Lo que) no me gusta de María es que es mitómana.
3. Felipe, _________ (el cual / lo que) es de Bolivia, se ha enfermado gravemente.
4. Mi profesor siempre llega tarde a clase, _________ (lo cual / los que) me molesta mucho.
5. Este es el apartamento en _________ (el que / lo que) vivimos.
6. Ahí está el marido de mi hermana, gritando como siempre, _________ (lo que / los que) me pone de muy mal genio.
7. ¡Qué problema! _________ (El que / Lo que) seguro ocurrió, fue que se robaron el dinero.
8. Luis planteó una hipótesis _________ (el que, que) nos pareció muy convincente.
9. La madre de Diego, _________ (la cual/ el cual) es muy bonita, quiere conocerte.
10. Marcela no nos invitó a su boda, _________ (la cual / lo que) nos ofendió mucho.

C. THE RELATIVE PRONOUN *CUYO*

The relative pronoun **cuyo** (*whose*) has some of the qualities of a noun, but is used as an adjective. **Cuyo** agrees **with the noun it modifies** in number and gender.

Example

La industria pesquera, **cuya explotación** es indiscriminada, plantea problemas ecológicos a corto plazo.
The fishing industry, whose exploitation is indiscriminate, poses short-term ecological problems.

La madre, **en cuyo rostro** se reflejaba una infinita alegría, dio a luz un varón.
The mother, whose face reflects an immense happiness, gave birth to a boy.

Exercise 23. Complete the following sentences using the correct relative pronoun.

1. Llamé a mi abuela, _________ (cuyo / cuyos / los cuales) consejos siempre me ayudan.
2. Se escuchaban pasos en la planta baja, ___________ (lo que / cuyo / los cuales) nos preocupó mucho.
3. Esta es la familia, _________ (cuya / cuyos / los cuales) gatos cuido en el verano.
4. Los estudiantes se portaron muy bien, ___________ (lo cual / cuyos / los cuales) llenó de orgullo a los maestros.
5. El campeón renunció a la medalla, ___________ (cuya / lo que / los cuales) sorprendió a sus admiradores.
6. El presidente, en _________ (cuyos/ cuyas / las cuales) manos se encuentra la solución, debe actuar pronto.
7. Gonzalo, en _________ (el que / lo que / cuyo) auto salimos anoche, tiene mucho dinero.
8. Tienes los ojos inflamados, ___________ (cuyos / lo que / los cuales) me hace pensar que estuviste llorando.
9. Estos son los libros _________ (las cuales / cuyas / las que) páginas debemos fotocopiar.
10. Subieron la colina muy deprisa, ___________ (lo cual / cuyo / cuyos) los dejó sin aliento.

V. Prepositional Pronouns

Prepositional pronouns are subject pronouns preceded by a preposition (**a**, **por**, **con**, **ante**, etc.) with the exception of the **yo** and **tú** forms.

Prepositional Pronouns	
mí	me
ti	you
él, ella	him, her
nosotros, nosotras	we
vosotros, vosotras	you
ellos, ellas	them

Example

Me gusta estar **contigo**.
I love to be with you.

Pilar habló muy bien de **ti**.
Pilar talked well about you.

La casa fue construida por **nosotros**.
The house was built by ourselves.

El jefe está hablando de **mí**.
The boss is talking about me.

TIP BOX

Note that subject pronouns differ from prepositional pronouns only in the forms **yo** and **tú**, which use the forms **mí** and **ti**. Also, it is important to notice that these two prepositional pronouns, when they are preceded by the preposition **con**, change to **conmigo** and **contigo**.

Exercise 24. Answer the following questions using the appropriate prepositional pronoun. Follow the example.

Example

—¿Hablaste con Alicia?
—Sí, hablé con ella.

1. —¿Te asombraste de los precios de los autos?

____

2. —¿Soñaste conmigo anoche?

____

3. —¿Hablaste con tu mamá sobre tu amiga Gloria?
____

4. —Según Alfonso, ¿cuánto dinero se necesita para viajar a Europa?
____

5. —¿Están los papás de Mimí preocupados por su hija?
____

6. —¿Voy a tener que ir sin que me acompañes?
____

Exercise 25. Lilo and Lola are twins. They are having an argument about one of the objects they have in their room. Fill in the blanks with the appropriate prepositional pronoun.

—Esta es mi silla. Papá la compró para __________ (me) el año pasado.
—¿Para __________(you)? Creo que te equivocas. Yo estaba con __________ (him) ese día.
—Si te sientas en ella no vuelvo a hablar con __________ (you) nunca más.
—Tú no puedes pasar ni un día sin hablar con __________ (me), hermanita.
—Tienes razón. Soy tan charlatana como tú.

REVIEW

Exercise 26. Fill in the blank with the appropriate personal, possessive, object, or relative pronoun.

Fernando: —Hola Clarita y Laura.
Clara y Laura: —Hola Fernando.
Fernando: —Quiero que vengan a la fiesta de inauguración de mi apartamento la próxima semana.
Laura: —¿_________ vas invitar a _________?
Fernando: —¡Sí, a _________!
Laura: —Muchas gracias. Y, ¿cómo está tu novia?
Fernando: —¡Uhm! No sé... ¿Y tu novio, Clarita?
Clara: ¿El _________? _________ no tengo novio.
Laura: ¿Cómo está tu familia?
Fernando—Muy bien, gracias. ¿Y la _________?
Laura: —La verdad, no muy bien. A mi padre _________ despidieron del trabajo ayer.
Clara: Y recién ha comprado un apartamento.
Laura: —Sí, _________ compró hace justo una semana.
Fernando: —Quisiera conocer_________.
Laura: ¡ _________ invito la próxima semana!
Clara: —¿Vieron la última película con Penélope Cruz?
Fernando: —No, no _________ he visto. De todas maneras no me gusta _________ como actriz.
Clara: —¡Laura! Olvidé mi bolso en la cafetería. Hasta luego.

Fernando: —¡Espera!
Clara: ¡ ________ vemos otro día!
Laura: —¡________ advertí que no ________ olvidara!
Fernando—¿Por qué no ________dijiste que esperara un momento?
Laura: —Mejor así, así podemos estar solos. Anoche soñé con________.
Fernando: —¿________?
Fernando: —¡Oh! ¡Qué suerte tengo!
Laura: —¿Por qué?
Fernando: —Allí hay un letrero ________ dice: "Se reparan relojes". Y debo llevar el ________ a que ________ reparen.
Laura: —Déja________ ver________, que ________ ________ acompaño.
Fernando: —No es necesario. Gracias. ¡Bueno...! ________ vemos otro día.
Laura: —¿Cuándo es la fiesta?
Fernando: —¿Cuál fiesta?
Laura: —¡________ a ________ que ________ invitaste a Clara y ________! ¡Idiota!
Fernando: —¡Espera Laura, no ________ enojes!... "¡A las mujeres no ________ entiende nadie!"

9

The Adverb

An adverb is a word that is used to modify a **verb**, an **adjective**, or **another adverb**. Adverbs indicate time, place, manner or quantity; unlike adjectives, they are **invariable**.

Example

Modifying a verb:
Margarita **acaricia** a su gato **suavemente**.
Margarita caresses her cat softly.

Modifying an adjective:
José es **muy simpático**.
José is very nice.

Modifying an adverb:
El avión vuela **muy rápido**.
The airplane flies very fast.

Adverbs derived from adjectives end in **-mente**, and are usually adverbs of manner. Adverbs without any particular ending are generally adverbs of manner, time, or place.

I. Adverbs Derived from Adjectives

Adverbs ending in **-mente** tell how something is done. They are formed by adding the suffix **-mente** to the feminine or to the invariable form of the adjective.

lenta → lentamente	(slow → slowly)
alegre → alegremente	(joy → joyfully)

TIP BOX

Adverbs ending in **-mente** are usually equivalent to the English suffix *-ly*. They are usually adverbs of manner because they denote the way in which something is done.

When two or more adverbs ending in **-mente** modify the same word, only the last adverb in the series retains the ending **-mente**, while the others remain in the feminine adjective form.

Example

El estudiante hizo su tarea rápida y correctamente.
The student did his homework fast and correctly.

Exercise 1. Rewrite the following sentences replacing the word in bold by an adverb ending in **-mente**.

Example

Todos comimos en el restaurante **con gusto**.
Todos comimos en el restaurante ***gustosamente****.*

1. El profesor habla **con rapidez**. ______________________.
2. Los gallos pelean **con violencia**. ______________________.
3. El pianista toca **con suavidad**. ______________________.
4. El jefe habla con sus empleados **de manera cortés**. ______________________.
5. El niño respondió a su maestro **de manera inteligente**. ______________________.
6. El padre juega con su hijo **con cariño.** ______________________.
7. Julián Sorel la miró **de manera tierna.** ______________________.
8. La profesora explicó la lección **de forma clara.** ______________________.
9. Anoche llovió **con intensidad.** ______________________.
10. El piano se cayó por las escaleras **con estrépito.** ______________________.

Exercise 2. Transform the following adjectives into adverbs and complete the sentences.

lento estupendo grosero alegre rápido enérgico suave ruidoso eficiente amable

Example

Los coches circulan *lentamente* porque hay mucho tráfico.

1. Luisa canta _______________ por eso ganó el concurso.
2. María es muy mal educada y rebelde—por eso le habló a la profesora _______________.
3. Los niños recibieron los juguetes y jugaron _______________.
4. El correcaminos es un animal muy veloz; atraviesa la autopista _______________.
5. A raíz de la crisis económica los desempleados protestan _______________.
6. Abre la puerta _______________ porque el bebé está durmiendo.
7. El avión rompió la barrera del sonido _______________.
8. Para sacar buenas notas tienes que hacer la tarea _______________.
9. La tortuga se desplaza _______________.
10. El portero de nuestro edificio es muy cortés. Siempre nos abre la puerta _______________.

Exercise 3. Transform the following adjectives to adverbs according to the model.

Example

hermoso → hermosamente

1. largo _______________
2. sincero _______________
3. alegre _______________
4. absoluto _______________
5. discreto _______________
6. secreto _______________
7. rápido _______________
8. frecuente _______________
9. enorme _______________
10. gentil _______________
11. loco _______________
12. suave _______________

II. Other Adverbs

Other adverbs, or those that do not have any particular ending, are varied in their function. Those adverbs may denote the **way** (adverb of manner), **the intensity or degree** (adverb of degree), the **time** (adverb of time), and the **place** (adverb of place) in which or where something is done.

TIP BOX

An adjective may act as an adverb when used with an intransitive verb or with a verb that expresses a state or condition. The adjective modifies both the subject and the verb simultaneously and agrees with the subject.

Example

Juan y María llegaron muy **contentos**.
Juan and María arrived very happy.

A. ADVERBS OF MANNER

Study the following examples.

así *(so, like this, like that, like what, thus)*

—¿Por qué te pones **así**?
"Why do you get worked up like that?"

—¿Cómo **así**?
"Like what?"

—**Así**, de mal genio.
"Like in a bad mood."

—Lo siento, pero **así** soy yo.
"I am sorry, but that's the way I am."

bien *(well, good)*

—Hola, ¿cómo estás?
"Hello, how are you?"

—**Bien**, gracias.
"Well, thanks."

—¿Dónde aprendiste español?
"Where did you learn Spanish?"

—En Costa Rica.
"In Costa Rica."

—Hablas muy **bien**.
"You speak [it] very well."

como *(like, as...as, about, around)*

—Ese queso se ve delicioso.
"That cheese looks delicious."

—Sí, sabe **como** a queso Manchego, ¿no?
"Yes, it tastes a bit like 'Manchego' cheese, doesn't it?"

—Pero es blanco **como** el queso fresco.
"But, it is white like farmer cheese."

—¿Quién lo trajo?
"Who brought it?"

—Lo trajo Liliana esta mañana **como** a las ocho.
"Liliana brought it this morning around eight."

despacio *(slowly)*

—¿Puedes hablar más **despacio**?
"Can you speak more slowly?"

mal *(badly)*

Los niños se portaron **mal** anoche.
The children behaved badly last night.

pronto (*soon, quickly*)

—¡Ven **pronto** que me muero por verte!
"Come soon. I am dying to see you!"

—¡Iré lo más **pronto** que pueda!
"I will come as soon as possible!"

Exercise 4. Underline the adjectives once and the adverbs twice.

1. Aquel hombre está como loco.
2. No me siento bien.
3. Quiero que vengas pronto.
4. Los caracoles se desplazan despacio.
5. Ese muchacho está pálido; anda muy mal de salud.
6. No es fácil trabajar así.

Exercise 5. Replace the underlined words using the following adverbs of manner: **pronto**, **mal**, **así**, **bien**, **como**, **despacio**.

Example

Los invitados llegaron rápidamente.
Los invitados llegaron pronto.

1. Tus amigos vendrán en un momento.

   ____

2. A nosotros nos gusta caminar lentamente.

   ____

3. Rosalba se siente apenada por lo que te dijo anoche.

____

4. No me gusta que me hables de esa manera.

____

5. No te preocupes, que estamos sin problemas.

____

6. Lo hice de la manera que me indicaste.

____

B. ADVERBS OF DEGREE

algo

As an adverb, the word *algo* means **a little** or **somewhat**.

Rosalba no puede ir al paseo porque se encuentra **algo** indispuesta.
Rosalba cannot go on the trip because she is somewhat indisposed.

apenas *(hardly, scarcely)*

Pobre hombre, **apenas** tiene para vivir.
Poor man, he scarcely has enough to live.

bastante *(enough, fairly, very, quit a bit)*

Anoche comimos **bastante**.
Last night we ate quite a bit.

La fiesta estuvo **bastante** divertida.
It was a very nice party.

casi *(almost, nearly)*

Casi todos los días voy al trabajo a pie.
Almost every day I walk to work.

Hoy, fui en coche y ¡**casi** me estrello!
Today I went by car and I almost crashed!

cuánto (*as, as much as*)

¡**Cuánto** sufrí al creer que te habías marchado!
How much I suffered when I thought you had left!

TIP BOX

The adverb **cuánto**, when followed by an adjective or an adverb, changes its form to **cuán**.

¡**Cuán** enorme fue mi sufrimiento cuando supe que te habías marchado!
How great was my suffering when I realized you had left!

¡**Cuán** lejos estás de creer que volveré a quererte!
How far are you from believing that I will love you again!

demasiado *(too, too much)*

—Vamos al restaurante *Gorditos*.
"Let's go to Gorditos *restaurant."*

—Ni loco, la comida allí es **demasiado** pesada, tiene mucha grasa.
"Are you crazy? The food there is too rich. It has too much fat."

—¿No será más bien, que tú comes **demasiado**?
"Maybe the problem is that you eat too much."

más* *(more, better, past)*

—Papá, ¿puedo comer postre?
"Dad, may I eat dessert?"

—Primero, come un poco **más** de carne.
"First, eat a little more meat."

—¡Papá! No me gusta la carne.
"Dad, I don't like meat."

—¿Te gusta **más** el pescado?
"Do you like fish better?"

—Sí.
"Yes."

—Apúrate, que son **más** de las ocho y tienes que acostarte.
"Hurry up, it's past eight o'clock, and you must go to bed."

menos* (*less, least, fewer, fewest*)

Ahora que estoy más viejo, salgo **menos**.
Now that I am older, I go out less.

mucho *(a lot)* and **muy** *(very)*
—¿Has oído la canción "Bésame **mucho**"?
"Have you heard the song 'Kiss me a lot?'"
—Por supuesto, ese bolero le gusta **mucho** a mi abuelita.
"Of course, my granny likes that bolero a lot."

The adverb **muy** is used before an adjective, before a participle acting as an adjective, and before an adverb.

Example

El profesor de química es **muy famoso**.
The chemistry professor is very famous.

Es un hombre **muy respetado**.
He is a very respected man.

Pero dicta clase **muy despacio**.
But he teaches class at a very slow pace.

*See Chapter 17, Comparatives and Superlatives.

TIP BOX

Note that the word **mucho** used as an adverb always follows the verb it qualifies. When modifying an adverb or an adjective, it is placed in front the adjectives *mejor, peor, mayor*, or *menor* and the adverbs *más, menos, antes,* or *después*. On the other hand, the adverb **muy** is **NEVER** followed by the adjectives *mejor, peor, mayor,* or *menor,* nor by the adverbs *más, menos, antes,* or *después*.

Example

Es <u>mucho</u> mejor que jueguen en el parque.
It is much better that they play in the park.

Por las malas, **es <u>mucho</u> peor** para todos.
By force, it is much worse for all of us.

Su esposa **es <u>mucho</u> mayor**, ¿no te parece?
His wife is much older, don't you think?

Jorge **sabe <u>mucho</u> más**.
Jorge knows much more.

Alicia **tiene <u>mucho</u> menos** dinero de lo que pensaba.
Alicia has less money than I thought.

Julio **llegó <u>mucho</u> antes** que nosotros.
Julio arrived a long time before we did.

Los invitados **llegaron <u>mucho</u> después** de lo previsto.
The guests arrived long after it was predicted they would.

nada *(not at all, by no means)*

Vivir en el país que no es el tuyo, no es **<u>nada</u>** fácil.
To live in a country that is not yours is not at all easy.

Lo que hiciste ayer, no me gusta **<u>nada</u>**.
What you did yesterday, I didn't like at all.

poco *(little)*

Ese coche cuesta **<u>poco</u>**.
This car doesn't cost much.

Es **<u>poco</u>** probable que te visite este fin de semana.
Is unlikely that I will visit you this weekend.

sólo *(only)*

Tengo **<u>sólo</u>** dieciocho años.
I am only eighteen years old.

también *(also)*

Yo **también** estoy cansado.
I am also tired.

tanto* (tan) *(as much as, as)*

No deberías comer **tanto**.
You shouldn't eat so much.

Exercise 6. Complete the following sentences using **mucho** or **muy**.

1. Liliana es una mujer ___________ elegante.
2. Hay ___________ que decir en la próxima reunión.
3. Me gusta ___________ menos la sopa.
4. Tu hermano conduce ___________ rápido.
5. ¡___________ gusto!
6. Quiero ___________ a mi novia.
7. ¡Perdóname! ¿Llevas ___________ más tiempo esperándome que de costumbre?
8. Es ___________ mejor ir al parque que perder el tiempo con juegos electrónicos.
9. Para aprender español hay que conversar ___________.
10. En agosto hace ___________ calor en Veracruz.

Exercise 7. Complete the following sentences using the correct adverb.

1. Hay ___________ (apenas / mucho) cinco naranjas en la mesa.
2. Hay ___________ (muy / mucho) poca gente en el parque.
3. Tú comes ___________ (muy / mucho) poco, menos de 400 calorías diarias.
4. ¿Es ___________ (muy / mucho) pedirte que laves los platos?
5. Lucía llegó a la fiesta___________ (muy / mucho) después que Laura.
6. A nosotros nos gustan ___________ (más / casi) las verduras frescas que la carne.
7. ___________ (Más / Casi) pierdo el examen de física; estaba bastante difícil.
8. Me siento ___________ (más / algo) enfermo y también un (más / poco) cansado.
9. No hay ___________ (nada / casi) que me guste; sólo dormir.
10. Hay ___________ (sólo / tanto) por aprender que es ___________ (demasiado / mejor) no dormir ___________ (también / tanto).

C. ADVERBS OF TIME

ahora *(now, soon)*

Ahora, creo que tenías razón.
Now, I think you were right.

—¿Cuándo vienes?
"When will you come?"

—**Ahora** voy.
"I'm coming soon."

*See Chapter 17, Comparatives and Superlatives.

anoche *(last night)*

Anoche me encontré con tu amigo Carlos.
Last night I bumped into your friend Carlos.

anteayer *(the day before yesterday)*

Anteayer fuimos a la playa.
The day before yesterday, we went to the beach.

antes *(before)*

Antes del mediodía estaremos en casa.
Before noon, we will be at home.

aún *(still, yet, even)*

Aún sigo sin ganas de trabajar.
I am still not in the mood to work.

ayer *(yesterday)*

Ayer era el Día de los muertos y fuimos de paseo al cementerio.
Yesterday it was the Day of the Dead, and so we took a trip to the cemetery.

cuando *(when)*

Cuando tengas tiempo, ven y nos tomamos una cerveza.
When you have a moment, let's have a beer together.

después *(after)*

Después del cine fuimos a bailar.
After the movie we went dancing.

entonces *(then)*

En aquel **entonces**, vivíamos en el campo.
Back then, we lived in the countryside.

hoy *(today)*

Hoy vivimos todos en la ciudad, menos mi abuelo.
Today we all live in the city, except my grandfather.

jamás and **nunca** *(never)*

Mi abuelo **jamás** quiso dejar el campo.
My grandfather never wanted to leave the countryside.

Nunca se acostumbró a la ciudad.
He never got used to living in the city.

TIP BOX

Note that **jamás** and **nunca** are synonyms. They are equivalent in meaning to both *never* and *ever*. Unlike in English, they can be used indiscriminately in negative sentences.

Nunca como helado. *or* **Jamás** como helado.
I never eat ice cream.
No como helado **nunca**. *or* No como helado **jamás**.
I don't ever eat ice cream.

luego *(then)*

Llegamos a la casa y **luego** preparamos la cena.
We came home and then we fixed dinner.

mañana *(tomorrow)*

Mañana saldremos para Bolivia.
Tomorrow we leave for Bolivia.

mientras *(meanwhile, while)*

Mientras mamá cocinaba, los niños jubagan.
While Mom cooked, the children played.

siempre *(always)*

Siempre me encuentro con tu tía en el cine.
I always bump into your aunt at the movies.

tarde *(late)*

Siempre llegamos **tarde** a clase.
We always arrive late to class.

todavía *(still, yet)* and **ya** *(already)*
–¿**Todavía** vas a ir a Francia?
"Are you still going to France?"
–Sí, **todavía** voy a ir.
"Yes, I'm still going."
–¿**Ya** compraste los boletos de avión?
"Did you already buy the plane tickets?"
–No, **todavía** no.
"No, not yet."

Exercise 8. Complete the following sentences using the correct adverb.

1. ___________ (Anteayer/Aún) estuvimos en la casa de mis tíos. Nunca ___________ (ahora/antes) había estado en casa de ellos.
2. ___________ (Ahora/Antes), ___________ (cuando/mientras) era niña, siempre jugaba en el parque. En aquel ___________ (después/entonces) tenía 8 años.
3. ___________ (Anoche/Mientras), ___________ (aún/jamás) después de visitarte, seguía extrañándote.
4. ___________ (Ayer/Aún) amanecí contento, ___________ (hoy/nunca) no lo estoy.
5. ___________ (Mientras/Mañana) iremos a la playa y ___________ (luego/ todavía) iremos a bailar.
6. ___________ (Hoy/Luego) todavía me siento un poco enfermo; ___________ (ayer/ahora) estaba peor.
7. (Cuando/Ahora) vamos a comer un helado; ___________ (todavía/luego) te invito a mi casa___________.
8. No he ido ___________ (nunca/siempre) a aquel restaurante. ¿Vamos?
9. ___________ (Todavía/Nunca) tengo un poco de dinero, yo te invito.
10. ___________ (Tarde/Mientras) comíamos llegó Adela con su estúpido novio.
11. ___________ (Ya/Anteayer) es hora de partir, es muy ___________ (ahora/tarde).

D. ADVERBS OF PLACE

- **abajo** *(below)* and **arriba** *(above)*

  Abajo está el infierno, **arriba** el cielo.
  Hell is below. Heaven above.

- **acá**, **aquí** *(here)* / **allí, ahí** *(there)* / **allá** *(over there)* / **donde** *(where)* / **cerca** *(near)* / **lejos** *(far)*

  Acá, **donde** vivo, es muy verde.
  Here, where I live, is very green.

  Cerca del río están los guaduales, y **allá**, a lo **lejos**, la sierra nevada.
  Near the river are the bamboo forests, and over there, in the distance, are the snow-peaked mountains.

  Ahí en el valle está el pueblo, **allá** en el cerro, la finca de mi abuelo.
  There in the valley is the village; over there, on the hill, is my grandfather's farm.

- **adentro** *(inside)* and **afuera** *(outside)*

  ¡Qué desesperación! **Adentro** de la casa hace un calor infernal y **afuera** un frío glacial.
  How frustrating! Inside the house it's hellishly hot and outside it's as cold as ice!

- **alrededor** *(around)*

  Puse una cerca **alrededor** de mi casa.
  I put a fence around my house.

- **debajo** *(under)* / **encima** *(on top)* / **detrás** *(behind)* / **delante** *(in front of)*

—¡Lola! ¿Dónde pusiste mis libros?
"Lola, where did you put my books?"

—Los puse **encima** de la mesa.
"I put them on top of the table."

—No, no están.
"They are not there."

—Entonces, búscalos **debajo** de la mesa.
"Then, look for them under the table."

—No, tampoco están.
"No, they are not there either."

—¡Míralos! Están ahí bajo tus narices.
"Look at them! They are there right under your nose."

—¿Dónde?
"Where?"

—**Detrás** de ti.
"Behind you."

—No los veo.
"I don't see them."

—¿Estás ciego? Los tienes **delante** y no los ves.
"Are you blind? You have them right in front of you and you don't see them!"

Exercise 9. Complete the following sentences using the correct adverb.

1. ___________ (Allá / Cerca) de tu casa hay un edificio grande.
2. ___________ (Cerca / Allá) a lo lejos veo un pájaro enorme.
3. ___________ (Encima / Abajo) está el sótano oscuro y frío y ___________ (arriba / debajo) el ático.
4. Ven ___________ (acá / alrededor), a mi lado ___________ (donde / detrás) pueda verte.
5. La tierra gira ___________ (alrededor / aquí) del Sol.
6. Las manzanas rojas están ___________ (afuera / encima) de la mesa.
7. ___________ (Detrás / Allá) de mi casa hay un parque muy lindo.
8. ¡Eres muy desordenado! Busca tus medias ___________ (debajo / aquí) de la cama.
9. ___________ (Debajo /Delante) de nosotros hay un coche sospechoso.
10. ¡No dejes la leche fresca ___________ (allá / afuera) de la nevera!

Exercise 10. Match each adverb with its opposite.

1. cerca	a. arriba
2. adentro	b. encima
3. debajo	c. afuera
4. detrás	d. delante
5. abajo	e. lejos

E. ADVERBIAL EXPRESSIONS

- **Adverbial Expressions of Manner**

a ciegas	*blindly*	**de memoria**	*by heart*
a cuestas	*at the expense of*	**de mala gana**	*unwillingly*
a diestra y siniestra	*disorderly*	**de prisa**	*fast*
a escondidas	*secretly*	**de pronto**	*suddenly*
a oscuras	*in the dark*	**de repente**	*suddenly*
a la moda	*stylish, in vogue*	**en resumen**	*in conclusion, in general*
al revés	*upside down, just the opposite*	**en vano**	*in vain*
de buena gana	*of good will*	**por desgracia**	*unfortunately*
de golpe	*suddenly, fast*	**sobre todo**	*above all, especially*

- **Adverbial Expressions of Time**

de ahora en adelante	*hereafter, from here on*	**de noche**	*at night, nightime*
al anochecer	*tonight, at dusk*	**de vez en cuando**	*sometimes, once in a while*
de antemano	*beforehand, before*		
de día	*during daytime*	**al fin**	*at last, finally*
de la noche a la mañana	*overnight*	**pasado mañana**	*the day after tomorrow*
		por ahora	*presently, for now*
de la tarde	*afternoon, P.M.*	**por último**	*at last, finally*
de mañana	*since morning; morningtime*		

- **Adverbial Expressions of Place**

a la derecha	*to the right*	**en cualquier parte**	*anywhere*
a la izquierda	*to the left*	**en el extranjero**	*abroad*
de arriba a bajo	*from top to bottom*	**en ninguna parte**	*nowhere*
de dónde	*where...from?*	**en otra parte**	*elsewhere*
dentro de	*within, inside, indoors*	**en todas partes**	*everywhere*
en alguna parte	*somewhere*	**por aquí**	*this way*
en casa	*at home*	**en ninguna parte**	*nowhere*

Exercise 11. Complete the following sentences using the appropriate adverbial expression.

1. Mi hijo se aprendió la poesía _____________ (a cuestas / de memoria).
2. María le respondió a su madre _____________ (de mala gana / al revés).
3. Los presos fueron encarcelados _____________ (en el extranjero / de ahora en adelante).
4. Todos corren _____________ (dentro de / de prisa) para llegar a tiempo.
5. _____________ (En resumen / Al fin), descubrió que ya no era un niño.
6. Todos los empleados hicieron su trabajo _____________ (por ahora / en vano).

10

The Subjunctive

There are three **moods** in Spanish—the indicative, the subjunctive, and the imperative,* which is used for direct commands.

WHAT IS THE SUBJUNCTIVE?

The subjunctive is used in hypothetical or subjective situations. The indicative, on the other hand, is always used to express a more objective or "real" action or situation.

The **subjunctive** is often used when we **desire** for something to occur, when we want to **influence** someone, when we **doubt** something, or when we express **emotions**.

Examples

Subjunctive Mood

- Desire or Influence

  El jefe quiere que **trabajemos** más.
  The boss wants us to work harder.

- Hope

  Los estudiantes esperan que no **haya** clase el lunes.
  The students hope that there is no class on Monday.

- Emotion

  Es maravilloso que hoy **sea** día festivo.
  It is wonderful that today is a holiday.

- Doubt

  Tal vez **llueva** mañana.
  It may rain tomorrow.

Quisiera un pescado.
(I would like a fish.)

*See Chapter 12, Commands.

Indicative Mood

El jefe dice que **tenemos** que trabajar más.
The boss says that we have to work harder.

Los estudiantes **están** contentos porque no **hay** clase el lunes.
The students are happy because there is no class on Monday.

Hoy **es** día festivo.
Today is a holiday.

Mañana **va** a llover.
It will rain tomorrow.

TIP BOX

Some grammar definitions
A **mood** indicates the point of view of the speaker toward what he or she is saying.

The **tense of a verb** refers to the time when the action of the verb takes place (present, past, or future).

The **aspect** refers to the manner in which a verb's action is distributed through the time-space continuum. The aspect may be **perfect** or **imperfect**. Perfect indicates that the action is seen by the speaker as complete, as ended, or as a fact. Imperfect indicates that the action is seen by the speaker as incomplete.

II. The Present Subjunctive

A. REGULAR FORMATION OF THE PRESENT SUBJUNCTIVE

The present tense of the subjunctive is formed by taking the root of a conjugated verb in the first person (**yo**) in the present tense of the indicative mood, and adding the following endings:

	Verb Endings of the Present Subjunctive	
	-ar	**-er / -ir**
yo	-e	-a
tú	-es	-as
él, ella, usted	-e	-a
nosotros/as	-emos	-amos
vosotros/as	-éis	-áis
ellos, ellas, ustedes	-en	-an

TIP BOX

To conjugate the verb **tener** *(to have)* in the present tense of the subjunctive, use the root of the first person of the present tense of the indicative: **Yo tengo**.

Add to the root **teng-** the corresponding verb ending for the verbs that end in **-er**: *-a,-as, -a, -amos, -áis, -an.*

Regular Formation of the Present Subjunctive				
		bail-ar (*to dance*)	**com-er** (*to eat*)	**viv-ir** (*to live*)
Present of the Indicative	yo	bail-**o**	com-**o**	viv-**o**
Present of the Subjunctive	yo tú él, ella, usted nosotros(as) vosotros(as) ustedes, ellos, ellas	bail-**e** bail-**es** bail-**e** bail-**emos** bail-**éis** bail-**en**	com-**a** com-**as** com-**a** com-**amos** com-**áis** com-**an**	viv-**a** viv-**as** viv-**a** viv-**amos** viv-**áis** viv-**an**

Exercise 1. Part A. Complete the following sentences in the present of the indicative and underline the root of the verb.

Example

Yo (tener) <u>teng</u>o una amiga increíble.

1. Yo (bailar) _____________ salsa todas las noches.
2. Yo (caminar) _____________ por el parque.
3. Yo (cocinar) _____________ para sus amigos.
4. Yo (compartir) _____________ las mismas aficiones de Julián.
5. Yo (vivir) _____________ en el mismo barrio.
6. Yo (ver) _____________ por las tardes la televisión en español.
7. Yo (poner) _____________ la música demasiado alta por las mañanas.
8. Yo (hacer) _____________ deporte con Carmen.

Part B. Using the preceding underlined roots complete the following sentences in the present subjunctive.

Example

Es maravilloso que (tener/tú) tengas una amiga increíble.

1. María quiere que (bailar/tú) _____________ con ella esta noche.
2. Carlos le dice a María que (caminar) _____________ más rápidamente.
3. Es fantástico que Julián (cocinar) _____________ para sus amigos.
4. Es bueno que Carmen (compartir) _____________ las mismas aficiones de Julián.
5. Es una pena que no todos (vivir) _____________ en el mismo barrio.
6. María no quiere que Carmen (ver) _____________ tanta televisión.
7. Los vecinos le piden a Carlos que no (poner) _____________ la música tan alta.
8. María no cree que Carmen (hacer) _____________ suficiente deporte.

B. IRREGULAR FORMATION OF THE PRESENT SUBJUNCTIVE

Not all verbs have a regular formation. Verbs ending in **-gar**, **-guar**, **-car**, **-zar**, and the following verbs are irregular:

dar (*to give*)	**estar** (*to be*)	**haber** (*to have*)
ir (*to go*)	**saber** (*to know*)	**ser** (*to be*)

a. Verbs ending in **-gar**, **-guar**, **-car**, and **-zar** do not have the same root in the first person either of the present indicative or in the present subjunctive. These verbs need to adopt the phonetic rules as shown in the examples below.

Verbs that end in **-gar** take the letter **u** after **g**:
yo juego → yo jue**gue**

Verbs that end in **-guar** take a **ü**:
yo desaguo → yo desa**güe**

Verbs that end in **-car** change to **qu**:
yo busco → yo bus**que**

Verbs that end in **-zar**, by an orthographic convention, change the **z** to a **c**:
yo almuerzo → yo almuer**ce**

Present Subjunctive of Verbs Ending in *-gar, -guar, -car, -zar*					
		peg-ar (*to hit*)	**averigu-ar** (*to investigate*)	**busc-ar** (*to look for*)	**rez-ar** (*to pray*)
Present of the Indicative	yo	peg-**o**	averigu-**o**	busc-**o**	rez-**o**
Present of the Subjunctive	yo	peg**u**-e	averig**ü**-e	bus**qu**-e	re**c**-e
	tú	peg**u**-es	averig**ü**-es	bus**qu**-es	re**c**-es
	él, ella, usted	peg**u**-e	averig**ü**-e	bus**qu**-e	re**c**-e
	nosotros(as)	peg**u**-emos	averig**ü**-emos	bus**qu**-emos	re**c**-emos
	vosotros(as)	peg**u**-éis	averig**ü**-éis	bus**qu**-éis	re**c**-éis
	ellos, ellas, ustedes	peg**u**-en	averig**ü**-en	bus**qu**-en	re**c**-en

Other Verbs Following the Same Pattern			
-gar	**-guar**	**-car**	**-zar**
agregar *(to add)*	amortiguar *(to cushion)*	acercar *(to bring near)*	abrazar *(to embrace)*
entregar *(to deliver)*	apaciguar *(to appease)*	adjudicar *(to award)*	alcanzar *(to reach)*
jugar *(to play)*	atestiguar *(to attest)*	buscar *(to search)*	almorzar *(to have lunch)*
llegar *(to arrive)*	averiguar *(to find out)*	cerrar *(to close)*	avanzar *(to advance)*
negar *(to deny)*	desaguar *(to drain)*	machacar *(to pound)*	danzar *(to dance)*
refregar *(to scrub)*	fraguar *(to conceive, to hatch)*	picar *(to sting)*	economizar *(to save)*
regar *(to water)*		salpicar *(to sprinkle)*	empezar *(to begin)*
rogar *(to beg)*	menguar *(to diminish)*	tocar *(to touch)*	enderezar *(to straighten)*

b. Verbs **haber, ir, saber, ser, dar, estar** are extremely irregular and they must be memorized.

Present Subjunctive of the Verbs *haber, ir, saber, ser, dar, estar*						
	haber (*to have*)	**ir** (*to go*)	**saber** (*to know*)	**ser** (*to be*)	**dar** (*to give*)	**estar** (*to be*)
yo	haya	vaya	sepa	sea	dé	esté
tú	hayas	vayas	sepas	seas	des	estés
él, ella, usted	haya	vaya	sepa	sea	dé	esté
nosotros(as)	hayamos	vayamos	sepamos	seamos	demos	estemos
vosotros(as)	hayáis	vayáis	sepáis	seáis	deis	estéis
ellos, ellas, ustedes	hayan	vayan	sepan	sean	den	estén

Exercise 2. Complete the following sentences in the present subjunctive.

1. Quiero que (dormir/tú) _____________ más, para que mañana trabajes mejor.
2. Me alegro de que (ir/vosotros) _____________ a mi boda.
3. Es necesario que (pagar/usted) _____________ sus facturas.
4. Les aconsejo que (ustedes empezar) _____________ a estudiar pronto.
5. Es importante que (cerrar/ella) _____________ la puerta antes de salir.
6. No creo que (saber/nosotros) _____________ la verdad de la historia.
7. Es mejor que (agregar/usted) _____________ la propina a la cuenta.
8. Es necesario que (desaguar/usted) _____________ la piscina.
9. Es importante que (refregar/vosotros) _____________ los platos todos los días.
10. Que maravilla que (ir/tú) _____________ a Madrid con tu esposa.
11. No creo que (buscar/ella) _____________ un apartamento para vivir con su novio.
12. Ojalá que (almorzar/ellas) _____________ con sus padres.
13. Es mejor que (dar/ella) _____________ el dinero para la matrícula pronto.
14. Quiero que (rogar/tú) _____________ por mí en la iglesia.
15. Le aconsejo al presidente que (apaciguar/él) _____________ a los manifestantes.
16. Me alegro de que (entregar/tú) _____________ tus trabajos.

C. USES OF THE SUBJUNCTIVE

THE SUBJUNCTIVE IN SUBORDINATE NOUN CLAUSES

The subjunctive is used in subordinate clauses when the main clause indicates **influence**, **desire**, or **doubt**.

TIP BOX

A *subordinate clause* is a dependent clause. This means that it cannot stand alone; it is always subordinated to a main clause. The main clause and the subordinate clause are linked by the conjunction **que**. Note that the verb in the main clause, which expresses influence, desire or doubt, is always in the indicative mood. Also, the main and the subordinate clauses must have different subjects. In many cases a Spanish subjunctive is expressed by an English infinitive construction or by a phrase containing a gerund.

Quiero que usted **llame** mañana.
I want you to call tomorrow.
No estoy de acuerdo en que ustedes **vengan** mañana.
I disapprove of your coming tomorrow.

a. The subjunctive in sentences that express **influence** or **desire**. When the subject in the main clause expresses a desire to influence the subject in the subordinate clause to perform an action, the use of the subjunctive is required in the subordinate clause.

No quiero que andes fuera de casa.
(I don't want you to go outside the house.)

Example

El profesor quiere que María **estudie** más español.
The teacher wants María to study more Spanish.

In this example, **el profesor** wants to influence the behavior of the subject in the subordinate clause, **María**, to perform the action (**que estudie más**).

Different verbs and expressions are used to express desire or influence. When those verbs or expressions are present in the main clause, the use of the subjunctive is required in the subordinate clause. The following verbs and expressions are used in this case.

Verbs That Express Influence or Desire		
Verb	**Example**	**Translation**
aconsejar (*to advise*)	Te aconsejo que vengas.	*I advise you to come.*
decir (*to say*)	Te digo que te apresures.	*I tell you to hurry.*
dejar (*to leave*)	Deja que se vaya.	*Let him go.*
desear (*to desire*)	Luis desea que Lucía venga.	*Luis wants Lucía to come.*
esperar (*to expect*)	Espero que cumplas tu promesa.	*I expect you to keep your promise.*
exigir (*to demand*)	Él exige que le des una explicación.	*He demands that you give him an explanation.*
mandar (*to order*)	El cura le manda que rece.	*The priest orders him to pray.*
ordenar (*to order*)	El capitán ordena que zarpemos.	*The captain orders us to set sail.*
pedir (*to request, to ask*)	Me pide que le disculpe.	*He asks me to forgive him.*
permitir (*to allow*)	No te permito que la insultes.	*I do not allow you to insult her.*
preferir (*to prefer*)	Prefiero que se queden.	*I prefer you to stay.*
prohibir (*to forbid*)	Te prohibo que salgas con Juan.	*I forbid you to go out with Juan.*
querer (*to want*)	Quiero que te cases conmigo.	*I want you to marry me.*
recomendar (*to recommend*)	Te recomiendo que te olvides de ella.	*I recommend you forget about her.*
rogar (*to beg*)	Les ruega que rectifiquen la ley.	*He begs them to amend the law.*
sugerir (*to suggest*)	Mi madre me sugiere que estudie más.	*My mother suggests that I study more.*

Impersonal Expressions That Express Influence or Desire		
Expressions	**Example**	**Translation**
Es esencial...	que sigas los consejos del médico.	***It is essential*** *for you to follow the doctor's advice.*
Es importante...	que prestes atención.	***It is important*** *for you to pay attention.*
Es mejor...	que nos demos prisa.	***It is better*** *for us to hurry.*
Es necesario...	que se cumplan las normas.	***It is necessary*** *to comply with the rules.*
Es preciso...	que me ayudes.	***It is essential*** *that you to help me.*
Es urgente...	que pagues la cuenta del gas.	***It is urgent*** *that you pay the gas bill.*
Es indispensable...	que llames al médico.	***It is essential*** *that you call the doctor.*
Es aconsejable...	que recojas tu desorden.	***It is advisable*** *that you pick up your mess.*

Exercise 3. Complete the following sentences in the present subjunctive. Imagine you are a teacher and it is your first day of class. Explain to your students the class rules. Use verbs and expressions that express influence or desire.

Example

preparar la tarea todos los días
Es esencial que ustedes preparen la tarea todos los días.

1. Llegar puntuales a clase
____
2. Corregir los ejercicios
____
3. Repasar con regularidad
____
4. Escribir los trabajos en procesador de texto
____
5. Leer con cuidado el programa
____
6. Participar en las actividades comunes
____
7. Estudiar con anticipación los temas que se van a ver en clase
____
8. Hacer preguntas para aclarar dudas
____
9. Participar en los trabajos en equipo
____
10. Practicar antes y después de clase
____

Exercise 4. You and your parents are packing yours bags to go on vacation and there still is much to do.

Example

comprar aspirinas
Quiero que compres aspirinas.

1. Ir al banco
2. Preparar tu ropa
3. Despedirte de tu hermana
4. Recoger los billetes de avión
5. Hacer la reserva del hotel
6. Regar las plantas
7. Llevar el perro a casa de tu primo
8. Cancelar la entrega del periódico
9. Avisar en la oficina de correos que estaremos de vacaciones
10. Empacar las vitaminas y los medicamentos

b. The subjunctive in sentences that express **doubt**. When the subject in the main clause expresses **doubt**, the subordinate clause requires the use of the subjunctive.

Dudo que la perrita <u>quiera</u> regresar a casa.
(I doubt that the nice doggie would like to go back home.)

Example

El profesor duda que María **<u>venga</u>** mañana a clase.
The teacher doubts that María will come to class tomorrow.

(Yo) No creo que los unicornios **<u>existan</u>**.
I don't believe that unicorns exist.

In the first example, **el profesor** doubts if **María** is coming to class tomorrow. In the second example the subject, **Yo**, doubts the existence of unicorns. In both examples the main clause expresses *doubt*. This is why the verb in the subordinate clause is in the subjunctive.

TIP BOX

When the main clause expresses **certainty** or a **belief**, the subordinate clause should be in the indicative.

El profesor **no duda** que María **viene** mañana.
The teacher has no doubt that María is coming tomorrow.

Creo que los unicornios **existen**.
I believe unicorns exist.

Pienso que **tienes** razón.
I think you are right.

In Spanish, different verbs and expressions are used to express **doubt**. When those expressions or verbs are present in the main clause, the use of the subjunctive is required in the subordinate clause. Those verbs and expressions are shown in the table that follows.

Verbs That Express *Doubt* (Subjunctive)		
Verbs	**Example**	**Translation**
no creer *(not to believe)*	No creo que tenga tiempo para comer contigo.	*I don't believe I will have time to eat with you.*
dudar *(to doubt)*	Nosotros dudamos que haya oro en esa cueva.	*We doubt that there is gold inside that cave.*
no estar seguro de *(not to be certain)*	Eva no está segura que su madre pueda venir.	*Eva is not certain that her mother can come.*
no pensar *(not to think)*	No pienso que sea buena idea invitarlo a la fiesta.	*I don't think it's a good idea to invite him to the party.*
no parecer* *(not to seem)*	No nos parece que tengas razón.	*It doesn't seem to us that you are right.*

* This verb is conjugated as *gustar*. See Chapter 15.

Impersonal Expressions That Express *Doubt* (Subjunctive)		
Expressions	**Example**	**Translation**
Es dudoso...	que llueva mañana.	*It is doubtful that it will rain tomorrow.*
Es improbable...	que haga sol hoy.	*It is unlikely that it will be sunny today.*
Es posible...	que todos los empleados sean despedidos.	*It is possible that all the employees will be fired.*
Es probable...	que te compre un regalo si te portas bien.	*If you behave, it is likely that I will buy you a gift.*
No es cierto...	que todos los políticos sean corruptos.	*It is not true that all the politicians are corrupt.*
No es claro...	que su marido sea muy inteligente.	*It is not clear that your husband is very intelligent.*
No es evidente...	que la economía se esté recuperando.	*It is not evident that the economy is recovering.*
No es obvio...	que los avances técnicos mejoren la calidad de vida.	*It is not obvious that the technological advances improve the quality of life.*
No es posible...	que volvamos juntos. Ya no te quiero.	*It's not possible for us to get back together. I don't love you anymore.*
No es seguro...	que apruebe el examen de matemáticas.	*It is not certain that I will approve the Math exam.*
No es verdad...	que me lo pase jugando todo el día en la computadora.	*It is not true that I spend all day long playing on the computer.*
Puede ser que...	vayamos de vacaciones a las Islas Canarias este verano.	*Maybe we will go to the Canary Islands for vacation this summer.*

Note that most of the verbs and expressions that convey **doubt** have a counterpart in verbs and expressions of **certainty** and **belief**. In these cases the use of the **indicative mood** is required.

Verbs That Express *Certainty* and *Belief* (Indicative)		
Verbs	**Example**	**Translation**
creer *(to believe)*	Creo que tengo tiempo para comer contigo.	*I believe I will have time to eat with you.*
no dudar *(not to doubt)*	Nosotros no dudamos que hay oro en esa cueva.	*We don't doubt that there is gold in that cave.*
estar seguro de *(to be certain)*	Eva está segura que su madre puede venir.	*Eva is certain that her mother can come.*
pensar *(to think)*	Pienso que es buena idea invitarlo a la fiesta.	*I think it's a good idea to invite him to the party.*
parecer* *(to seem)*	Nos parece que tienes razón.	*It seems to us that you are right.*

* This verb is conjugated as *gustar*. See Chapter 15.

Impersonal Expressions That Express *Certainty* and *Belief* (Indicative)		
Expressions	**Example**	**Translation**
Es cierto…	que todos los políticos son corruptos.	*It is true that all the politicians are corrupt.*
Es claro…	que su marido es muy inteligente.	*It is clear that your husband is very intelligent.*
Es evidente…	que la economía se está recuperando.	*It is evident that the economy is recovering.*
Es obvio…	que los avances técnicos mejoran la calidad de vida.	*It is obvious that the technological advances improve the quality of life.*
Es seguro…	que aprobaré el examen de matemáticas.	*It is not certain I will approve the Math exam.*
Es verdad…	que me lo paso jugando todo el día en la computadora.	*It is true that I spend all day long playing on the computer.*

TIP BOX

Special Attention: Interrogative Sentences!

In interrogative sentences the speaker's intent, viewpoint, or attitude determines whether the subjunctive or the indicative is to be used in the dependent clause after expressions of certainty or belief. If the speaker **doubts**, the verb in the subordinate clause should be in the subjunctive. But if the speaker **knows** or **has an opinion** about what he or she is asking, the verb in the subordinate clause should be in the indicative.

Example

¿Estás seguro de que Javier <u>tiene</u> hambre?
Are you sure Javier is hungry?

In this sentence the speaker has an opinion about whether Javier is or is not hungry. For this reason the indicative is used.

¿Estás seguro de que Javier <u>tenga</u> hambre?
Are you sure Javier might be hungry?

In this sentence the speaker has no opinion about whether Javier is or is not hungry. This is why the subjunctive is used here.

Exercise 5. Juan has many debatable opinions. Rewrite his opinions using expressions of doubt.

Example

Juan:—En Estados Unidos los estudiantes beben demasiado.
—No estoy seguro de que los estudiantes ***beban*** *demasiado.*

1. —Los políticos dicen siempre la verdad.
   —____
2. —El presidente no cobra suficiente dinero.
   —____
3. —Los ciudadanos no pagamos muchos impuestos.
   —____
4. —Los programas de televisión son muy educativos.
   —____
5. —Soy el mejor trabajador de mi empresa.
   —____
6. —Los vinos alemanes son los mejores.
   —____
7. —El fútbol americano es el deporte más inofensivo.
   —____
8. —El precio de la gasolina ha estado estable en los últimos diez años.
   —____
9. —Sólo los niños deben usar protector solar.
   —____
10. —La pizza es un alimento con bajo contenido de grasas.
   —____

Exercise 6. Rewrite the following sentences in the negative. Follow the example.

Example

Hay extraterrestres en la galaxia Andrómeda.
No creo que haya extraterrestres en la galaxia Andrómeda.

1. Es sano comer carne.
   ____
2. Tu esposa gasta mucho dinero en cosméticos.
   ____
3. Jorge está enamorado de ti.
   ____

4. La recesión económica va a cambiar nuestros hábitos de consumo.

____

5. Van a viajar al Amazonas.

____

6. Lucía quiere comprar una casa muy costosa.

____

Exercise 7. Imagine that María wants to go to the beach with her friend Roberto. Roberto doesn't want to go and he is absolutely sure of it. Complete the following sentences using the subjunctive or the indicative.

Example

Estoy seguro/ haber / mucha gente en la playa
Estoy seguro de que hay mucha gente en la playa.

1. No creo / ser / sano tomar el sol

____

2. Es posible / encontrarse / con tu ex-novio

____

3. ¿No es mejor / ir a un lugar / con menos gente?

____

4. Es evidente / tener / ganas de ver a Federico, tu ex-novio

____

5. Es posible / preferir / quedarme solo en casa

____

6. Es cierto / estar / celoso de Federico

____

7. Es probable / no tener / traje de baño

____

8. Me parece / ir a llover / esta tarde

____

9. Prefiero / quedarnos / en casa

____

10. Creer / ser / el concierto de Juana / mañana

____

c. The subjunctive in sentences that convey **emotion**. When the subject in the main clause expresses **emotion**, the subordinate clause requires the use of the subjunctive.

Es maravilloso que <u>pueda</u> escaparme.
(It's wonderful that I can run away from home.)

Example

Me alegro mucho de que María **<u>venga</u>** a clase.
I am very glad that María is coming to class.

Es terrible que **<u>haya</u>** guerra.
It is terrible that there is war.

In Spanish, different verbs and expressions are used to convey **emotion**. When those expressions or verbs are present in the main clause, the use of the subjunctive is required in the subordinate clause. Those verbs and expressions are shown in the table that follows.

Verbs That Express *Emotion*

Verbs	Example	Translation
alegrarse *(to be happy)*	Me alegro que puedas venir.	*I am happy that you can come.*
enojar* *(to make angry)*	¿Te enoja que haga ruido?	*Does it make you angry that I make noise?*
gustar* *(to like)*	Me gusta que sonrías.	*I like that you smile.*
lamentar *(to regret)*	Luis lamenta mucho que no vengas a la fiesta.	*Luis regrets a lot that you cannot come to the party.*
maravillar* *(to astonish)*	Nos maravilla que seas tan valiente.	*It astonishes us that you are so brave.*
molestar* *(to bother)*	¿Os molesta que escuche música?	*Does it bother you if I listen to music?*
quejarse *(to complain)*	Inés se queja de que no la escuches.	*Inés complains that you don't listen to her.*
sentir (*to be sorry*)	Siento mucho que no te puedas quedarte a comer.	*I am very sorry that you cannot stay for dinner.*
sorprender* *(to be surprised)*	Nos sorprende que seas tan indelicado.	*It surprises us that you are so inconsiderate.*

* These verbs are conjugated as *gustar*. See Chapter 15.

Impersonal Expressions That Express *Emotion*		
Expression	**Example**	**Translation**
Es difícil…	que podamos sobrevivir con tan poco dinero.	*It's difficult for us to survive with so little money.*
Es sorprendente…	que tengas tanto éxito.	*It's surprising that you have so much success.*
Es mejor…	que te relajes un poco.	*It's better if you relax a little bit.*
Es terrible…	que sufras tanto.	*It's terrible that you suffer so much.*
Es extraño…	que Luis nos llame; seguro que quiere un favor.	*It's strange for Luis to call us; he must need a favor.*
Es deplorable…	que comas como un cerdo.	*It's unfortunate that you eat like a pig.*
Es raro…	que él nos pida disculpas si es tan orgulloso.	*It's unusual for him to apologize since he is so proud.*
Es fácil…	que un político se convierta en un dictador.	*It is easy for a politician to become a dictator.*
Es estupendo…	que cumplas con tus promesas.	*It is wonderful that you keep your promises*
Es maravilloso…	que existas.	*It is marvelous that you exist.*
Es agradable…	que aún te acuerdes de mí con cariño	*It's nice that you still remember me with love.*
Es bueno…	que te laves las manos antes de comer.	*It's good that you wash your hands before eating.*
Es interesante…	que el asesino sea el bueno de la película.	*It's interesting that the assassin is the good character in the movie.*
¡Es el colmo…	que me grites de esa manera!	*It's unbelievable that you scream at me like that.*
Es increíble…	que por fin tengas un novio buena persona.	*It is incredible that finally you got yourself a nice boyfriend.*
Es normal…	que te enfermes si no te cuidas.	*It's normal for you to get sick if you don't take care of yourself.*
Es una lástima…	que Ana sea tan creída.	*It is a shame that Ana is so conceited.*
Es una pena	que tengamos que estudiar tanto.	*It is a shame we have to study so much.*
Es una desgracia…	que nuestro equipo favorito pierda siempre.	*It is disgraceful that our favorite team loses always.*
Es peor…	que no me digas la verdad.	*It is worse if you don't tell me the truth.*
Es vergonzoso…	que estés saliendo con otra mujer.	*It is shameful that you are going out with another woman.*
¿Es natural…	que tenga hambre a toda hora?	*Is it natural that I feel hungry all the time?*
Es lamentable…	que no goces tu tiempo libre.	*It's deplorable that you don't enjoy your free time.*
Es malo…	que trabajes tanto.	*It's bad that you work so much.*
Es una suerte...	que te tenga a ti.	*It is lucky that I have you.*

Exercise 8. Imagine that you are reacting towards your friend's most salient personality features, which are listed below. Write six sentences according to these features using verbs or expressions of emotion.

Example

(ser leal) Es estupendo que seas tan leal.

1. ______________________________ (ser sincero)
2. ______________________________ (ser honrado)
3. ______________________________ (ser de mal genio)
4. ______________________________ (ser desordenado)
5. ______________________________ (ser olvidadizo)
6. ______________________________ (ser imprudente)
7. ______________________________ (ser comprensivo)
8. ______________________________ (ser entrometido)
9. ______________________________ (ser divertido)
10. ______________________________ (ser muy inteligente)

Exercise 9. Write four sentences in accordance to the drawings above. Use the following expressions of emotion: *es una suerte, es el colmo, es una desgracia, es increíble*.

1. (haber escrito)

____

2. (ladrarme)

____

3. (no tener trabajo)

____

4. (ser irresponsable)

____

THE SUBJUNCTIVE IN ADJECTIVAL CLAUSES OR RELATIVE CLAUSES

The adjectival or relative subordinate clauses modify nouns. When the noun that is modified by the subordinated clause is hypothetical and exists only in the mind of the speaker, the verb in the subordinate clause takes the subjunctive.

Example

Necesito un profesor que **sepa** español.
I need a teacher who knows Spanish.

Conozco a un profesor que **sabe** español.
I know a teacher who knows Spanish.

In the sentence on the left, the noun modified by the subordinate clause **profesor** is hypothetical; it does not yet exist in the real world, only in the mind of the speaker. The verb in the subordinate clause should therefore be in the subjunctive. In the sentence on the right, the noun **profesor** is not hypothetical. The speaker knows him; therefore, the verb in the subordinate clause should be in the indicative mood.

Exercise 10. Answer the following questions according to the example.

Example

¿Conoces a alguien que sepa construir letrinas ecológicas?
No, no conozco a nadie que sepa construir letrinas ecológicas.
Sí, conozco a una persona que sabe construir letrinas ecológicas.

1. ¿Conoces a alguien que tenga un amigo en Madrid?
   No, ____
   Sí, ____
2. ¿Conoces a alguien que hable diez idiomas?
   No, ____
   Sí, ____
3. ¿Conoces a alguien que componga televisores?
   No, ____
   Sí, ____
4. ¿Conoces a alguien que trabaje en la NASA?
   No, ____
   Sí, ____
5. ¿Conoces a alguien que conduzca camiones?
   No, ____
   Sí, ____

Exercise 11. Imagine that you want to meet someone to share your leisure time. Write ten sentences describing the person that you are looking for.

Example

(saber cocinar)
Busco un amigo(a) que sepa cocinar.

1. (ser sincero)
____
2. (tener tiempo para mí)
____
3. (hablar y reírse mucho)
____
4. (trabajar poco)
____
5. (gozar la vida)
____
6. (saber bailar)
____
7. (disfrutar leer)
____
8. (no ser celoso)
____
9. (ser chistoso)
____
10. (ser muy inteligente)
____

Exercise 12. Write five sentences describing the man of Carol's dreams and five sentences describing her real husband. Follow the example.

Example

hablar español
Carol quiere un hombre que hable español.
Carol <u>está casada</u> <u>con</u> un hombre que <u>no</u> <u>habla</u> español.

1. tener dinero suficiente
____
____

2. amarla con locura

____

____

3. tratarla de igual a igual

____

____

4. ser verdaderamente guapo

____

____

5. querer tener hijos

____

____

Exercise 13. Imagine that you are looking for an apartment to share with a friend. Write ten sentences describing the apartment you are looking for.

Example

(tener dos dormitorios)
Necesitamos (queremos, buscamos) un apartamento que tenga dos dormitorios.

1. (tener una sala grande)

____

2. (estar bien ubicado)

____

3. (tener una cocina moderna)

____

4. (tener vista al mar)

____

5. (tener una sala amplia)

____

6. (tener garaje)

____

7. (tener portero)

____

8. (no ser costoso)

____

9. (estar en un último piso)

____

10. (ser luminoso)

____

Exercise 14. Complete the following text using the present subjunctive or present indicative.

Sonia y Javier ____________ (tener) un apartamento en Houston que ____________ (costar) mucho dinero. Ambos ____________ (querer) una vida más divertida y ____________ (aspirar) a vender el apartamento que ____________ (tener) en Estados Unidos y a comprar uno en España. Sonia ____________ (querer) que el apartamento ____________ (estar) ubicado en la ciudad de Granada. Javier está de acuerdo, pero además ____________ (querer) que el apartamento ____________ (quedar) en el Albaicín, el antiguo barrio moro. Sonia ____________ (desear) que ____________ (tener) vista a la Sierra Nevada y a la Alhambra. Javier, también ________________ (querer) que el apartamento no ____________ (ser) ruidoso y ____________ (tener) garaje.

THE SUBJUNCTIVE IN INDEPENDENT CLAUSES

- The subjunctive is used in independent clauses in exclamatory sentences.

Example

¡**Muera** el rey!
Death to the king!

- In sentences that express ***desire*** after the expression **ojalá** (*I hope*).

Example

Ojalá llegue la primavera pronto.
I hope spring will come soon.

- When you want to express ***doubt*** after the expressions **tal vez**, **quizá**, **a lo mejor**, **acaso**, **probablemente** (*maybe*).

Example

Tal vez vaya a tu casa mañana.
Maybe I will go tomorrow to your home.

Probablemente llueva mañana.
It might rain tomorrow.

Exercise 15. Write six sentences about your possible plans for this summer using the expressions **tal vez**, **quizá**, **a lo mejor**, **probablemente**.

Example

(ir de vacaciones a Madrid este verano)
Tal vez (quizá, a lo mejor, probablemente) vaya de vacaciones a Madrid este verano.

1. (trabajar durante el verano)
____

2. (ir a México este verano)

____

3. (tener que estudiar para los exámenes de doctorado)

____

4. (visitar a mi familia en España)

____

5. (tener suerte y poder [tú] venir a visitarme)

____

6. (comprar una casa este verano)

____

7. (jugar la final de la copa de fútbol)

____

8. (conseguir un perro)

____

9. (conducir a Montreal)

____

10. (ir al festival de cine en agosto)

____

THE PRESENT SUBJUNCTIVE IN ADVERBIAL CLAUSES

An adverbial subordinate clause acts as an adverb or an adverbial phrase. Adverbial clauses inform us about time, place, manner, condition, cause, purpose, and concession. They are introduced by a conjunction or conjunctive phrase from the main sentence. The verb in the adverbial clause may either be in the indicative or subjunctive, depending what is being expressed.

- **Adverbial Conjunctive Phrases That Always Use the Subjunctive**

The subjunctive is always used after the following conjunctive phrases:

a fin (de) que	*in order to*
a menos (de) que	*unless*
antes (de) que	*before*
con tal (de) que	*provided that*
en caso (de) que	*provided that*
para que	*in order to*
sin que	*without*

TIP BOX

If the subject of the main clause is the same as in the adverbial subordinate clause, the infinitive is used and a preposition should precede the verb.

Juan trabaja mucho **para** comprar su casa.
Juan works a lot to buy his house.

El banco le presta dinero a Juan **para que** (Juan) pueda comprar su casa.
The bank lends money to Juan so that he can buy his house.

Exercise 16. Complete the following sentences using the subjunctive or infinitive.

1. Iremos al cine a menos de que ___________ (llover).
2. Trabajas mucho para que los dueños de la compañía no te ___________ (despedir) del trabajo.
3. Te llevaremos al cine con tal de que no ___________ (llorar) más.
4. Saldremos antes de que ___________ (amanecer).
5. Iré a tu casa en caso de ___________ (tener) tiempo.
6. Te regalaré el dinero a fin de que no me ___________ (pedir) más.
7. No puedes vivir sin ___________ (trabajar).
8. Mi mamá me va a recoger antes de que ___________ (oscurecer).
9. No se puede comprar casa sin ___________ (ahorrar) antes.
10. Con tal de que ___________ (hacer) la tarea, te compraré el juego.

Exercise 17. Complete the following sentences with the appropriate form of the verb.

1. Graciela llama a todas sus amigas a fin de que _________ (enterarse) de la noticia.
2. Déjale tu número telefónico a la bibliotecaria para que te _________ (avisar) cuando tenga el libro.
3. Arreglemos las flores en el jarrón para que no _________ (caerse).
4. A fin de que todos ustedes _________ (poder) comprar casa, hemos reducido las tasas de interés.
5. Cómprale libros a tu hijo para que _________ (aprender) a leer.
6. Iremos a la fiesta sin que mi mamá _________ (darse) cuenta.
7. Seguro de que te visitaremos a menos que _________ (ocurrir) algo inesperado.
8. Salgamos del barco antes de que _________ (hundirse).
9. Yo firmaré el documento con tal de que el banco no nos _________ (quitar) la casa.

Exercise 18. As shown in the example below, answer the following questions.

Example

¿Pepe, llamo a Liliana? (venir a la fiesta)
Por supuesto, para que venga a la fiesta.

1. —¿Le dejo a José las llaves en la portería? (poder entrar)
   —____.
2. —¿Invitamos a Pedro? (traer cerveza)
   —____.
3. —¿Salgo ya? (llegar [tú] temprano)
   —____.
4. —¿Compro sillas? (tener donde sentarnos)
   —____.
5. —¿Comemos ahora? (no tener [nosotros] hambre después)
   —____.
6. —¿Aspiramos el apartamento? (estar limpio)
   —____.

- **Adverbial Phrases That Use Only the Indicative**

The indicative is always used after the following adverbial phrases:

como	*since, because*
de manera que	*in such a way that*
de modo que	*in such a way that*
porque	*because*
puesto que	*since, because*
ya que	*since, because*

Example

Como no hiciste la tarea, no **podrás** ver televisión.
Since you didn't finish your homework, you cannot watch television.

No **podré** comprarte el juguete **porque** no tengo dinero.
I will not be able to buy you that toy because I don't have any money.

TIP BOX

Como, de manera que, de modo que have other meanings:

como	*if*
de manera que	*so that*
de modo que	*so that*

When **como** has a conditional function *(if)*, it requires the use of the subjunctive in the subordinate clause.

Example

Como no hagas la tarea, no **podrás** ver televisión.
If you don't do your homework, you cannot watch television.

When the adverbial phrases **de modo que** and **de manera que** describe the purpose of an action, the subjunctive is required.

Julia habla español **de modo que** todos la **entiendan**.
Julia speaks Spanish so that everyone understands her.

Exercise 19. Complete the following sentences with the appropriate form of the verb.

1. Como no _________ (llegar/nosotros) temprano al concierto, no pudimos entrar.
2. Terminaré el trabajo como me ________ (decir/ustedes).
3. Las cosas no salieron como las ________ (haber/planeado/yo).
4. Los siento mucho, pero no podré ir al paseo con vosotros porque no _________ (tener) dinero.
5. Estos enfermos necesitan toda nuestra atención puesto que _________ (estar) desamparados.
6. Nicolás pintó el cuadro como se lo ________ (haber) imaginado.
7. Conecta el televisor así como (él) te ________. (indicar)
8. Te llamé anoche porque _________ (necesitar) tus consejos.
9. Aquí estamos, como te ________. (prometer)
10. Ya que _________ (llegar/tú), ayúdame a preparar la cena.

- **Adverbial Conjunctive Phrases That Use Either the Subjunctive or Indicative**

In adverbial conjunctive phrases of time, we use the subjunctive when the action of the subordinate clause has not yet occurred. When the action does happen, has happened, or is certain to happen, we use the indicative.

Adverbial conjunctive phrases of time	
cuando	*when*
después de que	*after*
en cuanto	*as soon as*
hasta que	*until*
luego que	*as soon as*
mientras	*as long as*
tan pronto como	*as soon as*

Example

Action has not yet occurred (subjuntive)

María vendrá a visitarnos **cuando tenga** tiempo.
María will visit us when she has time.

María vendrá a visitarnos **en cuanto pueda**.
María will visit us as soon as she can.

Action does happen, has happened, or is certain to happen (indicative)

Viajo **cuando tengo** dinero.
I travel when I have money.

Viajé **en cuanto recibí** el dinero.
I traveled as soon as I received the money.

Exercise 20. Answer the following questions with sentences in the indicative or the subjunctive. Use the conjunctive phrases in parentheses.

1. ¿Cuándo volveremos a París? (después de que/terminar/los estudios)

   ____.

2. ¿Cuánto tiempo nos quedaremos en esta esquina? (hasta que/aparecer/Luis)

   ____.

3. ¿Cuándo les escribirás a tus padres? (en cuanto/tener/tiempo)

   ____.

4. ¿En qué momento supieron que habían perdido el partido? (después de que/Jorge/tener que retirarse del juego)
________________________________.

5. ¿Cuándo regresaste a casa? (luego que/nosotros/despedirse)
________________________________.

6. ¿Cuándo dejaremos salir a jugar a los perros? (cuando/haber/comido)
________________________________.

7. ¿A qué hora abren las puertas del teatro? (tan pronto como/ser/las siete en punto)
________________________________.

8. ¿Cuándo pueden entregarnos el equipo de sonido? (cuando/repararlo/el técnico)
________________________________.

9. ¿En qué momento viste salir el avión? (mientras/estar/comiendo)
________________________________.

10. ¿Cuándo se puede tocar esta pintura? (en cuanto/estar/seca)
________________________________.

Exercise 21. Answer the following questions with sentences in the simple preterit (indicative) or the present subjunctive.

1. ¿Cuándo te mudarás de casa? (pintar la casa nueva)
Cuando ________________________________

2. ¿Cuándo supieron que habían ganado la lotería? (leer el periódico)
Después de que ________________________________

3. ¿Cuándo encontraremos el balón que se perdió? (derretirse la nieve)
Cuando ________________________________

4. ¿Cuándo fuiste a Lima por primera vez? (cumplir 16 años)
Luego que ________________________________

5. ¿Cuándo siembras las semillas de tomate? (comenzar la primavera)
Tan pronto como ________________________________

6. ¿Cuándo comenzó a trabajar Tania en esa oficina? (tener una entrevista con el jefe)
En cuanto ________________________________

7. ¿Cuándo podré pasar al equipo profesional de ciclismo de montaña? (cumplir 21 años)
Cuando ________________________________

8. ¿Cuándo me llamó Gonzalo? (dormir)
Tan pronto como te ________________________________

9. ¿A qué hora saldremos hacia Nueva York? (encontrar las llaves del auto)
En cuanto ________________________________

10. ¿Hasta cuándo estarán juntos? (acabarse el mundo)
Hasta que ________________________________

In adverbial phrases of place, we use the subjunctive when the location is unknown; otherwise we use the indicative.

Adverbial phrases of place	
donde	*where, wherever*
por donde	*through, which, where*
en donde	*where, wherever*
adonde	*where, wherever*

Example

Location unknown (subjunctive)

Te buscaré en donde **estés.**
I will look for you wherever you are.

Te llevo adonde **digas.**
I will take you wherever you say.

Location known (indicative)

Te espero donde nos vimos la última vez.
I will wait for you where we last saw each other.

Exercise 22. Fill in the blanks with the present indicative or the present subjunctive.

1. Espérame donde ________ (yo/poder) estacionar el auto.
2. Quiero que me lleves adonde ________ (ellos/vender) esas chaquetas de cuero tan hermosas.
3. Hay una grieta por donde ________ (entrar) la luz.
4. Caminaremos por donde no ________ (haber) lodo.
5. Vamos adonde _______ (nosotros/poder) hablar en privado.
6. Donde ________ (terminar) el camino, empieza mi propiedad.
7. Vamos a un lugar donde _______ (yo/poder) ir al baño.
8. No se preocupen, que nosotros los llevamos a donde _______ (ustedes/querer).
9. Irá detrás de ella a cualquier parte donde ella _______ (ir).
10. Vamos donde _______ (nosotros/verse) la última vez.

In adverbial phrases of concession, the subjunctive is required when there is no certainty that the action proposed by the adverbial clause will occur. If the action will occur without doubt or has already occurred, then the indicative is used.

Adverbial phrases of concession	
aunque	*though, although, even though*
bien sea que	*although*
pese a que	*even though*

Example

There is no certainty that the action will happen (subjunctive)

Saldré aunque **llueva.**
I will go out even though it is raining.

Aunque me **pida** disculpas, no lo perdonaré.
Even if he apologizes, I won't forgive him.

The action will happen without doubt or has already happened (indicative)

Aunque **tengo** dinero, no lo voy a gastar.
Even though I have money, I won't spend it.

Aunque me **pidió** disculpas, no lo perdonaré.
Even though he apologized, I won't forgive him.

Exercise 23. Complete the following sentences with the appropriate form of the verb.

1. Aunque _________ (tener/yo) noventa años, esta música me hace sentir romántico.
2. Bien sea que te _________ (inscribirse) o no, tendrás que pagar el curso.
3. Pese a que les _________ (advertir/nosotros), no nos hicieron caso.
4. Aunque _________ (querer/ellas) disimular, se les nota la curiosidad.
5. Aunque _________ (ver/nosotros) lo que pasó, no reconocimos al asaltante.
6. Mónica se levantó temprano, pese a que _________ (acostarse) tarde.
7. Aunque le _________ (rogar/tú) no quiso volver.
8. Bien sea que _________ (tratarse) de ti o no, la ley se aplica por igual.
9. Pese a que _________ (llegar/nosotros) temprano, ya no había boletos para el concierto.
10. Aunque _________ (vivir/nosotros) juntos, no pienso casarme nunca.

Exercise 24. Fill in the blanks with the present or preterit indicative or the present subjunctive.

1. Iremos a México a menos que ________ los planes. (ellos cambiar)
2. Te daré la fórmula con tal de que no se la ________ a nadie. (decir)
3. Le daremos el dinero del taxi con tal de que nos ________. (esperar)
4. Carmela se irá sin que nadie la ________. (ver)
5. Los niños se quedarán sin comer a menos que ________ de jugar pronto. (dejar)
6. Ana le contó a José las cosas como ________. (suceder)

7. Como bien ________ (saber/ustedes), este es el monumento más importante de la ciudad.
8. Me iré sin ti a menos que ________ a tiempo. (llegar)
9. Haz las tareas como te ________. (explicar/yo)
10. Los estudiantes escogieron esta clase porque ________ (ser) la más interesante.
11. Voy a perder la partida a menos que ________ (poder) salvar la reina.
12. El vecino me deja usar su podadora de césped con tal de que le ________ el jardín. (arreglar)
13. No olvides que las cosas son como ________. (ser)
14. Fernando nos explicó la película tal como ________. (ocurrir)
15. Te enfermarás a menos que ________ mejor. (comer)
16. Ya que ________ (tener) ganas de divertirte, te invitó a bailar.
17. ¿Sabes cómo envejecer sin que se ________? (notar)
18. Todo sucedió como ________ (pronosticar) aquel historiador famoso.

II. The Imperfect Subjunctive

A. REGULAR FORMATION OF THE IMPERFECT SUBJUNCTIVE

The imperfect of the subjunctive is formed by using the root of the conjugation of the third person plural **ellos**, **ellas**, **ustedes** in the simple preterit tense of the indicative, plus the corresponding verb endings for the imperfect subjunctive. The imperfect subjunctive has two sets of endings: **-ra**, **-ras**, **-ra**, **-ramos**, **-rais**, **-ran** (used more frequently in spoken language), and **-se**, **-ses**, **-se**, **-semos**, **-seis**, **-sen** (used more often in written language).

	Verb Endings of the Imperfect Subjunctive	**amar** root: ellos **amar~~on~~**	**comer** root: ellos **comier~~on~~**	**vivir** root: ellos **vivier~~on~~**
	(-ra) form			
yo	-ra	amar**a**	comier**a**	vivier**a**
tú	-ras	amar**as**	comier**as**	vivier**as**
él, ella, usted	-ra	amar**a**	comier**a**	vivier**a**
nosotros/as	-ramos	amár**amos**	comiér**amos**	viviér**amos**
vosotros/as	-rais	amar**ais**	comier**ais**	vivier**ais**
ellos, ellas, ustedes	-ran	amar**an**	comier**an**	vivier**an**
	(-se) form			
yo	-se	ama**se**	comie**se**	vivie**se**
tú	-ses	ama**ses**	comie**ses**	vivie**ses**
él, ella, usted	-se	ama**se**	comie**se**	vivie**se**
nosotros/as	-semos	amá**semos**	comié**semos**	vivié**semos**
vosotros/as	-seis	ama**seis**	comie**seis**	vivie**seis**
ellos, ellas, ustedes	-sen	ama**sen**	comie**sen**	vivie**sen**

TIP BOX

Note that since the formation of the imperfect subjunctive is formed using the root of the third person plural of the simple preterit, all irregular verbs maintain the same irregularity in the imperfect of the subjunctive.

See Chapter 4 to review verbs that have irregularities in the simple preterit.

Exercise 25. Conjugate the following verbs using the preterit indicative and underline the root of the verb.

Example

Ellos *leyeron* (leer)

1. Ellos _________ (incluir)
2. Ellos _________ (retirar)
3. Ellos _________ (repetir)
4. Ellos _________ (pagar)
5. Ellos _________ (influir)
6. Ellos ________ (explicar)
7. Ellos _________ (destrozar)
8. Ellos _________ (caminar)
9. Ellos _________ (temer)
10. Ellos _________ (reír)
11. Ellos _________ (reducir)
12. Ellos _________ (producir)
13. Ellos _________ (llegar)
14. Ellos _________ (fabricar)
15. Ellos _________ (decidir)
16. Ellos _________ (cruzar)

Exercise 26. Complete the following sentences using the imperfect subjunctive.

1. Era importante que Lucía_________ (incluir) a Jorge en la lista de invitados.
2. El director nos dijo que mejor nos_________ (retirar) del comité.
3. No me entenderías aunque te _________ (repetir) mil veces lo mismo.
4. Salomé dijo que compraría este vestido cuando le _________ (ellos pagar) su sueldo.
5. No creo que su madre _________ (influir) en su decisión de casarse.
6. Quisiera que me ________ (explicar/tú) este ejercicio.
7. Aunque me _________ (destrozar) el corazón, te seguiría queriendo.
8. Omar prometió que cuando _________ (caminar) de nuevo aprendería a esquiar.
9. Era increíble que Juan, siendo tan valiente, _________ (temer) a un simple ratoncito.
10. Me dijo que no me _________ (reír) de su peinado.
11. Era normal que el banco _________ (reducir) las tasas de interés.
12. Fue un milagro que no se _________ (producirse) un accidente peor.
13. ¡Te dije que _________ (llegar) temprano!
14. Jorge nos pidió que _________ (fabricar) una máquina fotográfica como las antiguas.
15. Era necesario que Carmen _________ (decidir) con quién se iba a casar.
16. Los autos se detuvieron para que la anciana_________ (cruzar) la calle.

B. USES OF THE IMPERFECT SUBJUNCTIVE

The imperfect subjunctive is used following the same rules used in the present subjunctive, but with the difference that the action referred to is in **the past.**

THE IMPERFECT SUBJUNCTIVE IN SUBORDINATED NOUN CLAUSES

- In sentences that express **influence** or **desire.**

Example

Necesitaba que **llegaras** pronto pero no apareciste.
I needed you to come quickly but you didn't show up.

Exercise 27. You are going camping with a couple of friends. On the day you are leaving, you find out that your friends did not do what they were supposed to. Express your disappointment using the imperfect subjunctive. Use verbs and expressions of influence or desire.

Example

comprar los víveres
Era importante que ustedes compraran los víveres.

1. preparar la tienda de campaña

   ____

2. conseguir combustible para la estufa portátil

   ____

3. traer un botiquín

   ____

4. hacer un mapa del recorrido

   ____

5. averiguar cómo llegar al sitio del campamento

   ____

6. comprar repelente de insectos

   ____

Exercise 28. Put the following text in the subjunctive according to the example.

Me parece que mi casa es un poco pequeña.	*Yo quería que fuera más grande...*
no tiene suficiente luz.	que ______________________ .
Me parece que la cocina no es moderna,	Yo quería que ______________________.
y el color de las paredes es triste.	y ______________________.
Además, no tiene clósets para guardar la ropa.	Además yo quería que ______________________ .
Tampoco hay restaurantes cerca.	y que ______________________ .

- In sentences that express **doubt**.

Example

Juan no creía que María **llegara** temprano a casa.
Juan did not believe that María would come home early.

Exercise 29. Use the following words to make sentences in the imperfect subjunctive. Use verbs and expressions of doubt.

Example

Pedro / dudar/ haber guerra
Pedro dudaba que hubiera guerra.

1. Nosotros / no pensar / tú / venir
____
2. Los ingenieros / no creer / el terreno / hundirse
____
3. La policía / dudar / producirse / un nuevo atentado
____
4. Mi madre / no estar segura / yo / venir / a ayudarla
____
5. El juez / no creer / el testigo / estar diciendo / la verdad
____
6. Quizás si nosotros / llevar / mucho dinero / poder / comprar anillo
____

- In sentences that express **emotion**.

Example

Él tenía miedo de que lo **mordieran** los perros.
He was afraid of being bitten by the dogs.

Exercise 30. Use the following words to make sentences in the imperfect subjunctive. Use verbs and expressions of emotion.

Example

ser terrible / haber / tanta contaminación.
Era terrible que hubiera tanta contaminación.

1. Marisela / temer / mojársele / el cabello
____
2. Yo / preocuparse / el dinero / perderse
____
3. ¡Qué miedo / haber / una avalancha!
____
4. Alegrarme / ir / juntos / a la fiesta
____
5. Me preocupar/ el gato/ no comer
____
6. La anciana / emocionarse / nosotros / venir / de visita
____

THE IMPERFECT SUBJUNCTIVE IN ADJECTIVAL CLAUSES OR RELATIVE CLAUSES

The imperfect subjunctive in relative clauses is used in the same way as explained on page 228.

Example

Necesitaba un profesor que **supiera** español
I needed a teacher who would know Spanish.

Conocí a un profesor que **sabía** español.
I met a teacher who knew Spanish.

Exercise 31. Imagine that last year you were looking for a car to buy. Write six sentences describing the car you were looking for.

Example

ser económico
Necesitaba un coche que fuera económico.

1. ser de color amarillo
____.
2. tener cuatro puertas
____.

3. marchar rápido

 ____.

4. frenar bien

 ____.

5. estar entre los diez mejores

 ____.

6. no ser muy costoso

 ____.

Exercise 32. Complete the following text using either the imperfect subjunctive or the imperfect indicative.

Carmen tenía un perro que ___________ (llamarse) Solovino y que ___________ (ladrar) mucho. Sus vecinos, que ___________ (ser) intolerantes, se quejaron. Carmen no quería regalar a Solovino. Ella pensó que necesitaba cambiarse de casa. Ella quería una casa que ___________ (estar) en el campo, que ___________ (tener) mucho espacio y que no ___________ (costar) mucho. Una mañana salió a buscar su casa ideal. Salió de la ciudad y en el camino a Veracruz vio una casa que ___________ (encontrarse) a la orilla de un lago, que ___________ (ser) muy bonita y que ___________ (parecer) deshabitada. Y lo mejor de todo era que en la entrada había un letrero que ___________ (decir): "Se vende barata".

THE IMPERFECT SUBJUNCTIVE IN ADVERBIAL CLAUSES

Read the explanation on adverbial subordinate clauses on pages 232–239 and follow the same rules.

Exercise 33. Complete the following sentences using the subjunctive or infinitive.

1. María dijo que nos iba a llevar al parque a menos de que __________ (llover).
2. Trabajé mucho para que los jefes no me __________ (despedir).
3. Te llevé a la playa con tal de que no __________ (molestar) más.
4. Los excursionistas salieron antes de que __________ (amanecer).
5. Cambié la cerradura a fin de que no __________ (poder) entrar nunca más.
6. Juan fue a la escuela de aviación para __________ (aprender) a volar.
7. No podrás ir a la boda sin __________ (ponerse) el traje que te compré.
8. Salimos a caminar antes de que __________ (oscurecer).

Exercise 34. Fill in the blanks with the past indicative tenses or the imperfect subjunctive.

1. Pedro no contestaba las cartas, a menos que________ (ser) de su madre.
2. Pintamos el exterior de la casa a fin de que ________ (conservarse) en buen estado.
3. La invitó a entrar para que no________ (mojarse) con la lluvia.
4. Los vendedores regalaban muestras del producto con tal de que lo ________. (probar/nosotros)
5. Quería llevarte adonde tú ________ (poder) comprar un vestido de novia.
6. Silvia dijo que iba a esperar hasta que Juan y José ________ (llegar).
7. Los músicos prometieron comenzar la serenata en cuanto________ (ser) las doce.
8. No podíamos dar marcha atrás a menos que ________ (nosotros/querer) reconocer nuestro error.
9. Pese a que ________ (nosotros/pagar) las deudas, nuestra reputación quedó arruinada.
10. La fotógrafa retrocedió unos pasos de modo que el sol no la ________. (deslumbrar)
11. El departamento de agricultura asesoró a los granjeros para que ________ (alternar) las cosechas.
12. Los gitanos iban de pueblo en pueblo, acampando en cualquier lugar donde________ (poder) pasar la noche.
13. Los niños le pidieron que comprara chocolates cuando ________ (ella/ir) a la tienda.
14. Revisamos todos los documentos de modo que ________ (cumplir) con todos los requisitos.
15. María se fue del país tan pronto como ________ (poder).

III. The Perfect Tenses of the Subjunctive

A. FORMATION OF THE PERFECT SUBJUNCTIVE TENSES

The perfect subjunctive tenses are formed with the present or imperfect subjunctive of the auxiliary verb **haber** and the past participle of the verb to be conjugated.

	Present Perfect	Past Perfect (-ra form)	Past Perfect (-se form)
yo	haya comido	hubiera comido	hubiese comido
tú	hayas comido	hubieras comido	hubieses comido
él, ella, usted	haya comido	hubiera comido	hubiese comido
nosotros/as	hayamos comido	hubiéramos comido	hubiésemos comido
vosotros/as	hayáis comido	hubierais comido	hubieseis comido
ellos, ellas, ustedes	hayan comido	hubieran comido	hubiesen comido

B. USES OF THE PRESENT PERFECT SUBJUNCTIVE

The present perfect subjunctive is used in a dependent clause that requires the subjunctive. When the verb in the main clause is in the present, present perfect, or future, the present perfect may be used in the subordinate clause when the action refers to a past action.

Example

No creo que María **haya pasado** el examen.
I don't believe María passed the exam.

Me ha dolido mucho que usted no **haya sido** capaz de llamarme.
It has hurt me very much that you have not called me.

No te imaginarás que te **haya creído** esa historia extraordinaria.
You could not have imagined that I would have believed that amazing story.

Exercise 35. Complete the following sentences using the present perfect subjunctive.

1. ¡No puedo creer que ________________ (tú/perder) tanto dinero!
2. Me preocupa mucho que papá ________________ (subir) tanto de peso.
3. Es imposible que no ________________ (nosotros/encontrar) ninguna huella.
4. ¿Cree usted que el centro comercial ________________ (cerrar) temprano?
5. No pienso que los espectadores ________________ (ver) el truco.
6. Cuando Beto y Daniel ________________ (demostrar) que son responsables, les enseñaremos a conducir.
7. No pensarás que ____________ (nosotros/gastar) nuestro dinero en ese aparato tan inútil.
8. Me ha parecido terrible que no le ____________ (tú/regalar) nada a tu esposa para el día de su cumpleaños.
9. Es una pena que Jorge ____________ (morir) en tales circunstancias.
10. Es increíble que muchos en las esferas altas de la sociedad ____________ (encubrir) a los culpables del desastre económico.

Exercise 36. Rewrite the following sentences as shown in the example.

Example

Es imposible que María llegue temprano.
Es imposible que María haya llegado temprano.

1. No creo que Luis te preste la motocicleta.

   ____.

2. ¡Es un milagro que Martín llegue sano y salvo!

   ____.

3. Es posible que la tía Magdalena venda su colección de sombreros.

   ____.

4. No se sabe si Nubia se vaya en el tren de las cuatro.

   ____.

5. ¡Qué bueno que consigamos todos los disfraces para la obra!

   ____.

6. No es cierto que me sienta solo.

   ____.

7. Espero que José separe la basura en orgánica e inorgánica.

   ____.

8. Es terrible que nosotros destruyamos el planeta.

   ____.

9. No creo que los niños pongan la mesa.

   ____.

10. Dudo que tu hermanito haga la tarea.

   ____.

Exercise 37. Rewrite the following sentences as shown in the example.

Example

No iremos a tu fiesta a menos de que **invites** a Paco.
No iremos a tu fiesta a menos de que hayas invitado a Paco.

1. En cuanto termine de trabajar, pasaremos por él para ir a la playa.

   ____.

2. Definitivamente voy a usar estos zapatos todos los días aunque cuesten mucho.

   ____.

3. Voy a hablarles después de que compren los boletos.

   ____.

4. Mañana iremos a la finca aunque llueva mucho.

   ____.

5. Estoy seguro de que me llamará por teléfono tan pronto como llegue al aeropuerto.

   ____.

6. La fiesta comenzará en cuanto resolvamos el problema con el equipo de sonido.

   ____.

C. USES OF THE PAST PERFECT SUBJUNCTIVE

The past perfect subjunctive is used in a dependent clause that requires the subjunctive. When the verb in the main clause is in the past tense (preterit, imperfect) or conditional and the verb of the subordinate clause refers to an action that was completed prior to that of the verb in the main clause, the past perfect subjunctive is used in the dependent clause.

Example

Era importante que todos hubiéramos ido a votar.
It was important that we all had gone to vote.

Todos te agradecieron que lo hubieras ayudado.
All of them thanked you for having helped him.

Todos habrían querido que no te hubieras aparecido a la reunión.
All of them would have wished that you had not showed up to the meeting.

Exercise 38. Complete the following sentences using the past perfect subjunctive.

1. Siento mucho que la carta no ____________ (llegar) a tiempo.
2. Nos alegró mucho que Julia ____________ (poder) viajar a Chile.
3. Me sorprendió que Jorge ____________ (resolver) aquel problema tan difícil.
4. Era increíble que la gata____________ (ponerse) tan gorda.
5. Era muy importante que tu padre ____________ (enviar) su carta a tiempo.
6. No era normal que nosotros ____________ (trabajar) tanto para nada.
7. Era improbable que esa empresa le ____________ (dar) el trabajo.
8. No me imaginaba que mi hijo ____________ (ser) capaz de hacer algo así.
9. Fue una lástima que esos insectos ____________ (destruir) mis plantas.
10. Todos dudamos que el testigo ____________ (decir) la verdad.

Exercise 39. Complete the following sentences using the past perfect subjunctive or perfect conditional.

1. Todos habríamos querido un coche que no nos ____________ (dejar) tirados en la autopista.
2. Mi padre habría trabajado con más gusto en una empresa que lo ____________ (apreciar) más.
3. Tu hermana habría preferido un trabajo en el que le ____________ (ellos/pagar) más.
4. Habría sido mejor para tu hijo que ____________ (estudiar) en una escuela pública.
5. A Julio le habría gustado un trabajo que le ____________ (ofrecer) mejores oportunidades.
6. En caso de que nos hubieran pagado a tiempo, ____________ (ir) al concierto.
7. Aunque hubieras invitado a Laura a la fiesta, ella no ____________ (ir) porque te odia.
8. Llamó a la policía pese a que su esposo no lo ____________ (permitir).
9. En toda su vida no tuvo a nadie que lo ____________ (querer).
10. Ana habría preferido unas vacaciones que no ____________ (ser) forzadas.
11. Aunque nos hubieras gritado en la cara, no te ____________ (nosotros/reconocer) con ese disfraz.
12. Habría seguido robando a menos de que la policía lo ____________ (poner) preso.

TIP BOX

Ojalá

It is possible to use either the present subjunctive, the imperfect subjunctive, or the present or past perfect subjunctive with the expression **ojalá**.

¡Ojalá llegue temprano!
God willing she will arrive early!

¡Ojalá llegara temprano!
Hopefully she would arrive early!

In the first sentence, we wish María to arrive on time and we are optimistic about the possibility. In the second case, we wish María to arrive on time but we doubt very much that she will.

We can also say:

Ojalá María haya llegado temprano.
God willing María will have arrived early.

¡Ojalá María hubiera llegado temprano.
Hopefully María would have arrived early.

In the first case, we do not know if María arrived early, but we hope she did. In the second case we know that María did not arrive on time and we regret it.

Exercise 40. Rewrite the following sentences using the past perfect subjunctive, as shown in the example.

Example

Ojalá María me llamara.
Ojalá María me hubiera llamado.

1. Ojalá tuviéramos suerte en el concurso.
 ______________________________.
2. Ojalá terminara de escribir el libro a tiempo.
 ______________________________.
3. Ojalá ganáramos el campeonato de fútbol.
 ______________________________.
4. Ojalá vinieras a mi graduación.
 ______________________________.
5. Ojalá nos escribieras.
 ______________________________.

11

Conditional Clauses

Conditional sentences in Spanish consist of a **si** clause (*If clause*) and a main clause. The main clause depends on the condition established by the **si** clause.

I. Factual Conditions

To express a factual or real condition we use mostly the following pattern:

Si + present indicative + future

Si no hay tráfico, llegaré temprano.
If there is no traffic, I will arrive early.

However, we may use the present tense or a command in the main clause and still express a sense of future.

Si no te acabas la sopa, no te daré postre.
If you don't finish your soup, I won't give you any dessert.

Example

Si te invito, ¿vienes?
If I invite you, will you come?

Si tienes demasiado trabajo, no vengas.
If you have too much work, don't come.

We may also express a factual or real condition in the past. In that case, we use the imperfect tense of indicative.

Example

Si no había tráfico, llegaba temprano.
Whenever there was no traffic, I used to arrive early.

Exercise 1. Connect the following sentences; make sure that they make sense.

1. Si come mucho,
2. Si no lo llamaba su novio,
3. Si no tengo nada que decir,
4. Si estoy haciendo fila,
5. Si mis compañeros hacen mucho ruido,
6. Si puedo,

a. siempre voy al trabajo caminando.
b. no abro la boca.
c. se engorda.
d. me aburro.
e. no me puedo concentrar.
f. se ponía a llorar

Exercise 2. Complete the following sentences using the appropriate form and tense of the verb.

1. Si podemos, _______________ (ir/nosotros) con ustedes al zoológico mañana.
2. Tendré éxito en la vida si me _______________(concentrarse/yo) un poco más.
3. Cuando era niña, lloraba si sus padres se _______________(burlarse) de ella.
4. Iremos al cine si ________ (venir/ustedes) por mí.
5. Te espero esta noche si ________ (salir/tú) del trabajo temprano.
6. Si me ________ (animarse/yo), participaré en el concurso.
7. Si estás enferma, mejor ________ (quedarse) en cama.
8. Si no vienen a trabajar les ________ (escribir/yo) un memorándum.
9. No vengas, si __________ (estar) ocupado.
10. Si (tú) __________ (poder), ven a las ocho de la noche.

Exercise 3. Make chain sentences, according to the example.
accidentarse ir al hospital no poder trabajar no tener dinero para las vacaciones no poder ir a Grecia aburrirse

Si conduces ebrio te accidentarás, si te accidentas ...

____

____

____

____

Exercise 4. Make a hypothesis for each drawing.

Example

ladrón/pasar/con el oro/caer/al vacío
Si el ladrón pasa con el oro, se caerá al vacío.

el niño/soltar/la copa/romperse

1. Si ______________________________.

la mujer/saltar/matarse

2. Si ______________________________.

el viejo/seguir/ mirando a la muchacha/ pegarse/contra el poste

3. Si ______________________________.

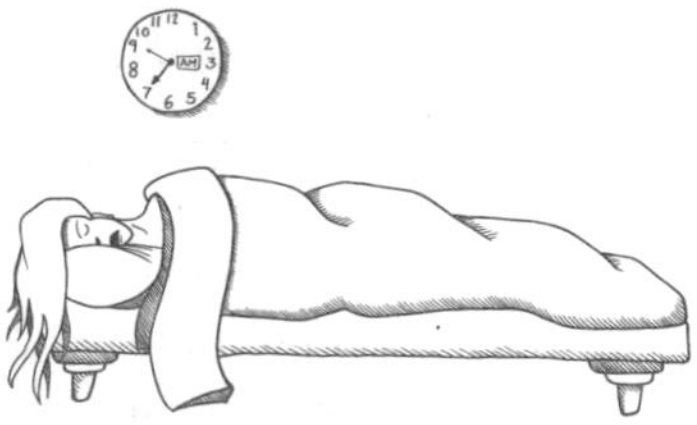

Julia/no /despertarse/pronto/llegar/ tarde al trabajo

4. Si ______________________________.

II. Nonfactual Conditions

A. UNREAL CONDITIONS IN PRESENT OR FUTURE

The **si** clause is also used to express an unreal condition in the present or future. In this case, the verb in the main clause is either in the conditional or perfect conditional and the verb in the **si** clause is in the imperfect subjunctive.

Examples

Si fuera rico, no trabajaría.
If I were rich, I would not work.

Si me amaras, no te habría abandonado.
If you loved me, I would not have left you.

¡Si tuviera dinero, comería como Dios manda!
(If I had money, I would eat like a king!)

Exercise 5. Complete the following sentences using the appropriate form and tense of the verb.

1. Si pudiera, te _______________ (comprar) el cielo.
2. Si tuvieras tiempo, _______________ (ir) a la fiesta.
3. Le _______________ (ayudar) si me lo pidiera.
4. Llamaría a Julia si _______________ (tener) su número de teléfono.
5. Te esperaría en la estación si me _______________ (decir) a qué horas llegas.
6. Si las encontráramos, las _______________ (saludar).
7. Si le pagaran lo suficiente, él _______________ (trabajar) más horas.
8. Si tú lo _______________ (intentar), lo _______________ (lograr).
9. Si te lo explicara, me _______________ (entender).
10. Si supieras lo que debes hacer, no _______________ (cometer) tantos errores.
11. ¡Qué objeto tenía correr, si cuando _________ (llegar/nosotros), sería demasiado tarde!
12. La máquina no se detendría si _________ (fabricar/nosotros) una fuente constante de energía.
13. Si Victoria _________ (decidir) aprender varios idiomas, podría hacerlo.

Exercise 6. According to the example answer the following sentences.

Example

Si volvieras a Nueva York, ¿dónde vivirías?
Si volviera a Nueva York, viviría en Manhattan.

1. Si invitaras a Carmen a comer, ¿dónde la llevarías? (a un restaurante elegante)
   ______________________________.
2. Si tuvieras dinero, ¿a dónde viajarías? (a Grecia)
   ______________________________.
3. Si hicieras una fiesta, ¿a quién invitarías? (a Carmen)
   ______________________________.
4. Si cambiaras de carro, ¿qué carro comprarías? (un Alfa Romeo)
   ______________________________.
5. Si fuera viernes, ¿qué harías? (ir a cine)
   ______________________________.

Exercise 7. Write sentences according to the example.

Example

(tú) cantar/mejor/ser/famoso
Si cantaras mejor serías famoso.

1. Memo/tener novia/no estar/triste
   ______________________________.
2. (nosotros)/consumir menos/vivir/mejor
   ______________________________.
3. Jorge y Ana/hablar/menos/(nosotros) los/invitar/a la reunión
   ______________________________.
4. Santiago/ser/más disciplinado/le /ir/mejor en la escuela
   ______________________________.
5. vosotros/poner/la casa/(nosotros) poder/hacer la fiesta
   ______________________________.
6. Teresa/comer/más/no/estar/tan flaca
   ______________________________.

7. ustedes/hacer/ejercicio/no/enfermarse/tanto

____.

8. yo/saber/conducir/no/depender/de ti

____.

9. (ellos) nos/regalar/los boletos/ir (nosotros)/al concierto

____.

10. Pedro/acostarse/temprano/no/estar/cansado/al otro día

____.

B. UNREAL CONDITIONS IN THE PAST

Si clauses are also used to express unreal conditions that have already occurred. In this case, the verb in the main clause uses either the conditional or perfect conditional and the **si** clause takes the past perfect subjunctive.

Example

Si hubieras bebido menos, no tendrías dolor de cabeza.
If you had drunk less, you would not have a headache.

Si hubieras terminado los deberes, habrías podido salir con tus amigos.
If you had finished your homework, you would have been able to go out with your friends.

Exercise 8. Complete the following sentences using the appropriate form and tense of the verb.

1. Si hubiéramos sabido que el museo estaba cerrado, no _______________ (venir).
2. Si se _______________ (detenerse) la tormenta, no se habrían inundado estos terrenos.
3. Si me hubiera casado más joven, _______________ (tener) más hijos.
4. Si Carlos hubiera visto el semáforo en rojo, no _______________ (tener) ese accidente.
5. Si mis padres no _____________ (llegar) temprano, habríamos podido hacer una fiesta.
6. Si me hubieras escuchado, no te _______________ (pasar) esa desgracia.
7. Si _______________ (estar) menos oscuro, no me habría tropezado.
8. Si el pastelero hubiera usado la receta, el pastel _____________ (quedar) más delicioso.
9. Si el gallo no hubiera cantado, no nos _______________ (despertar).
10. Si tu papá no _______________ (cargar) esa caja tan pesada, la espalda no se le habría maltratado.

Exercise 9. Answer the following sentences according to the example.

Example

necesitar/tú/dinero (ir a un cajero)
—Si hubieras necesitado dinero, ¿qué habrías hecho?
—Habría ido a un cajero.

1. tener/usted/una semana de vacaciones (ir a España)
   ______________________________________.
2. tener/yo/la oportunidad de escoger un coche (un Peugeot)
   ______________________________________.
3. perder/ustedes/el examen (retirarse de la universidad)
   ______________________________________.
4. Carmen/abandonarte/(ponerse a llorar)
   ______________________________________.
5. pasar/ustedes/el examen (entrar a la universidad)
   ______________________________________.
6. incendiarse/tu casa (llamar a los bomberos)
   ______________________________________.
7. tener que salir/tú/del país (irse a Italia)
   ______________________________________.
8. conocer/ustedes/a Einstein (pedirle un autógrafo)
   ______________________________________.
9. dar (a ti)/su teléfono (llamar [a ella])
   ______________________________________.
10. invitar (a mi)/(llevar un regalo [a ti])
   ______________________________________.

Exercise 10. Write sentences according to the example.

Example

Pilar/salir/temprano/no/llegar/ tarde
Si Pilar hubiera salido temprano, no habría llegado tarde

1. Claudia/no/salir/del país/no/conocer/a Federico
   ______________________________________.
2. ustedes/comprar/aquella casa/hoy/tener/un lugar donde vivir.
   ______________________________________.
3. la casa/tener/paneles solares/(nosotros)/la/comprar
   ______________________________________.

4. la gata/enfermarse/la/(tú)/llevar/al veterinario

¿____?

5. el volcán/hacer/erupción/la ciudad/cubrirse/de ceniza

____.

6. el piloto/no/reaccionar/tan diestramente/todos/morir/en el accidente

____.

7. la situación económica/no/empeorarse/no/haber/tantas protestas

____.

8. nosotros los humanos/no/tomar/conciencia/ecológica/la humanidad/extinguirse

____.

9. el planeta/no/calentarse/tanto/esas/islas/no/desaparecer

____.

10. los bomberos/llegar/a tiempo/la casa/no/quemarse.

____.

C. *COMO SI* CLAUSES

Como si or "as if" clauses are followed by the imperfect or past perfect subjunctive.

Example

Juanita le miró con complicidad, **como si le conociera** de toda la vida.
Juanita observed him with complicity as if she had known him all her life.

Fue **como si** Dios se **hubiera olvidado** de nosotros.
It was as if God had forgotten us.

TIP BOX

The order of the main and subordinate clause may be transposed in all **si** and **como si** clauses.

For example, it is correct to say:

Si tuviera dinero, viajaría por el mundo.
If I had money, I would travel the world.

or

Viajaría por el mundo, **si** tuviera dinero.
I would travel the world, if I had money.

Exercise 11. Complete the following sentences using the appropriate form of the imperfect subjunctive.

1. Me saludó con una sonrisa, como si me _______________ (conocer).
2. Caminó a pasos largos por el pasillo, como si _______________ (tener) prisa.
3. Miguel me miró como si yo _______________ (estar) loca.
4. Bailé toda la noche, como si aún _______________ (tener) veinte años.
5. Llovía como si _______________ (haberse/derretir) todas las nubes.
6. Los chiquillos nos miraban, como si _______________ (ser/nosotros) monstruos.
7. El perro arrastraba una de las patas, como si _______________ (estar) herido.
8. Pasaste por mi lado, como si no _______________ (existir).
9. Me acusas como si no me _______________ (conocer).
10. Nos despedimos, como si _______________ (ser) la última vez.

Exercise 12. According to the example below, answer the following questions.

Example

—¿Cómo reaccionó Lucía al verte? (nada/pasar)
—*Como si nada pasara.*

1. —¿Cómo reaccionó Lucía al verte? (no/conocerme)
   ____.
2. —¿Cómo encontraste al abuelo? (tener/quince años)
   ____.
3. —¿Cómo anduvo el coche? (ser/cohete)
   ____.
4. —¿Cómo se portaron los niños? (ser/unos ángeles)
   ____.
5. —¿Cómo habló el presidente? (estar/muerto de risa)
   ____.
6. —¿Cómo funcionó tu bote de vela? (ser/nuevo)
   ____.
7. —¿Cómo cantó Julieta? (tener/una papa en la boca)
   ____.
8. —¿Cómo bailó Carmen? (tener/una pata de palo)
   ____.
9. —¿Cómo te atendió el jefe? (ser/un/perro)
   ____.
10. —¿Cómo comieron los niños? (ser/marranos)
    ____.

Exercise 13. Complete the following sentences using the appropriate form of the past perfect subjunctive.

1. Puse todo mi empeño, como si _______________ (ser) mi última oportunidad.
2. El acusado bajó la cabeza, como si _______________ (saber) el veredicto.
3. Llovía como si _______________ (romperse) el cielo.
4. La mujer se estremeció como si _______________ (despertarse) de una pesadilla.
5. Julián se alegró mucho de su compañía, como si en toda su vida no _______________ (estar) siempre a su lado.
6. Julia regresó al otro día como si nada _______________ (pasar).
7. Jorge se veía como si _______________ (morirse).
8. Liliana sentía como si ella _______________ (descubrir) el gran secreto.
9. Óscar estaba muy cansado, como si _______________ (hacer) mil abdominales.
10. Todos se fueron en contra de él como si _______________ (decir) algo malo.

12

Commands

We conjugate verbs in the command or the imperative form when we are telling a person or a group of persons to accomplish a task. Commands in **usted**, **ustedes**, and **nosotros** form are conjugated using the present subjunctive. Informal commands (**tú** and **vosotros**) in negative sentences are conjugated in the present subjunctive as well. However, in the case of affirmative commands in **tú** and **vosotros** form, we use a different conjugation.

COMMANDS		
Cantar	**Affirmative Command**	**Negative Command**
yo	—	—
tú	canta	no cantes
usted	cante	no cante
nosotros	cantemos	no cantemos
vosotros	cantad	no cantéis
ellos	canten	no canten

= subjunctive

¡Come bien!
(Eat decently!)

¡No llores!
(Do not cry!)

¡Cállate! ¡No grites!
(Be quiet! Do not yell!)

¡No te rías!
(Do not laugh!)

¡No hables con la boca llena!
(Do not talk while eating!)

¡Siéntate bien!
(Sit down correctly!)

I. Formal Commands (*Usted, Ustedes*)

THE FORM OF FORMAL COMMANDS

Formal commands use the present subjunctive.*

caminar (*to walk*)	**responder** (*to answer*)	**ir** (*to go*)
camine (usted)	responda (usted)	vaya (usted)
caminen (ustedes)	respondan (ustedes)	vayan (ustedes)

TIP BOX

Note that reflexive and object pronouns are affixed to the endings of all commands in **affirmative sentences** only.

Example

No quiero verlo a usted más. **¡Váyase** de aquí!
I don't want to see you anymore. Leave!

No quiero perder ese trabajador. Por favor, ¡no **lo deje** ir!
I don't want to lose this worker. Please, don't let him go!

¡Dígaselo al jefe!
Tell it to the boss!

¡No **se lo diga** al jefe!
Don't tell that to the boss!

Exercise 1. Transform the following sentences to negative.

Example

¡Salga de ahí!
¡No salga de ahí!

1. ¡Cómpreles el juego! ____________________.
2. ¡Sea amable! ____________________.

*See Chapter 10, Regular and Irregular Formations of the Present Subjunctive.

3. ¡Dele todo a su hijo! ______________________.
4. ¡Tenga cuidado! ______________________.
5. ¡Guárdeme la ropa! ______________________.
6. ¡Pídale perdón! ______________________.
7. ¡Sírvale el desayuno! ______________________.
8. ¡Prepárenos café! ______________________.
9. ¡Súbanos la renta! ______________________.
10. ¡Apague la luz! ______________________.

Exercise 2. Answer the following questions according to the example.

Example

¿Envío la carta?
Sí, envíela. (or) *No, no la envíe.*

1. ¿Quiere que le empaque esta camisa? ______________________.
2. ¿Desea que la llame mañana? ______________________.
3. ¿Subo a ese autobús? ______________________.
4. ¿Podo todos estos árboles? ______________________.
5. ¿Quiere que le corte el cabello? ______________________.
6. ¿Lleno el tanque de la gasolina? ______________________.
7. ¿Digo la verdad? ______________________.
8. ¿Quiere que le cuente un secreto? ______________________.
9. ¿Apago las luces del corredor? ______________________.
10. ¿Me siento en esta silla? ______________________.

Exercise 3. Help write the instructions for submitting a short story to a local Spanish magazine. Use formal commands.

Example

(resumir el cuento) *Resuma el cuento.*

1. (escoger un título breve)

   ______________________.

2. (incluir el nombre del autor)

   ______________________.

3. (mencionar el tema del cuento)

____.

4. (hacer una lista de vocabulario nuevo)

____.

5. (enviar dibujos o fotografías que ilustren el cuento)

____.

6. (preparar tres originales en sobres diferentes)

____.

7. (poner los sobres al correo)

____.

8. (esperar con paciencia la respuesta del comité de publicación)

____.

II. Informal Commands (*Tú, Vosotros*)

THE FORM OF INFORMAL COMMANDS

Informal commands (**tú** and **vosotros**) are irregular in **affirmative** sentences. They do not take the subjunctive. In **negative** sentences, however, they use the present subjunctive.

a. AFFIRMATIVE SENTENCES

- **Tú** form

Affirmative **tú** commands are conjugated using the third person singular (**él**, **ella**, **usted**) of the present indicative; however, some verbs have an irregular form.

caminar (*to walk*)	**responder** (*to answer*)	**vivir** (*to live*)
camina (tú)	responde (tú)	vive (tú)

Irregular **tú** command verbs are:

Verb	**Irregular Form**	**Verb**	**Irregular Form**
venir *(to come)*	ven	decir *(to say)*	di
tener *(to have)*	ten	ir *(to go)*	ve
poner *(to put)*	pon	salir *(to go out)*	sal
hacer *(to do)*	haz	ser *(to be)*	sé

Example

¡Canta! (tú)
Sing!

¡**Ven** aquí!
Come here!

- **Vosotros** form

The informal command **vosotros** uses a special form that consists of the infinitive form of the verb, where the letter **r** is replaced by the letter **d**.

Example

(cantar)
¡Cantad! (vosotros)
Sing!

¡**Cantadle** una canción a Lucía! (vosotros)
Sing a song to Lucía!

(entregar)
¡**Entregad** aquello!
Bring that!

¡**Entregadle** la carta!
Bring him the letter!

b. NEGATIVE SENTENCES

- **Tú** form

In negative sentences, the informal **tú** command uses the second person singular (**tú**) of the present subjunctive.

Example

¡No vengas!
Don't come!

¡**No** le **entregues** las cartas!
Don't give the letters to him!

- **Vosotros** form

In negative sentences, the informal **vosotros** command takes the second person plural (**vosotros**) of the present subjunctive.

Example

¡No vengáis!
Don't come!

¡**No** le **entreguéis** las cartas!
Don't give the letters to him!

Exercise 4. Transform the following sentences to negative.

Example

¡Sal de ahí!
¡No salgas de ahí!

1. ¡Cómprales el juego! ______________________________.
2. ¡Sé amable! ______________________________.
3. ¡Dale todo a su hijo! ______________________________.
4. ¡Ten cuidado! ______________________________.
5. ¡Guárdame la ropa! ______________________________.
6. ¡Pídele perdón! ______________________________.
7. ¡Sírvele el desayuno! ______________________________.
8. ¡Prepáranos un café! ______________________________.
9. ¡Súbenos la renta! ______________________________.
10. ¡Apaga la luz! ______________________________.

Exercise 5. Answer the following sentences using informal commands.

Example

¿Cierro la puerta?
Sí, ciérrala. (or) *No, no la cierres.*

1. ¿Te presto algo de dinero?
   ______________________________.
2. ¿Mezclo la harina con el azúcar?
   ______________________________.
3. ¿Llamo por teléfono a Laura?
   ______________________________.
4. ¿Te busco a la salida del trabajo?
   ______________________________.
5. ¿Escribo esta carta?
   ______________________________.
6. ¿Te pago lo que te debo?
   ______________________________.
7. ¿Llevo las fotos de los niños?
   ______________________________.
8. ¿Anoto tu dirección?
   ______________________________.

9. ¿Preparo la cena esta noche?

   ____.

10. ¿Intento cruzar el río?

   ____.

Exercise 6. Miguel's mother needs to remind him of all the things he needs to help with at home. Fill in the blanks with the appropriate form of the verb, using informal commands.

Example

Miguel, ___________ los platos del desayuno. (lavar)
Miguel, lava los platos del desayuno.

1. ___________ a pasear al perro. (sacar)

①

2. ___________ tu ropa del piso. (levantar)

3. ___________ la cama antes de salir de casa. (tender)

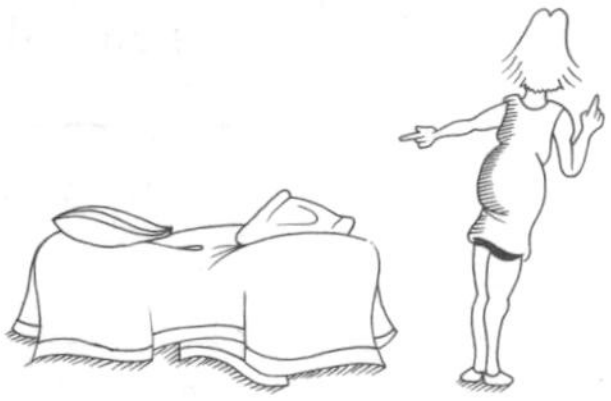

③

4. ___________ el periódico. (traer)

5. ___________ la alfombra de la sala. (aspirar)

⑤

6. ___________ a tu papá a cortar el césped. (ayudar)

7. ___________ las compras del auto. (sacar)

8. ___________ tus libros. (recoger)

⑥

9. ___________ gasolina al auto. (poner)

10. ___________ temprano esta noche. (llegar)

Exercise 7. Answer the following sentences as shown in the example below.

Example

Rewrite the following sentences using informal commands, negative commands, formal commands, and informal commands with **vosotros**, as shown in the example.

Example

Cuide las plantas del jardín.
Cuida las plantas del jardín.
No cuides las plantas del jardín.
Cuidad las plantas del jardín.
No cuidéis las plantas del jardín.

1. Juegue hasta que oscurezca.
   ________________________________.
   ________________________________.
   ________________________________.
   ________________________________.

2. Venga a almorzar con nosotros.
   ________________________________.
   ________________________________.
   ________________________________.
   ________________________________.

3. Sueñe con el futuro.
   ________________________________.
   ________________________________.
   ________________________________.
   ________________________________.

4. Compre pan.
   ________________________________.
   ________________________________.
   ________________________________.
   ________________________________.

5. Olvide los disgustos que hemos tenido.
   ________________________________.
   ________________________________.
   ________________________________.
   ________________________________.

6. Haga un diseño del mobiliario.
______________________.
______________________.
______________________.
______________________.

7. Diga sólo lo estrictamente necesario.
______________________.
______________________.
______________________.
______________________.

8. Coma todo lo que le sirvan.
______________________.
______________________.
______________________.
______________________.

9. Váyase de inmediato.
______________________.
______________________.
______________________.
______________________.

10. Entienda la gravedad de la situación.
______________________.
______________________.
______________________.
______________________.

Exercise 8. Use the words in parentheses to write negative commands.

Example

(arrancar las flores, tú)
No arranques las flores.

1. (cortarse el cabello, tú) ______________________.
2. (salir tan tarde, vosotros) ______________________.
3. (empujar, tú) ______________________.
4. (ser ingenuo, usted) ______________________.
5. (tocar esos cuadros, ustedes) ______________________.
6. (pensar en cosas tristes, vosotros) ______________________.
7. (olvidar tus promesas, tú) ______________________.
8. (cerrar los ojos, usted) ______________________.

III. The *Nosotros* Commands

When expressing a command using **nosotros**, the subjunctive is always used, with the exception of the verb **ir**.

Example

¡Juguemos! — *Let's play!*

¡No juguemos! — *Let's not play!*

The **nosotros** command for the verb **ir** is an exception; instead of using the subjunctive in affirmative sentences, we use the first person plural of the present indicative (**nosotros**).

Example

¡**Vamos** a comer!
Let's go eat!
¡**Vamos** al restaurante Los Girasoles!
Let's go to the restaurant Los Girasoles!
¡Buena idea! **¡Vámonos!**
Good idea! Let's go!
¡No, no **vayamos**!
No, let's not go!

TIP BOX

Note that reflexive and object pronouns are affixed to the endings of affirmative forms only. With affirmative commands, the final **s** of the verb form is dropped before adding the pronoun **nos**.

Example

¡**Vámonos** de aquí!
Let's get out of here!
¡**Hablémonos** mañana!
Let's talk to each other tomorrow!
¡No, nos **hablemos** mañana!
Let's not talk to each other tomorrow!

Exercise 9. Use the words in parentheses to write commands.

Example

(comprar leche, nosotros)
¡Compremos leche!

1. (comprar esa marca de jabón, nosotros)
______________________________________.
2. (ir a jugar al parque, nosotros)
______________________________________.
3. (no hablar de política, nosotros)
______________________________________.
4. (gritar, nosotros)
______________________________________.
5. (irse a la cafetería, nosotros)
______________________________________.
6. (mandar la carta a Julia, nosotros)
______________________________________.
7. (ir a bailar, nosotros)
______________________________________.
8. (no irse de aquí, nosotros)
______________________________________.
9. (no ir a cine, nosotros)
______________________________________.
10. (irse a la playa, nosotros)
______________________________________.

REVIEW

Exercise 10. Complete the following sentences, using the appropriate command.

1. Por favor ________________ (hablar/tú) más bajo que el bebé está durmiendo.
2. ________________ (venir/vosotros) pronto que el abuelo está solo.
3. ¡ ________________ (ir/nosotros) todos juntos a la fiesta!
4. ________________ (leer/vosotros) mucho en español, os ayudará mucho.
5. Por favor no ________________ (gritar/ustedes) que estamos en un hospital.
6. ¡ ________________ (poner/tú) las cosas en su lugar! ¡No las ________________ (dejar/tú) tiradas por ahí!
7. ¡ ________________ (correr/tú) que va a empezar a llover!
8. ________________ (sentarse/tú) a mi lado.
9. No ________________ (ir/nosotros) a la fiesta sin Laura.
10. ¡No le ________________ (hacer/tú) la tarea a tu hermano!

Exercise 11. Write a command for each of the following situations.

Example

Doctor a su paciente.
"Tomarse tres pastillas diarias después de cada comida."
–Tómese tres pastillas diarias después de cada comida.

1. La maestra a los alumnos
   "Hacer las tareas."
   – ________________________________

2. El padre a su hijo
   "Lavar el coche."
   – ________________________________

3. El sargento al soldado
   "Manejar el camión."
   – ________________________________

4. A nosotros
   "No ir a cine."
   – ________________________________

5. El padre a sus hijos
   "Portarse bien."
   – ________________________________

6. El novio a su novia
   "Venir a mi lado."
   — ____

7. Un amigo a su otro amigo
   "Correr más deprisa."
   — ____

8. La secretaria al presidente
   "Pagarse más."
   — ____

9. Un hermano a otro
   "Prestarse dinero."
   — ____

10. Un desconocido a otro
    "Cruzar a la derecha."
    — ____

Exercise 12. Transform the following recipe using formal commands.

Tortilla de papas
1¼ kilos de papas
1 decilitro de aceite de oliva
6 huevos
1 cebolla
Sal al gusto

Preparación
1. Picar la cebolla finamente.
2. Pelar las papas, lavarlas y cortarlas en rodajas muy delgadas.
3. Poner el aceite en una sartén.
4. Cuando esté caliente, echar la cebolla. Cocinar a fuego lento y, luego, echar las papas.
5. Añadirles sal y taparlas, moverlas de vez en cuando hasta que estén tiernas.
6. Sacarlas del aceite y dejarlas enfriar un poco.
7. Batir los huevos con un poco de sal y mezclar con las papas.
8. Poner todo de nuevo en la sartén.
9. Cuando la tortilla se cocine por un lado, darle la vuelta cuidadosamente.
10. Servir la tortilla en una fuente grande.

1. ____.
2. ____.
3. ____.
4. ____.
5. ____.
6. ____.
7. ____.
8. ____.
9. ____.
10. ____.

13

Affirmative, Negative, and Interrogative Sentences

I. Affirmative and Negative Sentences

To make a negative sentence, the word **no** is added to an affirmative sentence before the verbal expression.

Example

Marcos come carne.
Marcos eats meat.

Marcos **<u>no</u>** come carne
Marcos doesn't eat meat.

¿Me quiere?
(She loves me?)

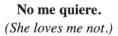

No me quiere.
(She loves me not.)

TIP BOX

Note that when answering a question negatively, the word **no** is used twice.

Example

—María, ¿Eres vegetariana?
"María, are you vegetarian?"

—<u>No, no</u> soy vegetariana.
"No, I am not a vegetarian."

The following are some common affirmative and negative words.

Affirmative Words		Negative Words	
alguien	*somebody*	nadie	*nobody*
algo	*something*	nada	*nothing*
algún (-o, -os, -a, -as)	*some, something*	ningún (-o, -os, -a, -as)	*no, no one, none, any*
alguna vez	*ever*	nunca, jamás	*never*
siempre	*always*	nunca, jamás	*never*
también	*also*	tampoco	*neither, not either*
todavía, aún	*still*	ya no	*no longer*
ya	*already*	todavía no	*not yet*
o	*or*	ni	*nor*
o...o	*either...or*	ni...ni	*neither...nor*

Example

—Alguna vez has preguntado: "¿Hay alguien ahí?" y te han respondido: "¡No, no hay nadie!"	*"Have you ever asked, 'Is anybody there?' and somebody answered, 'No, there isn't'?"*
—No, ¡nunca!	*"No. Never!"*
—¡Ah! A mi siempre me ocurre.	*"Oh! It always happens to me."*
—A mí, ¡ jamás!	*"It NEVER happens to me!"*
—Tal vez, algún día te ocurra a ti también algo parecido.	*"Maybe some day, something like that will happen to you."*
—Espero que nunca. Nadie se atrevería a hacerme un chiste como ese.	*"I hope not. Nobody would ever dare to play such a prank on me."*
—Yo tampoco creo que se deban hacer ese tipo de chistes, y nunca me imaginé que me ocurriera. De todas maneras no sé si fue una burla, o fue verdad.	*"I don't think it is right to play such pranks, and I never imagined that something like that would ever happen to me. In any case, I do not know if it was a joke or a true event."*
—¡No, hay nada que hable! Empiezo a creer que estás loco.	*"Things don't talk. I am beginning to think you are crazy."*
—Todavía no estoy loco, ni quiero estarlo, pero... algunas cosas hablan. Y siempre responden que no hay nadie.	*"I am not crazy yet, and I don't want to be, but... some things talk. And they always respond that there is nobody there."*
—No, ¡ jamás!	*"No. Never!"*
—¡Sí! Cuando hay alguien ahí que no quiere hablar contigo. ¡Ja! ¡Ja!	*"Of course! If that somebody doesn't want to talk to you!"*
—Me estás tomando del pelo, ¿no?	*"You are kidding, aren't you?"*

TIP BOX

Note that object pronouns always precede the verb in negative sentences.

Example

No le devolviste el libro a Juan.
You didn't bring the book back to Juan.

TIP BOX

When **nada**, **nadie**, or **ninguno** precedes the verb, there is no double negation.

Example

Nada le gusta.
He likes nothing.

Nadie lo quiere.
Nobody loves him.

Ningún amigo lo visita.
No friend visits him.

However, when **nada**, **nadie**, or **ninguno** follows the verb, there is double negation.

Example

No le gusta nada.
He doesn't like anything.

No lo quiere nadie.
Nobody loves him.

No lo visita ningún amigo.
No friend visits him.

Exercise 1. Complete the following, using negative words.

1. —¿Siempre haces los deberes tan pronto como llegas de la escuela?
   —No, yo __________ hago los deberes tan pronto como llego de la escuela.
2. —Alguien en tu casa sabe coser.
   —No, __________ sabe coser.
3. —¿Todavía compran en su casa la leche al repartidor?
   —No, __________ le compramos la leche al repartidor. La compramos en el super.
4. —¿Han ido alguna vez a Jamaica?
   —No, __________ hemos ido a Jamaica.

5. —¿Hay algunas cosas que te incomodan?
   —No, no hay __________.
6. —¿Conoces a alguien en esa empresa?
   —No, yo no conozco a __________.
7. —¿Quedan algunos días de vacaciones?
   —No, no queda __________.
8. —¿Hay algo típico para comer en ese restaurante?
   —No, no hay __________ típico.
9. —¿Te gusta el pollo o el pescado?
   —No, no me gusta el pollo __________ el pescado.
10. —¿Ya compraste el libro de gramática?
   —No, __________ no.

Exercise 2. Complete the following, using affirmative words.

1. —¿ __________ estás cansado?
   —No, ya no lo estoy. Dormí muy bien anoche.
2. —¿Hay __________ que te preocupa?
   —No, nada me preocupa.
3. —¿Crees que el coche tenga __________ problema?
   —No, no creo que tenga ningún problema.
4. —¿Quieres __________ de beber?
   —No, no quiero nada, gracias.
5. —Nunca sacas buenas notas.
   —No es verdad. __________ saco buenas notas.
6. —Jamás he comido erizos de mar.
   —__________ quisiera probarlos.
7. —¿Hay __________ en la oficina?
   —No, no hay nadie.
8. —¿Te gustaría ir a Chile __________ a España?
   —No, no me gustaría ir a Chile ni a España.
9. —¿Jorge también piensa ir a la fiesta?
   —No, ni yo __________.
10. —¿Siempre sientes dolor de cabeza después de comer?
   —No, __________.

Exercise 3. Complete the following sentences using negative and affirmative words.

1. —¿Haces algo esta tarde?
   —No, no hago _______.
2. —¿Comprendiste todo?
   —No, no comprendí _______.

3. —¿Vieron ustedes a alguien?
   —No había _______.
4. —¿Tienes algún amigo latinoamericano?
   —Sí, tengo _______.
5. —¿Todas tus amigas van a ir la fiesta?
   —No, no va _______.
6. —¿Hay algún problema?
   —No, no hay _______ problema.

Exercise 4. Complete the following dialogue using negative and affirmative words.

1. —¿Hay alguien en la oficina?
   —No, no hay ________.
2. —Hay algo horrible adentro.
   —Estás loco, si no hay ________.
3. —¿Siempre sientes miedo?
   —No, ________.
4. —¿Encontraste alguna pista en el lugar del crimen?
   —No, no encontré ________.
5. —¿Alguna vez has visto un extraterrestre?
   —No, ________.
6. —Sabes, voy a renunciar a mi cargo.
   —¿Sí?, yo ________.
7. —No me gusta mi jefe.
   —A mí ________, es un déspota.

II. Interrogative Sentences

The following are the interrogative words used most frequently in Spanish:

¿Cómo?	*How?*
¿Cuál(es)?	*Which (which ones)?*
¿Cuándo?	*When?*
¿Cuánto(o), (a)?	*How much?*
¿Cuánto(os), (as)?	*How many?*
¿Dónde?	*Where?*
¿Qué?	*What?*
¿Quién(es)?	*Who, whom?*

All interrogative words take a written accent when used to introduce an interrogative sentence, so they can be distinguished from other pronouns. A preposition may precede the interrogative word when needed.

Note that in interrogative sentences, when a stated subject is present, the subject follows either the verb or the complement of the verb.

Example

Notice that the underlined interrogatives all have accent marks.

En una tienda de animales
Cliente:—¿Cómo se llama ese perro y de dónde es?
Vendedor:—¿Cuál?
C:—El que tiene manchas.
V:—Pero si son todos casi idénticos. ¿Cuántas manchas tiene?
C:—El que tiene tres o cuatro manchas.
V:—Veamos, ¿dónde tiene las manchas?
C:—Una en la cola y las otras en las patas.
V:—¿En qué patas, las delanteras o las traseras?
C:—¿Cómo puedo saber si se mueven todo el tiempo?
V:—Entonces, explíqueme mejor. ¿Con quién está el perro? ¿Con ese de manchas chicas o grandes?

In a pet store
Customer: What is that dog's name and where is it from?
Salesman: Which one?
C: The one with the spots.
S: But they are almost identical! How many spots does it have?
C: The one with three or four spots.
S: Let's see... Where are the spots?
C: It has one on the tail and the other ones on the legs.
S: On which legs, the front or the rear?
C: How can I know, if they are moving all the time?
S: Then you should explain yourself better. Which other dog is it with? With the one with small spots or with the one with big spots?

C:—Está con el de manchas grandes y orejas caídas.
C: The one with big spots and droopy ears.

V:—¿Cuáles manchas, las redondas o las cuadradas?
S: Which spots? The round ones or the square ones?

C:—Las ovaladas.
C: The oval ones.

V:—Igual estos perros no vienen de ninguna parte, nacieron aquí y aún no tienen nombre. ¿Cuál quiere el señor?
S: Anyway, these dogs are not from any particular place. They were all born here and do not have a name. Which one do you want?

C:—No, ninguno, sólo preguntaba... Ese tiene cara de llamarse Pedro como yo.
C: None. I was just asking... That one looks like it could be a Pedro, just like me.

V:—¿Cuál?
S: Which one?

C:—¡El que tiene manchas!
C: The one with spots!

TIP BOX

It is important to note that **qué** and **cuél** followed by the verb **ser** are equivalent to *what* in English. In Spanish, **cuál** is used almost always as *what* with the verb **ser**, except when the verb **ser** is used in sentences that ask to characterize something, in which case **qué** is used instead.

Example

¿**Cuál** es el problema?
What's the problem?

¿**Qué** es la filosofía?
What is philosophy?

¿**Qué** es lo que te pasa?
What is wrong with you?

Exercise 5. Complete the following sentences using **qué** or **cuál(es)**.

1. ¿ _____ de estas dos camisas prefieres?
2. ¿ En _____ barrio de la ciudad vives?
3. ¿A _____ hora sales para el trabajo?
4. ¿De _____ es tu anillo? ¿De plata o platino?
5. David, ¿ _____ tienes en tu bolsillo?
6. Doctor, ¿ _____ es la solución a mi problema?
7. Doctor, ¿ _____ son los riesgos de beber alcohol?
8. José, ¿ _____ es la diferencia entre vivir en el campo o vivir en la ciudad?

9. Julia tengo hambre, ¿ _____ tienes en la nevera?
10. Laura, ¿ _____ ingredientes tiene una tortilla de patatas?
11. Liliana, ¿ _____ es tu hermana, la de ojos azules o la de ojos negros?
12. Profesor, ¿ _____ opina sobre la crisis económica?
13. Lucho, ¿ _____ es el avión más rápido del mundo?
14. Lucía, ¿ _____ de tus amigos sabe bailar?
15. Marta, ¿ _____ es tu hermano, médico o abogado?
16. Patricia, ¿ _____ es la mejor manera de enamorar a una mujer?
17. Profesor, ¿ _____ es un dromedario?
18. Santiago, ¿ _____ es tu color preferido?
19. Señorita, ¿ _____ síntomas tiene usted?
20. Tina, ¿ _____son los números telefónicos de tu oficina?

Exercise 6. Complete the following with the correct interrogative word.

1. —¿__________ fruta es esta?
   —Una guanábana.
2. —¿__________ es el día de la independencia de México?
   —El 16 de septiembre
3. —¿ __________ está la biblioteca?
   —En el centro de la ciudad.
4. —¿__________ es esa mujer tan simpática?
   —Es mi prima.
5. —¿__________ están tus abuelitos?
   —Muy bien, gracias.
6. —¿__________ son los dueños de ese negocio?
   —Los dueños son Santiago y Julieta.
7. —¿__________ es el cumpleaños de Natalia?
   —Es el 12 de enero.
8. —¿__________ está viviendo Jorge?
   —Está viviendo en Barcelona.
9. —¿__________ años tienes?
   —23 años.
10. —¿__________ es la capital de Chile?
   —Santiago de Chile.

14

Ser and *Estar*

The verb *to be* in Spanish corresponds (in most cases) to the verbs **ser** and **estar**. These two forms create some difficuties for English speakers.

I. Uses of *Ser*

The verb **ser** is used to denote the essential quality of something. **Ser** is always used to denote possession, origin, or the material from which something is made. It is also used to express time and when events take place.

¡Este hombre está loco!
(This man is being crazy!)

Example

Ese disco compacto es de mi hermana.
That compact disc belongs to my sister.

Don Quijote es de La Mancha.
Don Quixote comes from La Mancha.

El barco es de madera.
The ship is made of wood.

El concierto es a las siete de la noche.
The concert is at seven P.M.

¡Este hombre es loco!
(This man is crazy!)

TIP BOX

The verb **ser** is always used with a noun, a pronoun, or an infinitive.

Example

El esposo de Julia <u>es</u> arquitecto.
Julia's husband is an architect.

Ese coche azul <u>es</u> mío.
That blue car is mine.

Querer <u>es</u> poder.
Where there is a will there is a way.

Exercise 1. Complete the following sentences using the appropriate form of the verb **ser**.

Example

El periódico ________ de papel.
El periódico es de papel.

1. Adela ______ periodista.
2. Estas ______ las llaves de mi hermano.
3. La bicicleta _____ de metal.
4. Hoy _____ martes.
5. Esa pluma no _____ tuya.
6. ¿ _____ ustedes de Puerto Rico?
7. La conferencia _______ a las 7 de la tarde.
8. Francisco _______ pintor.
9. Maite y Lucas _______ de México.
10. Estas películas _______ de la filmoteca de la universidad.
11. La silla ______ de plástico.
12. La casa azul ______ de Lorena.

II. Uses of *Estar*

The basic function of **estar** is to denote position.

Example

María **está** en el trabajo.
María is at work.

Argentina **está** en América del Sur.
Argentina is in South America.

TIP BOX

Remember that the verb **estar** is also used to form the progressive tenses.

No me interrumpas, que **estoy** leyendo.
Don't interrupt me, I am reading.

Exercise 2. Complete the following sentences using the appropriate form of the verb **estar**.

Example

María _______ en la biblioteca.
María está en la biblioteca.

1. Tomás _____ en San Juan.
2. Carlos y yo _____ en la playa.
3. Ellos ______ viendo una obra de teatro.
4. ¿Qué _____ (tú) haciendo?
5. Julio _____ escribiendo unas postales.
6. Patricia no ______ en casa. Salió hace un rato.
7. Mario ______ escuchando música.
8. Luisa todavía _____ en la oficina.
9. Andrés y yo ______ buscando el museo.
10. La calculadora ______ en el cajón.
11. Margarita ______ esperando a que llegue el autobús.
12. ¿Sabes dónde ______ los libros que te presté?

III. *Ser* and *Estar* + Adjective

Both **ser** and **estar** may be used with an adjective. When denoting inherent, permanent qualities, **ser** is used. To describe temporary and changeable conditions, **estar** is used.

Example

Tatiana **es** muy alegre, pero hoy **está** muy triste porque su gato murió.
Tatiana is very happy, but today she is very sad because her cat died.

María Clara no **es** una mujer alegre, pero hoy **está** muy contenta.
María Clara is not generally a happy person, but today she is very happy.

Exercise 3. Complete the following sentences using the appropriate form of the verb **ser** or **estar**.

Example

La profesora _____ muy exigente con sus estudiantes.
La profesora es muy exigente con sus estudiantes.

1. El documental sobre El Salvador _____ fabuloso.
2. Carmen ______ alta.
3. Podemos cruzar. Este puente ______ seguro.
4. Martín y Maribel se casaron hace años y ______ muy felices juntos.
5. Las uvas ______ verdes.
6. Mi hermano ______ muy listo, por eso saca muy buenas notas.
7. Nosotros _______ aburridos porque llevamos treinta minutos esperando.
8. Las uvas _______ verdes, todavía no podemos comérnoslas.
9. Los niños _______ guapísimos hoy porque van a una fiesta de cumpleaños.
10. Romeo y Julieta _______ enamorados.
11. Podemos salir, ya ________ lista.
12. El gato ______ vivo.
13. Miguel _______ cansado porque trabajó mucho ayer.

REVIEW

Exercise 4. According to the illustration use the appropriate form of the verb **ser** or **estar** to describe each member of the family.

La madre	El padre	El adolescente	El bebé
1. *La madre está de mal humor.*	1. *El padre..*	1. *El adolescente...*	1. *El bebé...*
2. ______________	2. ______________	2. ______________	2. ______________
3. ______________	3. ______________	3. ______________	3. ______________
4. ______________	4. ______________	4. ______________	4. ______________
5. ______________	5. ______________	5. ______________	5. ______________

Exercise 5. Complete the following sentences using the appropriate form of the verb **ser** or **estar**.

1. Marco Antonio __________ de Lima y ahora __________ estudiando en Boston.
2. El profesor __________ furioso porque los estudiantes __________ muy groseros.
3. __________ lloviendo y Juan __________ todo mojado porque su chaqueta __________ de algodón.
4. La cita con el médico __________ en una semana. El médico __________ muy bueno.
5. Hoy __________ un poco cansados. El día ha __________ muy caluroso.
6. ¿Me podría traer otro café? Este café __________ frío y la taza no __________ muy limpia.
7. ¿Cómo __________ el novio de Julia? ¿__________ joven y guapo?
8. Roberto y Teresa __________ novios. Los dos __________ muy enamorados. La boda __________ en abril.
9. Mi tía __________ nerviosa porque su marido __________ cocinando.
10. ¿La casa de la esquina __________ la de tu hermana? ¿O __________ la que __________ al lado de la tuya?
11. Mi esposa __________ alemana. Siempre __________ hablando en alemán.
12. Tu esposo __________ un charlatán. ¡Siempre __________ haciendo alarde de que es muy rico!

13. ¿Qué hora __________? No sé. Mi reloj __________ en el baño.
14. Los niños __________ contentos porque su madre __________ de vacaciones.
15. Bernardo __________ celoso porque su novia __________ muy bonita y __________ de vacaciones en Brasil.

Exercise 6. Complete the following dialogue using the appropriate form of the verb **ser** or **estar**.

Alberto: —¡Hola! ¿Cómo te llamas?
Lola: —Me llamo Lola.
Alberto: —¿De dónde _________?
Lola: —_________ de España. ¿Y tú, cómo te llamas?
Alberto: —Yo me llamo Alberto y _________ argentino.
Lola: —¿Qué haces?
Alberto: —_________ matemático.
Lola: —¡_________ matemático!
Alberto: —Sí, la verdad es que _________ una profesión difícil pero divertida.
Lola: —Sabes, hoy _________ un poco aburrida. Te invito a una cerveza.
Alberto: —¡Genial! Vamos al bar "La Casita de Piedra", _________ buenísimo.
Lola: —¿Cuál? ¿El bar que _________ en la calle Bolívar?
Alberto: —Sí, _________ un bar tranquilo y además podemos oír tangos.
Lola: —¿Te gustan los tangos? _________ un poco pasado de moda, ¿no te parece?
Alberto: —Quizá. Y dime una cosa, ¿tú que haces?
Lola: —Yo _________ estudiante de administración de empresas.
Alberto: —¿Dónde estudias?
Lola: —En el Instituto de Negocios y Finanzas.
Alberto: —¿Dónde _________ ese instituto?
Lola: —_________ en la avenida Las Américas.
Alberto: —¡Ah! ¡Ya sé cuál _________! ¡Qué tal si vamos al bar!
Lola: —¡Vale! Vamos que me _________ muriendo de sed.

15

Special Constructions with Indirect Objects

In some Spanish and English verbs the action of the verb is received by an indirect object that is always a person or a personified object or a thing.

I. Nonreflexive Verbs

Example

Las serpientes me asustan.*
Snakes scare me.

Tu visita nos sorprendió.*
Your visit surprised us.

Le fastidia tu egoísmo.
Your selfishness annoys him (or *her*).

Lo siento, pero se me perdió la billetera.
(I am sorry, but I lost my wallet.)

*The verbs **asustarse** and **sorprenderse** are also used as reflexive verbs (when the subject of the verb and the pronoun correspond to the same person) and without an indirect object.

(Yo) <u>**Me**</u> asusto al ver serpientes. **(me = yo)**
I get scared when I see snakes.

(Nosotros) <u>**Nos**</u> sorprendimos con tu visita. **(nos = nosotros)**
We were surprised by your visit.

TIP BOX

However, in many cases this kind of verb does not function in the same way in English. In such cases the subject in the sentence in English becomes an indirect object in the Spanish sentence.

Example

Me gusta tu vestido.

In English we say *I like your dress*. We do not say *Your dress is pleasing to me*, which is the literal translation of the Spanish usage of the verb **gustar**.

Study the following verbs, comparing the English and Spanish versions.

agradar *(to please)*
Me agrada tu visita.
I am pleased by your visit.

alegrar *(to gladden)*
Me alegra que viniste.
I am glad you came.

apasionar *(to arouse passion, to love)*
A don Quijote le apasionaban los libros de caballería.
Don Quijote loved stories about knights.

apetecer *(to feel like)*
Me apetece una copa de vino con la comida.
I feel like having a glass of wine with my meal.

atraer *(to attract)*
Me atraen los coches deportivos.
I am attracted to sports cars.

bastar *(to be enough)*
Sólo me basta tu presencia para estar feliz.
Your mere presence is enough to make me happy.

caber *(to fit, to fill)*
Me cabrían más muebles en esta alcoba.
I could fit more furniture in this room.

convenir *(to be better for)*
Creo que me convendría mejor que vinieras en la tarde.
I think it would be better for me if you arrived in the afternoon.

corresponder *(to be responsibile for)*
A ti te corresponde lavar el baño esta semana.
*It is your responsibility [*or *turn] to clean the bathroom this week.*

costar *(to cost, to make an effort)*
Aquel abrigo me costó trescientos dólares.
That coat cost me 300 dollars.

encantar *(to please, to delight, to love)*
A Juanita le encantan los chocolates.
Juanita loves chocolates.

extrañar *(to be surprised)*
Me extraña mucho que no hayas venido a la fiesta.
I'm surprised that you didn't come to the party.

hacer falta *(to be lacking, to miss)*
A Andrea le hace falta mucho su hijo.
Andrea misses her son very much.

fascinar *(to like very much)*
Nos fascina ir a cine.
We like very much going to the movies.

fastidiar *(to annoy)*
A Rocío le fastidian los hombres.
Rocío finds men annoying.

gustar *(to be pleasing, to like)*
A nosotros nos gusta bailar salsa.
We like to dance salsa.

importar *(to matter)*
Me importa mucho que te alejes de mí.
It matters to me that you are distancing yourself from me.

interesar *(to interest)*
¿Os interesaría ir de compras?
Are you interested in going shopping?

molestar *(to be a nuisance, to bother)*
A Gabriel y Teresa les molesta el ruido.
Gabriel and Teresa are bothered by noise.

quedar *(to remain)*
A Julia le quedan un par de años para terminar sus estudios.
Julia has two more years remaining before finishing her studies.

sobrar *(to have left over, to be in excess)*
A Jacobo le sobra el dinero.
Jacob has money left over.

tocar (*to have to, to be responsible for*)
A muchas mujeres todavía les toca hacer la comida y los quehaceres de la casa.
Many women still have to [have the responsibility to] make meals and clean the house.

Exercise 1. Form sentences according to the example.

Example

Lucía/ gustar/ los tomates
A Lucía le gustan los tomates.

1. Pedro y José/corresponder/lavar la ropa
   ______________________________.
2. nosotros/convenir/no gastar tanto dinero
   ______________________________.
3. Daniel/tener/tanta hambre que/caber/un pollo entero
   ______________________________.
4. Jorge/extrañar/que María no haya vuelto
   ______________________________.
5. vosotros/bastar/una comida al día
   ______________________________.
6. ¿ti/apetecer/ una bebida?
   ______________________________.
7. yo/alegrar/que vengas pronto
   ______________________________.
8. ¿vosotros/atraer/ese hombre?
   ______________________________.
9. nosotros/agradar/tu visita
   ______________________________.
10. Pedro/apasionar/la literatura
    ______________________________.
11. nosotros/ese perro/costar/un ojo de la cara
    ______________________________.

Exercise 2. Complete the following sentences with the appropriate indirect object pronoun and form of the verb in the present tense.

1. A nosotros ___ ________ (encantar) tu cocina.
2. A Julia ___ ________ (hacer falta) un amigo simpático como yo.
3. A mi madre ___ ________ (fascinar) los pistachos.
4. Mañana a nosotros ___ ________ (tocar) limpiar la casa.

5. A Clara ___ ________ (sobrar) el dinero.
6. A Teresa y su marido ___ ________ (molestar) que tú los llames.
7. A vosotros ___ ________ (quedar) cinco minutos para terminar el examen.
8. A mí no ___ ________ (interesar) tu amistad.
9. A nosotros ___ ________ (importar) mucho el bienestar de todos.
10. A Santiago ___ ________ (gustar) ir a cine.
11. ¿A ti ___ ________ (fastidiar) estudiar gramática?

II. Reflexive Verbs

A similar construction occurs in Spanish when an accidental action occurs, such as losing one's keys or dropping one's eyeglasses. The following reflexive verbs are the most commonly used.

caerse (*to drop*)
Se me cayeron las gafas.
I dropped my eyeglasses.

olvidarse (*to forget*)
Se me olvidaron los libros.
I forgot my books.

perderse (*to lose*)
A Juan, se le perdieron las llaves.
Juan lost his keys.

romperse (*to break*)
A Rebeca se le rompieron los huevos.
Rebecca broke the eggs.

quemarse (*to burn*)
¡Se me quemó el arroz!
I burned the rice!

Exercise 3. Look at the illustrations and describe what is happening.

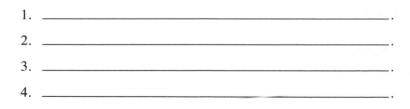

1. ____.
2. ____.
3. ____.
4. ____.

Exercise 4. Change the following according to the example.

Example

Ximena y yo quemamos nuestra casa.
A Ximena y a mí se nos quemó la casa.

1. Julio perdió su perro.
   ______________________________.
2. Pablo y Marcela perdieron su anillo de matrimonio.
   ______________________________.
3. Andrea rompió los platos.
   ______________________________.
4. Santiago dejó caer el armario.
   ______________________________.
5. Vosotros perdisteis las llaves del carro.
   ______________________________.
6. Clemente y yo olvidamos los pasaportes en la casa.
   ______________________________.
7. Federico quemó las tostadas del desayuno.
   ______________________________.
8. Teresa rompió el florero.
   ______________________________.
9. Ellos perdieron la maleta en el aeropuerto.
   ______________________________.
10. El niño dejó caer la pelota.
    ______________________________.

Exercise 5. Answer the following questions according to the example.

Example

¿Quién rompió la copa? (yo)
A mí se me rompió.

1. ¿Quién dejo caer el vaso? (Juan)
   ______________________________.
2. ¿Quién quemó la carne? (tú)
   ______________________________.

3. ¿Quién rompió los platos? (nosotros)

_______________________________________.

4. ¿Quién perdió las llaves? (vosotros)

_______________________________________.

5. ¿Quién olvidó los libros? (ellos)

_______________________________________.

6. ¿Quién quemó la casa? (yo)

_______________________________________.

7. ¿Quién olvidó el dinero? (nosotros)

_______________________________________.

8. ¿Quién perdió la billetera? (Pedro)

_______________________________________.

9. ¿Quién olvidó pagar las cuentas? (ustedes)

_______________________________________.

10. ¿Quién dejo caer el niño? (Lucía)

_______________________________________.

Exercise 6. Form sentences in the preterit according to the example.

Example

Marta / perderse / las llaves
A Marta se le perdieron las llaves.

1. El futbolista / romperse / la pierna

_______________________________________.

2. Yo / perderse / el cuaderno

_______________________________________.

3. Fernando / ensuciarse / la camisa

_______________________________________.

4. Nosotros / dañarse / el coche

_______________________________________.

5. Nicolás / olvidarse / hacer la tarea

_______________________________________.

6. Alina / romperse / el zapato

_______________________________________.

7. los niños / acabarse / los dulces

_______________________________________.

8. yo / caerse / los platos

____.

9. yo / perderse / tu número de teléfono

____.

10. nosotros / quemarse / la comida

____.

Exercise 7. Translate to Spanish, according to the example.

Example

I forgot my wallet at home.
Se me olvidó mi billetera en casa.

1. I dropped my glass.

____.

2. José broke his arm.

____.

3. We ran out of water.

____.

5. My mother forgot her keys inside the car.

____.

5. Susana burned the rice.

____.

6. We ran out of time.

____.

7. I lost my keys.

____.

8. Julia dropped the bottle.

____.

9. Your sister broke the eggs.

____.

10. Lucía forgot her books at school.

____.

16

Special Verbs and Verb Expressions

The following verbs and verb expressions have peculiar uses in Spanish, which is why it is necessary to study them carefully.

TIP BOX

In Spanish, many expressions are formed by combining two verbs. When this occurs, the first verb is conjugated, while the second verb remains in the infinitive form.

I. *Acabar*

The Spanish verb **acabar** usually means *to finish*; however, if the verb is followed by the preposition **de**, the meaning changes to *to have just*. Finally, if the verb is followed by the preposition **por**, the meaning changes to *to end up*.

- **Acabar** *(to finish)*

  Él **acabó** todo el helado.
  He finished all of the ice cream.

- **Acabar de + infinitive** (*to have just*)

  Acabo de llamar al teatro y me dicen que las entradas están agotadas.
  I have just called the theater and they told me the tickets are sold out.

- **Acabar por + infinitive** (*to end up*)

  Finalmente el policía **acabó por** creer en mi inocencia.
  The police finally ended up believing in my innocence

TIP BOX

Remember that a verb after a preposition is always in the infinitive.

Exercise 1. Complete the following sentences with the appropriate form of the verb **acabar**, **acabar de**, or **acabar por**.

1. Manuel __________ comer y se fue a jugar.
2. ¡Mamá! Ya __________ los deberes. ¿Puedo ver televisión?
3. Aunque Roberto no es simpático __________ invitarlo a la fiesta.
4. ¡Qué mala suerte! Se nos __________ la gasolina.
5. Todos en la clase __________ el ejercicio al mismo tiempo.
6. Mis padres __________ comprar un apartamento.
7. Lucía __________ volver de España
8. Se nos __________ la leche.

II. *Acordarse de*

The verb expression **acordarse de** is equivalent to the verb **recordar**, which means *to remember*.

Example

Anoche me **acordé de** nuestro viaje a Tulúm.
Last night I remembered our trip to Tulúm.

Anoche te **recordé**.
Last night I remembered you.

Exercise 2. Transform the following sentences using the verb expression **acordarse de**.

Example

Ayer te recordé.
Ayer me acordé de ti.

1. Siempre recordaré aquellos años dichosos.

   ____.
2. El abuelo no recuerda nada; ha perdido la memoria.

   ____.

3. Las tortugas recuerdan el lugar donde nacieron durante toda su vida.

   ____.

4. El niño no recordó que tenía que hacer los deberes.

   ____.

5. El otro día mientras comíamos te recordamos con alegría.

   ____.

III. *Ahorrar, Salvar*

The verb **ahorrar** (*to save*) means to save things, such as money or time, whereas **salvar** is used for *saving a life* or *surviving*.

Example

Tu padre **ahorra** mucho tiempo trabajando en casa.
Your father saves a lot of time by working at home.

El dodo no se **salvó** de la extinción.
The dodo bird did not survive extinction.

Exercise 3. Complete the following sentences with the appropriate form of the verb **ahorrar** or **salvar**.

1. Los ecologistas ____________ energía.
2. ¡Gracias! Me ____________ (tú) la vida.
3. El año pasado ____________ (nosotros) tres mil dólares.
4. Como no ganamos mucho no ____________ nada.
5. ¡Hay que ____________ las ballenas! Están en vía de extinción.

IV. *Andar, Ir, Irse*

The verb **andar** means *to walk* and *to go* when referring to walking or going without a specific destination. It also has the meaning of *running* when referring to nonanimated things (a car, a refrigerator). When talking about going to a specific destination, the verb **ir** is used instead. **Irse**, the pronominal form of the verb **ir,** means *to go away.*

Example

Ayer **anduvimos** por el parque.
Yesterday, we walked around the park.

Este coche **anda** muy bien.
This car runs well.

Anoche **fuimos** al teatro.
Last night we went to the theater.

Liliana se **fue** de la casa.
Liliana left home.

Exercise 4. Complete the following sentences with the appropriate form and tense of the verb **andar**, **ir**, or **irse**.

1. Los exploradores ____________ por aquí.
2. Mis padres ____________ a Roma el mes pasado.
3. ¿Por dónde ____________ los niños?
4. Este reloj no ____________ bien.
5. Esta mañana ____________ (ellos) por el bosque recogiendo setas.
6. ¡Es tarde! ¡____________! (nosotros)

V. *Bajar*

In Spanish the verb **bajar** corresponds to the English verbs *to lower, to go down, to descend,* and *to download.*

Example

Los intereses **han bajado** notablemente en los últimos meses.
Interest rates have gone down noticeably in the last months.

Vamos a **bajar** el piano lentamente.
Let's lower the piano very slowly!

Los buzos **bajaron** a las profundidades del océano.
The divers descended to the depths of the ocean.

Carlos **baja** muchos programas del internet.
Carlos downloads a lot of software from the internet.

Exercise 5. Complete the following sentences with the appropriate form of the verb **bajar**.

1. ¿Le ___________(tú) la temperatura al arroz, por favor?
2. Los estudiantes ____________las escaleras corriendo.
3. Por favor, ____________(ustedes) el volumen del radio.
4. Anoche, ___________(nosotros) varias fotos del internet.
5. Dante ____________ a las profundidades del infierno.

VI. *Convertirse en, Transformarse en*

In Spanish, the verbal expression **convertirse en** or **transformarse en** is used when a transformation is involved.

Example

Después de años de felicidad, su matrimonio se **convirtió en** un infierno.
After years of happiness, his marriage became a living hell.

Exercise 6. Complete the following sentences with either the appropriate form of the verb **convertirse en** or **transformarse en**.

1. Doctor, lo que pasa es que mi marido después de casarse ____________ en un monstruo.
2. Todas las noches sueño que (él) ____________ en un perro con tres cabezas.
3. Con el tiempo ____________ (yo, present perfect) en una mujer sin esperanzas.

VII. *Cuidar, Cuidarse*

The verb **cuidar** followed by the prepositions **a** or **de** means *to care for* or *to take care of*. The reflexive form **cuidarse** means *to take care of oneself,* while **cuidarse de** means *to be careful of.*

Example

La abuela **cuida a** los niños.
The grandmother takes care of the children.

Ella **cuida de** su apariencia.
She takes care of her appearance.

Gabriela trabaja mucho y no **se cuida** bien.
Gabriela works too much and she doesn't take care of herself.

Nosotros nos **cuidamos de** no enfermarnos.
We take care not to get sick. (or) We are careful not to get sick.

Exercise 7. Complete the following sentences with the appropriate form of the verb **cuidar** or **cuidarse**.

1. Jorge __________ de su salud.
2. ¡Fernando está loco! __________ su coche como si fuera su hijo.
3. Lucía __________ a su tía que está enferma.
4. Federico y Roberta comen mucho y no hacen ejercicio; parece que no se __________.

VIII. *Dar*

The verb **dar**, *to give,* is used in numerous expressions.

- **Dar un paseo** (*to take a walk*)

Los niños **dieron un paseo** por el parque.
The children took a walk in the park.

- **Dar las gracias** (*to give thanks*)

  ¿Le **diste las gracias**?
  Did you thank him?

- **Darse cuenta** (*to realize something*)

  Cuando llegué a casa me **di cuenta** que había perdido las llaves.
  When I arrived home, I realized I had lost my keys.

- **Dar la bienvenida** (*to welcome someone*)

  Le **dimos la bienvenida** cuando llegó.
  We welcomed him when he arrived.

- **Dar de comer** (*to feed*)

  La madre le **da de comer** a su hijo.
  The mother feeds her son.

- **Dar un examen** (*to give an exam*)

  El profesor **dio el examen** final de español en la tarde.
  The professor gave the Spanish final exam in the afternoon.

- **Darse + noun** (impersonal sentences) (*to make + noun*)

  Me da envidia.
  He makes me jealous.

  Me dan celos.
  It makes me jealous.

  Me da hambre.
  It makes me hungry.

  Me da pena.
  It makes me feel sorry.

  Me da tristeza.
  It makes me feel sad.

  Me da rabia.
  It makes me angry.

- **Dar la gana** (*to want to*)

  ¡Hago lo que quiero porque me **da la gana**!
  I do whatever I want because I want to!

Exercise 8. Complete the following sentences with the appropriate form of the verb **dar**.

1. Me________ pena pedirle su bicicleta prestada.
2. Él se fue porque le_________ susto ver a su madre.
3. Nosotros le ___________ la mejor educación a nuestros hijos.
4. Nos ___________ mucha pena no asistir a tu comida anoche.
5. No vinieron porque no les _________ la gana, ya que hubieran podido llegar un poco tarde.
6. Es que a Ana le ________ envidia de Victoria.
7. No te puedo ver porque a mi esposo le _____ celos desde la última vez que salimos juntos.
8. Cuando veo esa sopa me________ más hambre.
9. A los hijos les __________ rabia cuando sus padres les prohiben algo.

IX. *Dejar, Dejar de*

The verb **dejar** means *to leave*. When **dejar** is followed by the preposition **de**, it means *to stop doing something*.

Example

Francisco **dejó** las llaves del carro adentro.
Francisco left his car keys inside.

Por favor **deje de** fastidiarme.
Please stop bothering me.

TIP BOX

The verb **salir** means also to leave, specifically *to go out* or *to go away from* or *toward* a place.

Example

¿A qué hora **sales** del trabajo?
What time do you leave from work?

¡No me digas! ¿**Sales** para Madrid?
No kidding! Are you leaving for Madrid?

Exercise 9. Complete the following dialogue with the appropriate form of the verb **dejar** or **dejar de**.

—He ____________ quererte porque eres muy grosero. Anoche por ejemplo me __________ esperando en la entrada del teatro mientras estacionaba el carro.
—Mi amor, ____________ pensar en tonterías y trata de componer las cosas.
—No querido, voy a __________ para siempre. ¡Yo también tengo dignidad!

X. *Echar de Menos, Extrañar, Hacer Falta*

The expressions **echar de menos**, **extrañar**, **hacer falta**, all mean *to miss*.

Example

Cuando viajo lejos **echo de menos** mi familia.
When travelling far away, I miss my family.

¿Acaso te **hago falta**?
Do you mean you miss me?

Sí, te **extraño** mucho.
Yes, I miss you a lot.

Exercise 10. Complete the following sentences with the appropriate form of the verb **echar de menos**, **extrañar**, or **hacer falta**.

1. No me __________ el clima de Lima.
2. No __________ a su familia, será porque no los quiere.
3. Yo, personalmente, lo que más __________ son las tardes soleadas en el patio de mis abuelos.
4. Nosotros __________ las tertulias en el Café argentino del barrio Palermo.
5. Desde que vivimos en Toledo __________ las autopistas.
6. Siempre __________ (yo) los cuentos de mi abuelo desde cuando él murió.
7. A quien más __________ (yo) es a nuestro hijo menor.
8. Lo único que __________ (ellos) es la comida de su país.

XI. *Hacer, Hacerse*

The verb **hacer** means *to do*, in Spanish, but it is also used to talk about the weather.

Example

Anoche **hicimos** toda la tarea de ciencia.
Last night we did all of our science homework.

Hoy **hace** sol.
Today is sunny.

Mañana **hará** buen tiempo.
Tomorrow there will be nice weather.

En el verano **hace** calor.
Summer is hot.

The pronominal form **hacerse** means *to become* or *to pretend*.

Example

Con el pasar de los años la vida **se hace** más difícil.
With the passing of years, life becomes more difficult.

Julio **se hace** el que no me ve.
Julio always pretends he doesn't see me.

TIP BOX

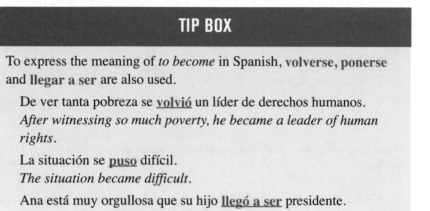

To express the meaning of *to become* in Spanish, **volverse, ponerse** and **llegar a ser** are also used.

De ver tanta pobreza se **volvió** un líder de derechos humanos.
After witnessing so much poverty, he became a leader of human rights.

La situación se **puso** difícil.
The situation became difficult.

Ana está muy orgullosa que su hijo **llegó a ser** presidente.
Ana is very proud that her son became President.

Exercise 11. Complete the following sentences with the appropriate form of the verbs **hacer**, **hacerse**, **ponerse**, **volverse**, **llegar a ser**.

1. Ayer, el gobierno ____________ lo imposible para obtener la mayoría de los votos.
2. Me gusta cuando ____________ calor.
3. Ojalá ____________ buen tiempo durante el fin de semana.
4. En el invierno ____________ mucho frío en Boston.
5. Una solución pacífica a la crisis política se ____________ cada día más difícil.
6. María se ____________ la muy interesante cada vez que hablo con ella.
7. Lucía se ____________ una falda preciosa ayer.
8. La situación se ____________ difícil.
9. Cuando seas grande ____________el mejor cantante de country.
10. Él siempre se _________ el que no sabe nada.
11. Nosotros _________ grandes amigos, si logramos superar nuestras diferencias.

XII. *Jugar, Tocar*

- The verb **jugar** (*to play*) is used to mean the playing of a sport or a game. The verb **tocar** (*to play*) is used to mean the playing of an instrument.

TIP BOX

The verb **tocar** means also *to touch, to ring, to take your turn,* and *to need to.*

El geólogo **toca** la superficie de la roca.
The geologist touched the surface of the rock.

¡Alguien **toca** el timbre!
Someone is ringing the doorbell!

Te **toca** jugar a ti.
It's your turn to play.

Me **toca** * trabajar mañana temprano.
I need to work tomorrow.

* See Chapter 15, Special Constructions with Indirect Objects.

Exercise 12. Complete the following sentences with the appropriate form of the verb **jugar** or **tocar**.

1. ¿Cuántas veces me _________ decirte las misma cosas?
2. ¿Quieres __________ baloncesto?
3. ¡Lo que me estás diciendo de mi familia no me _________ porque sé que no es cierto!
4. Él es el que mejor_________ la tambora.
5. Ella ________ mejor tenis que ping-pong.
6. Creo que les ________ irse a la cama porque mañana ___________ la final del campeonato.
7. A mí no me gusta _______ ajedrez.
8. A mí me _________ ir al trabajo todas las mañanas.
9. A ellos, lo que más les gusta es _________ la flauta.
10. ¡_________, te _________ a ti!

XIII. *Llevar, Llevarse*

The verb **llevar** means *to take, to carry* and *to wear*. In its reflexive form **llevarse** means *to take*.

Example

Abraham **llevа** a sus hijos todas las mañanas al colegio.
Abraham takes his sons every morning to school.

Estoy cansado de **llevar** la cruz.
I am tired of carrying the [proverbial] cross.

¡Cómo estás de guapa! ¡**Llevas** un vestido precioso!
How gorgeous you are! You are wearing a wonderful dress!

El ladrón se **llevó** la joyas.
The thief took the jewelry.

Exercise 13. Complete the following sentences with the appropriate form of the verbs **llevar**, **llevarse**.

1. El vendaval se ____________los techos de las viviendas.
2. Me gusta Aníbal cuando ____________ su camisa blanca.
3. ¿Me podrías_________ este sobre al correo?
4. Sólo Anita ________ nuestro noble apellido.
5 Los policías se ____________al reo a la estación y luego lo liberaron.
6. El Señor de los Anillos se _________las ovaciones del público.
7. Mis padres ________ treinta años casados.
8. Los vecinos nos __________ a la escuela porque a mi papá se le averió el coche.
9. Nosotros nos__________muy bien desde que nos divorciamos.

XIV. *Mover, Mudarse*

The verb **mover** means to move in the sense of changing the location of something, whereas **moverse** is used when the subject and the object that is moved are the same. However, to move from one place where you once lived to another, the verb **mudarse** is used instead.

Example

¡**<u>Mueve</u>** la silla!
Move the chair!

¡No cabemos aquí! ¡**<u>Muévete</u>** un poco!
We don't fit here! Move over a little bit!

El año pasado **<u>nos mudamos</u>** tres veces.
Last year we moved three times.

Exercise 14. Complete the following sentences with the appropriate form of the verb **mover** or **mudarse**.

1. Mi hermano se __________ con su novia a un nuevo apartamento.
2. Yo también quiero ver televisión. ¿Podrías _________ un poco?
3. La tropa se ____________ unos 1000 km. hacia atrás, evitando al enemigo.
4. Me enteré que compraron nueva casa. ¿Cuando se _________?
5. Pronto (nosotros) _________ a otro país.
6. Cuando me fui a sentar, alguien __________ la silla y por eso me fracturé la cadera.
7. ¿La tierra se ___________ alrededor del sol, pero también hacia el sol?
8. No te ____________ que te estoy poniendo alfileres, aun no acabo de medirte este vestido.

XV. *Pedir, Preguntar*

The verbs **pedir** and **preguntar** both mean *to ask*. When requesting someone to do something, or to order in a restaurant, the verb **pedir** is used. When requesting information, the verb **preguntar** is used instead.

Example

Julia me **pidió** que la acompañara a la fiesta.
Julia asked me to go with her to the party.

Pedimos una pizza enorme para todos.
We asked for a large pizza for all of us.

Pregúntale a Gabriel si tiene cerveza.
Ask Gabriel if he has any beer.

Exercise 15. Complete the following sentences with the appropriate form of the verb **pedir** or **preguntar**.

1. Te __________ que me des una explicación razonable de tu comportamiento.
2. Ustedes __________ demasiado y dan muy poco.
3. Ella me ___________ dónde había estado anoche y tuve que mentir.
4. Amalia le ______________ el divorcio a Joaquín.
5. Los sacerdotes no _________ nada, tú sólo vas y dices lo que quieres durante la confesión.
6. Te _______ que no me molestes más con tus preguntas.
7. Mis amigos _________ la cerveza y yo__________ la cuenta.
8. No me ____________ (ellos) nada de mi pasado.
9. No te ________ que me contaras toda tu vida, sólo por qué no estudiaste la lección.

XVI. *Perder, Perderse*

In Spanish the verb **perder** corresponds to the English verb *to lose*; however, in its pronominal form, **perderse** means *to get lost*.

Example

Perdí la paciencia contigo.
I lost my patience with you.

Ayer nos **perdimos** yendo a tu casa.
Yesterday, we got lost going to your home.

TIP BOX

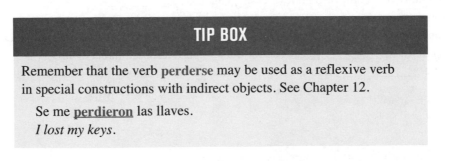

Remember that the verb **perderse** may be used as a reflexive verb in special constructions with indirect objects. See Chapter 12.

Se me **perdieron** las llaves.
I lost my keys.

Exercise 16. Complete the following sentences with the appropriate form of the verb **perder** or **perderse**.

1. Lucía __________ el sentido de la realidad.
2. Todos en el pueblo __________ todo a causa de la guerra.
3. ___________ todo lo que teníamos porque él apostaba en el casino y yo no lo sabía.
4. Rodrigo ___ ________ viniendo del trabajo.
5. Las ballenas ___ ________ cuando escuchan los sonares de los submarinos.
6. ___________ todo vuestro dinero en la bolsa.
7. Ayer José ________ la billetera y sus documentos de identificación.
8. A Andrea ___ ____ _________ las llaves.
9. Por perezoso _________ su carrera como actor.

XVII. *Prestar*

In Spanish, the verb **prestar** corresponds to the English verbs *to lend* and *to borrow*.

¡Devuélveme el libro que te **<u>presté</u>**!
Give me back the book I lent you!

Yo le pedí **<u>prestado</u>** el coche a María.
I asked to borrow Maria's car.

Exercise 17. Complete the following sentences with the appropriate form of the verb **prestar**.

1. No te voy a _____________mis colores, porque tú les partes la punta siempre que te los ___________.
2. ¿Me podrías __________ tu coche?
3. Si quieres yo te ___________ mi abrigo para la fiesta.
4. Toma mi maleta, yo te la _________.
5. ¿Tú crees que el banco me ___________ el dinero?

XVIII. *Poner*

The verb **poner** means *to put* or *to place*. In its pronominal form it may mean *to start, to wear,* and *to become*.

Example

Por favor, **<u>ponga</u>** música.
Please, put on some music.

El jefe los **<u>puso</u>** a todos en su sitio.
The boss put all of them in their place.

María se **<u>puso</u>** la chaqueta.
María put on her jacket.

Cuando Helena supo la noticia, se **<u>puso</u>** a llorar.
When Helena found out the news, she started to cry.

El jefe se **<u>puso</u>** furioso, pero a nosotros no nos importó.
The boss became angry but we didn't care.

TIP BOX

Remember that the verb **ponerse** may be used as a reflexive verb in special constructions with indirect objects. See Chapter 12.

Del susto, se me **pusieron** los pelos de punta.
I was so scared, my hair stood on end.

Exercise 18. Complete the following sentences with the appropriate form of the verb **poner** or **ponerse**.

1. No ___ __________ odioso porque te dejo hablando solo.
2. A Liliana ___ ___ __________ la piel roja cuando va a la playa.
3. Al oír sus palabras ___ __________ como una fiera y trató de morderlo.
4. ¡Te ves muy bien cuando ___ __________ el vestido rojo!
5. __________ en mi lugar y dime, tú, ¿qué harías?
6. Fue el fiscal Suárez quien logró __________ al gerente de la compañía en prisión.
7. No ___ __________ así, sólo te estoy diciendo que me voy por un año al Congo.
8. ¿__________ los sobres en el correo? Porque si no lo hiciste, ¡los __________ mañana a primera hora!
9. El perro ___ __________ a ladrar sin parar hasta el amanecer.

XIX. *Quedar, Quedarse*

The verb **quedar** means *to remain* or *to be located*. **Quedarse** means *to stay* but when followed by the preposition **en**, it means *to agree on something*.

- **Quedar** (*to remain*)

  ¿Cuánto tiempo **queda** para que termine la película?
  How much time remains [is left] for the movie to end?

- **Quedar** (*to be located*)

  ¿Dónde **queda** el teatro Colón?
  Where is Colón Theater located?

- **Quedar** (*to stay*)

  Es mejor que te **quedes** donde estás.
  It is better for you to stay where you are.

- **Quedar** (*to agree on something*)

  Sara y Felipe **quedaron** en ir juntos al cine.
  Sara and Felipe agreed to go together to the movies.

Exercise 19. Complete the following sentences with the appropriate form of the verb **quedar**, **quedar en**, or **quedarse**.

1. La estación de gasolina _________ a tres cuadras de aquí.
2. Fercho ___ _________ mudo cuando oyó la sentencia.
3. No olvides que _________ ___ pagar las bebidas.
4. ¡Este niñito no ___ _________ quieto un instante!
5. Hemos llegado tarde porque ___ _________ _________ dormidos.
6. La mujer del puerto ___ _________ esperando toda la vida y él nunca regresó.
7. No creo que ___ _________ a vivir en esta ciudad más de dos años.
8. ¡Mi amor! ¿Cuánto ___ _________ de dinero para este mes?
9. Todos _________ ___ encontrarnos en la puerta del teatro.

XX. *Saber, Conocer*

The verbs **saber** and **conocer** both mean *to know*. **Saber** is used when we need to know a fact, a reason, or something related to professional knowledge. **Conocer** is used for knowing things, persons, and places.

- **Saber** (*to know facts, reasons, or professional knowledge*)

  Juliana **sabe** hacer una paella deliciosa.
  Juliana knows how to make delicious paella.

  Fernando es físico y por eso **sabe** matemáticas.
  Fernando is a physicist, which is why he knows mathematics.

- **Conocer** (*to know things, persons, or places*)

  Tu padre **conoce** un libro interesante.
  Your father knows an interesting book.

  Sara **conoce** al presidente.
  Sara knows the president.

  Lucrecia no **conoce** España.
  Lucrecia doesn't know Spain.

TIP BOX

The verb *saber* means also *to taste*. **Saber** followed by the preposition **a** means *to taste like*.

Me fascinan los riñones al jerez. ¡**Saben** delicioso!
I love sherried kidneys. They taste delicious!

¡Este trago **sabe a** fruta!
This food tastes fruity!

Exercise 20. Complete the following sentences with either the verb **conocer** or the verb **saber**.

1. Samuel _________ Portugal pero no _________portugués.
2. Lo __________ desde que éramos niños y nunca he __________ quien es su padre.
3. Yo _________ a Stella pero no _____________ a su familia.
4. Ellos __________lo que quieren, por eso son tan amables contigo.
5. Toda la geografía que __________ sólo la __________ por los libros.
6. Vamos a __________ el nuevo restaurante marroquí. Parece que la comida ___________ delicioso.
7. Quisiera __________ las mezquitas de Sevilla.
8. Ese vino __________ ___ vinagre.
9. Perdóname, pero creo que no te ____________ a ti mismo.

XXI. *Servir, Servirse*

The verb **servir** means *to serve*, but it may also have other meanings, as follows.

- **Servir + para** (*to be useful*)

  Ese consejo no **sirve para** nada.
  That advice is not useful at all.

  No tires esa caja; me **sirve para** empacar mis cosas.
  Don't throw away that box; I can use it to pack my things.

- **Servir + de** (*to serve as*)

  Ese hombre le **sirve de** conductor.
  This man serves him as his chauffeur.

TIP BOX

Servirse de (pronominal form) (*to make use of*)

Él **se sirve de** sus empleados como si fueran esclavos.
He makes use of his employees as if they were slaves.

Exercise 21. Complete the following sentences with the appropriate form of the verb **servir de**, **servir para**, or **servirse de**.

1. Haz el favor y __________ el café que está sobre la estufa.
2. Angela ____ ________ _____ los demás para obtener siempre lo que quiere.
3. Esos muchachos no estudian y no trabajan, no ________ _____ nada.

4. ¡Regálame ese cuadro! Me ________ _____ adornar la sala.
5. Vosotros ____ ________ _____ vuestros procesadores de texto, sólo para escribir tonterías.
6. Todos los domingos los niños de la escuela ________ _____ ayudantes en la ceremonia de la iglesia.
7. Los meseros que ___________ en el restaurante Irlandés son muy informales, ¿no?
8. Me perdonas, pero esto que has escrito no ________ _____ el diario; tendrás que publicarlo en otra parte.
9. Tan caro este taladro y no ________ _____ nada.

XXII. *Tener, Tener que, Tener Lugar*

The verb **tener** (*to have*) is used in many expressions that in English translate to the expression *to be*.

tener hambre *to be hungry*	**tener fuerza** *to be strong*	**tener calor** *to be hot*	**tener cuidado** *to be careful*	**tener miedo** *to be scared*	**tener suerte** *to be lucky*
tener sed *to be thirsty*	**tener éxito** *to be successful*	**tener frío** *to be cold*	**tener sueño** *to be sleepy*	**tener razón** *to be right*	**tener ansias** *to be anxious*

- **Tener que** (*to have to*)

  Tienes que salir inmediatamente.
  You have to go immediately.

- **Tener lugar** (*to take place*)

  El concierto **tendrá lugar** en el teatro Real.
  The concert will take place at the Teatro Real.

- **Tener + age** (*age concepts*)

  Rocío **tiene** veinticinco años.
  Rocío is twenty-five years old.

Exercise 22. Complete the following sentences with the appropriate form of the verb **tener**.

1. Lucía, no ________ más de quince años. Es todavía una niña.
2. La ceremonia ______________ ______ en la capilla central de la universidad.
3. Mis padres ________________ veinte años de casados.
4. Creo que ese perro ___________ sólo dos años y es muy perezoso.
5. Seremos entonces cinco primos que __________ la misma edad.
6. Roberta __________ _____ salir de la oficina a las cinco si quiere llegar a tiempo al concierto.

REVIEW

①

②

③

④

Exercise 23. Make a sentence for each frame of the illustration above, telling what Lucía does during her vacation. Use the appropriate expressions studied in this chapter.

1. ______________________________

2. ______________________________

3. ______________________________

4. ______________________________

17

Comparatives and Superlatives

I. Comparisons of Inequality

a. To indicate the idea of **superiority** or the quality of ***more than***, the following structure is used in Spanish.

más	+	noun adjective adverb	+	que
verb	+	más	+	que

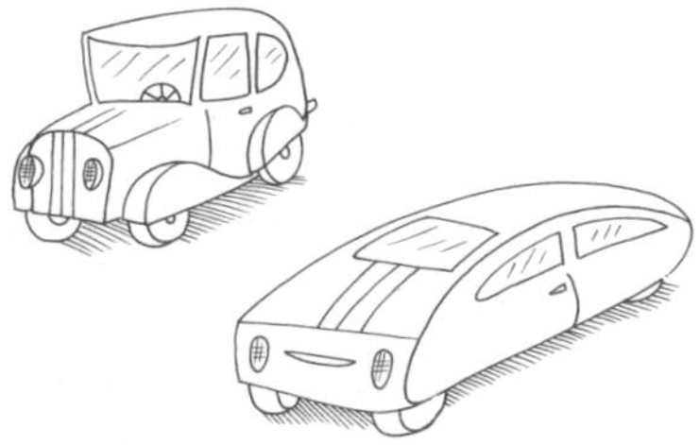

Example

David tiene **más dinero que** Sara.
David has more money than Sara.

Sara es **más amable que** David.
Sara is kinder than David.

Lucho corre **más rápidamente que** Luciano.
Lucho runs faster than Luciano.

Irene **habla más que** Teresa.
Irene talks more than Teresa.

Exercise 1. Complete the following exercises using comparatives of ***more than***.

1. Normalmente yo ________________________ (tener / tiempo) mi esposa para estar en casa porque yo ________________________ (regresar / temprano) ella. Mi mujer trabaja todo el día. Yo, sólo trabajo por las mañanas.
2. El vino ____________________ (ser / caro) la cerveza.
3. Mario ________________ (hacer deporte) yo, por eso él ________________ (estar delgado) yo.
4. Carlos ________________________ (hablar español / despacio) Sara, por eso le entiendo muy bien.
5. El nivel de vida de los países desarrollados ____________________(es/alto) el de los países subdesarrollados.
6. Las personas hoy día ____________________ (vivir/tiempo) las personas de antaño.
7. Federico es muy vanidoso, y ____________________(comprar/ropa) que su esposa.
8. Los franceses ____________________ (beber/vino) los americanos.
9. En el Caribe ____________________(hacer/calor) en Londres.
10. Ese coche ____________________ (andar/ rápido) esa moto.

b. To indicate the idea of **inferiority** or the quality of being ***less than***, the following structure is used in Spanish.

menos + { **noun** / **adjective** / **adverb** } + **que**

verb + **menos** + **que**

Example

Carlos tiene **menos hambre que** Lola.
Carlos is less hungry than Lola.

Liana es **menos apasionada que** Luisa.
Liana is less passionate than Luisa.

Lucía baila **menos bien que** Ana.
Lucía dances less well than Ana.

Irene **come menos que** Teresa.
Irene eats less than Teresa.

TIP BOX

Note that when **más** or **menos** is followed by a number, the preposition **de** is used instead of **que**.

Example

Hay **más de dos millones y medio** de argentinos sin trabajo.
There are more than two and a half million Argentineans without jobs.

In comparative sentences that are the result of a comparison of inequality, **de lo que** is used.

Example

Este examen es **más fácil de lo que** creía.
This exam is easier than I thought.

Esa camisa me costó **menos de lo que** me dijiste.
That shirt cost me less than what you told me.

Exercise 2. Complete the following exercises using comparatives of ***less than***.

1. Mi hermana Carmen ________________________ (ser / tímida) yo; por eso ella tiene muchos amigos.
2. Hoy estoy feliz porque ________________________ (tener / trabajo) yo pensaba.
3. La cena ________________________ (ser / cara) me dijiste.
4. Laura y Rosa ________________________ (ser / trabajador) Mónica. Ella siempre está en la oficina.
5. Roberto ________________________ (ser / divertido) Juan. Por eso yo prefiero salir con Juan los fines de semana.
6. José Alejandro ________________________ (tiene / entusiasmo) Lucía. Por eso, Lucía no quiere verlo más.
7. Carlos ________________________ (ser / amable) su esposa Carmen. Por eso, nos gusta más Carmen.
8. La vida ________________________ (ser / dura) uno se imagina.
9. Tomás ________________________(jugar / agresivamente al tenis) su hermano Luis.
10. Antes ________________________(haber / contaminación) ahora.

II. Comparisons of Equality or Sameness

a. To indicate the idea of ***equality or sameness***, the following structure is used in Spanish.

tan	+	**adjective** / **adverb**	+	**como**
tanto / **tanta** / **tantos** / **tantas**	+	**noun**	+	**como**
verb	+	**tanto**	+	**como**

Example

La nieve es **tan blanca como** el azúcar.
Snow is as white as sugar.

Caminas **tan lento como** una tortuga.
You walk as slowly as a turtle.

Hay **tantas realidades como** puntos de vista.
There are as many realities as there are points of view.

Carlos **duerme tanto como** tú.
Carlos sleeps as much as you do.

Exercise 3. Complete the following exercises using comparisons of equality.

1. Alberto y Marcos son hermanos gemelos y tienen muchas cosas en común. Por ejemplo, Carlos ______________________ (ser / alto) Marcos, y Marcos ______________________ (ser / activo) Carlos. Carlos ______________________ (comer) Marcos, así que los dos hermanos tienen más o menos el mismo peso.
2. ¿Tu hermano ____________________ (ser / guapo) tú?
3. Yo no ____________________ (dormir) tú. Para mí es suficiente dormir siete horas.
4. Julio es bilingüe y yo también. Él ____________________ (hablar / lenguas) yo.
5. Marta ____________________ (trabajar / horas) su hermano José.
6. Todos ellos ____________________ (tener / urgencia) nosotros. Lo mejor es que nos apuremos.
7. Aunque no lo creas, el cerdo ____________________ (tener / grasa) el pollo.
8. No te preocupes que todo va a salir bien. Yo ____________________ (tener / fe en que habrá paz) tú.
9. Liliana ____________________ (comer) Pilar. Por eso, ambas se entienden muy bien.
10. Jorge ____________________ (bailar / bien) Lola. Ambos han ganado varios concursos de baile.

III. Superlatives

a. To indicate the idea of ***comparison between persons or items***, the following structure is used in Spanish.

el / la / los / las } + **noun** + **más** + **adjective** + **de**

Example

María es **la mujer más alta de** todas sus amigas.
María is the tallest woman of all her friends.

Diego es **el niño más inteligente de** la clase.
Diego is the smartest child in the class.

Exercise 4. Complete the following exercises using superlatives.

1. Fabián dice que el café colombiano ________________________________ (ser / rico) del mundo.
2. Para María las playas del Caribe ________________________ (ser / divertido).
3. Este es el hotel ________________________ (elegante) de la ciudad.
4. Dicen que Tokio es la ciudad __________________ (caro) del mundo.
5. Las abuelas siempre piensan que sus nietos son ______________________ (inteligentes) del colegio.

IV. Irregular Comparatives and Superlatives

a. The following are ***irregular comparatives***.

mejor(es)	peor(es)	mayor(es)	menor(es)
better *best*	*worse* *worst*	*older* *higher*	*younger* *lower*

Example

Los españoles dicen que el vino español es **mejor** que el vino francés.
Spaniards say that wine from Spain is better than wine from France.

Sus ambiciones son **peores** de lo que me imaginaba.
His ambition is worse than what I had imagined.

Tus hermanas son **mayores** que tú.
Your sisters are older than you.

La abuela Laura es **menor** que su hermana Julieta.
Grandmother Laura is younger than her sister Julieta.

TIP BOX

Note that when these irregular comparatives are used, the words **más** and **menos** are omitted.

Also note that **mayor** and **menor** are used when comparing age and nouns that can be measured, such as speed, height, and weight.

Example

Aquel avión está a mayor altura que aquel otro.
This airplane is at a higher altitude than that other one.

El sonido tiene menor velocidad que la luz.
Sound is slower in speed than is light.

Exercise 5. Complete the following exercises using irregular comparatives.

1. Pedro es una persona muy orgullosa. Él siempre piensa que ________________ (ser / bueno) que los demás.
2. Este restaurante ________________ (ser / malo) el restaurante italiano que hay al lado de casa.
3. Mariela ____________________________ (ser / joven) que su esposo.
4. Mi prima Carmen ______________________ (ser / viejo) que yo.

b. The following are ***irregular superlatives***.

el, la, los, las mejor(es)	el, la, los, las peor(es)	el, la, los, las mayor(es)	el, la, los, las menor(es)
the best	*the worst*	*the oldest* *the highest*	*the youngest* *the lowest*

Example

La carne argentina es **la mejor** del mundo.
Argentinean meat is the best in the world.

Tus modales son **los peores** que he conocido.
Your manners are the worst I have ever seen.

José es **el mayor** de los hermanos.
José is the oldest of all the brothers.

Tu hija es **la menor** de la clase.
Your daughter is the youngest in the class.

Exercise 6. Complete the following exercises using irregular superlatives.

1. Este ________________________ (*ser / bueno*) restaurante de la ciudad. Lo recomiendan en todas las guías.
2. Diego ______________________________ (*ser / joven*) de sus hermanos.
3. El año pasado __________________________ (*tener / malo*) invierno en mucho tiempo.
4. Estoy pasando las__________________________ (*buenas*) vacaciones de mi vida.

V. The Suffix *-ísimo*

The suffix **-ísimo**, added to an adjective, intensifies the meaning of the adjective. It is more or less equivalent to **muy** or *very*. Note that **ísimo**-intensified adjectives agree in number and gender with the noun they qualify.

aburrido *bored*	aburridísimo *very bored*
bello *beautiful*	bellísimo *very beautiful*
bueno *good*	buenísimo *very good*
feo *ugly*	feísimo *very ugly*
guapo *handsome*	guapísimo *very handsome*
lindo *beautiful*	lindísimo *very beautiful*
pobre *poor*	pobrísimo *very poor*
rico *rich*	riquísimo *very rich*
simpático *nice*	simpatiquísimo *very nice*

Example

¡Esta comida está **buenísima**!
This meal is very good!

Ese perro es **feísimo**.
That dog is very ugly.

TIP BOX

Rules to add the suffix *-ísimo*

- For adjectives that end in vowels, drop the vowel and add a form of **-ísimo**.

Example

alto → **altísimo**
alta → **altísima**

- For adjectives that end in a consonant, simply add **-ísimo**.

Example

fácil → facilísimo
normal → normalísimo

- Adjectives that end in **-co** change the **c** to **qu** before adding **-ísimo**.

Example

loco → loquísimo
loca → loquísima

- Adjectives that end in **-go** change the **g** to **gu** before adding **-ísimo**.

Example

largo → larguísimo
larga → larguísima

- Adjectives that end in **-z+vowel** change the **z** to **c** before adding **-ísimo**.

Example

tenaz → tenacísimo
atroz → atrocísimo

Exercise 7. Complete the following exercises using the adjectives **bueno**, **malo**, **tarde**, **inteligente**, **interesante**, **difícil** with the suffix **-ísimo**.

1. Cristina tiene unas recetas ______________ para preparar el pavo.
2. La última vez que fui al cine vi una película excelente, pero la que vimos ayer fue ______________.
3. Esta mañana me levanté ______________ porque no oí el despertador.
4. Me gusta mi profesor de historia porque es ___________, y sus clases son ____________.
5. La clase de español es fácil, pero las de alemán son ______________.

REVIEW

Exercise 8. Answer using **más...que, menos...que, tan (to, tos, ta, tas)...como** as shown in the example below.

Example

Lisette trabaja 20 horas diarias, José 30 horas diarias.
Lisette trabaja menos que José.

1. Julio bebe tres cervezas, Lola bebe dos.
   ____.
2. Javier gana 2000 euros, Liliana gana 3000 euros.
   ____.
3. Susana duerme 8 horas, Santiago 8.
   ____.
4. Sebastián tiene muchos amigos, Marta no tiene ninguno.
   ____.
5. Jorge corre muy rápido, Susana también corre igual de rápido.
   ____.
6. La altura de Luna es 1,70 mts, la altura de Jorge es 1,70 mts.
   ____.

Exercise 9. Study the picture on the right. Write complete sentences using superlatives as shown in the example.

Example

Lola es la más alta de las tres.

1. Javier ______________________________. (pequeña)
2. María ______________________________. (pelo)
3. Javier ______________________________. (viejo)
4. Lola ______________________________. (joven)
5. María ______________________________.(vestida)

Exercise 10. Write complete sentences as shown in the example below.

Example

Alfredo es muy inteligente, pero Lucía *es más inteligente. Lucía es inteligentísima.*

1. Jorge es muy rico, pero Gabriel ______________________________.
2. Julio es muy amable, pero Santiago ______________________________.
3. Andrés es muy envidioso, pero Federico______________________________.
4. Melania es muy tacaña, pero Jonás ______________________________.
5. Andrea es muy dramática, pero Claudia ______________________________.
6. Sara es muy mala, pero María ______________________________.
7. Liliana es muy aburrida, pero Germán ______________________________.
8. Perión es muy valiente, pero Amadís ______________________________.
9. Mario es muy guapo, pero Gabriela ______________________________.
10. Kelly es muy nerviosa, pero Pedro ______________________________.

18 Prepositions

Prepositions are words used to show the relationship of one word to another in a sentence. Prepositions usually indicate location, direction, or time.

The prepositions are **a** (*to*); **ante** (*before, in the presence of*); **bajo** (*under*); **con** (*with*); **contra** (*against*); **de** (*of, from*); **desde** (*from, since*); **durante** (*during*); **en** (*in, on*); **entre** (*between, among*); **excepto** (*except*); **hacia** (*toward*); **hasta** (*until, up to*); **para** (*for*); **por** (*for, by, through*); **según** (*according to*); **sin** (*without*); **sobre** (*upon, on, above, around*); **tras** (*behind*).

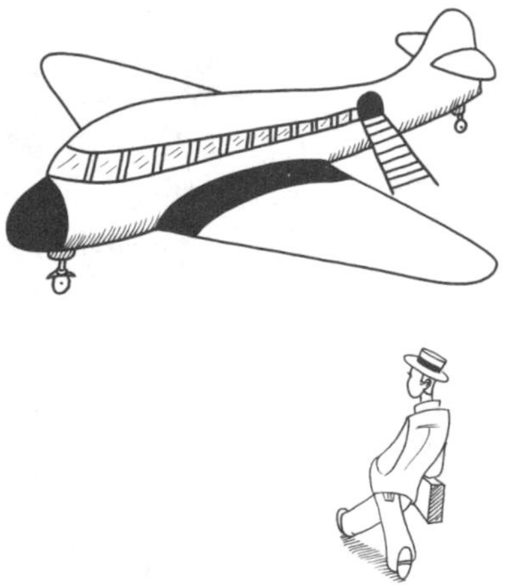

Viaja por avión.
(He travels by airplane.)

A. THE PREPOSITION *A*

Study the following sentences.

La familia Domínguez nos invitó **a** comer el domingo.
The Domínguez family invited us to eat over on Sunday.

¡Mi amor, ven **a** mis brazos!
My love, come in to my arms.

Llegaremos mañana **a** las once de la noche.
We will arrive at eleven P.M.

Esa alfombra es de Tabriz y está hecho **a** mano.
That carpet is from Tabriz, and it is handmade.

Trabaja para gozar.
(He works in order to enjoy life.)

TIP BOX

Remember that **al** is a Spanish contraction formed by the preposition **a** and the definite article **el**, and **del** is a contraction formed by the preposition **de** and the article **el**.

Example

Julia va al museo del Prado.
Julia goes to the Prado Museum.

Aquel juguete es del niño.
That toy belongs to that child.

TIP BOX

Note that in Spanish, **a** is used before a direct object that refers to human beings or personalized things.

Example

Tengo que llamar a Kelly.
I need to call Kelly.

¡Calla! ¡No llames a la muerte!
Shut up! Don't call on Death!

Exercise 1. Complete the following sentences with the preposition **a**, when required.

1. Anoche conocí ____ tu novio, ¡es muy guapo!
2. Mañana iré contigo ____ cenar, te lo prometo.
3. El otro día, me encontré ____ un anillo de oro en la calle.
4. Mi novia me invitó ____ Madrid.
5. Nos vemos ____ las ocho en el teatro.
6. Lucho me invitó ____ jugar billar.

B. THE PREPOSITION *DE*

- The preposition **de** is used to indicate possession.

Example

¿Te gustó la última novela **de** Vargas Llosa?
Did you like the last novel by Vargas Llosa?

Ese coche es **de** mi hermano.
That is my brother's car.

Exercise 2. Complete the following sentences with the preposition **de**.

1. Los libros son ____ la biblioteca.
2. La casa es ____ el banco, todavía no la hemos terminado de pagar.
3. Ese suéter es ____ tu hermano.
4. El aire y el agua es ____ todos.

- The preposition **de** is used to indicate origin, provenance, and cause.

Example

Los geólogos llegaron **de** Italia.
The geologists came from Italy.

Hace una hora salieron **de** su casa y no han llegado.
They left his home an hour ago and they haven't arrived.

Clareta es **de** Italia, y tiene 18 años.
Clareta is from Italy, and she is 18 years old.

Rafael se enfermó **de** tanto comer comida grasa.
Rafael got sick from eating greasy food.

Exercise 3. Complete the following sentences with the preposition **de**.

1. Los invitados llegaron ____ Perú.
2. Las anchoas son ____ el mar adriático.
3. Mi profesora de francés es ____ Lyon.
4. Estamos cansados, venimos ____ la montaña.

- The preposition **de** is used to indicate the material from which something is made.

Example

La silla es **de** madera.
This chair is made of wood.

Exercise 4. Complete the following sentences with the preposition **de**.

1. Los coches modernos son ____ plásticos.
2. Tú siempre estás pensando en castillos ____ arena.
3. Esas empanadas están deliciosas. Son ____ carne.
4. Me gusta el vino ____ La Rioja.

- The preposition **de** is used to indicate time.

Example

¡Vámonos! ¡Son las cuatro **de** la mañana!
Let's go! It's four in the morning!

Exercise 5. Complete the following sentences with the preposition **de**.

1. ¡Apúrate! Tu novio llega a las tres ____ la tarde.
2. ¿Qué hora es? ¡Las tres ____ la mañana!
3. Dentro ____ un año iré a visitarte.
4. A las dos ____ la madrugada nació.

C. THE PREPOSITION *EN*

The preposition **en** is used to indicate place, direction, time, and manner.

Example

El lápiz está **en** el escritorio.
The pencil is on the desk.

Susana entró **en** el almacén.
Susana entered the shop.

Jorge viajó a España **en** el verano.
Jorge traveled to Spain in the summer.

Lucho partió **en** avión.
Lucho left [on a trip] on an airplane.

Exercise 6. Complete the following sentences with the preposition **en**.

1. ¡Tráeme los libros! Están ____ la mesa.
2. Las golondrinas llegan ____ grupos de a miles.
3. Los osos duermen ____ el invierno.
4. La botella está ____ el piso.

D. THE PREPOSITIONS *PARA* AND *POR*

The use of **por** and **para** poses many difficulties, because both correspond to the English preposition *for* as well as the preposition *to*.

a. *Para*

- To indicate destination and purpose, **para** is used as *for, to,* and *in order to*.

Example

La próxima semana voy **para** Mérida.
Next week I am going to Mérida.

Esta olla es sólo **para** hervir el agua.
This pot is [used] only for boiling water.

Exercise 7. Complete the following sentences with the preposition **para**.

1. Ese avión va ____ Europa.
2. Las niñas están listas ____ partir.
3. ____ poder jugar bien al fútbol hay que practicar.
4. Esa llave no sirve ____ abrir esa puerta.

- To indicate time, **para** is used as *by*.

Example

Terminaré este trabajo **para** mañana.
I will finish this work by tomorrow.

Exercise 8. Complete the following sentences with the preposition **para**.

1. ____ el próximo año ya habrás terminado tu doctorado.
2. La tarea es ____ mañana.
3. Tenemos que tener listo el vestido ____ el jueves
4. Lo siento, ya me comprometí ____ el próximo viernes.

b. *Por*

- To indicate reason or motive, **por** is the equivalent of *because.*

Example

Lo despidieron **por** inepto.
He was fired because of his ineptitude.

Exercise 9. Complete the following sentences with the preposition **por**.

1. Ella hace cualquier cosa ______ dinero.
2. Lo premiaron ____ su gran talento.
3. ____ no estudiar, Diana vivió aburrida toda su vida.
4. A vosotros os invitaron ____ cumplir con el protocolo.

- To introduce the agent in the passive voice, **por** is the equivalent of *by.*

Example

Ese retrato fue pintado **por** Botero.
That portrait was painted by Botero.

Exercise 10. Complete the following sentences with the preposition **por**.

1. Esa catedral fue construida ____ Gaudí.
2. La imprenta fue inventada ____ Gutenberg.
3. La ley de la relatividad fue propuesta ____ Einstein.

- To indicate purpose, **por** is used in the espression **ir + por**, and is the equivalent of *going for something.*

Example

Enrique fue **por** las llaves.
Enrique went for the keys.

Exercise 11. Complete the following sentences with the preposition **por**.

1. Vamos ____ aquel camino. Es más corto.
2. ¡María! Ve a la tienda ____ aceite, que se terminó.
3. Voy ____ el camino tropical.
4. Fueron ____ lana y salieron trasquilados.

- **Por** is used to indicate the means or manner by which something is done or accomplished.

Example

El jefe llegó **por** avión.
The boss arrived by plane.

Exercise 12. Complete the following sentences with the preposition **por**.

1. Las ondas sonoras viajan _____ el aire.
2. Robert viajó _____ tierra.
3. El hombre viaja ____aire, mar y tierra.
4. Todos los invitados llegaron ____ barco.

- **Por** is used to indicate substitution.

Yo trabajaré **por** ella.
I will work in her place.

Exercise 13. Complete the following sentences with the preposition **por**.

1. Juaco está enfermo. Liliana vendrá ____ él.
2. Rocío cambió su reloj ____ el vestido de flores.
3. Tomás y Helena reemplazaron su perro pastor alemán ____ un conejo.
4. Te cambio este coche ____ el tuyo.

REVIEW

Exercise 14. Complete the following paragraph with the appropriate preposition **a**, **de**, **en**, **por**, or **para** (use elisions if needed).

Eran las ocho ___ la noche, cuando Julio fue ___ comida al restaurante chino ___ el barrio. ___ el apartamento lo esperaba su novia Graciela. Como eran las once ___ la noche y Julio no llegaba, Graciela se acostó ___ el sofá ___ la sala ___ esperar. Graciela había conocido ___ Julio ___ suerte, una mañana ___ abril. Aquel día, Graciela había sido invitada ___ el señor Felipe Naranjo, dueño del periódico "El Vespertino", ___ que conociera su empresa. El señor Naranjo pensaba, ___ su imaginación, que Graciela sería la madre ___ sus hijos. Cuando Graciela llegó ___ las instalaciones ___ periódico, fue recibida ___ Felipe con un exquisito desayuno con panecillos hechos ___ harina ___ maíz. Felipe le habló ___ Graciela y le insinuó que si se casaba con él, ella sería tratada como una reina. Le propuso inclusive que ___ luna ___ miel la llevaría ___ su propio yate hasta su isla privada ___ el mar Caribe, y que luego viajarían ___ avión ___ París. Después del desayuno Felipe le presentó ___ los redactores ___ el periódico. Entre ellos estaba Julio, que había ido aquel día ___ reemplazar ___ Paco, uno ___ los periodistas ___ periódico, que ___ suerte ___ Julio se encontraba enfermo aquel día.

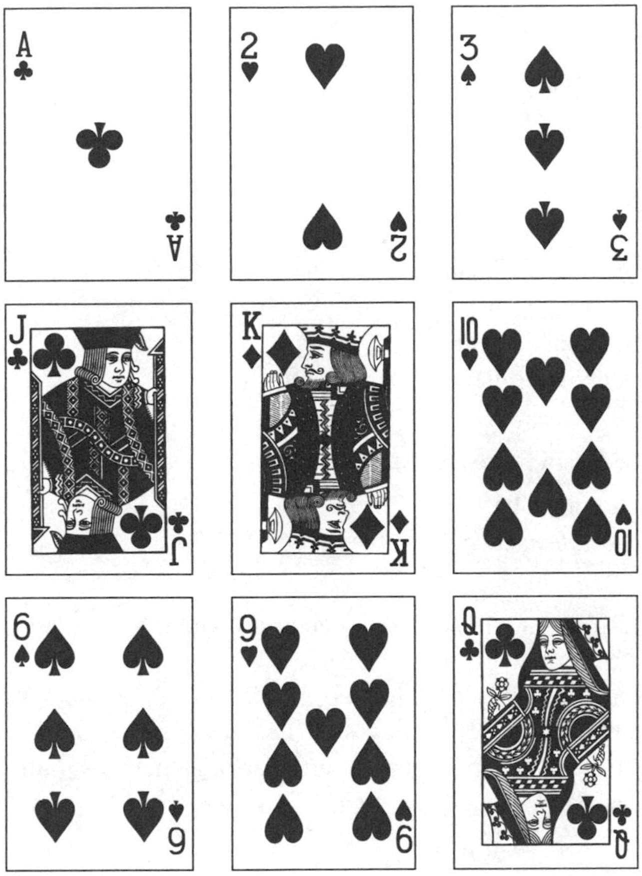

Exercise 15. According to the illustration, complete the following sentences using the appropriate prepositions.

1. El as ____ tréboles (A♣) está ____ la primera fila, junto ____ el dos ____ corazones (2♥) y el tres ____ picas (3♠).
2. El rey ____ diamantes (K♦) está ____ el valet ____ tréboles (J♣) y el 10 ____ corazones (10♥).
3. ____ el rey de diamantes (K♦) está el 2 ____ corazones (2♥).
4. ____ la derecha del rey ____ diamantes (K♦) está el 10 ____ corazones (10♥).
5. ____ el 10 ____ corazones (10♥) se encuentra la reina ____ tréboles (Q♣).

Answer Keys

CHAPTER 1

Exercise 1.

1. e; 2. p; 3. h; 4. c; 5. g; 6. x; 7. c, t; 8. d; 9. b; 10. a; 11. v; 12. j; 13. u; 14. f, l; 15. m; 16. o; 17. k, q; 18. w; 19. s; 20. r; 21. i; 22. n

Exercise 2.

1. ✔; 2. ✔; 3. ✗; 4. ✔; 5. ✗; 6. ✗; 7. ✔; 8. ✗; 9. ✗; 10. ✔; 11. ✔; 12. ✗; 13. ✗; 14. ✗; 15. ✗; 16. ✔; 17. ✔; 18. ✗

Exercise 3.

1.	fu/ria	muer/to	ra/bia
2.	hue/vo	Dia/na	cui/da/do
3.	tiem/po	ver/de	Juan
4.	jue/go	a/gua	viu/da
5.	via/ja	ca/rro/ña	gua/ri/da
6.	ciu/dad	tre/gua	len/gua
7.	puen/te	re/cuer/do	a/bue/lo
8.	nie/ve	tiem/po	reu/ma/tis/mo
9.	viu/da	Lui/sa	vi/rue/la
10.	pa/ñue/lo	a/za/le/a	Eu/ro/pa
11.	an/ti/guo	cuan/to	cua/dro

Exercise 4.

1. /**e**-rre-ko-**ne**-rre-si-g**a**-rro/
/**e**-rre-ko-**ne**-rre-ba-rr**il**/
/rr**a**-pi-do-k**o**-rren-los-k**a**-rros/
/kar-g**a**-dos-de-a-s**u**-ka-ral-fe-rro-ka-rr**il**/

2. /t**re**s-tr**i**s-tes-t**i**-gres-ko-m**i**-an-tr**i**-go/
   /en-tr**e**s-tr**i**s-tes-tr**a**s-tos-rre-pl**e**-tos-de-tr**i**-go/

3. /kom-p**a**-drel k**o**m-pra-m**eu**n-k**o**-ko/
   /kom-p**a**-drel k**o**-ko-no-k**o**m-pro/
   /k**e**l-ke-p**o**-ko-k**o**-ko-k**o**-me/
   /p**o**-ko-k**o**-ko-k**o**m-pra/

4. /pa-bl**i**-to-kla-b**ou**n-kla-v**i**-to/
   /k**e**-kla-b**i**-to-kla-b**o**-pa-bl**i**-to/

5. /e-la-m**o**r-es-**u**-na-lo-k**u**-ra/
   /ke-s**o**-loel-k**u**-ra-lo-k**u**-ra/
   /p**e**-roel-k**u**-ra-ke-lo-k**u**-ra/
   /ko-m**e**-teu-na-gr**a**n-lo-k**u**-ra/

Exercise 5.

/n**ue**s-tras-b**i**-das-son-los-rr**i**-os/
/ke-b**a**-na-d**a**r-en-la-m**a**r/
/k**e**s-el-mo-r**i**r/

/b**e**r-de-ke-te-k**ie**-ro-b**e**r-de/
/b**e**r-de-bien-tol b**e**r-des-rr**a**-mas/
/el-b**a**r-ko-s**o**-bre-la-m**a**r/
/yel-ka-b**a**-yo-en-la-mon-t**a**-ña/

/hu-ben-t**u**dl di-b**i**-no-te-s**o**-ro/
/ya-te-b**a**s-p**a**-ra-no-bol-b**e**r/
/kuan-do-k**ie**-ro-yo-r**a**rl no-y**o**-ro/
/ya-b**e**-ses-y**o**-ro-sin-ke-r**e**r/

/la-mas-b**e**-ya-n**i**-ña/
/de-n**ue**s-tro-lu-g**a**r/
/oi-vi**u**-dai-s**o**-la/
/ya-y**e**r-por-ka-s**a**r/
/v**ie**n-do-ke-su-s**o**-jos/
/a-la-g**e**-rra-b**a**n/
/a-su-m**a**-dre-d**i**-se/
/kes-k**u**-ča-su-m**a**l/
/de-j**a**d-me-yo-r**a**r/
/a-o-r**i**-yas-del-m**a**r/

Exercise 6.

ac/cio/nis/ta
a/cei/tu/na
ad/ver/bio
ai/re
a/plau/dir
as/tro/nau/ta
a/tri/buir
au/tor
bai/le
béis/bol
bue/no
bui/tre
can/ción
cau/sa
cien/to
cons/truir
con/ti/nuo
cui/dar
deu/da
eu/ca/lip/to
Eu/ro/pa
i/dio/ma
in/fluen/cia
in/ge/nuo
i/ta/lia/no
Li/lia/na
Lui/sa
ma/jes/tuo/so
muer/to
nai/pes
pai/sa/je
pei/ne
pia/no
pie/dra
rei/na
reu/nir
siem/pre
sue/la
su/per/fluo
tien/da
true/no

Exercise 7.

1.	a/ho/ra	i/de/a	des/ha/cer	to-a-lla	cuer/da	ma/es/tro	ciu/dad
2.	a/diós	cien/cia	ins/pi/rar	du/raz/no	abs/trac/to	com/ple/to	des/truir
3.	re/cons/truir	cui/da/do	tem/pra/no	sep/tiem/bre	pe/li/gro	res/plan/dor	lá/piz
4.	em/pe/ra/triz	ai/re	Eu/ge/nia	ba/úl	frí/o	al/co/hol	lec/ción
5.	a/zul	ca/lle	Is/lam	des/pla/zar	in/fluir	le/ón	ce/re/al
6.	bai/le	hé/ro/e	mer/ca/der	fe/liz	pe/lí/cu/la	tí/tu/lo	gra/má/ti/ca

Exercise 8.

1.	**jó**ven	re**loj**	**lá**piz	**án**gel	**dé**bil	ho**tel**	se**gún**
2.	a**mor**	**cé**lebre	ol**vi**do	pe**lí**cula	musul**mán**	**jó**venes	**án**geles
3.	direc**tor**	**ór**denes	**tí**tulo	**cré**dito	**tér**mino	ter**mi**no	**víc**tima
4.	infe**liz**	fe**liz**	ani**mal**	**ú**nico	mu**jer**	se**ñor**	sim**pá**tico
5.	**vír**genes	inte**rés**	es**tá**	**es**ta	gra**má**tica	pe**li**gro	ameri**ca**nos
6.	chimene**a**	**sa**la	e**xa**men	e**xá**menes	ra**zón**	ra**zo**nes	**ár**bol
7.	aza**le**a	ta**re**a	mu**jer**	hipo**pó**tamo	pa**pá**	an**ti**guo	**pa**pa

Exercise 9.

1. solo.
2. té
3. Te
4. té
5. ¿Cuánto, aquel
6. Como, aún
7. él
8. Sólo, si
9. Tú, sí
10. mas

CHAPTER 2

Exercise 1.

1. la nieta, la abuela
2. El hermano
3. el esposo
4. la suegra
5. la prima
6. el perro (la mascota)
7. la madre
8. el tío
9. la cuñada
10. la tía

Exercise 2.

1. La hermana
2. La vecina
3. El amigo
4. La sobrina
5. El abuelo
6. La sicóloga
7. La gata
8. El perro
9. El tío
10. La prima

Exercise 3.

1. El
2. El
3. La
4. El
5. La
6. la
7. El
8. La
9. El
10. La

Exercise 4.

1. El patrón
2. La señora
3. El doctor
4. La rectora
5. El director
6. La embajadora
7. El vendedor
8. La conductora
9. La exploradora
10. La administradora

Exercise 5.

1. María, **la** estudiante, está contenta.
   José, **el** estudiante, está contento.
2. Juan es **el** testigo del crimen.
   Marta es **la** testigo del crimen.

3. El señor Rodríguez es **el** visitante más importante.
   La señora Rodríguez es **la** visitante más importante.
4. **La** cliente es amig**a** de mi padre.
   El cliente es amig**o** de mi padre.
5. **El** agente es amig**o** de mi madre.
   La agente es amig**a** de mi madre.
6. **La** novelista es muy famos**a**.
   El novelista es muy famos**o**.
7. **La** astronauta, Julia, se prepara para viajar a Marte.
   El astronauta, Carlos, se prepara para viajar a Marte.
8. Teresa, **la** adolescente, juega para el equipo de fútbol de su escuela.
   Jorge, **el** adolescente, juega para el equipo de fútbol de su escuela.
9. **La** cantante, Isabel, recibió muchos aplausos anoche en el concierto.
   El cantante, Romeo, recibió muchos aplausos anoche en el concierto.

Exercise 6.

1. La
2. La
3. la
4. Los
5. Las
6. los
7. las
8. la
9. Los

Exercise 7.

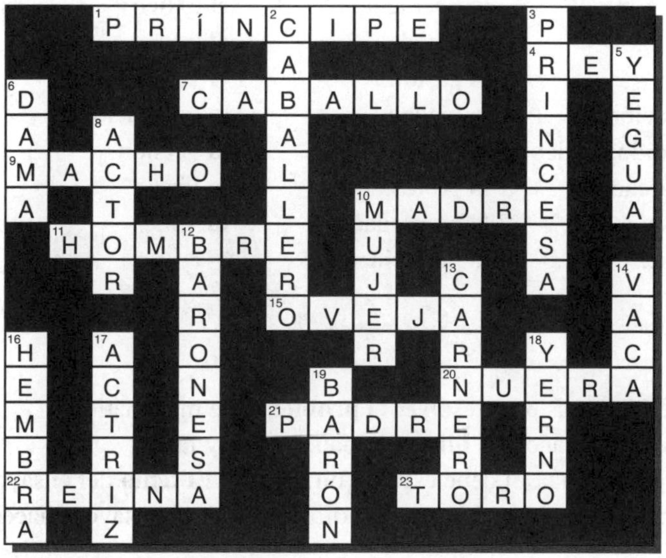

Exercise 8.

1. **La; la**
2. **la; el; la; el; la; la**
3. **La; el**
4. **el; el**
5. **El**
6. **el**

Exercise 9.

1. la
2. el
3. la
4. el; la
5. el
6. la, la

Exercise 10.

el acné
la actividad
la admiración
el afiche
la agresividad
el aljibe
la amabilidad
la ambición
el amplificador
la ansiedad
el antibiótico
la aptitud
el arco
la atracción
el baile
el banco
el barco
la bondad
el cable
el cacao
el café
la calefacción
la cantidad
la capacidad
la circulación
la ciudad
la claridad
la coalición
el coco
la composición
el cruce
la cruz
la decisión
la declaración
la depresión
el destornillador
la dirección
el domingo
el dulce
la educación
el electrodoméstico
la embarcación
el equipaje
la escasez
la estupidez
la evaluación
la habilidad
el humidificador
la infección
la liberación
la libertad
la luz
la madurez
el meteoro
el monitor
la nación
la nariz
la niñez
la operación
la pared
la pasión
la piedad
la prisión
la profesión
la propiedad
la publicidad
el reflector
el retrovisor
la revolución
la salud
la sed
la selección
la sencillez
la superstición
el tabaco
la televisión
el televisor
la tempestad
la tensión
la timidez
el tóxico
el tronco
el vapor
la vegetación
la versión
la virtud
la voz

Exercise 11.

María Sol utilizó **el teorema** de Pitágoras para resolver **el problema** de matemáticas.
Ahora tiene que terminar la tarea de español. **El idioma** español es muy fácil.
La tarea de ciencias es más difícil. María Sol debe escribir un ensayo. **El tema** del ensayo es sobre **el clima** tropical. **El dilema** de María es escribir directamente el ensayo o hacer primero **el esquema.**

Exercise 12.

1. el mapa
2. el ataúd
3. el arroz
4. el lápiz
5. la avestruz
6. el ajedrez
7. el pez
8. el planeta
9. el tranvía

Exercise 13.

1. la mano
2. la llave
3. la calle
4. la carne
5. la nieve
6. la noche
7. la nube
8. la sangre
9. la sal

Exercise 14.

1. la fiebre
2. la foto
3. la nube
4. la llave
5. la mano

Exercise 15.

1. La modelo
2. El orden
3. El papa
4. La guía
5. La cura
6. La capital
7. La corte
8. El modelo
9. El policía, la orden
10. El corte
11. La papa
12. El guía

Exercise 16.

1. el capital
2. el corte
3. el cura
4. la modelo
5. la papa
6. el papa

Exercise 17.

1. Los chocolates están sobre la mesa.
2. Las camas están sin tender.
3. Las casas están al norte de la ciudad.
4. Los tigres están en la jaula.
5. Los problemas están en los gobernantes.
6. Las tiendas están en el barrio.

Exercise 18.

1. el hermano
2. la amiga
3. la almendra
4. el edificio
5. el coche
6. la candidata
7. el sindicato
8. la modelo
9. el cura
10. la máquina
11. la noche
12. la calle

Exercise 19.

1. **las** casas, **los** perros, **las** gatas
2. **los** dormitorios, **los** problemas, **las** manos
3. **el** teorema, **los** días, **las** motos
4. **las** noches, **la** luna, **la** Tierra
5. **los** sistemas, **el** viaje, **los** planetas
6. **los** mapas, **los** poemas, **los** programas

Exercise 20.

1. Los hornos microondas son negros.
2. Las batidoras son verdes.
3. Los fregaderos son metálicos.
4. Las ollas son grandes.
5. Las cafeteras son eléctricas.
6. Las estufas son blancas.

Exercise 21.

1. Los refrigeradores del hotel son blancos.
2. Los congeladores de mi casa son eficientes.
3. Los trenes son lentos.
4. Las leyes son obsoletas.
5. Los ataúdes son de madera.
6. Los sartenes son de hierro.

Exercise 22.

1. El empleado está cansado.
2. El motor está encendido.
3. El rey está preso.
4. El actor está desesperado.
5. El maniquí está en la vitrina.
6. El pan está crujiente.

Exercise 23.

Todos los días la abuela Rosario entra a **la sala** y mira **el cuadro** pintado por su hijo. Luego toma uno de **los libros** que están en **la estantería** al lado de la mesita y se sienta en **el sillón** cerca de la ventana. Cuando hace frío, enciende **la calefacción** o prende **el fuego en la chimenea**. En **la mesita** coloca **la taza** de té. A la abuela Rosario le encantan **las flores** frescas.

Exercise 24.

1. Las nueces
2. Los lápices
3. Los peces
4. Los pies
5. Los cafés
6. Los papás

Exercise 25.

	Masculine	Feminine	Singular	Plural
planetas	✔			✔
leyes		✔		✔
jarrones	✔			✔
temas	✔			✔
dilemas	✔			✔
actrices		✔		✔
perdiz		✔	✔	
cafés	✔			✔
peces	✔			✔
teoremas	✔			✔

Exercise 26.

1. **los**
2. **La**
3. **los**
4. **El**
5. **La**
6. **Las**

Exercise 27.

1. los microbuses
2. los compases
3. los gases
4. los meses
5. los entremeses
6. los burgueses

Exercise 28.

1. apendicitis
2. artritis
3. caries
4. escocés
5. fotosíntesis
6. francés
7. inglés
8. jueves
9. lunes
10. miércoles
11. oasis
12. viernes
13. virus
14. tenis

Exercise 29.

1. la abeja africana
   las abejas africanas
2. el agua mineral
   las aguas minerales
3. el águila calva
   las águilas calvas
4. el ala del avión
   las alas del avión
5. la alcaparra en vinagre
   las alcaparras en vinagre
6. el alma muerta
   las almas muertas
7. la almendra tostada
   las almendras tostadas
8. la almohada de plumas
   las almohadas de plumas
9. el arma de fuego
   las armas de fuego
10. la azalea es una flor
    las azaleas son unas flores
11. el hacha de piedra
    las hachas de piedra
12. la hambruna
    las hambrunas

Exercise 30.

1. **la**
2. **al**
3. **del**
4. **al**
5. **del, las**
6. **al**
7. **la**
8. **la**

Exercise 31.

1. del guante rojo
2. de la mariposa
3. al infierno
4. el agua del río
5. del Duque
6. de la hermana

Exercise 32.

1. unos problemas
2. una balanza
3. una decisión
4. un perfume
5. un hombre
6. un escritor
7. un idioma
8. una toalla
9. unas canciones
10. un príncipe
11. unas yeguas
12. unos leones

Exercise 33.

1. **un**
2. **una**
3. **un**
4. **una**
5. **un**
6. **unos**

Exercise 34.

1. **El, la**
2. **La**
3. **El**
4. **La, la**
5. **El**
6. **Las, la**

Exercise 35.

1. **El**
2. **La**
3. **El, el**
4. **La**
5. **El**
6. **Las, la**

Exercise 36.

1. Quiero beber vino de California.
2. Hay leche en el supermercado.
3. Rosario compra azúcar de caña.
4. No hay justicia en algunos países.
5. Sin tiempo, no podré terminar **el** ensayo de español.
6. Estudia matemáticas y física en la universidad.
7. Nosotros hablamos inglés.

Exercise 37.

1. **Una**
2. **Un**
3. **Una, una**
4. **un**
5. **un**
6. **Un, un**

Exercise 38.

1. **El** domingo pasado vimos **unos** globos en **el** parque del barrio.
2. **Un** niño encontró **un** guante en **la** puerta del teatro.
3. Necesitamos **una** libra de azúcar y **un** par de huevos para preparar **el** postre preferido de papá.
4. Juan tuvo que esperar **unos** minutos antes de entrar a **la** oficina de su jefe.
5. En **el** zoológico de la ciudad vimos **una** jirafa, **un** león, **un** elefante, **un** tigre y **unas** tortugas.
6. **El** animal preferido de todos fue **el** gorila.

Exercise 39.

El joven Javier, todos **los** días se levanta a **las** seis de **la** mañana. Se baña, se viste y bebe **una** taza de café con **una** galleta. Luego, se cepilla **los** dientes y toma **el** bus para ir a **la** universidad. **El** martes a **las** ocho de **la** mañana tiene clase de estadística. Javier es **el** mejor estudiante de la clase. **Una** vez a la semana juega fútbol con **unos** amigos que conoció en la universidad.

REVIEW

Exercise 40.

1. una señora triste
2. una mujer fiel
3. una esposa feliz
4. una oficial capaz
5. una policía valiente
6. una gata angora
7. un reina déspota
8. una gobernadora popular

Exercise 41.

1. La señora Gómez es una artista famosa.
2. Lucía es una actriz famosa.
3. Martina es una campeona de tenis.
4. María es una cantante excepcional.

Exercise 42.

1. Tengo una perra valiente,
2. una yegua inteligente,
3. una gata paciente,
4. una ratona inocente,
5. y una esposa desesperante.

Exercise 43.

1. John Glenn y Neil Armstrong son unos astronautas intrépidos.
2. Nicole Kidman y Tom Cruise son unos actores famosos.
3. Lance Armstrong y Robbie McEwen son unos ciclistas veloces.
4. Batistuta y Romario son unos futbolistas estupendos.

Exercise 44.

1. la, el, la
2. los, un
3. la, una
4. el, una
5. las, los
6. la, el

CHAPTER 3

Exercise 1.

1. delgado
2. sucia
3. cara
4. largas
5. costosos
6. alta

Exercise 2.

1. d
2. f
3. e
4. a
5. b
6. c

Exercise 3.

1. español.
2. ecuatoriana.
3. americano.
4. suecos.
5. japoneses.
6. suizas.
7. inglesa.
8. franceses.
9. portuguesa.
10. boliviana.
11. alemanes
12. panameñas
13. salvadoreña
14. argentinas

Exercise 4.

1. importante
2. alegre
3. grande
4. interesante
5. rebelde
6. verde

Exercise 5.

1. homicidas
2. fuerte
3. insignificantes
4. inteligentes
5. excelente
6. reconfortante

Exercise 6.

1. atroz
2. cruel
3. gris
4. peor
5. joven
6. feliz

Exercise 7.

1. c
2. f
3. d
4. b
5. e
6. a

Exercise 8.

1. trabajadores
2. jóvenes
3. azul
4. útil
5. especiales
6. mejores

Exercise 9.

1. San
2. gran
3. grande
4. Santa
5. mal
6. malas

Exercise 10.

1. pobre
2. blanca
3. delicado
4. excelente
5. triste
6. feliz

Exercise 11.

1. **El pobre** está sin trabajo.
2. **La joven** ganó el concurso de belleza.
3. **Los trabajadores** pidieron un aumento de salario.
4. **El alemán** viajó por Sudamérica.
5. **Las argentinas** son muy simpáticas.
6. **El negro** es mi preferido.

Exercise 12.

1. estas
2. Aquel
3. estos
4. esas
5. Este
6. estos

Exercise 13.

—Mamá, compremos **este** jabón.
—Vamos a comprar **aquel** jabón rosado, Gabriela. Es mi marca favorita.
—Pero no me gusta el perfume de **esa** marca de jabón, mamá.
—¿Qué te parece **este** jabón cremoso?
—Me gusta mucho más. ¿Ves **esas** flores?
—¡Qué lindas! Quedan perfectas en **aquel** jarrón que te regaló papá.

Exercise 14.

Estoy buscando **mi** mochila. Me voy de viaje con **mis** primos Arturo y Gonzalo. **Nuestra** tía Carmen y **su** esposo tienen una casa en el campo y vamos a visitarlos. Préstame **tu** auto y devuélveme **mis** maletas. Las voy a necesitar.

Exercise 15.

1. Así son, <u>tus</u> amigos. Esa es la pura verdad.
2. Dame <u>tu</u> teléfono. Te llamo mañana.
3. Lucía y Marta dejaron <u>sus</u> maletas en el hotel.
4. El panadero comienza <u>su</u> trabajo muy temprano.
5. Mi hermana y yo donamos <u>nuestra</u> ropa vieja a los pobres.
6. Pensad en la felicidad de <u>vuestras</u> familias.

Exercise 16.

1. Francisco me invitó a **la** finca **suya** el fin de semana.
2. Pero, yo prefiero quedarme en **la** casa **mía**.
3. Felipe, **el** novio **mío**, llega de Chile mañana.
4. Iremos a un bar el viernes en la noche con **unas** amigas **nuestras** de la universidad.
5. El sábado en la tarde iremos con **los** hijos **tuyos** a la playa.
6. Santiago perdió **los** libros **tuyos**.
7. Lola no puede abrir **el** coche **suyo** porque perdió **las** llaves **suyas**.
8. El futuro **del** país **vuestro** no es muy prometedor.

Exercise 17.

1. doscientos cuarenta y cinco coches
2. cuarenta y cinco televisores
3. mil doscientas ochenta y dos manzanas
4. ciento cuarenta y cinco mil setecientos sesenta y cinco personas
5. quinientos cincuenta y cuatro mil ochocientos noventa y ocho trabajadores
6. un millón doscientas ochenta y nueve mil novecientas ocho naranjas
7. doscientos nueve muchachos
8. doscientas veintinueve mil mujeres
9. ciento una niñas
10. quinientas noventa naranjas
11. veintiún balones
12. treinta y tres almacenes

Exercise 18.

1. 7,5 Kg.
2. $3.500
3. €1.300.000
4. 6,03 Kg.
5. $140.000.000.000

Exercise 19.

1. Son las nueve.
2. Son las diez y ocho.

3. Es la una y cuarto *or* Es la una y quince.
4. Son las cuatro y veinte.
5. Son las cuatro menos cuarto *or* Son las cuatro menos quince.
6. Son las tres menos cinco.
7. Son las doce menos cuarto *or* Son las doce menos quince.
8. Es la una y media or Es la una y treinta.

Exercise 20.

1. primer
2. tercera
3. primero, primer
4. tercer, cuarto
5. primeros
6. decimotercer

Exercise 21.

1. quinto
2. tercer
3. primer
4. sexto
5. cuarto
6. segundo

REVIEW

Exercise 22.

1. Marta es colombiana.
2. Mi tía es española.
3. Mi hermana es guapa.
4. Mi amiga está contenta.
5. Liliana es inteligente.
6. Mi tía es simpática.
7. Tu abuela es amable.
8. El perro está enfermo.
9. Tu profesora es alemana.
10. Lucía es hipócrita.

Exercise 23.

1. Un helicóptero eficiente y un avión **eficiente**.
2. Un jugo refrescante y una fruta **refrescante**.
3. Un amigo fiel y una compañera **fiel**.
4. Un actor famoso y una actriz **famosa**.
5. Un empleado perezoso y una empleada **perezosa**.
6. Un profesor exigente y una profesora **exigente**.
7. Un niño inteligente y una niña **inteligente**.
8. Un país interesante y una ciudad **interesante**.
9. Unos animales inmensos y unos árboles **inmensos**.
10. Un coche rojo y una moto **roja**.

Exercise 24.

1. Hay sesenta y ocho mil soldados en Afganistán.
2. Tenemos tres mil seiscientos setenta y tres francos suizos.
3. José ganó quinientos setenta y ocho millones de pesos.
4. Ese toro pesa setecientos ochenta y siete kilos.
5. El premio mayor de la lotería es doscientos treinta y un millones quinientos treinta y siete mil dólares.
6. Ese anillo de oro pesa dieciocho onzas.
7. Al concierto asistieron más de doscientas personas.
8. La Luna se encuentra a trescientos ochenta y cuatro mil cuatrocientos kilómetros de la Tierra.
9. Entre todos reunimos más de veintidós mil doscientos cincuenta pesos.
10. Colón viajó a América en mil cuatrocientos noventa y dos.

Exercise 25.

1. ese
2. esta
3. Estos
4. Esa
5. esa
6. Esta
7. Estos
8. aquella
9. esa
10. aquel

Exercise 26.

1. **Estos** pantalones son **mis** pantalones. **Tus** pantalones están sobre la cama.
2. **Aquellos** muchachos están compitiendo con **sus** bicicletas.
3. **Esa** señora tiene **tus** libros de español.
4. ¿**Aquel** muchacho tiene **su** perro?
5. **Este** es **nuestro** amigo Marco.
6. **Esta** es **vuestra** casa, ¿verdad?
7. La emoción de **aquellos** recuerdos le humedecieron **sus** ojos.
8. Para salir de **esta** crisis económica lo mejor es consumir poco.
9. ¿Recuerdas **aquella** noche, **mis** perros ladrando?
10. ¿No te acuerdas? **Esa** tarde **tu** hermana se desmayó.

Exercise 27.

1. primeros
2. tercera
3. primer
4. quinto
5. sexta
6. tercer
7. Quinto
8. primer
9. quinceava

CHAPTER 4

Exercise 1.

1. llego
2. tememos
3. creen
4. viven
5. respondes
6. miran
7. insiste
8. comprende
9. necesitan
10. hablan
11. saltáis
12. rompen
13. aplauden
14. dibuja
15. prometes
16. oprimes
17. gana
18. ceden
19. partimos
20. retroceden

Exercise 2.

1. zurzo; zurces
2. ejerzo; ejerces
3. aborrece; aborrezco
4. apetezco; apeteces
5. reduzco; reducen
6. frunce; frunzo

Exercise 3.

1. reconoce, reconozco
2. Venzo
3. Esparzo
4. desaparezco
5. introduzco
6. agradezco
7. Aborrezco
8. convenzo
9. Conduzco

Exercise 4.

1 recojo; recoges
2. eliges; elijo
3. emerjo; emergéis
4. corriges; corrijo
5. exiges; exijo
6. encoges; encojo
7. infrinjo; infringes
8. afligen, aflijo
9. resurjo; resurges
10. escojo; escoges

Exercise 5.

1. recojo, exijo, protejo, acojo, restringes, finjo
2. escojo, dirijo, sumerjo

Exercise 6.

1. consigo; consiguen
2. sigo; sigues
3. yergo; erguís
4. persigo; persigues

Exercise 7.

1. distingo
2. prosigo
3. sigo
4. extingo
5. yergo
6. consigo
7. persigo

Exercise 8.

1. atribuyes; atribuyo
2. huimos; huyen
3. incluyo; incluimos
4. influyen; influyo
5. arguyen; arguyo
6. constituyes; constituyo

Exercise 9.

1. distribuyes
2. concluyes
3. diluyen
4. destruyen
5. reconstruimos
6. obstruye
7. disminuís
8. recluye
9. sustituye
10. contribuyen

Exercise 10.

1. evalúan
2. ampliáis
3. enfría
4. sitúas
5. guía
6. perpetúa
7. insinuáis
8. devalúan
9. efectúan
10. continúa

Exercise 11.

1. acentúas; acentuamos
2. ansiamos; ansían
3. confío; confías
4. evacúan; evacúa
5. variamos; varías
6. insinuáis; insinuamos

Exercise 12.

1. enciendo; calentáis
2. confiesa; mentimos
3. quiere; defiendes
4. atiendo; encerráis
5. gobiernan; consentimos
6. descendemos; niegas
7. comienza; empezamos
8. divierte; sentamos
9. sugiere; entiendo

Exercise 13.

Visita al psiquiatra

—Doctor, siempre temo cuando él **atraviesa** la calle y yo **pienso** que algo le va a pasar.

—¿Qué es lo que (tú) **sientes**?

—No sé Dr. Algo **gobierna** mis sentidos y (yo) **prefiero** alzarlo en mis brazos. Mis amigos me **recomiendan** comprar un cargador para bebés y (ellos) se **divierten** burlándose de mi. Y me preguntan con quién me **despierto** en las mañanas... Pero yo soy normal, sólo temo cuando (nosotros) **atravesamos** la calle...

—Por favor empieza de nuevo, es que (yo) **pierdo** el hilo con mucha facilidad. ¿Qué raza es tu perro?

Exercise 14.

1. viste
2. repite, consigue
3. corrige
4. mide
5. eliges
6. despedís
7. impedimos
8. sigues
9. persigue

Exercise 15.

Exercise 16.

1. adquieren
2. adquiere
3. inquiere
4. adquirís

Exercise 17.

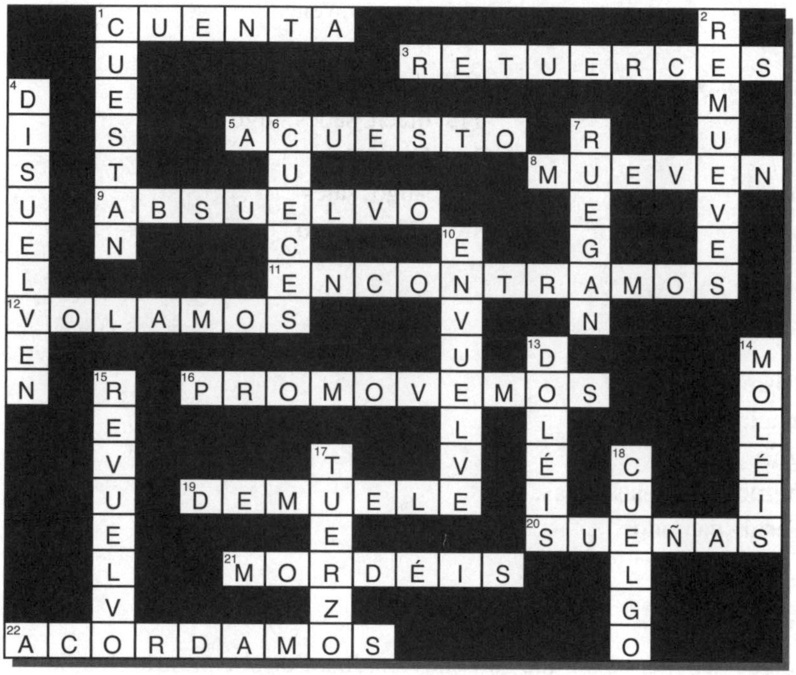

Exercise 18.

1. encuentran; encontramos
2. acuerdas; acuerdo
3. Llueve
4. almuerzan; almorzamos
5. recuerdo; recuerdan
6. devuelve; devolvéis
7. movemos; mueves
8. volvemos; vuelves
9. disuelve; disuelven
10. mostramos; muestras

Exercise 19.

1. vuelves
2. muere
3. resuelve
4. suenan
5. almorzamos
6. dormís
7. puede
8. huelo
9. recuerdan
10. devuelves

Exercise 20.

1. juegas
2. juego
3. juegan
4. juegan
5. juega

Exercise 21.

1. trae, traigo
2. dais, doy
3. dices, haces, digo, hago
4. viene, vengo
5. cabe, quepo
6. poneis, pongo
7. viene, vengo
8. ve, veo, ven
9. tengo, tienes
10. saben, sé
11. dicen, sabes, digo
12. Oigo, oyes
13. salgo, sales
14. vales, valgo

Exercise 22.

1. La niña **está** triste.
2. Los niños **van** a la escuela.
3. Yo **voy** contigo.
4. Nosotros no **hemos** hecho las tareas.
5. Julio y María están cansados.

Exercise 23.

Me gustan los libros de caballerías porque **son** entretenidos. Por el contrario, los libros de gramática que (yo) **he** estudiado me aburren. Un libro de aventuras **es** siempre más divertido, y aún más, cuando **está** escrito con humor. Porque si vosotros **estáis** leyendo algo aburrido, **vais** directo a dormir. De todas maneras, recuerda que con voluntad y entusiasmo **es** más fácil aprender cualquier idioma.

Exercise 24.

1. Sonia se levanta.
2. Sonia se ducha.
3. Sonia se pone los zapatos.
4. Sonia camina por la playa.
5. Sonia come en un restaurante.
6. Sonia va al museo.
7. Sonia conoce a un amigo.
8. Sonia baila en una discoteca.

Exercise 25.

Paco: —Hola, ¿Cómo te **llamas**?

Pilar: —Me **llamo** Pilar.

Paco: —Yo me **llamo** Paco. ¿Qué **haces**? ¿**Trabajas** o **estudias**?

Pilar: —**Trabajo** en una librería. ¿Y tú, qué **haces**?

Paco: —**Estudio** administración de empresas. ¿Quieres una cerveza?

Pilar: —¡Vale!

Paco: —Esta noche **vamos** a ir con unos amigos a un concierto de música de Senegal. ¿**Quieres** venir?

Pilar: —¡Estupendo!

Paco: —Entonces, nos **vemos** en el Teatro Real a las ocho en punto.

Pilar: —De acuerdo. Hasta entonces.

Paco: —Hasta luego.

REVIEW

Exercise 26.

Marta y Carlos **son** novios. Ambos **asisten** a la Universidad Nacional y **estudian** biología. En un mes **van** a graduarse, y por eso Marta **busca** un trabajo urgentemente. **Viven** juntos porque no **pueden** estar separados un minuto. Los viernes **juegan** tenis por la tarde y por la noche **bailan** salsa. Los sábados, Marta **duerme** hasta las ocho de la mañana, se **viste** y **corre** siete kilómetros. Cuando Carlos **decide** ir con ella, siempre le dice: "Marta, esta vez sí te **venzo**", pero la verdad es que nunca la **vence**. Cuando ella lo **socorre,** Carlos le **contesta**: "Mi amor te lo **agradezco**". Yo les **confieso** algo: "Carlos **es** un flojo" y Marta siempre lo **protege**. Yo lo **conozco** desde hace dos años. A Marta le **reconozco** su ternura. Pero, también le **exijo** prudencia. Ese hombre **es** un vividor. **Persigue** a las muchachas dulces y las **hace** sentir diosas. Pero luego, cuando **adquiere** confianza, se **muda** a su apartamento. Allí, **almuerza**, **come** y **duerme** y no **trae** nada, sólo **distribuye** sonrisas y palabras bonitas, y una las **oye** como venidas del cielo. Luego que una se **ha** ilusionado, **tiene** la desfachatez de decir que algo extraño le **sucede** y dice: "Mi pasión se **enfría**, lo **siento** corazón pero me **voy**". Cuando **dice** aquello, no **cabe** la menor duda que **es** porque **ha** visto otra mujer. Lo **digo** yo, que lo **he** vivido en carne propia.

Exercise 27.

1. amó
2. aprendí
3. abrió, encontró
4. bailaron
5. corrí
6. asististe
7. socorrí
8. decidisteis
9. caminó
10. emprendió
11. escribieron
12. alisté
13. insistió
14. compraste
15. comió
16. hablé

Exercise 28.

1. comprendimos
2. subió
3. llegó
4. vivió
5. miró
6. respondió
7. necesité; prestó
8. temimos
9. retornó
10. vendieron
11. trabajaron
12. viajaron
13. permitieron
14. envió
15. bebió
16. recibieron

Exercise 29.

1. ubicaron
2. toqué
3. supliqué
4. secaron
5. sacó
6. publicó
7. pesqué
8. fabricasteis
9. explicó
10. empacaron
11. duplicó
12. dediqué
13. busqué
14. ataqué
15. calificaron
16. Coloqué
17. aparqué
18. clasifiqué
19. criticaron
20. falsificó

Exercise 30.

1. apagó
2. arriesgasteis
3. cargué
4. Colgué
5. encargó
6. fumigué
7. jugamos
8. llegaste
9. pagó
10. regué
11. amargué
12. halagó
13. sosegué
14. devengaron
15. embargó

Exercise 31.

1. apaciguó
2. atestiguó
3. averigüé
4. desaguó
5. fragüé
6. santiguó
7. atestigüé
8. amortiguaron
9. menguó
10. averigüé

Exercise 32.

1. abrazó
2. adelgazaron
3. Alcancé
4. almorzamos
5. alzamos
6. analicé
7. cazaron
8. cruzaron
9. destrozaron
10. empezaste
11. encabezó
12. lancé
13. organizaste
14. reemplazó
15. memorizaron
16. localizasteis
17. tranquilizó
18. tropezó
19. danzó
20. analicé

Exercise 33.

1. corroyó
2. cayó
3. poseyó
4. royeron
5. recayeron
6. creí
7. proveyó
8. decayeron
9. releyeron
10. royeron

Exercise 34.

1. oyó
2. atribuyó
3. concluyó
4. reconstruyeron
5. destruyeron
6. disminuyó
7. distribuyó
8. incluiste
9. influisteis
10. sustituyó
11. desoyó
12. construyeron
13. obstruyó
14. Diluiste
15. recluyeron

Exercise 35.

1. consintieron
2. divirtió
3. mentimos
4. prefirió
5. sugirió
6. sintieron
7. asentí
8. resintieron
9. invirtieron
10. convertiste

Exercise 36.

1. consiguió
2. corrigió
3. despidió
4. eligió
5. impidió
6. midió
7. persiguió
8. rieron
9. repitieron
10. siguió
11. sonreísteis
12. vestimos
13. despidieron
14. eligieron
15. consiguió

Exercise 37.

1. durmió
2. murieron
3. durmieron
4. murieron
5. dormiste

Exercise 38.

1. Carlos le **dio** las gracias al taxista.
2. María y José le **dieron** un regalo de cumpleaños a su hijo.
3. Tú **diste** dinero para proteger el medio ambiente.
4. Nosotros le **dimos** la bienvenida al astronauta.
5. Yo **di** lo mejor de mí.

Exercise 39.

1. anduvimos
2. estuvo
3. tuvieron
4. viniste
5. cupiste
6. dijeron
7. Hubo
8. produjeron
9. redujeron
10. pudieron
11. traje
12. retrajo
13. pusieron
14. supimos
15. hice
16. quisiste

Exercise 40.

1. El Sr. Urrutia vino de compras a Miami.
2. Yo hice la tarea por la mañana.
3. El presidente no pudo convencer a los congresistas.
4. Los niños anduvieron en bicicleta por la mañana.
5. La herida le produjo mucho dolor.
6. Los niños trajeron sus mochilas a clase, pero vacías.
7. Antes de salir, hicimos la comida.
8. Yo no le dije la verdad.
9. No supe adonde fue.
10. Ana no vino a clase el lunes.

Exercise 41.

1. incluyó
2. retiraste
3. repetí
4. pagamos
5. influyó
6. explicaron
7. destrocé
8. caminamos
9. temí
10. rió
11. reduje
12. llegaron
13. fabricaron
14. decidimos
15. cruzaron

Exercise 42.

1. sugirió
2. socorrieron
3. proveyó
4. pescamos
5. persiguió
6. necesité
7. jugamos
8. Hubo
9. distribuyeron
10. cazó
11. sentimos
12. respondió
13. publicó
14. midió
15. fumigué
16. disminuyeron

Exercise 43.

1. abrazó
2. pudieron
3. emprendiste
4. empezó
5. empacamos
6. anduve
7. ubicaste
8. oyeron
9. durmieron
10. consiguió
11. comprendieron
12. apagó
13. amó

Exercise 44.

1. *El abuelo Marco nació el 21 de mayo de 1920,*
2. se casó el 5 de junio de 1941.
3. El 7 de marzo de 1942 tuvo un hijo.
4. El 23 de julio de 1945 se graduó de la escuela de arquitectura.
5. El 3 de mayo de 1950 se accidentó.
6. El 3 de agosto de 1955 ganó un concurso de arquitectura.
7. El 5 de mayo de 1969 arrestaron a su hijo.
8. El 3 de abril de 1970 fue al matrimonio de su hijo.

Exercise 45.

1. recogía
2. hacía
3. almorzabas
4. protegían
5. insistíais
6. escribía
7. decidíamos
8. asistían
9. vendía
10. temían
11. respondía
12. creían
13. comprendía
14. buscaba
15. bailaba
16. tenían
17. dormía

Exercise 46.

1. iba
2. íbamos
3. erais
4. era
5. veíamos
6. eran
7. iban
8. eran
9. iba
10. veía
11. era
12. veías
13. era

Exercise 47.

Ahora recuerdo que cuando **estábamos** en la escuela secundaria, para poder ir de paseo **organizábamos** rifas. En los paseos, muchos de mis compañeros **bebían** aguardiente a escondidas y les **enviaban** serenatas a sus prometidas sin el consentimiento de sus padres. En casa, nuestros padres eran muy estrictos. Todos los días **comíamos** en una mesa diferente a la de los adultos. Allí, en esa mesa exclusiva para nosotros los niños, nos **divertíamos** monstruosamente, especialmente con mis primos que todos los años, **venían** en las vacaciones a visitarnos. Después de comer, durante el verano todas las tardes **íbamos** a la playa y **jugábamos** voleibol. A veces **caminábamos** por la montaña y nos **escondíamos** de mi hermano menor.

Exercise 48.

1. Ricardo tiene dos novias, **pero antes tenía sólo una**.
2. Adriana canta rock, **pero antes cantaba tango**.
3. Alberto y Daniel escriben para el diario más importante del país, **pero antes escribían para el diario local**.
4. Mi madre sonríe sólo de vez en cuando, **pero antes sonreía todo el tiempo**.
5. Lucrecia no duerme mucho, **pero antes dormía muchas horas**.
6. Ahora nunca miento, **pero antes mentía todo el tiempo**.
7. Rosa corre tres kilómetros, **pero antes corría diez kilómetros**.
8. Mi padre no tiene mucho dinero, **pero antes tenía mucho**.
9. Hoy, mi madre no posee nada, **pero antes poseía una fortuna**.

Exercise 49.

1. Mi perra **era** grande y blanca y **era** muy juguetona.
2. Mi profesora **tenía** el cabello negro y **era** muy estricta.
3. Los niños **eran** muy inquietos y **tenían** mucha energía.
4. María y Josefa **eran** altas y bondadosas, y además **tenían** mucha paciencia.
5. Rosa **era** muy simpática y se **vestía** muy elegante.
6. Fernando **era** guapo, **tenía** los ojos negros y el cabello oscuro. Además **era** inteligente.

Exercise 50.

Julia **se sentía** agobiada cuando nuestra madre la **reprendía**. A ninguno nos **gustaba** estudiar. La escuela nos **aburría** y **llorábamos** desconsoladamente todos los lunes cuando **íbamos** camino a la escuela. **Mirábamos** a los pescadores y al mar con nostalgia. **Pensábamos** que la libertad era lanzar piedras desde el acantilado. Julia además siempre **sentía** miedo cuando **entraba** a la clase de latín. Muchas veces para no ir a la escuela **decía** que **estaba** enferma y que **tenía** náuseas. Pero mamá nunca le **creía**.

Exercise 51.

1. Mis padres **pensaban** que **era** un perezoso.
2. Yo **creía** que **tenía** una enfermedad grave.
3. Mi hermana **estaba** segura de mi lealtad.
4. Raúl nos **aseguraba** que **tenía** un secreto.

5. Andrea **pensaba** que yo nunca **tenía** la razón, y **era** cierto.
6. Yo no **reconocía** que me **equivocaba**.
7. Clemente **insinuaba** que yo **perdía** todo.
8. Yo **insistía** en ser astronauta.
9. Ellas siempre **averiguaban** dónde **era** la fiesta.

Exercise 52.

1. hacía
2. miraban
3. vivíamos
4. trabajaba
5. recogía
6. encendían
7. aparcaba
8. rezabas
9. leía
10. vendían

Exercise 53.

1. era
2. hacía
3. Llovía
4. seguía, nevaba
5. Hacía
6. estaba, hacía
7. Era
8. había
9. corría

Exercise 54. Cuando la madre llegó:

1. Un niño pintaba en la pared de la sala.
2. El otro niño rompía los libros de arte.
3. El padre bebía cerveza.
4. El padre también miraba televisión.

Exercise 55.

Past Imperfect

Era alrededor de las ocho de la mañana
Afuera, **había** miles de personas gritando
Era un día de verano
el cielo **estaba** completamente azul
Todos, en la calle, **iban** vestidos con
disfraces de variados colores
(todos) **cantaban**
(todos) **bailaban** como locos
Todos nos **miraban** de manera extraña.
No **había** duda
teníamos cara de turistas.

Simple Preterit

oímos gritos en la calle.
Marta y yo nos **levantamos** y
nos **asomamos** a la ventana
—Ya **comenzó** el Carnaval—
le **dije** a Marta.
Nos **vestimos** rápidamente
tomamos la cámara
salimos a la calle.

Exercise 56.

El Bogotazo

El señor Torres **era** un hombre maduro, casado con una mujer que **trabajaba** en la oficina de correos. El 9 de abril de 1948, se **encontraba** bebiendo una cerveza en el Café Royal, sobre la calle Séptima. De repente, **escuchó** una multitud de hombres armados que **venían** enfurecidos de todas partes, con palos y machetes. Como no **tuvo** tiempo suficiente para levantarse y salir corriendo, **decidió** refugiarse en el bar. Desde la ventana **vio** cómo hombres enfurecidos **destruían** y **saqueaban** todo lo que **estaba** a su alrededor. Todo el centro de la ciudad de Bogotá **estaba** en llamas. El señor Torres **pasó** la noche en el bar y sólo al día siguiente **logró** salir. Se **dirigió** a su casa, preocupado por su mujer. No **sabía** si **estaba** viva. Aunque **había** muertos por todas partes, el señor Torres **encontró** a su mujer sana y salva.

Exercise 57.

Answers may vary

1. Porque hacía mucho calor.
2. Porque no funcionaba bien.
3. Porque no tenía tu número de teléfono y no pude llamarte.
4. Porque estaba cansado.
5. Porque estaba enfermo y no tenía ganas de trabajar.

Exercise 58.

El barbero se **quedó** mirando a Evaristo, no **dio** crédito al cuento, y **pensó** que más bien **tenía** delante a uno de esos temibles bandidos, quizá cómplice o el mismo asesino de Tules, pues ya **había** leído en los periódicos el suceso; pero **tuvo** miedo; **hizo** sentar al cliente en la silla, le **ató** una toalla en el cuello y **comenzó** a cortar aquellas greñas espesas, pegadas con la sangre que **había** brotado de la herida que le **hizo** Juan con el serrote. Después lo **rasuró** y le **presentó** un espejito. Evaristo mismo no se **reconocía** . . .

Exercise 59.

1. Paco está tocando la guitarra.
2. Pedro está leyendo el periódico.
3. Daniel está durmiendo.
4. Natalia está comprando un boleto.

Exercise 60.

1. estoy encendiendo
2. estamos despidiendo
3. está lloviendo
4. estás alistando
5. está apareciendo
6. estás escribiendo
7. Estoy leyendo
8. está asistiendo
9. Estoy comprando
10. estás comiendo

Exercise 61.

1. Durante el otoño, las hojas **estuvieron cayendo** sobre el jardín.
2. El año pasado, Tomás **estuvo escribiendo** sus memorias.
3. Anoche, Nicolás **estuvo alistando** todo su equipaje.
4. Ayer, nosotros **estuvimos mirando** su última obra de teatro pero no nos gustó.
5. Ayer en la tarde el profesor **estuvo corrigiendo** las partes mal escritas de las composiciones.
6. ¿Por qué ayer **estuvieron recogiendo** las uvas si aún no estaban maduras?
7. ¡Durante toda la comida **estuviste sonriendo** con el esposo de tu amiga!
8. Nos duelen las piernas porque **estuvimos caminando** ayer toda la tarde.
9. ¿Cómo se llamaba esa muchacha con la que **estuviste viviendo** en Bruselas?
10. Los niños están cansados, toda la tarde **estuvieron subiendo** los muros de los vecinos.

Exercise 62.

1. estaban bebiendo
2. estaba vendiendo
3. estaba buscando
4. estaban bailando
5. estaban viajando
6. estaba oyendo
7. estabas leyendo
8. estábamos asistiendo
9. estaban construyendo
10. estábamos jugando

Exercise 63.

1. escribirá
2. alistaré
3. leeremos
4. insistirá
5. comprará
6. comerá
7. permitirán
8. enviará
9. beberás
10. recibirás

Exercise 64.

1. cabrán
2. habré
3. sabrás
4. cabrá
5. podremos
6. habrá
7. querrán
8. habremos
9. sabrán

Exercise 65.

1. compondrás
2. tendremos
3. saldrán
4. pondrá
5. valdrá
6. sobresaldréis
7. entretendremos
8. vendrá
9. equivaldrá
10. intervendrán

Exercise 66.

1. dirán
2. harás
3. contradiré
4. dirás
5. desharán
6. diremos
7. reharán
8. hará
9. satisfará
10. rehará

Exercise 67.

1. A las 4:45 P.M. los niños harán sus tareas.
2. A las 5:45 P.M. los niños jugarán en la computadora.
3. A las 6:30 P.M. los niños comerán.
4. A las 8:00 P.M. los niños verán televisión.

Exercise 68.

1. Ahora no tengo bastante dinero, pero el próximo año tendré bastante.
2. Ahora no hablo muy bien español, pero el próximo año hablaré muy bien.
3. Ahora trabajo en Estados Unidos, pero el próximo año trabajaré en España.
4. Ahora no hago mucho ejercicio, pero el próximo año haré mucho.
5. Ahora te obedezco en todo, pero el próximo año no te obedeceré más.
6. Ahora soy muy responsable, pero el próximo año no lo seré.

Exercise 69.

irás, celebrará, harás, compraré, regalaré, irás, visitaré, pasará, dejará, estará, llegará, sorprenderá, presentarás, organizaremos, prestarás, ganaré

Exercise 70.

—¿Quién crees que **ganará** las elecciones para el cargo de alcalde?
—No sé, pero dicen que Guerra de seguro **tratará** de hacer trampa.

—En el futuro cercano todo lo que haces y dices lo **sabrá** el gobierno.
—¿Dijiste lo **sabrá?** Hace tiempo ya lo saben.

—Ayer un virus atacó el internet a nivel mundial. ¿Cómo sabremos que esto no se **producirá** de nuevo?
—Creo que eso nadie lo **garantizará**.

Exercise 71.

—Mañana viernes, como de costumbre, Ana se levantará, tomará el bus, irá a trabajar, hablará con los clientes, hará ejercicio, comerá y bailará.

Exercise 72.

1. Estará enfermo.
2. Estarán jugando fútbol.
3. Estarán viendo televisión.
4. Estará en la corte.
5. Estará en un embotellamiento de tráfico.
6. Estará hablando con sus amigos.
7. Estará escuchando música.

Exercise 73.

1. ¿Saldrá a bailar todas las noches?
2. ¿Tendrá nuevas amigas?
3. ¿Querrá volver?
4. ¿Irá a muchos bares?
5. ¿Nadará en el río con amigas?

Exercise 74.

1. Las golondrinas **van a salir** con el sol.
2. El precio de la carne **va a aumentar**.
3. Las computadoras **van a ser** más baratas en unos años.
4. **Voy a tener** una entrevista para un nuevo empleo el próximo mes.
5. Tú **vas a emprender** un largo viaje.
6. Tus planes **van a ser** exitosos.
7. Esta historia **va a tomar** un rumbo impredecible.
8. Dos grandes editoriales españolas se **van a fusionar** en el transcurso de este año.
9. Si todo sale bien **vamos a comprar** un yate en abril.
10. La crisis económica **va a afectar** especialmente a las pobres.

Exercise 75.

1. Antes de gritar, Julio debería razonar.
2. Antes de salir a jugar, deberían comer.
3. Antes de comenzar un nuevo proyecto, deberíamos terminar este.
4. Antes de precipitarte, deberías calmarte.
5. Antes de regalarle dinero a los bancos, el presidente debería reflexionar un poco más.
6. Antes de subir la montaña, deberíais preparar el equipo.
7. Antes de comprar una casa, debería comprar un coche.
8. Antes de comer, deberías lavarte las manos.

Exercise 76.

1. —Yo que usted, no iría *or* Yo que tú, no iría.
2. —Yo que ustedes, no invertiría *or* Yo que vosotros, no invertiría.

3. —Yo que usted, no me retiraría *or* Yo que tú, no me retiraría.
4. —Yo que usted, no me saldría *or* Yo que tú, no me saldría.
5. —Yo que ustedes, no me los pondría *or* Yo que vosotros, no me los pondría.
6. —Yo que usted, no saldría *or* Yo que tú, no saldría.

Exercise 77.

1. Nos gustaría tener más tiempo libre.
2. Le gustaría conocer más gente.
3. Me gustaría vivir en Granada.
4. Les gustaría salir más a menudo por la noche.
5. Os gustaría ir con más frecuencia a cine.
6. Nos gustaría tener más libertad.

Exercise 78.

1. ¿Me podría usted traer pan, por favor?
2. Por favor, ¿me podría usted traer un vaso de agua?
3. ¿Podría usted traerme una garrafa de vino?
4. ¿Me podría traer usted una paella? Por favor.
5. Por favor, ¿podría usted traerme flan de postre?
6. ¿Me podría usted traer la cuenta, por favor?

Exercise 79.

1. —De entrada, ¿me podría usted traer un plato de jamón y lomo ibérico, por favor?
2. —De carne, ¿me podría usted traer un solomillo al oporto con setas, por favor?
3. —De postre, ¿me podría usted traer una cuajada de leche de oveja con miel, por favor?
4. —Para beber, ¿me podría usted traer una botella de vino, por favor?

Exercise 80.

1. —Quisiera azúcar *or* Quisiera miel.
2. —Quisiera una tostada *or* Quisiera un panecillo.
3. —Quisiéramos agua *or* Quisiéramos jugo de naranja.
4. —Quisiera huevos fritos *or* Quisiera huevos revueltos.
5. —Quisiéramos fruta o Quisiéramos helado.
6. —Quisiéramos pagar en efectivo *or* Quisiéramos pagar con tarjeta de crédito.

Exercise 81.

1. —Que recogerían el niño en la guardería.
2. —Que retiraría la demanda.
3. —Que aprobarían la ley.
4. —Que terminaría la guerra.
5. —Que protestarían hasta el final.
6. —Que metería a la cárcel a los ladrones.

Exercise 82.

1. Estaría enferma.
2. Estaría discutiendo de política.
3. Estaría escuchando un concierto.
4. Estaría hablando por teléfono.
5. Estaría en una reunión muy importante.
6. Estaría redactando la composición.
7. Estaría visitando a su médico.

Exercise 83.

1. Encontraría a otra mujer.
2. Tendría un problema en el aeropuerto.
3. Compraría una finca.
4. Despilfarraría el dinero.
5. Extraviaría su pasaporte.

CHAPTER 5

Exercise 1.

1. Leer
2. Hacer
3. Bailar
4. Beber
5. Ir
6. Correr
7. Comer
8. Caminar
9. Dormir
10. Conducir

Exercise 2.

1. **Quiero pasear** en el parque.
2. **Quiero nadar** con frecuencia para sentirme bien.
3. **Quiero cortar** el césped del jardín durante el fin de semana.
4. **Quiero ir** al cine porque estrenan una película interesante.
5. **Quiero leer** una novela antes de dormirme.
6. **Quiero ir** a un concierto de jazz con mis amigos.

Exercise 3.

1. Observé a mi abuela preparar la tarta.
2. Escuché la orquesta ensayar para el concierto.
3. Oí a un chico pedir auxilio en la calle.
4. ¿Ves salir el sol desde tu habitación?
5. Miramos a los niños patinar sobre el hielo.

6. ¿Escuchaste al guitarrista dar un concierto?
7. Sentiste a tu hermano cerrar la puerta.
8. Contemplaremos a Óscar hacer una escultura.
9. Vi a Patricia entrar en correos.
10. Oyes sonar el teléfono.

Exercise 4.

1. Al graduarme, viajé a Chile.
2. Al abrir la puerta, escuché a alguien hablar dentro de la casa.
3. Al leer el libro, aprendí mucho sobre la cultura azteca.
4. Al ver las noticias, nos enteramos de que nevaría mañana.
5. Al hablar con Laura por teléfono, me dijo que no estabas.
6. Al salir del museo, nos encontramos a Pepe.
7. Al hacer la compra, descubriste que habías olvidado el dinero.
8. Al abrir el mapa, supe dónde estaba.
9. Al tomar un café, me quemé la lengua.
10. Al manejar al trabajo, escuchaba las noticias por la radio.

Exercise 5.

1. Lisa está feliz de no tener clase.
2. Santiago está interesado en leer *El siglo de la luces*.
3. Marta está empeñada en visitar el museo del Prado.
4. Nunca voy a vivir pobre para morir rico.
5. ¿Todavía Sonia está con deseos de terminar con su novio?

Exercise 6.

1. El municipio nos dio el permiso para construir.
2. El congreso aprobó el dinero para reconstruir las escuelas.
3. Los estudiantes leyeron el libro para comentar en clase.
4. María trajo cerveza para dar y convidar.
5. Zoraida compró un vino delicioso para beber.

Exercise 7.

1. Jorge y Ana hicieron ejercicio después de nadar.
2. Julia compró palomitas antes de comenzar la función.
3. Esa lámpara además de iluminar sirvió para calentar.
4. Luego de llegar a un acuerdo firmaron el contrato.
5. Jorge, con tal de ganar dinero, engañó a sus conciudadanos.

Exercise 8.

1. plantando
2. comiendo
3. dando
4. construyendo
5. durmiendo
6. leyendo

Exercise 9.

1. Viviendo en Madrid conocí a Pepe.
2. Haciendo ejercicio, te sentirás mejor.
3. Viajando a Guatemala aprendí a cocinar tamales.
4. Viendo el partido de tenis, me tomé una cerveza.
5. Leyendo el periódico, estarás informado.
6. Entrando a la oficina, me dijeron que había una reunión importante.

Exercise 10.

1. Benito llegó a ser presidente estudiando.
2. La profesora enseña a los niños cantando.
3. Los niños salieron de la escuela corriendo.
4. Juan atravesó el Canal de la Mancha nadando.

Exercise 11.

1. salido
2. entrenado
3. llevado
4. divertido
5. trabajado
6. decidido
7. abierto
8. preferido
9. dicho
10. mandado

Exercise 12.

1. escritos
2. firmado
3. puesta, preparada
4. encontradas
5. construida
6. elegido
7. cerrada
8. rescatados
9. tomada
10. resuelto

Exercise 13.

1. borrado
2. pintado
3. usados
4. tenido
5. ido
6. preocupado
7. hecho
8. conocido
9. construida
10. corrido

Exercise 14.

1.	abierto	abriendo
2.	absuelto	absolviendo
3.	amado	amando
4.	bebido	bebiendo
5.	comido	comiendo
6.	cubierto	cubriendo
7.	dicho	diciendo
8.	descubierto	descubriendo
9.	encubierto	encubriendo
10.	escrito	escribiendo
11.	estado	estando
12.	hablado	hablando
13.	hecho	haciendo
14.	jugado	jugando
15.	leído	leyendo
16.	muerto	muriendo
17.	pedido	pidiendo
18.	podrido	pudriendo

CHAPTER 6

Exercise 1.

1. He caminado
2. ha escrito
3. ha leído
4. hemos comprado
5. han comido
6. hemos permitido
7. Habéis bebido
8. He insistido
9. has conseguido
10. ha enviado

Exercise 2.

1. he escrito
2. has dicho
3. he vuelto
4. hemos muerto
5. han frito
6. han leído
7. has visto
8. han descubierto
9. han abierto
10. han cubierto

Exercise 3.

1. —No, todavía no he ido.
2. —Sí, ya la limpié.
3. —Sí, ya comí.
4. —No, todavía no lo he conocido.
5. —No, todavía no los he hecho.
6. —No, todavía no lo he terminado.
7. —Sí, ya los grabé.
8. —Sí, ya los hizo.
9. —No, todavía no lo han terminado.
10. —No, todavía no se ha ido.

Exercise 4.

1. había abierto
2. habías bailado
3. había estudiado
4. había venido
5. habían vivido
6. habíamos roto
7. habían comido
8. había visitado
9. había llegado
10. habían muerto

Exercise 5.

1. —¿Ya **viste** la última película de Penélope?
   —¿Cuál? ¿Una en que **hizo** el papel de monja?
   —¡No! Esa ya la **había hecho** antes de venir a Hollywood.
2. —Cuando Martín **entró** a la casa, ya Andrea **había hecho** sus maletas y se disponía a partir.
   —¿Y él qué **hizo**?
   —Le pidió la llave del buzón del correo, pero ella le dijo que ya la **había dejado** encima de la nevera con una carta para él.
3. —¡La última vez que te vi aún no **habías dejado** los pantalones cortos! ¡Y mira ya hasta te **ha salido** bigote!
   —Sí es verdad, la última vez que la **vi** fue cuando **vino** a visitar a mi padre. Ud. recientemente **ha publicado** su primer libro, ¿verdad?

Exercise 6.

1. habré terminado
2. te habrás casado; habrás tenido
3. habrá despilfarrado
4. habrá conseguido
5. habremos hecho
6. habré comenzado
7. habrás ido
8. habré oído
9. habré llegado
10. habremos partido

Exercise 7.

1. Los asesinos se habrán llevado el cadáver.
2. La policía habrá perdido la pista de los delincuentes.
3. Un testigo habrá estado en el lugar del crimen.
4. El testigo lo habrá visto todo.
5. La policía habrá entrevistado al testigo.
6. El testigo habrá sido uno de los asesinos.

Exercise 8.

1. Probablemente el perro habrá comido basura.
2. Probablemente habrá recorrido la ciudad con otros perros.
3. Probablemente habrá entrado a un restaurante a comer.

4. Probablemente habrá mordido un policía.
5. Probablemente habrá jugado con los niños en el parque.
6. Probablemente habrá corrido entre los coches.

Exercise 9.

1. Aquel día nosotros habríamos comido, pero no teníamos hambre.
2. Esa noche habría ido al cine con ustedes, pero no tenía tiempo.
3. Aquella mañana María lo habría besado, pero no lo conocía lo suficiente.
4. Esa tarde habría jugado contigo al fútbol, pero no tenía el balón.
5. Aquel año habría estudiado, pero no tuve dinero para pagar la matrícula.
6. Aquella noche te habría dicho la verdad, pero no tuve la valentía de decírtela.
7. Ese día nosotros nos habríamos quedado en casa viendo películas, pero teníamos que trabajar.
8. Jorge y Tomás habrían ido a la fiesta, pero tenían que estudiar para un examen.
9. Ellos habrían construido la casa, pero no tenían los medios.
10. Aquel día, el presidente nos habría atendido, pero estaba muy ocupado.

Exercise 10.

1. Marcela ya habría probado las albóndigas en casa de su abuela.
2. El señor Rodríguez ya habría muerto cuando llegó al hospital.
3. Mi madre ya habría llamado cuando yo llegué a casa.
4. Roberto ya habría salido del trabajo cuando yo lo llamé.
5. Filomena y su hija ya habrían hecho las maletas cuando llegó el taxi.
6. El presidente ya habría tomado la decisión de ir a la guerra cuando asumió la presidencia.
7. Lucía ya habría pensado abandonar a su esposo cuando se marchó.

CHAPTER 7

Exercise 1.

1. Lucía se maquilla todas las mañanas.
2. El buzo se ahogó en el mar.
3. Tú siempre te emborrachas en las fiestas.
4. El bebé se levanta muy temprano todos los días.
5. Lucía se presenta al jefe como una buena empleada.
6. Fernando se mezcló entre los invitados.
7. Julia se duchó con agua caliente.
8. María se miró en el espejo.
9. Pablito se escondió en el clóset.
10. Liliana se vistió elegantemente para la fiesta.

Exercise 2.

1. Julio bent over.
2. Gabriel cut himself and complained.
3. Marta leaned on the table.
4. Lucía knelt down during mass.
5. The girl takes a bath in the tub.
6. The priest punished himself.
7. We freeze outside.
8. Poor countries govern themselves.
9. The ship sunk.
10. I injured myself.

Exercise 3.

1. se turnaron
2. se reunieron
3. se besaron
4. se abrazaron
5. se miraron
6. se pelearon
7. nos conocimos
8. se separaron
9. se miraron
10. os reunisteis

Exercise 4.

1. Juan and Pedro hate each other.
2. Luis and Felipe congratulated each other.
3. Luna and Liliana said good-bye to each other.
4. The boyfriend and girlfriend kissed each other.
5. The mother and daughter wrote to each other.

Exercise 5.
Después de una larga siesta, Juana **se frotó** los ojos, **se lavó** la cara, **se pintó** los labios, **se abrochó** los pantalones y **se puso** un cinturón nuevo para ir a la fiesta. Al salir, tuvo un accidente y **se fracturó** la pierna.

Exercise 6.

1. Felipe got his shirt dirty.
2. The children washed their hands.
3. I cleaned my shoes.
4. You washed your hair.
5. Laura and José both broke their foot.

Exercise 7.
Muy a menudo, los adolescentes **se rebelan** contra sus padres. Muchas veces **se jactan** de saberlo todo y **se quejan** de que nadie los comprende. Los padres a veces **se abstienen** de darles dinero y entonces los adolescentes **se arrepienten** de ser rebeldes.

Exercise 8.

1. Te fijaste
2. se abonó
3. encontró
4. se marcharon
5. se burlaron
6. se condujeron
7. se ocupó
8. se comió
9. se fían
10. abonaron

Exercise 9.

1. se enfermaron
2. me perdí
3. se alegró
4. se animó
5. nos sorprendimos
6. se quedó
7. se acostumbró
8. se desilusionaron
9. se fastidiaron
10. se enojaron

Exercise 10.

1. Se sabe la verdad.
2. Se dicen mentiras en tu casa.
3. Se tomarán las fotos.
4. Se firmó la ley.
5. Se compraron muchos dulces.

Exercise 11.

1. Se retiró ese producto del mercado.
2. Se encerraron los animales en el corral.
3. Se sacaron las abejas de la colmena.
4. Se retiró el dinero de los bancos.
5. Se llevaron los coches al taller.

Exercise 12.

1. Se cortan las papas y la cebolla en rodajas.
2. Se les añade un poco de sal a las papas.
3. Se sofríen en aceite a fuego lento.
4. Una vez cocinadas, se sacan las papas del aceite.
5. Aparte en un recipiente, se baten los huevos.
6. Se añaden las papas a lo huevos.
7. A fuego alto en una sartén y con una gota de aceite se colocan las papas y los huevos.
8. Se le da la vuelta a la tortilla y se cocina a fuego bajo por cuatro minutos.
9. Se sirve la tortilla en un plato y se come.

Exercise 13.

1. Se encierra a los presos.
2. Se castiga a los niños.

3. Se necesitan inmigrantes para recoger fresas.
4. Se elogió a los ejecutivos.
5. Se recogió a los invitados en el aeropuerto.

Exercise 14.

1. se corre
2. se camina
3. se preocupa
4. se ocupa
5. se habla
6. se nada
7. se llega
8. se viaja
9. se come
10. se dedica

REVIEW

Exercise 15.

1. Jorge se afeita a las seis y media de la mañana.
2. Jorge se baña a las seis y cuarenta y cinco de la mañana.
3. Jorge se viste a las siete de la mañana.
4. Jorge se pone su sombrero y se despide de su esposa a las siete y cuarenta y cinco de la mañana.
5. Jorge se sube en el autobús a las ocho de la mañana.

CHAPTER 8

Exercise 1.

1. Él
2. Ellas
3. Nosotros
4. Tú
5. Ellos

Exercise 2.

1. nosotros
2. tú
3. yo
4. ellas
5. él
6. ella
7. ellos
8. vosotros

Exercise 3.

1. usted *or* ustedes
2. ella
3. ellos
4. tú
5. Yo
6. nosotros
7. él
8. ellas

Exercise 4.

1. lo
2. La
3. Las
4. La
5. comprar**los**
6. la
7. Ábre**la**

Exercise 5.

1. En la reunión el presidente **lo** discutió.
2. La multitud **los** aprobó.
3. **Las** leí.
4. **Los** estoy buscando.
5. No **la** conozco.
6. Los científicos **la** encontraron.
7. Gabriela **las** vende en la feria.

Exercise 6.

1. le
2. le
3. Nos
4. te
5. Os
6. les
7. me

Exercise 7.

1. a mí
2. a ti
3. a él
4. a ustedes
5. a ellos
6. a nosotros
7. a ella

Exercise 8.

1. Roberto **se la** entregó.
2. No olvides de entregár**selo**.
3. Luis **se las** regaló.
4. Mi madre **me la** lavó.
5. Tu hermano **te lo** compró.
6. Desafortunadamente no **nos la** dieron.
7. El profesor **se la** explicó muy bien.
8. Finalmente el banco **nos lo** devolvió.
9. Raúl **se lo** dibujó muy bonito.
10. Rita **se los** pidió.

Exercise 9.

—¡Qué desorden hay en este cuarto! ¿Has visto mis zapatos?
—No **los** he visto. ¿Dónde los dejaste?
—Dentro de una caja blanca. ¿**La** viste por aquí?

—Sí. **La** dejé sobre el escritorio.
—No veo el escritorio. ¿Dónde **lo** pusiste?
—**Lo** saqué a la calle para que alguien se lo lleve.
—¡No puede ser! ¿Desocupaste los cajones?
—Ni **los** miré. ¿Tenías algo dentro?
—Mi colección de postales. ¿Cómo voy a recuperar**las**?
—Estaba bromeando. Aquí están tus postales. **Las** guardé en este sobre.
—Casi **me** matas del susto. Me alegro de que no **las** hayas perdido.

Exercise 10.

1. Sí, es suyo.
   No, no es suyo.
2. Sí, son nuestras.
   No, no son nuestras.
3. Sí, son suyos
   No, no son suyos
4. Sí, es mía.
   No, no es mía.
5. Sí, son nuestros.
   No, no son nuestros.
6. Sí, es suya.
   No, no es suya.
7. Sí, es suya.
   No, no es suya.
8. Sí, es mío.
   No, no es mío.

Exercise 11.

1. mío
2. vuestra
3. nuestro
4. suya
5. tuya
6. tuyo, mío
7. nuestra
8. míos
9. suyas
10. suya

Exercise 12.

1. mío; nuestro
2. nuestra
3. tuyo, mío
4. vuestros, nuestros
5. suyo, mío

Exercise 13.

1. aquellas
2. Esto
3. esa
4. este
5. esos
6. Éste
7. ese
8. Aquel
9. Eso
10. aquella

Exercise 14.

1. Aquellos
2. esta; esa
3. este; aquel
4. estos; aquellos
5. esas; aquellas
6. ese; esos
7. Este; aquel

Exercise 15.

1. Perdí un collar <u>que</u> **tiene** unas cuentas de marfil.
2. Me invitó un amigo <u>que</u> **es** arquitecto.
3. Ese perro, <u>el que</u> **está** allá junto al árbol, es el mío.
4. La única recesión <u>que</u> **se parece** a ésta es la de 1929.
5. Los perros <u>que</u> **ladran** en la noche son de Julia.
6. La profesora, <u>la que</u> **dicta** francés, es muy amable.
7. Es un amigo de tu hermana, <u>el cual</u> **habla** alemán, francés y español.
8. Las personas <u>que</u> **esperan** en la fila tiritan de frío.
9. Los amigos de Sol, <u>quienes</u> **están** enfermos, no pueden venir.
10. Siento una pena <u>que</u> me **oprime** la garganta.

Exercise 16.

1. Las flores que están en el jarrón son de muchos colores.
2. El collar de perlas que costó mucho dinero es de Julián.
3. Presentamos el examen de química, el cual fue muy fácil.
4. Es un pasaje de avión que costó 300 dólares.
5. Vivo en un apartamento que tiene cinco alcobas.
6. Vimos una película de horror que se llama "La pesadilla".
7. Juan vende una computadora que tiene un disco duro de 1T.
8. Silvia tiene una casa en la playa que es muy valiosa.
9. Encontré unos libros en el parque que eran de Gustavo.
10. El camino que lleva a la laguna está lleno de baches.

Exercise 17.

1. Nos robaron <u>el coche</u> **que** *tú* nos vendiste.
2. No crean los <u>rumores</u> **que** *ellos / ustedes* escuchan en la calle.
3. Encontraste a <u>la mujer</u> **que** *tú* buscabas por el internet.
4. Les compramos <u>el café</u> **que** *ellos / ustedes* nos pidieron.
5. ¡Encontraste <u>el gato</u> **que** *ellos / ustedes* nos regalaron!
6. Roberto trajo <u>unos dulces horribles</u> **que** *él* compró en el aeropuerto.
7. Finalmente compramos <u>la casa</u> **que** *ustedes / ellos* nos aconsejaron.
8. Llevamos a reparar <u>la máquina de café</u> **que** *tú* me obsequiaste.
9. Mi madre envió <u>el paquete</u> **que** *tú* le diste.
10. ¿Hallaste a <u>la señora</u> **a quien** *nosotros* buscábamos?

Exercise 18.

1. Lucía vendió la casa que compró en abril.
2. Juan no quiso el regalo que tú le obsequiaste ayer.
3. Visitamos los países que Juan nos sugirió.
4. Pedimos una cita con el médico que tu padre nos sugirió.
5. ¿Hablasteis con el agente que te dije?

Exercise 19.

1. quien
2. el que
3. el cual
4. los que
5. quienes
6. que
7. los cuales
8. el que
9. la que
10. quienes

Exercise 20.

1. que
2. que
3. la que
4. que
5. a quien
6. quien
7. el que
8. que
9. quien
10. los cuales
11. a quién
12. que
13. las que
14. que
15. a quienes
16. que
17. que
18. la cual
19. que

Exercise 21.

1. Lo que quiero es salir con él.
2. Lo que quiero es viajar a caballo y no a pie.
3. Lo que quiero es salir temprano para no perder el tren.
4. Lo que quiero es apagar la televisión para no distraerme.
5. Lo que quiero es verte pronto.
6. Lo que quiero es casarme contigo.
7. Lo que quiero es un buen trabajo.
8. Lo que quiero es descansar.
9. Lo que quiero es besarte.
10. Lo que quiero es decirte la verdad.

Exercise 22.

1. el que
2. Lo que
3. el cual
4. lo cual
5. el que
6. lo que
7. lo que
8. que
9. la cual
10. lo que

Exercise 23.

1. cuyos
2. lo que
3. cuyos
4. lo cual
5. lo que
6. cuyas
7. cuyo
8. lo que
9. cuyas
10. lo cual

Exercise 24.

1. Sí, me asombré de ellos.
2. Sí, soñé contigo.
3. Sí, hablé con ella.
4. Según él, se necesita...
5. Sí, están preocupados por ella.
6. Sí, vas a tener que ir sin mí.

Exercise 25.

—Esta es mi silla. Papá la compró para **mí** (me) el año pasado.
—¿Para **ti** (you)? Creo que te equivocas. Yo estaba con **él** (him) ese día.
—Si te sientas en ella no vuelvo a hablar **contigo** (you) nunca más.
—Tú no puedes pasar ni un día sin hablar **conmigo** (me), hermanita.
—Tienes razón. Soy tan charlatana como tú.

REVIEW

Exercise 26.

Fernando:—Hola Clarita y Laura.
Clara y Laura:—Hola Fernando.
Fernando:—Quiero que vengan a la fiesta de inauguración de mi apartamento la próxima semana.
Laura:—¿**Nos** vas invitar a **nosotras**?
Fernando:—¡Sí, a **ustedes**!
Laura:—Muchas gracias. Y, ¿cómo está tu novia?
Fernando:—¡Uhm! No se... ¿Y tu novio Clarita?
Clara: ¿El **mío**? **Yo** no tengo novio.
Laura: ¿Cómo está tu familia?
Fernando—Muy bien, gracias. ¿Y la **tuya**?
Laura:—La verdad, no muy bien. A mi padre **lo** despidieron del trabajo ayer.
Clara: Y recién ha comprado un apartamento.
Laura:—Sí, **lo** compró hace justo una semana.
Fernando:—Quisiera conocer**lo**.
Laura: ¡**Te** invito la próxima semana!
Clara:—¿Vieron la última película con Penélope Cruz?
Fernando:—No, no **la** he visto. De todas maneras no me gusta **ella** como actriz.
Clara: —¡Laura! Olvidé mi bolso en la cafetería. Hasta luego.
Fernando:—¡Espera!
Clara: ¡**Nos** vemos otro día!
Laura:—¡**Le** advertí que no **la** olvidara!
Fernando—¿Por qué no **le** dijiste que esperara un momento?
Laura:—Mejor así, así podemos estar solos. Anoche soñé con**tigo.**
Fernando:—¿**Conmigo**?
Fernando:—¡Oh! ¡Qué suerte tengo!
Laura:—¿Por qué?

Fernando:—Allí hay un letrero **que** dice: "**Se** reparan relojes". Y debo llevar el **mío** a que **lo** reparen.
Laura:—¡Déja**me** ver**lo**, que **yo te** acompaño!
Fernando:—No es necesario. Gracias. ¡Bueno...! **Nos** vemos otro día.
Laura:—¿Cuándo es la fiesta?
Fernando:—¿Cuál fiesta?
Laura:—¡**Aquella** a **la** que **nos** invitaste a Clara y **a mí**! ¡Idiota!
Fernando:—¡Espera Laura, no **te** enojes...! "¡A las mujeres no **las** entiende nadie!"

CHAPTER 9

Exercise 1.

1. El profesor habla **rápidamente**.
2. Los gallos pelean **violentamente**.
3. El pianista toca **suavemente**.
4. El jefe habla con sus empleados **cortésmente**.
5. El niño respondió a su maestro **inteligentemente**.
6. El padre juega con su hijo **cariñosamente**.
7. Julián Sorel la miró **tiernamente**.
8. La profesora explicó la lección **claramente**.
9. Anoche llovió **intensamente**.
10. El piano se cayó por las escaleras **estrépitosamente**.

Exercise 2.

1. estupendamente
2. groseramente
3. alegremente
4. rápidamente
5. enérgicamente
6. suavemente
7. ruidosamente
8. eficientemente
9. lentamente
10. amablemente

Exercise 3.

1. largamente
2. sinceramente
3. alegremente
4. absolutamente
5. discretamente
6. secretamente
7. rápidamente
8. frecuentemente
9. enormemente
10. gentilmente
11. locamente
12. suavemente

Exercise 4.

1. Aquel hombre está como loco.
2. No me siento bien.
3. Quiero que vengas pronto.
4. Los caracoles se desplazan despacio.

5. Ese muchacho está pálido; anda muy mal de salud.
6. No es fácil trabajar así.

Exercise 5.

1. Tus amigos vendrán **pronto**.
2. A nosotros nos gusta caminar **despacio**.
3. Rosalba se siente **mal** por lo que te dijo anoche.
4. No me gusta que me hables **así**.
5. No te preocupes, que estamos **bien**.
6. Lo hice **como** me indicaste.

Exercise 6.

1. muy
2. mucho
3. mucho
4. muy
5. Mucho
6. mucho
7. mucho
8. mucho
9. mucho
10. mucho

Exercise 7.

1. apenas
2. muy
3. muy
4. mucho
5. mucho
6. más
7. Casi
8. algo; poco
9. nada
10. tanto; mejor; tanto

Exercise 8.

1. Anteayer; antes
2. Antes; cuando; entonces
3. Anoche; aún
4. Ayer; hoy
5. Mañana; luego
6. Hoy; ayer
7. Ahora; luego
8. nunca
9. Todavía
10. Mientras
11. Ya; tarde

Exercise 9.

1. Cerca
2. Allá
3. Abajo; arriba
4. acá; donde
5. alrededor
6. encima
7. Detrás
8. debajo
9. Delante
10. afuera

Exercise 10.

1. e
2. c
3. b
4. d
5. a

Exercise 11.

1. de memoria
2. de mala gana
3. en el extranjero
4. de prisa
5. Al fin
6. en vano

CHAPTER 10

Exercise 1.

Part A.

1. Yo bailo.
2. Yo camino.
3. Yo cocino.
4. Yo comparto.
5. Yo vivo.
6. Yo veo.
7. Yo pongo.
8. Yo hago.

Part B.

1. bailes
2. camine
3. cocine
4. comparta
5. vivamos
6. vea
7. ponga
8. haga

Exercise 2.

1. duermas
2. vayáis
3. pague
4. empiecen
5. cierre
6. sepamos
7. agregue
8. desagüe
9. refreguéis
10. vayas
11. busque
12. almuercen
13. dé
14. ruegues
15. apacigüe
16. entregues

Exercise 3.

1. Es importante que lleguen puntuales a la clase.
2. Es necesario que corrijan los ejercicios.
3. Es bueno que repasen con regularidad.
4. Es necesario que escriban los trabajos en procesador de texto.
5. Es aconsejable que lean con cuidado el programa.
6. Es esencial que participen en las actividades comunes.
7. Es importante que estudien con anticipación los temas que se van a ver en clase.
8. Es recomendable que hagan preguntas para aclarar dudas.
9. Es importante que participen en los trabajos en equipo.
10. Es esencial que practiquen antes y después de clase.

Exercise 4.

1. Quiero que **vayas** al banco.
2. Quiero que **prepares** tu ropa.
3. Quiero que te **despidas** de tu hermana.
4. Quiero que **recojas** los billetes de avión.
5. Quiero que **hagas** la reserva del hotel.
6. Quiero que **riegues** las plantas.
7. Quiero que **lleves** el perro a casa de tu primo.
8. Quiero que **canceles** la entrega del periódico.
9. Quiero que **avises** en la oficina de correos que estaremos de vacaciones.
10. Quiero que **empaques** las vitaminas y los medicamentos.

Exercise 5.

1. No creo que los políticos **digan** siempre la verdad.
2. Dudo que el presidente no **cobre** suficiente dinero.
3. Es posible que los ciudadanos no **paguemos** muchos impuestos.
4. No creo que los programas de televisión **sean** muy educativos.
5. No estoy seguro que **seas** el mejor trabajador de tu empresa.
6. No creo que los vinos alemanes **sean** los mejores.
7. No es verdad que el fútbol americano **sea** el deporte más inofensivo.
8. No pienso que el precio de la gasolina **haya estado** estable en los últimos diez años.
9. No es cierto que sólo los niños **deban** usar protector solar.
10. No es cierto que la pizza **sea** un alimento con bajo contenido de grasas.

Exercise 6.

1. No creo que sea sano comer carne.
2. No creo que tu esposa gaste mucho dinero en cosméticos.
3. No creo que Jorge esté enamorado de ti.
4. No creo que la recesión económica vaya a cambiar nuestros hábitos de consumo.
5. No creo que vayan a viajar al Amazonas.
6. No creo que Lucía quiera comprar una casa muy costosa.

Exercise 7.

1. No creo que sea sano tomar el sol.
2. Es posible que te encuentres con tu ex-novio.
3. ¿No es mejor que vayamos a un lugar con menos gente?
4. Es evidente que tienes ganas de ver a Federico, tu ex-novio.
5. Es posible que prefiera quedarme solo en casa.
6. Es cierto que estoy celoso de Federico.
7. Es probable que no tenga traje de baño.
8. Me parece que va a llover esta tarde.
9. Prefiero que nos quedemos en casa.
10. Creo que el concierto de Juana es mañana.

Exercise 8.

1. Me encanta que seas sincero.
2. Me maravilla que seas honrado.
3. Me molesta que seas de mal genio.
4. Es terrible que seas desordenado.
5. Es una pena que seas olvidadizo.
6. Es una desgracia que seas imprudente.
7. Es estupendo que seas comprensivo.
8. Es lamentable que seas entrometido.
9. Es maravilloso que seas divertido.
10. Es bueno que seas muy inteligente.

Exercise 9.

1. Es una suerte que haya escrito.
2. Es el colmo que me ladre.
3. Es una desgracia que no tenga trabajo.
4. Es increíble que seas tan irresponsable.

Exercise 10.

1. No, no conozco a nadie que tenga un amigo en Madrid.
   Sí, conozco a una persona que tiene un amigo en Madrid.
2. No, no conozco a nadie que hable diez idiomas.
   Sí, conozco a una persona que habla diez idiomas.
3. No, no conozco a nadie que componga televisores.
   Sí, conozco a una persona que compone televisores.
4. No, no conozco a nadie que trabaje en la NASA.
   Sí, conozco a una persona que trabaja en la NASA.
5. No, no conozco a nadie que conduzca camiones.
   Sí, conozco a una persona que conduce camiones.

Exercise 11.

1. Busco un amigo que sea sincero.
2. Busco un amigo que tenga tiempo para mí.
3. Busco un amigo que hable y se ría mucho.
4. Busco un amigo que trabaje poco.
5. Busco un amigo que goce la vida.
6. Busco un amigo que sepa bailar.
7. Busco un amigo que disfrute leer.
8. Busco un amigo que no sea celoso.
9. Busco un amigo que sea chistoso.
10. Busco un amigo que sea muy inteligente.

Exercise 12.

1. Carol quiere un hombre que tenga dinero suficiente.
   Carol está casada con un hombre que no tiene dinero suficiente.
2. Carol quiere un hombre que la ame con locura.
   Carol está casada con un hombre que no la ama con locura.
3. Carol quiere un hombre que la trate de igual a igual.
   Carol está casada con un hombre que no la trata de igual a igual.
4. Carol quiere un hombre que sea verdaderamente guapo.
   Carol está casada con un hombre que no es verdaderamente guapo.
5. Carol quiere un hombre que quiera tener hijos.
   Carol está casada con un hombre que no quiere tener hijos.

Exercise 13.

1. Necesitamos un apartamento que tenga una sala grande.
2. Queremos un apartamento que esté bien ubicado.
3. Buscamos un apartamento que tenga una cocina moderna.
4. Queremos un apartamento que tenga vista al mar.
5. Necesitamos un apartamento que tenga una sala amplia.
6. Buscamos un apartamento que tenga garaje.
7. Queremos un apartamento que tenga portero.
8. Necesitamos un apartamento que no sea costoso.
9. Buscamos un apartamento que esté en un último piso.
10. Queremos un apartamento que sea luminoso.

Exercise 14.

Sonia y Javier tienen un apartamento en Houston que cuesta mucho dinero. Ambos quieren una vida más divertida y aspiran a vender el apartamento que tienen en Estados Unidos y a comprar uno en España. Sonia quiere que el apartamento esté ubicado en la ciudad de Granada. Javier está de acuerdo, pero además quiere que el apartamento quede en el Albaicín, el antiguo barrio moro. Sonia desea que tenga vista a la Sierra Nevada y a la Alhambra. Javier, también quiere que el apartamento no sea ruidoso y tenga garaje.

Exercise 15.

1. Tal vez trabaje durante el verano.
2. Quizás vaya a México este verano.
3. A lo mejor tenga que estudiar para los exámenes de doctorado.
4. Probablemente visite a mi familia en España.
5. Quizás tenga suerte y puedas venir a visitarme.
6. Tal vez compre una casa este verano.
7. Quizás juegue la final de la copa de fútbol.
8. Tal vez consiga un perro.

9. Probablemente conduzca a Montreal.
10. A lo mejor vaya al festival de cine en agosto.

Exercise 16.

1. llueva
2. despidan
3. llores
4. amanezca
5. tener
6. pidas
7. trabajar
8. oscurezca
9. ahorrar
10. hagas

Exercise 17.

1. se enteren
2. avise
3. se caigan
4. puedan
5. aprenda
6. se dé
7. ocurra
8. se hunda
9. quite

Exercise 18.

1. Por supuesto, para que pueda entrar.
2. Por supuesto, para que traiga cerveza.
3. Por supuesto, para que llegues temprano.
4. Por supuesto, para que tengamos donde sentarnos.
5. Por supuesto, para que no tengamos hambre después.
6. Por supuesto, para que esté limpio.

Exercise 19.

1. llegamos
2. dijeron
3. había planeado
4. tengo
5. están
6. había
7. indicó
8. necesitaba
9. prometí
10. llegaste

Exercise 20.

1. Después de que terminemos los estudios.
2. Hasta que aparezca Luis.
3. En cuanto tenga tiempo.
4. Después de que Jorge tuvo que retirarse del juego.
5. Luego que nosotros nos despedimos.
6. Cuando hayan comido.
7. Tan pronto como sean las siete en punto.
8. Cuando lo repare el técnico.
9. Mientras estaba comiendo.
10. En cuanto esté seca.

Exercise 21.

1. Cuando pinte la casa nueva.
2. Después de que leyeron el periódico.
3. Cuando se derrita la nieve.
4. Luego que cumplí 16 años.
5. Tan pronto como comience la primavera.
6. En cuanto tuvo una entrevista con el jefe.
7. Cuando cumplas 21 años.
8. Tan pronto como te dormiste.
9. En cuanto encontremos las llaves del auto.
10. Hasta que se acabe el mundo.

Exercise 22.

1. pueda
2. venden
3. entra
4. haya
5. podamos
6. termina
7. pueda
8. quieran
9. vaya
10. nos vimos

Exercise 23.

1. tenga
2. inscribas
3. advertimos
4. quieran
5. vimos
6. se acostó
7. rogaste
8. se trate
9. llegamos
10. vivamos

Exercise 24.

1. cambien
2. digas
3. espere
4. vea
5. dejen
6. sucedieron
7. saben
8. llegues
9. expliqué
10. era
11. pueda
12. arregle
13. son
14. ocurrió
15. comas
16. tenías
17. note
18. pronosticó

Exercise 25.

1. Ellos incluyeron
2. Ellos retiraron
3. Ellos repitieron
4. Ellos pagaron
5. Ellos influyeron
6. Ellos explicaron
7. Ellos destrozaron
8. Ellos caminaron
9. Ellos temieron
10. Ellos rieron
11. Ellos redujeron
12. Ellos produjeron
13. Ellos llegaron
14. Ellos fabricaron
15. Ellos decidieron
16. Ellos cruzaron

Exercise 26.

1. incluyera
2. retiráramos
3. repitiera
4. pagaran
5. influyera
6. explicaras
7. destrozaras
8. caminara
9. temiera
10. riera
11. redujera
12. produjera
13. llegaras
14. fabricáramos
15. decidiera
16. cruzara

Exercise 27.

1. Era importante que ustedes prepararan la tienda de campaña.
2. Era esencial que consiguieran combustible para la estufa portátil.
3. Era necesario que trajeran un botiquín.
4. Era importante que hicieran un mapa del recorrido
5. Era clave que averiguaran cómo llegar al sitio del campamento.
6. Ere necesario que compraran repelente de insectos.

Exercise 28.

Yo quería que fuera más grande...

tuviera suficiente luz.
la cocina fuera moderna,
el color de las paredes no fuera triste.
tuviera clósets para guardar la ropa,
hubiera restaurantes cerca.

Exercise 29.

1. Nosotros no pensábamos que vinieras.
2. Los ingenieros no creían que el terreno se hundiera.
3. La policía dudaba que se produjera un nuevo atentado.
4. Mi madre no estaba segura que yo viniera a ayudarla.
5. El juez no creía que el testigo estuviera diciendo la verdad.
6. Quizá si nosotros llevaramos mucho dinero podríamos comprar el anillo.

Exercise 30.

1. Marisela temía que se le mojará el cabello.
2. Yo me preocupé de que el dinero se perdiera.
3. ¡Qué miedo que hubiera una avalancha!
4. Me alegré que fuéramos juntos a la fiesta
5. Me preocupó que el gato no comiera.
6. La anciana se emocionó que nosotros viniéramos de visita.

Exercise 31.

1. Necesitaba un coche que fuera de color amarillo.
2. Necesitaba un coche que tuviera cuatro puertas.
3. Necesitaba un coche que marchara rápido.
4. Necesitaba un coche que frenara bien.
5. Necesitaba un coche que estuviera entre los diez mejores.
6. Necesitaba un coche que no fuera muy costoso.

Exercise 32.

Carmen **tenía** un perro que **se llamaba** Solovino y que **ladraba** mucho. Sus vecinos, que **eran** intolerantes, se quejaron. Carmen no **quería** regalar a Solovino. Ella pensó que necesitaba cambiarse de casa. Ella quería una casa que **estuviera** en el campo, que **tuviera** mucho espacio y que no **costara** mucho. Una mañana salió a buscar su casa ideal. Salió de la ciudad y en el camino a Veracruz vio una casa que **se encontraba** a la orilla de un lago, que **era** muy bonita, y que **parecía** deshabitada. Y lo mejor de todo era que en la entrada había un letrero que **decía:** "Se vende barata".

Exercise 33.

1. lloviera
2. despidieran
3. molestaras
4. amaneciera
5. pudieras
6. aprender
7. ponerte
8. oscureciera

Exercise 34.

1. fueran
2. se conservara
3. se mojara
4. probáramos
5. pudieras
6. llegaran
7. fueran
8. quisiéramos
9. pagamos
10. deslumbrara
11. alternaran
12. pudieran
13. fuera
14. cumplieran
15. pudo

Exercise 35.

1. hayas perdido
2. haya subido
3. hayamos encontrado
4. haya cerrado
5. hayan visto
6. hayan demostrado
7. hayamos gastado
8. hayas regalado
9. haya muerto
10. hayan encubierto

Exercise 36.

1. No creo que Luis te **haya prestado** la motocicleta.
2. ¡Es un milagro que Martín **haya llegado** sano y salvo!
3. Es posible que la tía Magdalena **haya vendido** su colección de sombreros.
4. No se sabe si Nubia **se haya ido** en el tren de las cuatro.
5. ¡Qué bueno que **hayamos conseguido** todos los disfraces para la obra!
6. No es cierto que **me haya sentido** solo.
7. Espero que José **haya separado** la basura en orgánica e inorgánica.
8. Es terrible que nosotros **hayamos destruido** el planeta.
9. No creo que los niños **hayan puesto** la mesa.
10. Dudo que tu hermanito **haya hecho** la tarea.

Exercise 37.

1. En cuanto **haya terminado** de trabajar, pasaremos por él para ir a la playa.
2. Definitivamente voy a usar estos zapatos todos los días aunque **hayan costado** mucho.
3. Voy a hablarles después de que **hayan comprado** los boletos.
4. Mañana iremos a la finca aunque **haya llovido** mucho.
5. Estoy seguro de que me llamará por teléfono tan pronto como **haya llegado** al aeropuerto.
6. La fiesta comenzará en cuanto **hayamos resuelto** el problema con el equipo de sonido.

Exercise 38.

1. hubiera llegado
2. hubiera podido
3. hubiera resuelto
4. se hubiera puesto
5. hubiera enviado
6. hubiéramos trabajado
7. hubiera dado
8. hubiera sido
9. hubieran destruido
10. hubiera dicho

Exercise 39.

1. hubiera dejado
2. hubiera apreciado
3. hubieran pagado
4. hubiera estudiado
5. hubiera ofrecido
6. habríamos ido
7. habría ido
8. habría permitido
9. hubiera querido
10. hubieran sido
11. habríamos reconocido
12. hubiera puesto

Exercise 40.

1. Ojalá hubiéramos tenido suerte en el concurso.
2. Ojalá hubiera terminado de escribir el libro a tiempo.
3. Ojalá hubiéramos ganado el campeonato de fútbol.
4. Ojalá hubieras venido a mi graduación.
5. Ojalá nos hubieras escrito.

CHAPTER 11

Exercise 1.

1. c
2. f
3. b
4. d
5. e
6. a

Exercise 2.

1. iremos
2. concentro
3. burlaban
4. llegan
5. sales
6. animo
7. quédate
8. escribiré
9. estás
10. puedes

Exercise 3.

Si conduces ebrio, te accidentarás, si te accidentas, irás al hospital, si vas al hospital, no podrás trabajar, si no puedes trabajar, no tendrás dinero para las vacaciones, si no tienes dinero para las vacaciones, no podrás ir a Grecia, si no puedes ir a Grecia te aburrirás.

Exercise 4.

1. Si el niño suelta la copa, la copa se romperá.
2. Si la mujer salta, la mujer se matará.
3. Si el viejo sigue mirando a la muchacha, el viejo se pegará contra el poste.
4. Si Julia no se despierta pronto, Julia llegará tarde al trabajo.

Exercise 5.

1. compraría
2. irías
3. ayudaría
4. tuviera
5. dijeras
6. saludaríamos
7. trabajaría
8. intentaras, lograrías
9. entenderías
10. cometerías
11. llegáramos
12. fabricáramos
13. decidiera

Exercise 6.

1. Si invitara a Carmen a comer, la llevaría a un restaurante elegante.
2. Si tuviera dinero, viajaría a Grecia.
3. Si hiciera una fiesta, invitaría a Carmen.
4. Si cambiara de carro, compraría un Alfa Romeo.
5. Si fuera viernes, iría a cine.

Exercise 7.

1. Si Memo tuviera novia no estaría triste.
2. Si consumiéramos menos viviríamos mejor.
3. Si Jorge y Ana hablaran menos los invitaríamos a la reunión.
4. Si Santiago fuera más disciplinado le iría mejor en la escuela.
5. Si vosotros pusierais la casa podríamos hacer la fiesta.
6. Si Teresa comiera más no estaría tan flaca.
7. Si ustedes hicieran ejercicio no se enfermarían tanto.
8. Si yo supiera conducir no dependería de ti.
9. Si nos regalaran los boletos iríamos al concierto.
10. Si Pedro se acostara temprano no estaría cansado al otro día.

Exercise 8.

1. habríamos venido
2. hubiera detenido
3. habría tenido
4. habría tenido
5. hubieran llegado
6. habría pasado
7. hubiera estado
8. habría quedado
9. habría despertado
10. hubiera cargado

Exercise 9.

1. —Si hubiera tenido una semana de vacaciones, ¿qué habría hecho?
   —Habría ido a España.
2. —Si hubiera tenido la oportunidad de escoger un coche, ¿qué habría hecho?
   —Habría escogido un Peugeot.
3. —Si hubieran perdido el examen, ¿qué habrían hecho?
   —Nos habríamos retirado de la universidad.
4. —Si Carmen te hubiera abandonado, ¿qué habrías hecho?
   —Me habría puesto a llorar.
5. —Si hubieran pasado el examen, ¿qué habrían hecho?
   —Habríamos entrado a la universidad.
6. —Si se hubiera incendiado tu casa, ¿qué habrías hecho?
   —Habría llamado a los bomberos.
7. —Si hubieras tenido que salir del país, ¿qué habrías hecho?
   —Habría ido a Italia.
8. —Si hubieran conocido a Einstein, ¿qué habrían hecho?
   —Le habríamos pedido un autógrato.
9. —Si te hubiera dado su teléfono, ¿qué habrías hecho?
   —La habría llamado.
10. —Si te hubiera invitado, ¿qué habrías hecho?
    —Te habría llevado un regalo.

Exercise 10.

1. Si Claudia no hubiera salido del país no habría conocido a Federico.
2. Si ustedes hubieran comprado aquella casa hoy habrían tenido un lugar donde vivir.
3. Si la casa hubiera tenido paneles solares la habríamos comprado.
4. ¿Si la gata se hubiera enfermado la habrías llevado al veterinario?
5. Si el volcán hubiera hecho erupción la ciudad se habría cubierto de ceniza.
6. Si el piloto no hubiera reaccionado tan diestramente todos habrían muerto en el accidente.
7. Si la situación económica no se hubiera empeorado no habría habido tantas protestas.
8. Si nosotros los humanos no hubiéramos tomado conciencia ecológica la humanidad se habría extinguido.
9. Si el planeta no se hubiera calentado tanto esas islas no habrían desaparecido.
10. Si los bomberos hubieran llegado a tiempo la casa no se habría quemado.

Exercise 11.

1. conociera
2. tuviera
3. estuviera
4. tuviera
5. se hubieran derretido
6. fuéramos
7. estuviera
8. existiera
9. conocieras
10. fuera

Exercise 12.

1. —Como si no me conociera.
2. —Como si tuviera quince años.
3. —Como si fuera un cohete.
4. —Como si fueran unos ángeles.
5. —Como si estuviera muerto de risa.
6. —Como si fuera nuevo.
7. —Como si tuviera una papa en la boca.
8. —Como si tuviera una pata de palo.
9. —Como si fuera un perro.
10. —Como si fueran marranos.

Exercise 13.

1. hubiera sido
2. hubiera sabido
3. se hubiera roto
4. se hubiera despertado
5. hubiera estado
6. hubiera pasado.
7. se hubiera muerto
8. hubiera descubierto
9. hubiera hecho
10. hubiera dicho

CHAPTER 12

Exercise 1.

1. ¡No les compre el juego!
2. ¡No sea amable!
3. ¡No le dé todo a su hijo!
4. ¡No tenga cuidado!
5. ¡No me guarde la ropa!
6. ¡No le pida perdón!
7. ¡No le sirva el desayuno!
8. ¡No nos prepare café!
9. ¡No nos suba la renta!
10. ¡No apague la luz!

Exercise 2.

1. Sí, empáquela.
   No, no la empaque.
2. Sí, llámala mañana.
   No, no la llames mañana.
3. Sí, suba.
   No, no suba.
4. Sí, pódalos todos.
   No, no los podes todos.
5. Sí, córtemelo.
   No, no me lo corte.
6. Sí, llénelo.
   No, no lo llene.
7. Sí, dígala.
   No, no la diga.
8. Sí, cuéntemelo.
   No, no me lo cuente.
9. Sí, apáguelas.
   No, no las apague.
10. Sí, siéntese.
    No, no se siente.

Exercise 3.

1. Escoja un título breve.
2. Incluya el nombre del autor.
3. Mencione el tema del cuento.
4. Haga una lista de vocabulario nuevo.
5. Envíe dibujos o fotografías que ilustren el cuento.
6. Prepare tres originales en sobres diferentes.
7. Ponga los sobres al correo.
8. Espere con paciencia la respuesta del comité de publicación.

Exercise 4.

1. ¡No les compres el juego!
2. ¡No seas amable!
3. ¡No le des todo a tu hijo!
4. ¡No tengas cuidado!
5. ¡No me guardes la ropa!
6. ¡No le pidas perdón!
7. ¡No le sirvas el desayuno!
8. ¡No nos prepares un café!
9. ¡No nos subas la renta!
10. ¡No apagues la luz!

Exercise 5.

1. Sí, préstamelo.
   No, no me lo prestes.
2. Sí, mézclala.
   No, no la mezcles.
3. Sí, llámala.
   No, no la llames.
4. Sí, búscame.
   No, no me busques.
5. Sí, escríbela.
   No, no la escribas.
6. Sí, págame lo que me debes.
   No, no me pagues lo que me debes.
7. Sí, llévalas.
   No, no las lleves.
8. Sí, anótala.
   No, no la anotes.
9. Sí, prepárala.
   No, no la prepares.
10. Sí, inténtalo.
    No, no lo intentes.

Exercise 6.

1. Saca a pasear al perro.
2. Levanta tu ropa del piso.
3. Tiende la cama antes de salir de casa.
4. Trae el periódico.
5. Aspira la alfombra de la sala.
6. Ayuda a tu papá a cortar el césped.
7. Saca las compras del auto.
8. Recoge tus libros.
9. Pon gasolina al auto.
10. Llega temprano esta noche.

Exercise 7.

1. Juega hasta que oscurezca.
   No juegues hasta que oscurezca.
   Jugad hasta que oscurezca.
   No juguéis hasta que oscurezca.
2. Ven a almorzar con nosotros.
   No vengas a almorzar con nosotros.
   Venid a almorzar con nosotros.
   No vengáis a almorzar con nosotros.
3. Sueña con el futuro.
   No sueñes con el futuro.
   Soñad con el futuro.
   No soñéis con el futuro.
4. Compra pan.
   No compres pan.
   Comprad pan.
   No compréis pan.

5. Olvida los disgustos que hemos tenido.
   No olvides los disgustos que hemos tenido.
   Olvidad los disgustos que hemos tenido.
   No olvidéis los disgustos que hemos tenido.
6. Haz un diseño del mobiliario.
   No hagas un diseño del mobiliario.
   Haced un diseño del mobiliario.
   No hagáis un diseño del mobiliario.
7. Di sólo lo estrictamente necesario.
   No digas sólo lo estrictamente necesario.
   Decid sólo lo estrictamente necesario.
   No digáis sólo lo estrictamente necesario.
8. Come todo lo que te sirvan.
   No comas todo lo que te sirvan.
   Comed todo lo que os sirvan.
   No comáis todo lo que os sirvan.
9. Vete de inmediato.
   No te vayas de inmediato.
   Idos de inmediato.
   No os vayáis de inmediato.
10. Entiende la gravedad de la situación.
    No entiendas la gravedad de la situación.
    Entended la gravedad de la situación.
    No entendáis la gravedad de la situación.

Exercise 8.

1. No te cortes el cabello.
2. No salgáis tan tarde.
3. No empujes.
4. No sea ingenuo.
5. No toquen esos cuadros
6. No penséis en cosas tristes.
7. No olvides tus promesas.
8. No cierre los ojos.

Exercise 9.

1. Compremos esa marca de jabón.
2. Vamos a jugar al parque.
3. No hablemos de política.
4. Gritemos.
5. Vamos a la cafetería.
6. Mandemos la carta a Julia.
7. Vamos a bailar.
8. No nos vayamos de aquí.
9. No vayamos al cine.
10. Vamos a la playa.

REVIEW

Exercise 10.

1. habla
2. venid
3. Vamos
4. Leed
5. griten
6. Pon; dejes
7. Corre
8. Siéntate
9. vayamos
10. hagas

Exercise 11.

1. Hagan las tareas.
2. Lava el coche.
3. Maneja el camión.
4. No vayamos a cine.
5. Pórtense bien.
6. Ven a mi lado.
7. Corre más de prisa.
8. Págueme más.
9. Préstame dinero.
10. Cruce a la derecha.

Exercise 12.

1. **Pique** la cebolla finamente.
2. **Pele** las papas, **lávelas** y **córtelas** en rodajas muy delgadas.
3. **Ponga** el aceite en una sartén.
4. Cuando esté caliente, **eche** la cebolla. **Cocine** a fuego lento y, luego, **eche** las papas.
5. **Añádales** sal y **tápelas**, **muévalas** de vez en cuando hasta que estén tiernas.
6. **Sáquelas** del aceite y **déjelas** enfriar un poco.
7. **Bata** los huevos con un poco de sal y mezcle con las papas.
8. **Ponga** todo de nuevo en la sartén.
9. Cuando la tortilla se cocine por un lado, **déle** la vuelta cuidadosamente.
10. **Sirva** la tortilla en una fuente grande.

CHAPTER 13

Exercise 1.

1. nunca *or* jamás
2. nadie
3. ya no
4. nunca *or* jamás
5. ninguna
6. nadie
7. ninguno
8. nada
9. ni
10. todavía

Exercise 2.

1. Todavía *or* Aún
2. algo
3. algún
4. algo
5. Siempre
6. Alguna vez
7. alguien
8. o
9. tampoco
10. nunca

Exercise 3.

1. nada
2. nada
3. nadie
4. algunos
5. ninguna
6. ningún

Exercise 4.

1. nadie
2. nada
3. nunca
4. ninguna
5. nunca
6. también
7. tampoco

Exercise 5.

1. Cuál
2. qué
3. qué
4. qué
5. qué
6. cuál
7. cuáles
8. cuál
9. qué
10. qué
11. cuál
12. qué
13. cuál
14. cuál
15. qué
16. cuál
17. qué
18. cuál
19. qué
20. cuáles

Exercise 6.

1. Qué
2. Cuál
3. Dónde
4. Quién
5. Cómo
6. Quiénes
7. Cuándo
8. Dónde
9. Cuántos
10. Cuál

CHAPTER 14

Exercise 1.

1. es
2. son
3. es
4. es
5. es
6. Son
7. es
8. es
9. son
10. son
11. es
12. es

Exercise 2.

1. está
2. estamos
3. están
4. estás
5. está
6. está
7. está
8. está
9. estamos
10. está
11. está
12. están

Exercise 3.

1. es
2. es
3. es
4. están
5. son
6. es
7. estamos
8. están
9. están
10. están
11. estoy
12. está
13. está

REVIEW

Exercise 4. (Answers will vary.)

La madre

1. La madre está de mal humor.
2. Está ocupada.
3. Ella es alta.
4. Está en la cocina

El padre

1. El padre está contento.
2. Él está sentado leyendo el periódico.
3. Él es bajo y calvo.
4. Él también es gordo.

El adolescente

1. El adolescente está parado tocando la guitarra.
2. Él es alto y flaco.
3. Él es un artista.
4. Él está cantando.

El bebé

1. El bebé es muy pequeño.
2. Él está en la cuna.
3. Él está llorando.
4. El bebé es muy bonito.

Exercise 5.

1. Marco Antonio **es** de Lima y ahora **está** estudiando en Boston.
2. El profesor **está** furioso porque los estudiantes **son** muy groseros.
3. **Está** lloviendo y Juan **está** todo mojado porque su chaqueta **es** de algodón.
4. La cita con el médico **es** en una semana. El médico **es** muy bueno.
5. Hoy **estamos** un poco cansados. El día ha **sido** muy caluroso.
6. ¿Me podría traer otro café? Este café **está** frío y la taza no **está** muy limpia.
7. ¿Cómo **es** el novio de Julia? ¿**Es** joven y guapo?
8. Roberto y Teresa **son** novios. Los dos **están** muy enamorados. La boda **es** en abril.
9. Mi tía **está** nerviosa porque su marido **está** cocinando.
10. ¿La casa de la esquina **es** la de tu hermana? ¿O **es** la que **está** al lado de la tuya?
11. Mi esposa **es** alemana. Siempre **está** hablando en alemán.
12. Tu esposo **es** un charlatán. ¡Siempre **está** haciendo alarde de que es muy rico!
13. ¿Qué hora **es?** No sé. Mi reloj **está** en el baño.
14. Los niños **están** contentos porque su madre **está** de vacaciones.
15. Bernardo **está** celoso porque su novia **es** muy bonita y **está** de vacaciones en Brasil.

Exercise 6.

Alberto: —¡Hola! ¿Cómo te llamas?
Lola: —Me llamo Lola.
Alberto: —¿De dónde eres?
Lola: —Soy de España. ¿Y tú, cómo te llamas?

Alberto: —Yo me llamo Alberto y soy argentino.
Lola: —¿Qué haces?
Alberto: —Soy matemático.
Lola: —¡Eres matemático!
Alberto: —Sí, la verdad que es una profesión difícil pero divertida.
Lola: —Sabes, hoy estoy un poco aburrida. Te invito a una cerveza.
Alberto: —¡Genial! Vamos al bar "La Casita de Piedra", es buenísimo.
Lola: —¿Cuál? ¿El bar que está en la calle Bolívar?
Alberto: —Sí, es un bar tranquilo y además podemos oír tangos.
Lola: —¿Te gustan los tangos? Eres un poco pasado de moda, ¿no te parece?
Alberto: —Quizás. Y dime una cosa, ¿tú que haces?
Lola: —Yo soy estudiante de administración de empresas.
Alberto: —¿Dónde estudias?
Lola: —En el Instituto de Negocios y Finanzas.
Alberto: —¿Dónde está ese instituto?
Lola: —Está en la avenida Las Américas.
Alberto: —¡Ah! ¡Ya sé cuál es! ¡Qué tal si vamos al bar!
Lola: —¡Vale! Vamos que me estoy muriendo de sed.

CHAPTER 15

Exercise 1.

1. A Pedro y José les corresponde lavar la ropa.
2. A nosotros nos conviene no gastar tanto dinero.
3. Daniel tiene tanta hambre que le cabría un pollo entero.
4. A Jorge le extraña que María no haya vuelto.
5. A vosotros os basta una comida al día.
6. ¿A ti te apetece una bebida?
7. Me alegra que vengas pronto.
8. ¿A vosotros os atrae ese hombre?
9. A nosotros nos agrada tu visita.
10. A Pedro le apasiona la literatura.
11. A nosotros ese perro nos costó un ojo de la cara.

Exercise 2.

1. nos encanta
2. le hace falta
3. le fascinan
4. nos toca
5. le sobra
6. les molesta
7. os quedan
8. me interesa
9. nos importa
10. le gusta
11. te fastidia

Exercise 3.

1. Al señor se le cayó su copa encima de la señora.
2. A la señora se le perdió algo.
3. A la señora se le quemó la comida.
4. Al señor se le rompió el florero.

Exercise 4.

1. A Julio se le perdió su perro.
2. A Pablo y Marcela se les perdió su anillo de matrimonio.
3. A Andrea se le rompieron los platos.
4. A Santiago se le cayó el armario.
5. A vosotros se os perdieron las llaves del carro.
6. A Clemente y a mí se nos olvidaron los pasaportes en la casa.
7. A Federico se le quemaron las tostadas del desayuno.
8. A Teresa se le rompió el florero.
9. A ellos se les perdió la maleta en el aeropuerto.
10. Al niño se le cayó la pelota.

Exercise 5.

1. A Juan se le cayó el vaso.
2. A ti se te quemó la carne.
3. A nosotros se nos rompieron los platos.
4. A vosotros se os perdieron las llaves.
5. A ellos se les olvidaron los libros.
6. A mí se me quemó la casa.
7. A nosotros se nos olvidó el dinero.
8. A Pedro se le perdió la billetera.
9. A ustedes se les olvidó pagar las cuentas.
10. A Lucía se le cayó el niño.

Exercise 6.

1. Al futbolista se le rompió la pierna.
2. Se me perdió el cuaderno.
3. A Fernando se le ensució la camisa.
4. Se nos dañó el coche.
5. A Nicolás se le olvidó hacer la tarea.
6. A Alina se le rompió el zapato.
7. A los niños se les acabaron los dulces.
8. Se me cayeron los platos.
9. Se me perdió tu número de teléfono.
10. Se nos quemó la comida.

Exercise 7.

1. Se me cayó la copa.
2. A José se le rompió su brazo.
3. Se nos acabó el agua.
4. A mi madre se le olvidaron las llaves dentro del coche.
5. A Susana se le quemó el arroz.
6. Se nos acabó el tiempo.
7. Se me perdieron las llaves.
8. A Julia se le cayó la botella.
9. A tu hermana se le rompieron los huevos.
10. A Lucía se le olvidaron los libros en la escuela.

CHAPTER 16

Exercise 1.

1. acabó de
2. acabé
3. acabé por
4. acabó
5. acabaron
6. acabaron de
7. acabó de
8. acabó

Exercise 2.

1. Siempre me acordaré de aquellos años dichosos.
2. El abuelo no se acuerda de nada; ha perdido la memoria.
3. Las tortugas se acuerdan del lugar donde nacieron durante toda su vida.
4. El niño no se acordó de que tenía que hacer los deberes.
5. El otro día mientras comíamos nos acordamos de ti con alegría.

Exercise 3.

1. ahorran
2. salvaste
3. ahorramos
4. ahorramos
5. salvar

Exercise 4.

1. andan
2. fueron
3. andan
4. anda
5. anduvieron
6. Vámonos

Exercise 5.

1. bajas
2. bajan
3. bajen
4. bajamos
5. bajó

Exercise 6.

1. se convirtió *or* se transformó
2. se convierte *or* se transforma
3. me he convertido *or* me he transformado

Exercise 7.

1. cuida
2. Cuida
3. cuida
4. cuidan

Exercise 8.

1. da
2. dio
3. dimos
4. dio
5. dio
6. da
7. dan
8. da
9. da

Exercise 9.

—He **dejado de** quererte porque eres muy grosero. Anoche por ejemplo me **dejaste** esperando en la entrada del teatro mientras estacionaba el carro.

—Mi amor, **deja de** pensar en tonterías y trata de componer las cosas.

—No querido, voy a **dejarte** para siempre. ¡Yo también tengo dignidad!

Exercise 10.

1. hace falta
2. echa de menos *or* extraña *or* le hace falta
3. echo de menos *or* extraño *or* me hace falta
4. echamos de menos *or* extrañamos *or* nos hacen falta
5. echamos de menos *or* extrañamos *or* nos hacen falta
6. echo de menos *or* extraño *or* me hacen falta
7. echo de menos *or* extraño
8. echan de menos *or* extrañan *or* les hace falta

Exercise 11.

1. hizo
2. hace
3. haga
4. hace
5. hace
6. hace
7. puso
8. puso
9. llegarás a ser
10. hace
11. llegaremos a ser

Exercise 12.

1. toca
2. jugar
3. toca
4. toca
5. juega
6. toca, juegan
7. jugar
8. toca
9. tocar
10. juega, toca

Exercise 13.

1. llevó
2. lleva
3. llevar
4. lleva
5. llevaron
6. llevó
7. llevan
8. llevan
9. llevamos

Exercise 14.

1. mudó
2. moverte
3. movió
4. mudan
5. nos mudaremos
6. había movido
7. mueve
8. muevas

Exercise 15.

1. pido
2. piden
3. preguntó
4. pidió
5. preguntan
6. pido
7. piden, pido
8. preguntaron
9. pedí

Exercise 16.

1. perdió
2. perdieron
3. Perdimos
4. se perdió
5. se pierden
6. Perdisteis
7. perdió
8. se le perdieron
9. perdió

Exercise 17.

1. prestar, presto
2. prestar
3. presto
4. presto
5. prestará

Exercise 18.

1. te pongas
2. se le pone
3. se puso
4. te pones
5. Ponte
6. poner
7. te pongas
8. Pusiste, pongo
9. se puso

Exercise 19.

1. queda
2. se quedó
3. quedaste en
4. se queda
5. nos hemos quedado
6. se quedó
7. se quede
8. nos queda
9. quedamos en

Exercise 20.

1. conoce, sabe
2. conozco, sabido
3. conozco, conozco
4. saben
5. sé, conozco
6. conocer, sabe
7. conocer
8. sabe a
9. conoces

Exercise 21.

1. sirve
2. se sirve de
3. sirven para
4. sirve para
5. os servís de
6. sirven de
7. sirven
8. sirve para
9. sirve para

Exercise 22.

1. tiene
2. tuvo lugar
3. tienen
4. tiene
5. tenemos
6. tiene que

REVIEW

Exercise 23.

1. Lucía cuida sus plantas.
2. Lucía le da de comer a su gato.
3. Lucía da un paseo por la playa.
4. Lucía juega tenis.

CHAPTER 17

Exercise 1.

1. Normalmente yo tengo **más tiempo que** mi esposa para estar en casa porque yo regreso **más temprano que** ella. Mi mujer trabaja todo el día. Yo, sólo trabajo por las mañanas.
2. El vino es **más caro que** la cerveza.
3. Mario **hace más deporte que** yo, por eso él **está más delgado que** yo.
4. Carlos **habla español más despacio que** Sara, por eso le entiendo muy bien.
5. El nivel de vida de los países desarrollados **es más alto que** el de los países subdesarrollados.
6. Las personas hoy día viven **más tiempo que** las personas de antaño.
7. Federico es muy vanidoso, y **compra más ropa** que su esposa.
8. Los franceses **beben más vino que** los americanos.
9. En el Caribe **hace más calor que** en Londres.
10. Ese coche **anda más rápido que** esa moto.

Exercise 2.

1. Mi hermana Carmen **es menos tímida que** yo; por eso ella tiene muchos amigos.
2. Hoy estoy feliz porque **tengo menos trabajo de lo que** yo pensaba.
3. La cena **fue menos cara de lo que** me dijiste.
4. Laura y Rosa **son menos trabajadoras que** Mónica. Ella siempre está en la oficina.
5. Roberto **es menos divertido que** Juan. Por eso yo prefiero salir con Juan los fines de semana.
6. José Alejandro **tiene menos entusiasmo que** Lucía. Por eso, Lucía no quiere verlo más.
7. Carlos **es menos amable que** su esposa Carmen. Por eso, nos gusta más Carmen.
8. La vida **es menos dura de lo que** uno se imagina.
9. Tomás **juega menos agresivamente al tenis que** su hermano Luis.
10. Antes **había menos contaminación que** ahora.

Exercise 3.

1. Alberto y Marcos son hermanos gemelos y tienen muchas cosas en común. Por ejemplo, Carlos **es tan alto como** Marcos, y Marcos **es tan activo como** Carlos. Carlos **come tanto como** Marcos, así que los dos hermanos tienen más o menos el mismo peso.
2. ¿Tu hermano **es tan guapo como** tú?
3. Yo no **duermo tanto como** tú. Para mí, es suficiente dormir siete horas.
4. Julio es bilingüe y yo también. Él **habla tantas lenguas como** yo.
5. Marta **trabaja tantas horas como** su hermano José.
6. Todos ellos **tienen tanta urgencia como** nosotros. Lo mejor es que nos apuremos.
7. Aunque no lo creas, el cerdo **tiene tanta grasa como** el pollo.
8. No te preocupes que todo va a salir bien. Yo **tengo tanta fe en que habrá paz como** tú.
9. Liliana **come tanto como** Pilar. Por eso, ambas se entienden muy bien.
10. Jorge **baila tan bien como** Lola. Ambos han ganado varios concursos de baile.

Exercise 4.

1. Fabián dice que el café colombiano **es el más rico** del mundo.
2. Para María las playas del Caribe **son las más divertidas**.
3. Este es el hotel **más elegante de** la ciudad.
4. Dicen que Tokio es la ciudad **más cara del** mundo.
5. Las abuelas siempre piensan que sus nietos son **los más inteligentes del** colegio.

Exercise 5.

1. Pedro es una persona muy orgullosa. Él siempre piensa que **es mejor que** los demás.
2. Este restaurante **es peor que** el restaurante italiano que hay al lado de casa.
3. Mariela **es menor** que su esposo.
4. Mi prima Carmen **es mayor** que yo.

Exercise 6.

1. Este **es el mejor** restaurante de la ciudad. Lo recomiendan en todas las guías.
2. Diego **es el menor** de sus hermanos.
3. El año pasado **tuvimos el peor** invierno en mucho tiempo.
4. Estoy pasando las **mejores** vacaciones de mi vida.

Exercise 7.

1. Cristina tiene unas recetas **buenísimas** para preparar el pavo.
2. La última vez que fui al cine vi una película excelente, pero la que vimos ayer fue **malísima**.
3. Esta mañana me levanté **tardísimo** porque no oí el despertador.
4. Me gusta mi profesor de historia porque es **inteligentísimo**, y sus clases son **interesantísimas.**
5. La clase de español es fácil, pero las de alemán son **dificilísimas**.

REVIEW

Exercise 8.

1. Julio bebe más cervezas que Lola.
2. Javier gana menos euros que Liliana.
3. Susana duerme tantas horas como Santiago.
4. Sebastián tiene más amigos que Marta.
5. Jorge corre tan rápido como Susana.
6. Luna es tan alta como Jorge.

Exercise 9.

1. Javier es el más pequeño de los tres.
2. María es la que tiene más pelo de los tres.
3. Javier es el mayor de los tres.
4. Lola es la más joven de los tres.
5. María es la mejor vestida de los tres.

Exercise 10.

1. Jorge es muy rico, pero Gabriel es más rico. Gabriel es riquísimo.
2. Julio es muy amable, pero Santiago es más amable. Santiago es amabilísimo.
3. Andrés es muy envidioso, pero Federico es más envidioso. Federico es envidiosísimo.
4. Melania es muy tacaña, pero Jonás es más tacaño. Jonás es tacañísimo.
5. Andrea es muy dramática, pero Claudia es más dramática. Claudia es dramatiquísima.
6. Sara es muy mala, pero María es peor. María es malísima.
7. Liliana es muy aburrida, pero Germán es más aburrido. Germán es aburridísimo.
8. Perión es muy valiente, pero Amadís es más valiente. Amadís es valientísimo.
9. Mario es muy guapo, pero Gabriela es más guapa. Gabriela es guapísima.
10. Kelly es muy nerviosa, pero Pedro es más nervioso. Pedro es nerviosísimo.

CHAPTER 18

Exercise 1.

1. Anoche conocí **a** tu novio, ¡es muy guapo!
2. Mañana iré contigo **a** cenar, te lo prometo.
3. El otro día, me encontré un anillo de oro en la calle.
4. Mi novia me invitó **a** Madrid.
5. Nos vemos **a** las ocho en el teatro.
6. Lucho me invitó **a** jugar billar.

Exercise 2.

1. Los libros son **de** la biblioteca.
2. La casa es **del** banco, todavía no la hemos terminado de pagar.
3. Ese suéter es **de** tu hermano.
4. El aire y el agua es **de** todos.

Exercise 3.

1. Los invitados llegaron **de** Perú.
2. Las anchoas son **del** mar Adriático.
3. Mi profesora de francés es **de** Lyon.
4. Estamos cansados, venimos **de** la montaña.

Exercise 4.

1. Los coches modernos son **de** plásticos.
2. Tu siempre estás pensando en castillos **de** arena.
3. Esas empanadas están deliciosas. Son **de** carne.
4. Me gusta el vino **de** La Rioja.

Exercise 5.

1. ¡Apúrate! Tu novio llega a las tres **de** la tarde.
2. ¿Qué hora es? ¡Las tres **de** la mañana!
3. Dentro **de** un año iré a visitarte.
4. A las dos **de** la madrugada nació.

Exercise 6.

1. ¡Tráeme los libros! Están **en** la mesa.
2. Las golondrinas llegan **en** grupos de a miles.
3. Los osos duermen **en** el invierno.
4. La botella está **en** el piso.

Exercise 7.

1. Ese avión va **para** Europa.
2. Las niñas están listas **para** partir.
3. **Para** poder jugar bien al fútbol hay que practicar.
4. Esa llave no sirve **para** abrir esa puerta.

Exercise 8.

1. **Para** el próximo año ya habrás terminado tu doctorado.
2. La tarea es **para** mañana.
3. Tenemos que tener listo el vestido **para** el jueves.
4. Lo siento, ya me comprometí **para** el próximo viernes.

Exercise 9.

1. Ella hace cualquier cosa **por** dinero.
2. Lo premiaron **por** su gran talento.
3. **Por** no estudiar, Diana vivió aburrida toda su vida.
4. A vosotros os invitaron **por** cumplir con el protocolo.

Exercise 10.

1. Esa catedral fue construida **por** Gaudí.
2. La imprenta fue inventada **por** Gutenberg.
3. La ley de la relatividad fue propuesta **por** Einstein.

Exercise 11.

1. Vamos **por** aquel camino. Es más corto.
2. ¡María! Ve a la tienda **por** aceite, que se terminó.
3. Voy **por** el camino tropical.
4. Fueron **por** lana y salieron trasquilados.

Exercise 12.

1. Las ondas sonoras viajan **por** el aire.
2. Robert viajó **por** tierra.
3. El hombre viaja **por** aire, mar y tierra.
4. Todos los invitados llegaron **por** barco.

Exercise 13.

1. Juaco está enfermo. Liliana vendrá **por** él.
2. Rocío cambió su reloj **por** el vestido de flores.
3. Tomás y Helena reemplazaron su perro pastor alemán **por** un conejo.
4. Te cambio este coche **por** el tuyo.

Exercise 14.

Eran las ocho **de** la noche, cuando Julio fue **por** comida al restaurante chino **del** barrio. **En** el apartamento lo esperaba su novia Graciela. Como eran las once **de** la noche y Julio no llegaba, Graciela se acostó **en** el sofá **de** la sala **a** esperar. Graciela había conocido **a** Julio **por** suerte, una mañana **de** abril. Aquel día, Graciela había sido invitada **por** el señor Felipe Naranjo, dueño del periódico "El Vespertino", **para** que conociera su empresa. El señor Naranjo pensaba, **en** su imaginación, que Graciela sería la madre **de** sus hijos. Cuando Graciela llegó **a** las instalaciones **del** periódico, fue recibida **por** Felipe con un exquisito desayuno con panecillos hechos **de** harina **de** maíz. Felipe le habló **a** Graciela y le insinuó que si se casaba con él, ella sería tratada como una reina. Le propuso inclusive que **de** luna **de** miel la llevaría **en** su propio yate hasta su isla privada **en** el mar Caribe, y que luego viajarían **por** avión **a** París. Después del desayuno Felipe le presentó **a** los redactores **del** periódico. Entre ellos estaba Julio, que había ido aquel día **para** reemplazar **a** Paco, uno **de** los periodistas **del** periódico, que **por** suerte **para** Julio se encontraba enfermo aquel día.

Exercise 15. According to the illustration complete the following sentences, using the appropriate prepositions.

1. El as **de** tréboles (A♣) está **en** la primera fila, junto **con** el dos **de** corazones (2♥) y el tres **de** picas (3♠).
2. El rey **de** diamantes (K♦) está **entre** el valet **de** tréboles (J♣) y el 10 **de** corazones (10♥).
3. **Sobre** el rey de diamantes (K♦) está el 2 **de** corazones (2♥).
4. **A** la derecha del rey **de** diamantes (K♦) está el 10 **de** corazones (10♥).
5. **Bajo** el 10 **de** corazones (10♥) se encuentra la reina **de** tréboles (Q♣).

SPANISH-ENGLISH GLOSSARY

This vocabulary includes the words used in this book. (Some exceptions are ordinal and cardinal numbers, and proper nouns.) Each word is followed by its grammatical function and its corresponding English definition. The definition is limited to the context in which the word is used in this book. Nouns, adjectives, and participles appear in masculine form. If the word is both masculine and feminine, it is so noted. The following abbreviations are used.

adj.	adjective
adj. dem.	demonstrative adjective
adv.	adverb
dem. pron.	demonstrative pronoun
def. art.	definite article
indef. art.	indefinite article
f.	feminine
g.	gerund
ind. pron.	indefinite pronoun
interj.	interjection
interr. pron.	interrogative pronoun
inv.	invariable
loc. adv.	adverbial locution
m.	masculine
n.	noun
part.	participle
pers. pron.	subject pronoun
poss. adj.	possessive adjective
poss. pron.	possessive pronoun
prep.	preposition
sup. adj.	superlative adjective
v.	verb

A

¡Ah! *(interj.)*	Oh!
a *(prep.)*	to
a menudo *(loc. adv.)*	often
abajo *(adv.)*	below
abandonado *(adj.)*	abandoned
abandonar *(v.)*	to abandon
abdominales *(n., m.)*	sit-ups
abeja *(n., f.)*	bee
abierto *(part.)*	open
abochornarse *(v.)*	to be shamed
abogado *(n.)*	lawyer
abonar *(v.)*	to credit; to fertilize
aborrecer *(v.)*	to hate
abrazar *(v.)*	to embrace
abrazarse *(v.)*	to embrace each other
abrazo *(n., m.)*	hug
abrigo *(n., m.)*	coat
abril *(n., m.)*	April
abrir *(v.)*	to open
abrocharse *(v.)*	to buckle up
absoluto *(adj.)*	absolute
absolver *(v.)*	to absolve
absolviendo *(g.)*	absolving
abstener *(v.)*	to abstain
abstenerse *(v.)*	to abstain
abstracto *(adj.)*	abstract
absuelto *(adj.)*	acquitted
abuela *(n., f.)*	grandmother
abuelita *(n., f.)*	granny
abuelo *(n., m.)*	grandfather
aburridísimo *(sup. adj.)*	extremely bored
aburrido *(adj.)*	bored
aburrir *(v.)*	to bore
aburrirse *(v.)*	to be bored
acá *(adv.)*	here
acabar *(v.)*	to finish
acabarse *(v.)*	to run out
acampando *(g.)*	camping
acantilado *(n., m.)*	cliff
acaso *(adv.)*	perhaps
accidentarse *(v.)*	to have an accident
accidente *(n., m.)*	accident
accionista *(n., m.)*	shareholder
aceite *(n., m.)*	oil
aceituna *(n., f.)*	olive
acentuar *(v.)*	to accentuate
acerca *(adv.)*	about
acercar *(v.)*	to approach
ácido *(adj.)*	acid
aclarar *(v.)*	to clarify
acné *(n., m.)*	acne
acoger *(v.)*	to receive
acompañar *(v.)*	to accompany
aconsejable *(adj., m./f.)*	advisable

aconsejar *(v.)*	to advise
acordado *(adj.)*	agreed
acordar *(v.)*	to agree
acordarse *(v.)*	to remember
acostar *(v.)*	to put to bed
acostarse *(v.)*	to go to bed
acostumbrarse *(v.)*	to get used
acreedor *(n., m.)*	creditor
actividad *(n., f.)*	activity
activo *(adj.)*	active
acto *(n., m.)*	act
actor *(n., m.)*	actor
actriz *(n., f.)*	actress
actualmente *(adv.)*	at present
actuar *(v.)*	to act
acudir *(v.)*	to respond
acuerdo *(n., m.)*	agreement
acumulado *(adj.)*	accumulated
acusado *(n., m.)*	defendant
acusar *(v.)*	to accuse
adelantado *(adj.)*	advanced
adelante *(adv.)*	ahead
adelgazar *(v.)*	to lose weight
además *(adv.)*	besides
adentro *(adv.)*	inside
adiós *(n., m.)*	good-bye
adjudicar *(v.)*	to award
administración *(n., f.)*	administration
administrador *(n., m.)*	administrator
admiración *(n., f.)*	admiration
admirador *(n., m.)*	admirer
admirador *(n., m.)*	admirer
admirar *(v.)*	to admire
adolescente *(n., m./f.)*	adolescent
adonde *(adv.)*	where
adorado *(part.)*	worshipped
adornar *(v.)*	to adorn
adquirir *(v.)*	to acquire
adquisitivo *(adj.)*	acquisitive
adulto *(n., m.)*	adult
advertir *(v.)*	to notify
aeropuerto *(n., m.)*	airport
afectar *(v.)*	to affect
afeitarse *(pron. v.)*	to shave
afiche *(n., m.)*	poster
afición *(n., f.)*	hobby
afligir *(v.)*	to afflict
afortunadamente *(adv.)*	fortunately
africano *(adj.)*	African
afuera *(adv.)*	outside
agacharse *(v.)*	to bend over
agente *(n., m.)*	agent
agobiado *(adj.)*	burdened
agosto *(n., m.)*	August
agradar *(v.)*	to please
agradecer *(v.)*	to thank
agradecido *(adj.)*	thankful
agregar *(v.)*	to add
agresividad *(n., f.)*	aggressiveness
agricultor *(n., m.)*	farmer
agricultura *(n., f.)*	agriculture
agua *(n., m.* if sing., *f.* if pl.*)*	water
aguacero *(n., m.)*	heavy rain
aguardiente *(n., m.)*	schnapps
águila *(n., m.* if sing., *f.* if pl.*)*	eagle
ahí *(adv.)*	there
ahogarse *(v.)*	to drown
ahora *(adv.)*	now
ahorrado *(part.)*	saved
ahorrar *(v.)*	to save
aire *(n., m.)*	air
ajedrez *(n., m.)*	chess
al (a+el) *(prep. + def. art., m. sing.)*	to the
ala *(n., m.* if sing., *f.* if pl.*)*	wing
alacena *(n., f.)*	pantry cupboard
alarde *(n., m.)*	boast
alberca *(n., f.)*	swimming pool
albóndiga *(n., f.)*	meatball
alcalde *(n., m.)*	mayor
alcanzar *(v.)*	to reach
alcaparra *(n., f.)*	caper
alcoba *(n., f.)*	bedroom
alcohol *(n., m.)*	alcohol
alegrar *(v.)*	to cheer
alegrarse *(v.)*	to be happy
alegre *(adj., inv.)*	happy
alegría *(n., f.)*	happiness
alemán *(adj.)*	German
alfabético *(adj.)*	alphabetical
alfiler *(n., m.)*	pin
alfombra *(n., f.)*	carpet
algo *(adv.)*	something
algodón *(n., m.)*	cotton
alguien *(ind. pron., m./f.)*	someone
algún *(ind. adj.)*	some
aliento *(n., m.)*	breath
alimento *(n., m.)*	food
alistando *(g.)*	getting ready
alistar *(v.)*	to prepare
aljibe *(n., m.)*	well
allá *(adv.)*	there
allá a lo lejos *(adv.)*	way off in the distance
allí *(adv.)*	there
alma *(n., m.* if sing., *f.* if pl.*)*	soul
almacén *(n., m.)*	store
almendra *(n., f.)*	almond
almohada *(n., f.)*	pillow
almorzar *(v.)*	to have lunch
alojarse *(v.)*	to stay

alquilar *(v.)*	to rent
alquiler *(n., m.)*	rent
alrededor *(adv.)*	around
alternar *(v.)*	to alternate
altísimo *(sup. adj.)*	highest
alto *(adj.)*	high
altura *(n., f.)*	height
alumno *(n., m.)*	student
alzar *(v.)*	to raise
amabilidad *(n., f.)*	amiability
amabilísimo *(sup. adj.)*	extremely kind
amable *(adj., inv.)*	kind
amablemente *(adv.)*	kindly
amado *(part.)*	beloved
amanecer *(v.)*	to dawn
amar *(v.)*	to love
amargar *(v.)*	to make bitter
amarillo *(adj.)*	yellow
ambición *(n., f.)*	ambition
ambicioso *(adj.)*	ambitious
ambiente *(n., m.)*	environment
ambos *(adj. pl.)*	both
ameno *(adj.)*	pleasant
americano *(adj.)*	American
amigo *(n., m.)*	friend
amistad *(n., f.)*	friendship
amor *(n., m.)*	love
amortiguador *(n., m.)*	shock absorber
amortiguar *(v.)*	to muffle
ampliar *(v.)*	to expand
amplificador *(n., m.)*	amplifier
amplio *(adj.)*	extensive
añadidura (por) *(n., f.)*	in addition
añadir *(v.)*	to add
analizar *(v.)*	to analyze
anchoa *(n., f.)*	anchovy
anciano *(n., m.)*	elderly man
andar *(v.)*	to walk
anécdota *(n., f.)*	anecdote
ángel *(n., m.)*	angel
anillo *(n., m.)*	ring
ánima *(n., m.* if sing., *f.* if pl.*)*	soul
animado *(adj.)*	animated
animal *(n., m.)*	animal
animarse *(v.)*	to encourage oneself
año *(n., m.)*	year
anoche *(adv.)*	last night
anochecer *(v.)*	evening
anotar *(v.)*	to write down
ansiar *(v.)*	to desire
ansiedad *(n., f.)*	anxiety
antaño *(adv.)*	long ago
ante *(adv.)*	before
anteayer *(adv.)*	the day before yesterday
antemano *(adv.)*	beforehand
antes *(adv.)*	before
antibiótico *(n., m.)*	antibiotic
anticipación *(n., f.)*	anticipation
antiguo *(adj.)*	old
antipático *(adj.)*	unpleasant
anunciar *(v.)*	to announce
anzuelo *(n., m.)*	fishhook
apaciguar *(v.)*	to appease
apagar *(v.)*	to put out, to turn off
apagón *(n., m.)*	blackout
aparato *(n., m.)*	apparatus
aparcar *(v.)*	to park
aparecer *(v.)*	to appear
aparecido *(part.)*	appeared
apariencias engañan (las) (idiom.)	appearances can be deceptive
apartamento *(n., m.)*	apartment
aparte *(adv.)*	aside
apasionarse *(v.)*	to be passionate about something
apellido *(n., m.)*	surname
apenado *(adj.)*	embarrassed
apenas *(adv.)*	barely
apendicitis *(n., f.)*	appendicitis
apetecer *(v.)*	to desire
aplaudir *(v.)*	to applaud
aplauso *(n., m.)*	applause
aplicado *(adj.)*	diligent
aplicar *(v.)*	to apply
apostar *(v.)*	to bet
apoyarse *(v.)*	to lean on
apoyo *(n., m.)*	support
apreciar *(v.)*	to appreciate
aprender *(v.)*	to learn
apresar *(v.)*	to capture
aprisa *(adv.)*	hurriedly
aprobar *(v.)*	to approve
aptitud *(n., f.)*	aptitude
apunte *(n., m.)*	annotation
apurarse *(pron v.)*	to hurry oneself
aquel *(adj. dem. m.)*	that
aquí *(adv.)*	here
arar *(v.)*	to plough
árbol *(n., m.)*	tree
archivo *(n., m.)*	file
arco *(n., m.)*	arch
ardilla *(n., f.)*	squirrel
arena *(n., f.)*	sand
argentino *(adj.)*	Argentinean
argüir *(v.)*	to argue
argumento *(n., m.)*	argument
arma *(n., m.* if sing., *f.* if pl.*)*	arm
armado *(adj.)*	armed
armario *(n., m.)*	cabinet
armonía *(n., f.)*	harmony
aro *(n., m.)*	hoop

arqueólogo *(n., m.)*	archaeologist
arquitecto *(n., m.)*	architect
arquitectura *(n., f.)*	architecture
arrancar *(v.)*	to start
arrastrar *(v.)*	to drag
arreglar *(v.)*	to fix
arreglarse *(v.)*	to get oneself ready
arrepentirse *(v.)*	to be sorry
arrestar *(v.)*	to arrest
arriba *(adv.)*	above; up
arriba *(adv.)*	up
arriesgar *(v.)*	to risk
arroz *(n., m.)*	rice
arruinado *(adj.)*	ruined
arte *(n. m.)*	art
artista *(n., m./f.)*	artist
artritis *(n., f.)*	arthritis
asaltante *(n., m./f.)*	assailant
asar *(v.)*	to roast
asegurar *(v.)*	to assure; to ensure; to insure
asentir *(v.)*	to agree
asesinar *(v.)*	to murder
asesinato *(n., m.)*	murder
asesino *(n., m.)*	murderer
asesorar *(v.)*	to advise
así *(adv.)*	thus
asistencia *(n., f.)*	aid
asistir *(v.)*	to attend
asomarse *(v.)*	to appear oneself
asombrarse *(v.)*	to be amazed
aspirando *(g.)*	aspiring
aspirar *(v.)*	to vacuum, to aspire
aspirina *(n., f.)*	aspirin
asqueroso *(adj.)*	filthy
astronauta *(n., m./f.)*	astronaut
astucia *(n., f.)*	cunning, ruse
asustar *(v.)*	to frighten
atacar *(v.)*	to attack
atar *(v.)*	to tie
ataúd *(n., m.)*	coffin
atención *(n., f.)*	attention
atender *(v.)*	to attend
atentado *(n., m.)*	attack
atestiguar *(v.)*	to testify
ático *(n., m.)*	attic
atleta *(n., inv.)*	athlete
atracción *(n., f.)*	attraction
atraer *(v.)*	to attract
atrapar *(v.)*	to trap
atrás *(adv.)*	behind
atravesar *(v.)*	to cross
atreverse *(v.)*	to dare
atribuir *(v.)*	to attribute
atroz *(adj., inv.)*	atrocious
aumentar *(v.)*	to enlarge; to increase
aumento *(n., m.)*	increase
aún *(adv.)*	still
aun *(conj.)*	even
aunque *(conj.)*	although
auto *(n., m.)*	car
autobús *(n., m.)*	bus
automático *(adj.)*	automatic
autónomo *(adj.)*	autonomous
autopista *(n., f.)*	freeway
autor *(n., m.)*	author
auxilio *(n., m.)*	help
avalancha *(n., f.)*	avalanche
avanzar *(v.)*	to advance
avenida *(n., f.)*	avenue
aventura *(n., f.)*	adventure
averiar *(v.)*	to damage
averiguar *(v.)*	to find out
avestruz *(n., m.)*	ostrich
aviación *(n., f.)*	aviation
avión *(n., m.)*	airplane
avisar *(v.)*	to notify
ayer *(adv.)*	yesterday
ayuda *(n., f.)*	aid
ayudado *(part.)*	helped
ayudante *(n., m.)*	assistant
ayudar *(v.)*	to help
azalea *(n., f.)*	azalea
azteca *(adj., m./f.)*	Aztec
azúcar *(n., m.)*	sugar
azul *(adj., m./f.)*	blue

B

bache *(n., m.)*	pothole
bailando *(g.)*	dancing
bailar *(v.)*	to dance
baile *(n., m.)*	dance
bajar *(v.)*	to descend; to download; to bring down
bajo *(adj.)*	short, lower
bajo *(adv.)*	low
bajo *(prep.)*	under
balanza *(n., f.)*	scale
balcón *(n., m.)*	balcony
ballena *(n., f.)*	whale
balón *(n., m.)*	ball
baloncesto *(n., m.)*	basketball
bañando *(g.)*	bathing
bañar *(v.)*	to bathe
bañarse *(v.)*	to take a bath
banco *(n., m.)*	bank
bandido *(n., m.)*	bandit
bañera *(n., f.)*	bathtub
baño *(n., m.)*	bath
banquero *(n., m.)*	banker
bar *(n., m.)*	bar
baratija *(n., f.)*	trifle

barato *(adj.)*	cheap
barbero *(n., m.)*	barber
barco *(n., m.)*	ship
barón *(n., m.)*	baron
baronesa *(n., f.)*	baroness
barrera *(n., f.)*	barrier
barril *(n., m.)*	barrel
barrio *(n., m.)*	neighborhood
base *(n., f.)*	base, basis
bastante *(adj., m./f.)*	enough
bastar *(v.)*	to suffice
basura *(n., f.)*	trash
bata *(n., f.)*	dressing gown
batería *(n., f.)*	battery
batidora *(n., f.)*	electric mixer
batir *(v.)*	to beat
baúl *(n., m.)*	trunk
bebé *(n., m./f.)*	baby
beber *(v.)*	to drink
bebida *(n., f.)*	beverage
bebido *(part.)*	drunk
bebiendo *(g.)*	drinking
beca *(n., f.)*	scholarship
béisbol *(n., m.)*	baseball
belleza *(n., f.)*	beauty
bellísimo *(sup. adj.)*	most beautiful
bello *(adj.)*	beautiful
bendito *(adj.)*	blessed
besarse *(v.)*	to kiss each other
biberón *(n., m.)*	baby bottle
Biblia *(n., f.)*	Bible
biblioteca *(n., f.)*	library
bibliotecaria *(n., f.)*	librarian
bibliotecario *(n., m.)*	librarian
bicicleta *(n., f.)*	bicycle
bien *(adj., m./f.)*	well
bien *(adv.)*	well
bienestar *(n., m.)*	welfare
bienvenida *(n., f.)*	welcome
bigote *(n., m.)*	mustache
bilingüe *(adj.)*	bilingual
billar *(n., m.)*	billiards
billete *(n., m.)*	bill
billetera *(n., f.)*	wallet
biología *(n., f.)*	biology
blanco *(adj.)*	white
blusa *(n., f.)*	blouse
boca *(n., f.)*	mouth
boda *(n., f.)*	wedding
bohío *(n., m.)*	hut
bola *(n., f.)*	ball
bolero *(n., m.)*	bolero (ballad with traditional Caribbean rhythm)
boleto *(n., m.)*	ticket
boliviano *(adj.)*	Bolivian
bolsa *(n., f.)*	stock market
bolsillo *(n., m.)*	pocket
bolso *(n., m.)*	bag
bombero *(n., m./f.)*	fireman
bondad *(n., f.)*	kindness
bondadoso *(adj.)*	kind
bonito *(adj.)*	pretty
bordado *(n., m.)*	embroidered
borrado *(part.)*	erased
borrar *(v.)*	to erase
bosque *(n., m.)*	forest
bota *(n., f.)*	boot
bote *(n., m.)*	boat
botella *(n., f.)*	bottle
botiquín *(n., m.)*	first aid kit
botón *(n., m.)*	button
brazo *(n., m.)*	arm
breve *(adj., m./f.)*	brief
británico *(adj.)*	British
bromeando *(g.)*	joking
brotado *(part.)*	sprouted
buen *(adj.)*	good
buenísimo *(sup. adj.)*	excellent
bueno *(adj.)*	good
buitre *(n., m.)*	vulture
burgués *(n., m.)*	bourgeois; middle class
burlar *(v.)*	to deceive
burlarse *(v.)*	to mock; to make fun
bus *(n., m.)*	bus
buscando *(g.)*	seeking
buscar *(v.)*	to seek
buzo *(n., m.)*	scuba diver
buzón *(n., m.)*	mailbox

C

caballería *(n., f.)*	cavalry
caballero *(n., m.)*	gentleman
caballo *(n., m.)*	horse
cabaña *(n., f.)*	cabin
cabello *(n., m.)*	hair
caber *(v.)*	to fit
cabeza *(n., f.)*	head
cable *(n., m.)*	cable
cacao *(n., m.)*	cocoa; chocolate; cacao
cachorro *(n., m.)*	puppy
cada *(adj., inv.)*	each
cadáver *(n., m.)*	cadaver; corpse
cadera *(n., f.)*	hip
caer *(v.)*	to fall
caerse *(v.)*	to fall down
café *(n., m.)*	coffee; coffee shop
cafetera *(n., f.)*	coffee pot
cafetería *(n., f.)*	cafeteria
caída *(n., f.)*	fall
caído *(part.)*	fallen

caja *(n., f.)*	box
cajero *(n., m.)*	cashier
cajón *(n., m.)*	drawer
calamar *(n., m.)*	squid
calcetín *(n., m.)*	sock
calculadora *(n., f.)*	calculator
calefacción *(n., f.)*	heater; heating
calentado *(part.)*	heated
calentamiento *(n., m.)*	warm-up
calentar *(v.)*	to heat
calidad *(n., f.)*	quality
cálido *(adj.)*	warm
caliente *(adj.)*	hot
calificación *(n., f.)*	assessment; evaluation
calificar *(v.)*	to grade
cáliz *(n., m.)*	chalice
callarse *(v.)*	to be quiet
calle *(n., f.)*	street
calma *(n., f.)*	calm
calmarse *(v.)*	to calm down
calor *(n., m.)*	heat
caloría *(n., f.)*	calory
caluroso *(adj.)*	hot
calva *(n., f.)*	bald head
calvo *(adj.)*	bald
cama *(n., f.)*	bed
cámara *(n., f.)*	chamber; camera
camarada *(n., m./f.)*	comrade
cambiar *(v.)*	to change
cambiarse *(v.)*	to be changed
cambio *(n., m.)*	change
camello *(n., m.)*	camel
caminando *(g.)*	walking
caminar *(v.)*	to walk
camino *(n., m.)*	road
camión *(n., m.)*	truck
camioneta *(n., f.)*	van
camisa *(n., f.)*	shirt
campamento *(n., m.)*	camp
campana *(n., f.)*	bell
campaña *(n., f.)*	campaign
campeón *(n., m.)*	champion
campeonato *(n., m.)*	championship
campesino *(n., m.)*	peasant
campo *(n., m.)*	field
caña *(n., f.)*	cane; fishing rod
canal *(n., m.)*	channel
canasta *(n., f.)*	basket
cancelar *(v.)*	to cancel
cáncer *(n., m.)*	cancer
canción *(n., f.)*	song
candidata *(n., f.)*	candidate
cansado *(adj.)*	tired
cansarse *(v.)*	to get tired
cantando *(g.)*	singing
cantante *(n., m./f.)*	singer
cantar *(v.)*	to sing
cántaros, llover a *(loc. adv)*	to rain cats and dogs
cantidad *(n., f.)*	quantity
caótico *(adj.)*	chaotic
capacidad *(n., f.)*	capacity
capaz *(adj., m./f.)*	capable; able
capilla *(n., f.)*	chapel
capital *(n., f.)*	capital (city)
capital *(n., m.)*	capital (money)
capricho *(n., m.)*	whim
captura *(n., f.)*	capture
cara *(n., f.)*	face
caracol *(n., m.)*	snail
cárcel *(n., f.)*	jail
cargador de bebé *(n., m.)*	baby carrier
cargar *(v.)*	to charge, to carry
cargo *(n., m.)*	post
See also *hacerse cargo de*	
caridad *(n., f.)*	charity
caries *(n., f.)*	tooth decay
cariño *(n., m.)*	affection
carnaval *(n., m.)*	carnival
carne *(n., f.)*	meat
carnero *(n., m.)*	ram
caro *(adj.)*	expensive
caro *(adj.)*	expensive
carpintero *(n., m.)*	carpenter
carrera *(n., f.)*	career; race
carretera *(n., f.)*	road
carrito *(n., m.)*	little cart
carro *(n., m.)*	car
carta *(n., f.)*	letter
cartero *(n., m.)*	mailman
casa *(n., f.)*	house
casado *(adj.)*	married
casarse *(v.)*	to get married
casi *(adv.)*	almost
casino *(n., m.)*	casino
casita *(n., f.)*	little house
caso *(n., m.)*	See *hacer caso*
castigar *(v.)*	to punish
castigo *(n., m.)*	punishment
castillo *(n., m.)*	castle
catedral *(n., f.)*	cathedral
causa *(n., f.)*	cause
cava *(n., f.)*	wine cellar
caverna *(n., f.)*	cavern
cayendo *(g.)*	falling
caza *(n., f.)*	hunt
cazador *(n., m.)*	hunter
cazar *(v.)*	to hunt
cebolla *(n., f.)*	onion
cebra *(n., f.)*	zebra
ceder *(v.)*	cede, relinquish

cejas *(n., f.)*	brows
celebración *(n., f.)*	celebration
celebrar *(v.)*	to celebrate
célebre *(adj., m./f.)*	famous
celos *(n., m.)*	jealousy
celoso *(n., m.)*	jealous
cena *(n., f.)*	supper
cenar *(v.)*	to have dinner
ceniza *(n., f.)*	ash
ceño *(n., m.)*	frown
centímetro *(n., m.)*	centimeter
central *(adj., inv.)*	central
centro *(n., m.)*	center
cepillarse *(v.)*	to brush
cerca *(adv.)*	nearby
cercano *(adj.)*	close
cercar *(v.)*	to surround
cerdo *(n., m.)*	pig; pork
cereal *(n., m.)*	cereal
cerebro *(n., m.)*	brain
ceremonia *(n., f.)*	ceremony
cerrado *(adj.)*	closed
cerrar *(v.)*	to close
cerveza *(n., f.)*	beer
césped *(n., m.)*	lawn
chaqueta *(n., f.)*	jacket
charlatán *(n., m.)*	charlatan
cheque *(n., m.)*	check
chica *(n., f.)*	girl
chico *(n., m.)*	boy
chimenea *(n., f.)*	chimney
chimpancé *(n., m.)*	chimpanzee
chino *(adj.)*	Chinese
chiquillo *(n., m.)*	kid
chistoso *(adj.)*	funny
chocante *(adj., m./f.)*	shocking
chocar *(v.)*	to collide
chocolate *(n., m.)*	chocolate
chofer *(n., m.)*	driver
ciclismo *(n., m.)*	cycling
ciclista *(n., f.)*	biker
cicuta *(n., f.)*	hemlock
ciegamente *(adv.)*	blindly
cielo *(n., m.)*	sky
ciencia *(n., f.)*	science
científico *(adj.)*	scientific
científico *(n., m.)*	scientist
cierto *(adj.)*	certain
cifra *(n., f.)*	figure
cine *(n., m.)*	movies
circulación *(n., f.)*	traffic; circulation
circular *(v.)*	to circulate
cita *(n., f.)*	meeting
ciudad *(n., f.)*	city
ciudadano *(n., m.)*	citizen
claridad *(n., f.)*	clarity
claro *(adj.)*	clear
clase *(n., f.)*	class
clemencia *(n., f.)*	clemency
cliente *(n., m./f.)*	client
clima *(n., m.)*	climate
clóset *(n., m.)*	closet
coalición *(n., f.)*	coalition
cobrar *(v.)*	to charge
cocer *(v.)*	to cook
coche *(n., m.)*	car
cocina *(n., f.)*	kitchen
cocinado *(adj.)*	cooked
cocinar *(v.)*	to cook
cocinero *(n., m.)*	cook
coco *(n., m.)*	coconut
cohete *(n., m.)*	rocket
colección *(n., f.)*	collection
colegio *(n., m.)*	school
colgar *(v.)*	to hang
colina *(n., f.)*	hill
collar *(n., m.)*	necklace
colmena *(n., f.)*	beehive
colmo	See *Es el colmo.*
colocar *(v.)*	to place
colombiano *(adj.)*	Colombian
color *(n., m.)*	color
combustible *(n., m.)*	combustible; flammable
comentar *(v.)*	to comment
comenzar *(v.)*	to begin
comer *(v.)*	to eat
comercial *(adj., m./f.)*	commercial
comestible *(adj., m./f.)*	edible
cometer *(v.)*	to commit
comida *(n., f.)*	food
comido *(part.)*	eaten
comiendo *(g.)*	eating
comité *(n., m.)*	committee
como *(adv.)*	how
cómo *(adv.)*	how?
como *(prep.)*	as
compañero *(n., m.)*	companion
compañía *(n., f.)*	company
compartir *(v.)*	to share
compás *(n., m.)*	compass
competencia *(n., f.)*	competence
compitiendo *(g.)*	competing
completamente *(adv.)*	completely
completar *(v.)*	to complete
completo *(adj.)*	complete
complicar *(v.)*	to complicate
cómplice *(n., m.)*	accomplice
complot *(n., m.)*	conspiracy
componente *(n., m.)*	component
componer *(v.)*	to compose

comportamiento *(n., m.)*	behavior
composición *(n., f.)*	composition
compra *(n., f.)*	purchase
comprado *(part.)*	bought
comprar *(v.)*	to buy
comprender *(v.)*	to understand
comprensible *(adj., inv.)*	understandable
comprensivo *(adj.)*	comprehensive
comprometer *(v.)*	to commit
compuesto *(n., m.)*	compound
computador *(n., m.)*	computer
computadora *(n., f.)*	computer
común *(adj., m./f.)*	common
con *(prep.)*	with
concentrar *(v.)*	to concentrate
concentrarse *(pron. v.)*	to concentrate oneself
concepto *(n., m.)*	concept
conciencia *(n., f.)*	consciousness
concierto *(n., m.)*	concert
concluir *(v.)*	to conclude
concurso *(n., m.)*	contest
condenar *(v.)*	to condemn
conducir *(v.)*	to drive
conducirse *(v.)*	to behave
conductor *(n., m.)*	driver; chauffeur
conectar *(v.)*	to connect
conejito *(n., m.)*	little rabbit
conejo *(n., m.)*	rabbit
conferencia *(n., f.)*	conference
confesar *(v.)*	to confess
confesión *(n., f.)*	confession
confianza *(n., f.)*	confidence
confiar *(v.)*	to confide; to trust
congelador *(n., m.)*	freezer
congelarse *(v.)*	to freeze
congresista *(n., m/f)*	congress member
congreso *(n., m.)*	congress
conmigo *(pers. pron.)*	with me
conocer *(v.)*	to know
conocido *(part.)*	known
conocimiento *(n., m.)*	knowledge
conquistar *(v.)*	to conquer
consecuencia *(n., f.)*	consequence
conseguir *(v.)*	to obtain
consejo *(n., m.)*	counsel
consentimiento *(n., m.)*	consent
consentir *(v.)*	to spoil; to allow
conservarse *(v.)*	to preserve
constante *(adj., m./f.)*	constant
constituir *(v.)*	to constitute
construido *(part.)*	constructed; built
construir *(v.)*	to build
consultorio *(n., m.)*	doctor's office
consumir *(v.)*	to consume
consumo *(n., m.)*	consumption
contagioso *(adj.)*	contagious
contaminación *(n., f.)*	contamination
contaminar *(v.)*	to contaminate
contar *(v.)*	to count; to tell a story
contemplar *(v.)*	to contemplate
contener *(v.)*	to contain
contenido *(n., m.)*	content
contento *(adj.)*	content; happy
contestar *(v.)*	to answer
contigo *(pers. pron.)*	with you
continuar *(v.)*	to continue
contra *(prep.)*	against
contradecir *(v.)*	to contradict
contraer *(v.)*	to contract
contrario *(n., m.)*	contrary
contrato *(n., m.)*	contract
contravenir *(v.)*	to contravene
contribuir *(v.)*	to contribute
contrincante *(n., m.)*	opponent
convencer *(v.)*	to convince
convencido *(part.)*	convinced
convenir *(v.)*	to agree
conversar *(v.)*	to converse
convertido *(part.)*	converted
convertir *(v.)*	to convert
convertirse *(pron. v.)*	to became or change into
convidar *(v.)*	to invite
convincente *(adj.)*	convincing
copa *(n., f.)*	cup; glass (wine)
corazón *(n., m.)*	heart
cordillera *(n., f.)*	mountain range
corral *(n., m.)*	corral
correcaminos *(n., m.)*	roadrunner
corredor *(n., m.)*	hall
corregir *(v.)*	to correct
correo *(n., m.)*	mail
correo electrónico *(n., m.)*	e-mail
correos *(n., m.)*	post office
correr *(v.)*	to run
correspondencia *(n., f.)*	correspondence; mail
corresponder *(v.)*	to correspond
corrido	moved
corriendo *(g.)*	running
corroer *(v.)*	to corrode
cortar *(v.)*	to cut
cortarse *(v.)*	to cut oneself
corte *(n., f.)*	court
corte *(n., m.)*	cut
cortés *(adj., m./f.)*	courteous
cortesía *(n., f.)*	courtesy
cortina *(n., f.)*	curtain
corto *(adj.)*	short
cosa *(n., f.)*	thing
cosecha *(n., f.)*	crop; harvest
coser *(v.)*	to sew

cosméticos *(n., m.)* cosmetics
costa *(n., f.)* coast
costar *(v.)* to cost
costo *(n., m.)* cost
costoso *(adj.)* costly
cotidiano *(adj.)* quotidian; routine
crear *(v.)* to create
creciendo *(g.)* growing
crédito *(n., m.)* credit
creer *(v.)* to believe
crema *(n., f.)* cream
cremoso *(adj.)* creamy
criar *(v.)* to raise; to rear children or animals
crimen *(n., m.)* crime
crisis *(n., f.)* crisis
cristal *(n., m.)* crystal
cristalino *(adj.)* crystalline
criticar *(v.)* to criticize
cruce *(n., m.)* crossing
cruel *(adj., m./f.)* cruel
crujiente *(adj.)* crusty
cruz *(n., f.)* cross
cruzar *(v.)* to cross
cuadra *(n., f.)* block (city)
cuadro *(n., m.)* picture
cuajada *(n., f.)* farm cheese
cual *(indef. pron. sing.)* which
cuál *(interr. pron. sing.)* which?
cualquier *(indef. adj.)* any
cuando *(adv.)* when
cuándo *(adv.)* when?
cuanto *(adv.)* as much as
cuánto *(pron., interr.)* how much?
cuarto *(n., m.)* room
cubierto *(part.)* covered
cubriendo *(g.)* covering
cubrir *(v.)* to cover
cubrirse *(v.)* to cover
cucharadita *(n., f.)* teaspoon
cuello *(n., m.)* neck
cuenta *(n., f.)*, See also *darse cuenta* account
cuento *(n., m.)* story
cuerda *(n., f.)* cord
cuerdo *(adj.)* sane
cuero *(n., m)* leather
cuidado *(n., m.)* care
cuidar *(v.)* to take care of
cuidarse *(v.)* to be taken care of
culpable *(n., m.)* culprit
cultivar *(v.)* to cultivate
cultura *(n., f.)* culture
cumpleaños *(n., m.)* birthday
cumplido *(part.)* compliment
cumplir *(v.)* to comply; to have a birthday
cuñado *(n., m.)* brother-in-law
cuota *(n., f.)* quota; payment
cura *(n., f.)* cure
cura *(n., m.)* priest
curiosidad *(n., f.)* curiosity
curioso *(n., m.)* curious
curso *(n., m.)* course
cuyo *(relative pron.)* whose

D

dama *(n., f.)* lady
damnificado *(n., m.)* victim
dañarse *(v.)* to be damaged
dando *(g.)* giving
danzar *(v.)* to dance
dar *(v.)* to give
dar la vuelta *(v.)* to flip; to turn around
darse cuenta *(v.)* to realize
dato *(n., m.)* datum; fact
de *(prep.)* of
de modo que *(loc. adv.)* so that
de pura *(loc. adv.)* excessively
de repente *(loc. adv.)* suddenly
de veras *(loc. adv.)* truly
debacle *(n., f.)* debacle
debajo *(adv.)* under
deber *(v.)* to owe
deberes *(n., m.)* homework; chores
débil *(adj. m./f.)* weak
decaer *(v.)* to decay
decidir *(v.)* to decide
decilitro *(n., m.)* deciliter
decir *(v.)* to say
decisión *(n., f.)* decision
declaración *(n., f.)* declaration; statement
dedicado *(adj.)* dedicated
dedicar *(v.)* to dedicate
dedo *(n., m.)* finger
defender *(v.)* to defend
definitivamente *(adv.)* definitively
dejando *(g.)* leaving
dejar *(v.)* to leave
del (de + el) *(prep. + def. art.)* of the
delante de *(adv.)* in front of
delegado *(n., m.)* delegate
delgado *(adj.)* thin
delicado *(adj.)* delicate
delicioso *(adj.)* delicious
delincuente *(n., m.)* delinquent; offender
demanda *(n., f.)* demand
demás *(adj., inv., pl.)* others
demasiado *(adj.)* too much
democráticamente *(adv.)* democratically

demoler *(v.)*	to demolish
demostrar *(v.)*	to show
dentro *(adv.)*	inside
departamento *(n., m.)*	department
depender *(v.)*	to depend
deponer *(v.)*	to depose
deporte *(n., m.)*	sport
depositar *(v.)*	to deposit
depresión *(n., f.)*	depression
depresión *(n., f.)*	depression
deprisa *(adv.)*	quickly; fast
derecha *(n., f.)*	right
derechos *(n., m.)*	rights
derretido *(adj.)*	melted
derretirse *(v.)*	to melt
derrumbar *(v.)*	to bring down
derrumbe *(n., m.)*	collapse
desafortunadamente *(adv.)*	unfortunately
desaguar *(v.)*	to drain
desamparado *(adj.)*	abandoned
desaparecer *(v.)*	to disappear
desaparecido *(part.)*	missing
desapercibido *(adj.)*	unnoticed
desarrollado *(adj.)*	developed
desastre *(n., m.)*	disaster
desayuno *(n., m.)*	breakfast
descansar *(v.)*	to rest
descanso *(n., m.)*	rest
descargar *(v.)*	to discharge
descender *(v.)*	to descend
descendiente *(n., m.)*	descendant
descomponer *(v.)*	to break down
desconcertante *(adj.)*	disconcerting
descongelar *(v.)*	to defrost
desconocido *(n., m.)*	unknown
desconsoladamente *(adv.)*	hopelessly
descubierto *(adj.)*	discovered
descubriendo *(g.)*	discovering
descubrir *(v.)*	to discover
desde *(adv.)*	since
desear *(v.)*	to desire
desempleado *(n., m.)*	unemployed
desempleo *(n., m.)*	unemployment
desenfundar *(v.)*	to draw
deseo *(n., m.)*	desire
desesperado *(adj.)*	desperate
desesperante *(adj., m./f.)*	maddening; infuriating
desfachatez *(n., f.)*	shamelessness; insolence
desgano *(n., m.)*	reluctance
desgracia *(n., f.)*	misfortune
deshacer *(v.)*	to undo
deshonesto *(adj.)*	dishonest
desilusionarse *(v.)*	to be disappointed
deslumbrar *(v.)*	to dazzle
desmayarse *(v.)*	to faint
desobediente *(adj., m./f.)*	disobedient
desocupar *(v.)*	to empty
desorden *(n., m.)*	disorder
desordenado *(adj.)*	disorderly
despacio *(adv.)*	slowly
despedir *(v.)*	to fire from a job
despedirse *(v.)*	to say good-bye
desperdicio *(n., m.)*	waste; remains
despertador *(n., m.)*	alarm clock
despertar *(v.)*	to awake
despertarse *(v.)*	to wake up
despierto *(adj.)*	awake
despilfarrar *(v.)*	to squander
desplazar *(v.)*	to displace
déspota *(adj. m./f.)*	despot
después *(adv.)*	later
destornillador *(n., m.)*	screwdriver
destripador *(n., m.)*	ripper (as in Jack the Ripper)
destrozar *(v.)*	to wreck; to smash
destruido *(adj.)*	destroyed
destruir *(v.)*	to destroy
detective *(n., m.)*	detective
detener *(v.)*	to stop
detenerse *(pron. v.)*	to stop oneself
detenido *(n., m.)*	detained
deterioro *(n., m.)*	deterioration
determinar *(v.)*	to determine
detestar *(v.)*	to hate
detrás *(adv.)*	behind
deuda *(n., f.)*	debt
deudor *(n., m.)*	debtor
devaluar *(v.)*	to devalue
devolver *(v.)*	to return
día *(n., m.)*	day
diabetes *(adj., f.)*	diabetes
diablo *(n., m.)*	devil
diario *(adj.)*	daily
diario *(n., m.)*	newspaper
dibujar *(v.)*	to draw
dibujo *(n., m.)*	drawing
dicho *(part.)*	said
dichoso *(adj.)*	happy
diciendo *(g.)*	saying
dictar *(v.)*	to dictate
diente *(n., m.)*	tooth
diestra, a *(loc. adv.)*	right side
diestramente	skillfully
diferencia *(n., f.)*	difference
diferente *(adj., m./f.)*	different
difícil *(adj., m./f.)*	difficult
dificilísimo *(sup. adj.)*	most difficult
dignarse *(v.)*	to deign
dignidad *(n., f.)*	dignity
dilema *(n., m.)*	dilemma

diluir *(v.)* to dilute
dinero *(n., m.)* money
dinosaurio *(n., m.)* dinosaur
dios *(n., m.)* god
dirección *(n., f.)* direction
directamente *(adv.)* directly
directo *(adj.)* direct
director *(n., m.)* director
dirigente *(n., f./m.)* leader
dirigir *(v.)* to direct
disciplina *(n., f.)* discipline
disco *(n., m.)* record; disk
discoteca *(n., f.)* discotheque
discreto *(adj.)* discreet
disculpa (n.,f.) excuse
discutiendo *(g.)* arguing; discussing
discutir *(v.)* to argue; to discuss
diseñador *(n., m.)* designer
diseño *(n., m.)* design
disfraz *(n., m.)* disguise
disgusto *(n., m.)* displeasure
disimular *(v.)* to pretend
disminuir *(v.)* to diminish
disolver *(v.)* to dissolve
disponer *(v.)* to arrange
dispuesto *(adj.)* ready; available for
distinguir *(v.)* to distinguish
distinto *(adj.)* distinct; different
distraerse *(v.)* to amuse
distraído *(adj.)* distracted; absentminded
distribuir *(v.)* to distribute
divagación *(n., f.)* digression
divertido *(adj.)* amusing
divertir *(v.)* to entertain
divertirse *(pron. v.)* to entertain oneself
divisa *(n., f.)* currency
divorciarse *(pron. v.)* to get divorced
divorcio *(n., m.)* divorce
doctor *(n., m.)* doctor
documental *(n., m.)* documentary
documento *(n., m.)* document
dólar *(n., m.)* dollar
doler *(v.)* to hurt
dolor *(v.)* pain
domingo *(n., m.)* Sunday
don *(n., m.)* Mr.
donar *(v.)* to donate
donde *(adv.)* where
dónde *(adv.)* where?
dormido *(part.)* asleep
dormir *(v.)* to sleep
dormirse *(v.)* to fall asleep
dormitorio *(n., m.)* bedroom
dragón *(n., m.)* dragon
dramático *(adj.)* dramatic
dramatiquísimo *(sup. adj.)* most dramatic
droga *(n., f.)* drug
ducha *(n., f.)* shower
ducharse *(v.)* to take a shower
duda *(n., f.)* doubt
dudar *(v.)* to doubt
dueño *(n., m.)* owner
dulce *(adj., m./f.)* sweet
dulces *(n., m.)* sweets; candy
dulzura *(n., f.)* sweetness
duplicar *(v.)* to duplicate
duque *(n., m.)* duke
durante *(adv.)* during
durazno *(n., m.)* peach
durmiendo *(g.)* sleeping
duro *(adj.)* hard

E

ebrio *(n., m.)* drunk
echar de menos *(v.)* to miss
ecológico *(adj.)* ecological
ecologista *(n., m./f.)* ecologist
económico *(adj.)* economic
economista *(n., m./f.)* economist
economizar *(v.)* to economize
ecuatoriano *(adj.)* Ecuadorian
edad *(n., f.)* age
edificio *(n., m.)* building
editorial *(n., f.)* publishing house
educación *(n., f.)* education
educado *(adj.)* educated
educar *(v.)* to educate
educativo *(n., m.)* educational
efectivo (en) *(adj.)* in cash
efectuar *(v.)* to carry out; to perform
eficiente *(adj., m./f.)* efficient
egoísmo *(n., m.)* selfishness
ejecutivo *(n., m.)* executive
ejemplo *(n., m.)* example
ejercer *(v.)* to exercise
ejercicio *(n., m.)* exercise
ejército *(n., m.)* army
el *(def. art., m., sing.)* the
él *(pers. pron., m., sing.)* he
elaborar *(v.)* to elaborate; to make; to devise
elecciones *(n., m.)* elections
eléctrico *(adj.)* electric
electrodoméstico *(n., m.)* appliance
electrónico *(adj.)* electronic
See also *correo electrónico*
elefante *(n., m.)* elephant
elegante *(adj., m./f.)* elegant
elegantemente *(adv.)* elegantly
elegido *(part.)* elected

elegir *(v.)*	to elect
eliminatorias *(n., f.)*	playoffs
ella *(pers. pron., f., sing.)*	she
ellas *(pers. pron., f., pl.)*	they
ellos *(pers. pron., m., pl.)*	they
embajador *(n., m.)*	ambassador
embarcación *(n., f.)*	boat
embargar *(v.)*	to levy
embargo *(n., m.)*	embargo
emborracharse *(v.)*	to get drunk
embotellamiento *(n., m.)*	traffic jam
emerger *(v.)*	to emerge
emoción *(n., f.)*	emotion
emocionarse *(v.)*	to be moved by something
empacar *(v.)*	to pack
empanada *(n., f.)*	turnover
empaque *(n., m.)*	package
emparedado *(n., m.)*	sandwich
empeñado *(adj.)*	pawned
empeño *(n., m.)*	effort
empeorado *(part.)*	worsened
empeorarse *(v.)*	to get worse
emperatriz *(n., f.)*	empress
empezar *(v.)*	to begin
empleado *(n., m.)*	employee
empleo *(n., m.)*	employment
emprender *(v.)*	to undertake
empresa *(n., f.)*	business
empujando *(g.)*	pushing
empujar *(v.)*	to push
en *(prep.)*	in
enamorado *(adj.)*	in love
enamorar *(v.)*	to court
encabezar *(v.)*	to head
encantar *(v.)*	to like
encarcelado *(adj.)*	imprisoned
encargar *(v.)*	to entrust
encender *(v.)*	to light; to turn on
encendido *(adj.)*	on; lighted
encendiendo *(g.)*	lighting
encerrado *(adj.)*	enclosed
encerrar *(v.)*	to enclose
encima *(adv.)*	on top
encoger *(v.)*	to shrink
encontrado *(part.)*	found
encontrar *(v.)*	to find
encontrarse *(v.)*	to find oneself
encubierto *(part.)*	concealed
encubrir *(v.)*	to conceal
enderezar *(v.)*	to straighten
enemigo *(n., m.)*	enemy
energía *(n., f.)*	energy
enérgicamente *(adv.)*	vigorously
enérgico *(adj.)*	energetic
enero *(n., m.)*	January
enfermarse *(v.)*	to become ill
enfermedad *(n., f.)*	illness
enfermo *(adj.)*	sick
enfermo *(n., m.)*	sick person
enfriar *(v.)*	to chill
enfriarse *(v.)*	to get chilled
enfurecido *(adj.)*	enraged
engañar *(v.)*	to deceive
engaño *(n., m.)*	deceit
engordarse *(v.)*	to get fat
enojado *(adj.)*	angry
enojarse *(v.)*	to get angry
enorme *(adj., m./f.)*	enormous
enormemente *(adv.)*	enormously
ensayar *(v.)*	to practice
ensayo *(n., m.)*	attempt; trial
enseñar *(v.)*	to teach
ensuciarse *(v.)*	to get dirty
entender *(v.)*	to understand
enterarse *(v.)*	to get informed
entero *(adj.)*	entire
entierro *(n., m.)*	burial
entonces *(adv.)*	then
entrada *(n., f.)*	entrance
entrando *(g.)*	entering
entrante *(adj., m./f.)*	coming
entrar *(v.)*	to enter
entre *(prep.)*	between
entrega *(n., f.)*	delivery
entregar *(v.)*	to deliver
entrenado *(part.)*	trained
entrenadora *(n., f.)*	trainer; coach
entrenar *(v.)*	to train; to coach
entretener *(v.)*	to entertain
entretenido *(adj.)*	entertained
entrevista *(n., f.)*	interview
entrevistado *(part.)*	interviewed
entristecerse *(v.)*	to get sad
entrometido *(adj.)*	meddlesome
entusiasmo *(n., m.)*	enthusiasm
envejecer *(v.)*	to age
enviar *(v.)*	to send
envidia *(n., f.)*	envy
envidioso *(adj.)*	envious
envolver *(v.)*	to wrap
equipaje *(n., m.)*	luggage
equipo *(n., m.)*	team
equivaler *(v.)*	to equal
equivocado *(adj.)*	wrong
equivocarse *(v.)*	to be mistaken
erguir *(v.)*	to straighten up
erizo de mar *(n., m.)*	sea urchin
error *(n., m.)*	error
erupción *(n., f.)*	eruption
Es el colmo. *(idiom.)*	You really take the cake.

esa *(adj. dem.; pron., f.)*	that; that one; that thing
esas *(adj. dem.; pron., f., pl.)*	those; those ones; those things
escaleras *(n., f., pl.)*	stairs
escasear *(v.)*	to become scarce
escasez *(n., f.)*	shortage
escena *(n., f.)*	scene
escocés *(adj.)*	Scottish
escoger *(v.)*	to choose
escolar *(adj.)*	school-related
esconderse *(v.)*	to hide
escondido *(part.)*	hidden
escondite *(n., m.)*	hideout
escribiendo *(g.)*	writing
escribir *(v.)*	to write
escrito *(adj.)*	written
escrito *(part.)*	written
escritor *(n., m.)*	writer
escritorio *(n., m.)*	desk
escuchado *(part.)*	listened
escuchando *(g.)*	listening
escuchar *(v.)*	to listen
escuela *(n., f.)*	school
escultura *(n., f.)*	sculpture
ese *(adj. dem.; pron., m.)*	that; that one; that thing
esencial *(adj., m./f.)*	essential
esfera *(n., f.)*	sphere
esfuerzo *(n., m.)*	effort
esfumarse *(v.)*	to vanish
eso *(pron. neut., m.)*	that
esos *(adj. dem.; pron., m., pl.)*	those; those ones; those things
espacial *(adj., m./f.)*	spatial; related to outer space
espacio *(n., m.)*	space
espacioso *(adj.)*	spacious
espada *(n., f.)*	sword
espaguetis *(n., m.)*	spaghetti
espalda *(n., f.)*	back
español *(adj.)*	Spanish
español *(n., m.)*	Spanish language
esparcir *(v.)*	to spread
especial *(adj., m./f.)*	special
especialmente *(adv.)*	especially
especies *(n., f.)*	species
espectáculo *(n., m.)*	spectacle
espectador *(n., m.)*	spectator
espejo *(n., m.)*	mirror
esperando *(g.)*	expecting
esperanza *(n., f.)*	hope
esperar *(v.)*	to expect
espesar *(v.)*	to thicken
espía *(n., m./f.)*	spy
espiritual *(adj., m./f.)*	spiritual
esposa *(n., f.)*	wife
esposas *(n., f., pl.)*	handcuffs
esposo *(n., m.)*	husband
esquema *(n., m.)*	plan; scheme
esquiar *(v.)*	to ski
esquimal *(n., m.)*	Eskimo
esquina *(n., f.)*	corner
esta *(adj. dem.; pron., f.)*	this; this one; this thing
estabilizar *(v.)*	to stabilize
estable *(adj., m./f.)*	stable
establecer *(v.)*	to establish
estación *(n., f.)*	station
estacionado	parked
estacionar *(v.)*	to park
estadística *(n., f.)*	statistics
estado *(n., m.)* See *golpe de estado*	state
estado *(part.)*	been
estafa *(n., f.)*	fraud
estantería *(n., f.)*	bookcase
estar *(v.)*	to be
estas *(adj. dem.; pron., f.)*	these; these ones; these things
este *(adj. dem.; pron., m.)*	this; this one; this thing
esto *(pron. neut., m.)*	this
estos *(adj. dem.; pron., m.)*	these; these ones; these things
estrella *(n., f.)*	star
estrellarse *(v.)*	to crash
estrenar *(v.)*	to premiere
estrépito *(n., m.)*	din
estrepitosamente *(adv.)*	boisterously
estrictamente *(adv.)*	strictly
estricto *(adj.)*	strict
estudiado *(part.)*	studied
estudiando *(g.)*	studying
estudiante *(n., m./f.)*	student
estudiar *(v.)*	to study
estudios *(n., m.)*	studies
estufa *(n., f.)*	stove
estupendamente *(adv.)*	stupendously
estupendo *(adj.)*	stupendous
estupidez *(n., f.)*	stupidity
estúpido *(adj.)*	stupid
eucalipto *(n., m.)*	eucalyptus
euro *(n., m.)*	euro (currency)
Europa *(n., f.)*	Europe
europeo *(adj.)*	European
evacuar *(v.)*	to evacuate
evadir *(v.)*	to avoid
evaluación *(n., f.)*	evaluation
evaluar *(v.)*	to evaluate
evidencia *(n., f.)*	evidence
evidente *(adj., m./f.)*	evident
evitando *(g.)*	avoiding
evitar *(v.)*	to avoid

evolución *(n., f.)*	evolution
exactamente *(adv.)*	exactly
exacto *(adj.)*	exact
examen *(n., m.)*	exam
examinar *(v.)*	to examine
excederse *(v.)*	to exceed
excelente *(adj., m./f.)*	excellent
excepcional *(adj., m./f.)*	exceptional
exclusivo *(adj.)*	exclusive
excursionista *(n., m.)*	excursionist
exigente *(adj., m./f.)*	demanding
exigir *(v.)*	to demand; to require
exilio *(n., m.)*	exile
existir *(v.)*	to exist
éxito *(n., m.)*	success
exitoso *(adj.)*	successful
expandirse *(v.)*	to expand
experiencia *(n., f.)*	experience
experimento *(n., m.)*	experiment
explicación *(n., f.)*	explanation
explicar *(v.)*	to explain
explorador *(n., m.)*	explorer
exportaciones *(n., f.)*	exports
exquisito *(adj.)*	exquisite
exterior *(n., m.)*	exterior
exterminar *(v.)*	to exterminate
externo *(adj.)*	external
extinción *(n., f.)*	extinction
extinguir *(v.)*	to extinguish
extinguirse *(v.)*	to extinguish
extracto *(n., m.)*	extract
extrañar *(v.)*	to miss
extranjero *(n., m.)*	foreigner
extraño *(adj.)*	strange
extraordinario *(adj.)*	extraordinary
extraterrestre *(n., m.)*	extraterrestrial
extraviarse *(v.)*	to get lost; to lose one's way

F

fabricar *(v.)*	to manufacture
fabuloso *(adj.)*	fabulous
fácil *(adj., inv.)*	easy
facilidad *(n., f.)*	facility
factura *(n., f.)*	invoice
facturar *(v.)*	to invoice; to bill
falda *(n., f.)*	skirt
falsificar *(v.)*	to falsify
falso *(adj.)*	false
falta *(n., m.)*	fault
fama *(n., f.)*	fame
familia *(n., f.)*	family
famoso *(adj.)*	famous
fantástico *(adj.)*	fantastic
fascinar *(v.)*	to fascinate
fastidiar *(v.)*	to bother
favor *(n., m.)*	favor
favorito *(adj.)*	favorite
fe *(n., f.)*	faith
febrero *(n., m.)*	February
fecha *(n., f.)*	date
felicidad *(n., f.)*	happiness
felicitar *(v.)*	to congratulate
feliz *(adj., inv.)*	happy
felpa *(n., f.)*	felt
fenicio *(n.)*	Phoenician
fénix *(n., m.)*	phoenix
feo *(adj.)*	ugly
feria *(n., f.)*	fair
ferrocarril *(n., m.)*	railroad
festival *(n., m.)*	festival
fiar *(v.)*	to give credit
fiarse *(v.)*	to trust
ficción *(n., f.)*	fiction
fiebre *(n., f.)*	fever
fiel *(adj., inv.)*	faithful
fiera *(n., f.)*	wild animal
fiesta *(n., f.)*	festival
fijar *(v.)*	to fix
fila *(n., f.)*	row
filmoteca *(n., f.)*	film library
filosofía *(n., f.)*	philosophy
fin *(n., m.)*	end
final *(n., m.)*	final
finalmente *(adv.)*	finally
finamente *(adv.)*	finely
financiero *(adj.)*	financial
finanzas *(n., f., pl.)*	finances
finca *(n., f.)*	farm
fingir *(v.)*	to pretend
finlandés *(adj.)*	Finnish
firmar *(v.)*	to sign
firme *(adj., m./f.)*	firm
fiscal *(n., m.)*	fiscal
física *(n., f.)*	physics
flaco *(adj.)*	thin
flan *(n., m.)*	custard
flauta *(n., f.)*	flute
flojo *(adj.)*	weak
flor *(n., f.)*	flower
florero *(n., m.)*	flower pot
foca *(n., f.)*	seal
forma *(n., f.)*	shape, form
fórmula *(n., f.)*	formula
fortuna *(n., f.)*	fortune
forzado *(part.)*	forced
foto *(n., f.)*	photograph
fotocopiar *(v.)*	to photocopy
fotografía *(n., f.)*	photography
fotográfico *(adj.)*	photographic
fotógrafo *(n., m.)*	photographer

fotosíntesis *(n., f.)*	photosynthesis
fracturar *(v.)*	to fracture
fraguar *(v.)*	to forge
francés *(adj.)*	French
Francia *(n., f.)*	France
franco suizo *(n., m.)*	Swiss franc
frecuencia *(n., f.)*	frequency
frecuente *(adj.)*	frequent
fregadero *(n., m.)*	sink
freír *(v.)*	to fry
fresa *(n., f.)*	strawberry
fresco *(adj.)*	cool air
frescos *(adj.)*	fresh
frío *(n., m.)*	cold
frito *(adj.)*	fried
frotarse *(v.)*	to rub
fruncir *(v.)*	to frown
fruta *(n., f.)*	fruit
fuego *(n., m.)*	fire
fuente *(n., f.)*	source
fuera de *(adv.)*	out from
fuerte *(adj., inv.)*	strong
fuerza *(n., f.)*	force
fugaz *(adj., inv.)*	fleeting
fumar *(v.)*	to smoke
fumigar *(v.)*	to fumigate
función *(n., f.)*	function
funcionar *(v.)*	to function
fundador *(n., m.)*	founder
fundamental *(adj., inv.)*	fundamental
furia *(n., f.)*	furious
furioso *(adj.)*	furious
fusionar *(v.)*	to fuse
fútbol *(n., m.)*	soccer
futbolista *(n., m./f.)*	soccer player
futuro *(n., m.)*	future

G

galaxia *(n., f.)*	galaxy
galleta *(n., f.)*	cookie; cracker
gallo *(n., m.)*	rooster
galón *(n., m.)*	gallon
gana *(n., f.)*	desire
ganado *(n., m.)*	cattle
ganado *(part.)*	won
ganando *(g.)*	winning
ganar *(v.)*	to win
ganso *(n., m.)*	goose
garaje *(n., m.)*	garage
garantizar *(v.)*	to guarantee
garganta *(n., f.)*	throat
garrafa *(n., f.)*	bottle
gas *(n., m.)*	gas
gasolina *(n., f.)*	gasoline
gastado *(part.)*	worn-out
gastar *(v.)*	to spend
gasto *(n., m.)*	expense
gato *(n., m.)*	cat
gaveta *(n., f.)*	drawer
gaviota *(n., f.)*	seagull
gemelos *(n., m.)*	twins
genial *(adj., m./f.)*	genial
genio *(n., m./f.)*	genius
gente *(n., f.)*	people
gentil *(adj., m./f.)*	genteel
geografía *(n., f.)*	geography
gerente *(n., m.)*	manager
gimnasio *(n., m.)*	gymnasium
girar *(v.)*	to spin
gitano *(n., m.)*	gypsy
global *(adj., m./f.)*	global
globo *(n., m.)*	globe
gobernador *(n., m.)*	governor
gobernante *(n., m.)*	ruler
gobernar *(v.)*	to govern
gobierno *(n., m.)*	government
golondrina *(n., f.)*	swallow (bird)
golpe *(n., m.)*	strike
golpe de estado *(n., m.)*	coup d'état; military overthrow
golpear *(v.)*	to hit
gordo *(adj.)*	fat
gorila *(n., m.)*	gorilla
gota *(n., f.)*	drop
gozar *(v.)*	to enjoy
grabar *(v.)*	to record
gracias *(n., f.)*	thanks
gracioso *(adj.)*	funny
grado *(n., m.)*	degree
graduarse *(v.)*	to graduate
gramática *(n., f.)*	grammar
gran *(adj., m./f.)*	great
grande *(adj., m./f.)*	large
grandemente *(adv.)*	largely
granja *(n., f.)*	farm
granjero *(n., m.)*	farmer
grano *(n., m.)*	grain
grasa *(n., f.)*	grease
grasas *(n., f.)*	fatty foods
grave *(adj., m./f.)*	serious
gravedad *(n., f.)*	gravity
gravemente *(adv.)*	gravely
greñas *(n., f.)*	untidy hair
grieta *(n., f.)*	crack
grillo *(n., m.)*	cricket
gris *(adj., m./f.)*	gray
gritando *(g.)*	yelling; screaming
gritar *(v.)*	to yell; to scream
grito *(n., m.)*	yell; scream
grosero *(adj.)*	impolite

grupo *(n., m.)*	group
guanábana *(n., f.)*	soursop (tropical fruit)
guante *(n., m.)*	glove
guapísimo *(sup. adj.)*	very handsome
guapo *(adj.)*	handsome
guardado *(part.)*	kept
guardar *(v.)*	to keep
guardería *(n., f.)*	preschool
guarecerse *(v.)*	to take shelter
guarida *(n., f.)*	den; lair
guerra *(n., f.)*	war
guía *(n., f.)*	guidebook
guía *(n., m.)*	guide
guiar *(v.)*	to guide
guitarra *(n., f.)*	guitar
guitarrista *(n., m./f.)*	guitarist
gustado *(part.)*	liked
gustar *(v.)*	to like; to please
gusto *(n., m.)*	taste
gustosamente *(adv.)*	gladly

H

haber *(v.)*	to have
habilidad *(n., f.)*	ability
habitación *(n., f.)*	room
habitante *(n., m./f.)*	inhabitant
hábito *(n., m.)*	habit
hablando *(g.)*	speaking
hablar *(v.)*	to speak
hacer *(v.)*	to do; to make
hacer caso *(idiom.)*	to obey
hacerse *(v.)*	to pretend to be
hacerse cargo de *(idiom.)*	to take charge of
hacha *(n., m.* if sing., *f.* if pl.)	ax
hacia *(prep.)*	toward
hacienda *(n., f.)*	ranch
haciendo *(g.)*	doing
halagar *(v.)*	to flatter
hambre *(n., m.* if sing., *f.* if pl.)	hunger
hambruna *(n., f.)*	famine
harina *(n., f.)*	flour
hasta *(prep.)*	to
hay See also *haber*	there is; there are
hecho *(n., m.)*	fact
hecho *(part.)*	made
helado *(n., m.)*	ice cream
helicóptero *(n., m.)*	helicopter
hembra *(n., f.)*	female
heredar *(v.)*	to inherit
herencia *(n., f.)*	inheritance
herida *(n., f.)*	wound
herido *(adj.)*	injured; wounded
herir *(v.)*	to wound
hermana *(n., f.)*	sister
hermanita *(n., f.)*	little sister
hermano *(n., m.)*	brother
hermosamente *(adv.)*	beautifully
hermoso *(adj.)*	beautiful
héroe *(n., m.)*	hero
hidrógeno *(n., m.)*	hydrogen
hielo *(n., m.)*	ice
hierba *(n., f.)*	herb
hierro *(n., m.)*	iron
hija *(n., f.)*	daughter
hijo *(n., m.)*	son
hilo *(n., m.)*	thread
hinchar *(v.)*	to swell
hindú *(adj.)*	Hindu
hipócrita *(adj., m./f.)*	hypocritical
hipopótamo *(n., m.)*	hippopotamus
hipoteca *(n., f.)*	mortgage
hipótesis *(n., f.)*	hypothesis
historia *(n., f.)*	history
historiador *(n., m.)*	historian
hoja *(n., f.)*	leaf
Hola. *(interj.)*	Hello.
hombre *(n., m.)*	man
hombro *(n., m.)*	shoulder
homicida *(n., m./f.)*	murderer
honrado *(adj.)*	honest
hora *(n., f.)*	hour
hormiga *(n., f.)*	ant
horno *(n., m.)*	oven
horno microondas *(n., m.)*	microwave oven
horrible *(adj., m./f.)*	horrible
horror *(n., m.)*	horror
hospital *(n., m.)*	hospital
hospitalario *(adj.)*	hospitable
hotel *(n., m.)*	hotel
hoy *(adv.)*	today
hueco *(n., m.)*	hole; hollow
huella *(n., f.)*	print; track
huerta *(n., f.)*	orchard
hueso *(n., m.)*	bone
huésped *(n., m./f.)*	guest
huevo *(n., m.)*	egg
huir *(v.)*	to escape
humanidad *(n., f.)*	humanity
humano *(n., m.)*	human
humedecer *(v.)*	to humidify
húmedo *(adj.)*	humid
humidificador *(n., m.)*	humidifier
humor *(n., m.)*	humor
hundirse *(v.)*	to sink
huracán *(n., m.)*	hurricane

I

idea *(n., f.)*	idea
ideal *(n., m.)*	ideal
identificación *(n., f.)*	identification

idioma *(n., m.)*	language
idiota *(n., m./f.)*	idiot
iglesia *(n., f.)*	church
ignominia *(n., f.)*	ignominy
igual *(adj., m./f.)*	equal
iluminar *(v.)*	to illuminate
ilusión *(n., f.)*	illusion
ilusionado *(adj.)*	hopeful
ilustración *(n., f.)*	illustration
imagen *(n., f.)*	image
imaginación *(n., f.)*	imagination
imaginado *(part.)*	imagined
imaginarse *(v.)*	to imagine
impedir *(v.)*	to impede
imperio *(n., m.)*	empire
imponer *(v.)*	to impose
importante *(adj., m./f.)*	important
importar *(v.)*	to import
imposible *(adj., m./f.)*	impossible
impredecible *(adj., m./f.)*	unpredictable
imprenta *(n., f.)*	press
improbable *(adj.)*	unlikely
imprudente *(adj., m./f.)*	imprudent
impuesto *(n., m.)*	tax
impulso *(n., m.)*	impulse
inauguración *(n., f.)*	inauguration
inca *(n., m.)*	Inca
incendiado *(part.)*	burned
incendiarse *(v.)*	to catch fire
incendio *(n., m.)*	fire
inclinado *(adj.)*	inclined
incluir *(v.)*	to include
inclusive *(adv.)*	inclusive
incomodar *(v.)*	to inconvenience
inconstitucional *(adj., m./f.)*	unconstitutional
increíble *(adj., m./f.)*	incredible
independiente *(adj., m./f.)*	independent
indicar *(v.)*	to indicate
indígena *(n., inv.)*	indigenous; native
indispensable *(adj., m./f.)*	essential
industria *(n., f.)*	industry
inesperado *(adj.)*	unexpected
infarto *(n., m.)*	heart attack
infección *(n., f.)*	infection
infeliz *(adj., m./f.)*	unhappy
infierno *(n., m.)*	hell
inflamado *(adj.)*	inflamed
influencia *(n., f.)*	influence
influir *(v.)*	to influence
informado *(adj.)*	informed; reported
informal *(adj., m./f.)*	informal
informe *(n., m.)*	report
infringir *(v.)*	to infringe
infusión *(n., f.)*	infusion
ingeniero *(n., m./f.)*	engineer
ingenuo *(adj.)*	naive; ingenuous
inglés *(adj.)*	Englishman
inglés *(n., m.)*	English
ingrediente *(n., m.)*	ingredient
iniciar *(v.)*	to initiate
inmediatamente *(adv.)*	immediately
inmediato (de) *(loc. adv.)*	immediate
inmenso *(adj.)*	huge
inmigrante *(n., m.)*	immigrant
inocencia *(n., f.)*	innocence
inofensivo *(adj.)*	inoffensive
inoportuno *(adj.)*	inopportune
inquieto *(adj.)*	restless
inquirir *(v.)*	to inquire
inscribirse *(v.)*	to register
insecto *(n., m.)*	insect
inseparable *(adj., m./f.)*	inseparable
insignificante *(adj., m./f.)*	insignificant
insinuar *(v.)*	to insinuate
insistido *(part.)*	insisted
insistir *(v.)*	to insist
insomnio *(n., m.)*	insomnia
inspirar *(v.)*	to inspire
instalación *(n., f.)*	installation
instante *(n., m.)*	instant
instituto *(n., m.)*	institute
instrumento *(n., m.)*	instrument
insultar *(v.)*	to insult
inteligente *(adj., m./f.)*	intelligent
inteligentísimo *(sup. adj.)*	very intelligent
intensamente *(adv.)*	intensely
intensidad *(n., f.)*	intensity
intentar *(v.)*	to try; to attempt
interés *(n., m.)*	interest
interesante *(adj., m./f.)*	interesting
interesantísimo *(sup. adj.)*	very interesting
interesar *(v.)*	to interest
interesarse *(v.)*	to be interested
internado *(adj.)*	inmate; boarder
interrupción *(n., f.)*	interruption
intervenir *(v.)*	to intervene
intolerante *(adj.)*	intolerant
intrépido *(adj.)*	intrepid
intriga *(adj.)*	intrigue
introducir *(v.)*	to introduce
inundado *(part.)*	flooded
inundarse *(v.)*	to flood
inútil *(adj., m./f.)*	useless
inventado *(adj.)*	invented
inversionista *(n., inv.)*	investor
invertir *(v.)*	to invest
investigación *(n., f.)*	investigation; research
invierno *(n., m.)*	winter
invitación *(adj.)*	invitation
invitado *(n., m.)*	guest

invitar *(v.)* to invite
ir *(v.)* to go
irlandés *(adj.)* Irish
irse *(pron. v.)* to leave
isla *(n., f.)* island
italiano *(adj.)* Italian
izquierda *(n., f.)* left

J

jabalí *(n., m.)* boar
jabón *(n., m.)* soap
jactarse *(v.)* to boast
jamás *(adv.)* never
japonés *(adj.)* Japanese
jardín *(n., m.)* garden
jardinería *(n., f.)* gardening
jarrón *(n., m.)* vase
jaula *(n., f.)* cage
jefe *(n., m.)* chief
jirafa *(n., f.)* giraffe
jornada *(n., f.)* day
joven *(adj., m./f.)* young
joven *(n., m.)* young one
joya *(n., f.)* jewel
juego *(n., m.)* game
jueves *(n., m.)* Thursday
juez *(n., m.)* judge
jugador *(n., m.)* player
jugando *(g.)* playing
jugar *(v.)* to play
jugarse la vida *(v.)* to risk one's life
jugo *(n., m.)* juice
juguete *(n., m.)* toy
juguetón *(adj.)* playful
juicio *(n., m.)* judgment
julio *(n., m.)* July
junio *(n., m.)* June
junto *(adj.)* together
junto *(adv.)* close to
jurado *(n., m.)* jury
justicia *(n., f.)* justice
justo *(adj.)* just

K

kilo *(n., m.)* kilogram
kilómetro *(n., m.)* kilometer

L

la *(def. art., f. sing.)* the
labio *(n., m.)* lip
labor *(n., f.)* labor
lado *(n., m.)* side
ladrar *(v.)* to bark
ladrón *(n., m.)* thief
lago *(n., m.)* lake
laguna *(n., f.)* pond
lamentable *(adj., m./f.)* lamentable
lámpara *(n., f.)* lamp
lana *(n., f.)* wool
langosta *(n., f.)* lobster
lanzar *(v.)* to throw
lápiz *(n., m.)* pencil
largo *(adj.)* long
larguísimo *(sup. adj.)* very long
las *(def. art., f., pl.)* the
lástima *(n., f.)* pity
lastimar *(v.)* to injure
lastimarse *(v.)* to get hurt
lata *(n., f.)* tin can
latín *(n., m.)* Latin
latinoamericano *(adj.)* Latin American
lavabo *(n., m.)* washroom
lavadora *(n., f.)* washing machine
lavaplatos *(n., m.)* dishwasher
lavar *(v.)* to wash
lavarse *(v.)* to wash oneself
le *(obj. pron.)* him *or* her
leal *(adj., m./f.)* loyal
lealtad *(n., f.)* loyalty
lección *(n., f.)* lesson
leche *(n., f.)* milk
leer *(v.)* to read
legal *(adj.)* legal
lejos *(adv.)* distant; far away
lengua *(n., f.)* language
lengua *(n., f.)* tongue
lentamente *(adv.)* slowly
lento *(adj.)* slow
león *(n., m.)* lion
les *(obj. pron.)* them
letrero *(n., m.)* sign
levantar *(v.)* to wake; to lift; to raise
levantarse *(v.)* to wake up
ley *(n., f.)* law
leyendo *(g.)* reading
libanés *(adj.)* Lebanese
liberación *(n., f.)* liberation
liberar *(v.)* to free
libertad *(n., f.)* liberty
libertador *(adj.)* liberator
libra *(n., f.)* pound
libre *(adj., m./f.)* free
librería *(n., f.)* bookstore
libreta *(n., f.)* notebook
libro *(n., m.)* book
licuar *(v.)* to blend
liebre *(n., f.)* hare
limpiar *(v.)* to clean
limpiarse *(v.)* to clean

limpio *(adj.)* clean
lindísimo *(sup. adj.)* very pretty
lindo *(adj.)* pretty
lingote *(n., m.)* ingot
linterna *(n., f.)* flashlight; lantern
liso *(adj.)* flat
lista *(n., f.)* list
listo *(adj.)* ready
literatura *(n., f.)* literature
llamado *(part.)* called
llamar *(v.)* to call
llamarse *(v.)* to be called
llanto *(n., m.)* wail; cry
llave *(n., f.)* key
llegado *(part., adj.)* arrived
llegar *(v.)* to arrive
llenarse *(pron. v.)* to be filled
lleno *(adj.)* full
llevar *(v.)* to carry
llorando *(g.)* crying
llorar *(v.)* to cry
llover *(v.)* to rain
lluvia *(n., f.)* rain
lo *(obj. pron.)* it
lobo *(n., m.)* wolf
local *(adj., m./f.)* local
localizado *(adj.)* located
localizar *(v.)* to locate
loco *(adj.)* crazy
locura *(n., f.)* madness
lodo *(n., m.)* mud
lograr *(v.)* to achieve
loquísimo *(sup. adj.)* very crazy
los *(ind. art., m., pl.)* the
lotería *(n., f.)* lottery
loza *(n., f.)* dishware; china
luchar *(v.)* to fight
lucir *(v.)* to display; to wear; to shine
luego *(adv.)* then
lugar *(n., m.)* place
luminoso *(adj.)* luminous
luna *(n., f.)* moon
lunes *(n., m.)* Monday
lupa *(n., f.)* magnifying glass
luz *(n., f.)* light
luz *(n., f.)* light

M

machete *(n., m.)* machete
macho *(n., m.)* male
madera *(n., f.)* wood
madre *(n., f.)* mother
madriguera *(n., f.)* burrow
madrugada *(n., f.)* early morning
madurez *(n., f.)* maturity
maduro *(adj.)* mature
maestro *(n., m.)* master; teacher
mafia *(n., f.)* mafia
maíz *(n., m.)* corn
mal *(n., m.)* evil
malcriado *(adj.)* bad-mannered
maleta *(n., f.)* suitcase
malo *(adj.)* bad
maltratado *(part.)* mistreated
mamá *(n., f.)* mom
mamífero *(n., m.)* mammal
mamut *(n., m.)* mammoth
mañana *(adv.)* morning
mañana *(n., f.)* tomorrow
manantial *(n., m.)* spring
mancha *(n., f.)* stain
mandar *(v.)* to send
manejar *(v.)* to drive
manera *(n., f.)* way; manner
manicomio *(n., m.)* asylum
manifestación *(n., f.)* demonstration
manifestante *(n., m.)* demonstrator
maniquí *(n., m./f.)* mannequin; model
mano *(n., f.)* hand
mansión *(n., f.)* mansion
mantener *(v.)* to maintain
manzana *(n., f.)* apple
mapa *(n., m.)* map
maquillarse *(v.)* to put on makeup
máquina *(n., f.)* machine
mar *(n., m.)* sea
maratón *(n., f.)* marathon
maravilla *(n., f.)* marvel; wonder
maravillar *(v.)* to amaze
maravilloso *(adj.)* marvelous
marca *(n., f.)* label; brand
marcha *(n., f.)* rally
marchar *(v.)* to walk; to go; to march
marcharse *(v.)* to leave
marco *(n., m.)* frame; framework
marfil *(n., m.)* ivory
marido *(n., m.)* husband
marinero *(n., m.)* sailor
mariposa *(n., f.)* butterfly
marisco *(n., m.)* shellfish
marrano *(n., m.)* pig
marrón *(adj., m./f.)* brown
marroquí *(adj., m./f.)* Moroccan
Marte *(pers. n., m.)* Mars
martes *(n., m.)* Tuesday
marzo *(n., m.)* March
más *(adv.)* more
mas *(prep.)* but
mascota *(n., f.)* mascot; pet

mata *(n., f.)*	plant
matar *(v.)*	to kill
matemáticas *(n., f.)*	mathematics
matemático *(n., m.)*	mathematician
matrícula *(n., f.)*	registration
matrimonio *(n., m.)*	marriage
mayo *(n., m.)*	May
mayor *(adj., m./f.)*	greater
mayoría *(n., f.)*	majority
me *(obj. pron.)*	me
medalla *(n., f.)*	medal
media *(n., f.)*	sock
medicamento *(n., m.)*	medication
medicina *(n., f.)*	medicine
médico *(n., m.)*	physician
medio *(adj.)*	half
medio ambiente *(n., m.)*	environment
medioevo *(n., m.)*	Middle Ages
medios *(n., m.)*	means
medir *(v.)*	to measure
mejor *(adj., m./f.)*	better
mejorado *(part.)*	improved
mejorarse *(v.)*	to get better
memorándum *(n., m.)*	memorandum
memoria *(n., f.)*	memory
memorizar *(v.)*	to memorize
mencionar *(v.)*	to mention
menguar *(v.)*	to decrease
menor *(adj., m./f.)*	smaller
menos *(adv.)*	less
mensaje *(n., m.)*	message
mensual *(adj., m./f.)*	monthly
mentir *(v.)*	to lie
mentira *(n., f.)*	lie
menú *(n., m.)*	menu
menudo	See *a menudo*
mercader *(n., m./f.)*	merchant
mercado *(n., m.)*	market
mercancía *(n., f.)*	merchandise
mero *(n., m.)*	grouper
mes *(n., m.)*	month
mesa *(n., f.)*	table
mesero *(n., m.)*	waiter
mesita *(n., f.)*	little table
meta *(n., f.)*	goal
metal *(n., m.)*	metal
metálico *(adj.)*	metallic
meteorito *(n., m.)*	meteorite
meteoro *(n., m.)*	meteor
meter *(v.)*	to insert
metro *(n., m.)*	meter
mezclar *(v.)*	to mix
mezclarse *(v.)*	to mix
mezquita *(n., f.)*	mosque
mi *(poss. adj., sing.)*	my
mí *(poss. pron.)*	me
mía *(poss. pron. & adj., f., sing.)*	mine
mías *(poss. pron. & adj., f., pl.)*	mine
microbús *(n., m.)*	bus
microondas See also *horno microondas*	microwave
miedo *(n., m.)*	fear
miel *(n., f.)*	honey
mientras *(adv.)*	while
miércoles *(n., m.)*	Wednesday
milagro *(n., m.)*	miracle
mina *(n., f.)*	mine
mineral *(n., m.)*	mineral
ministro *(n., m.)*	minister
minuciosamente *(adv.)*	meticulously
minuto *(n., m.)*	minute
mío *(poss. pron. & adj., m., sing.)*	mine
míos *(poss. pron. & adj., m., pl.)*	mine
mirada *(n., f.)*	look
mirando *(g.)*	looking
mirar *(v.)*	to look
mirarse *(v.)*	to look at oneself
mis *(poss. adj., pl.)*	my
misa *(n., f.)*	mass
miserable *(adj., m./f.)*	miserable
misión *(n., f.)*	mission
misionero *(n., m.)*	missionary
mismo *(adj.)*	same
mitómano *(adj.)*	mythomaniac
mobiliario *(n., m.)*	furniture
mochila *(n., f.)*	backpack
mochila *(n., f.)*	backpack
moda *(n., f.)*	fashion
modelo *(n., m.)*	model
moderno *(adj.)*	modern
modista *(n., f.)*	seamstress
modo	See *de modo que*
mojado *(adj.)*	wet
mojarse *(v.)*	to get wet
molecular *(adj.)*	molecular
moler *(v.)*	to mill
molestar *(v.)*	to bother
momento *(n., m.)*	moment
moneda *(n., f.)*	currency; coin
monitor *(n., m.)*	monitor
monja *(n., f.)*	nun
monopolio *(n., m.)*	monopoly
monstruo *(n., m.)*	monster
monstruosamente *(adv.)*	monstrously
montaña *(n., f.)*	mountain
monumento *(n., m.)*	monument
morder *(v.)*	to bite

mordido *(part.)* bitten
morir *(v.)* to die
moro *(n., m.)* Moor
mostrar *(v.)* to show
moto *(n., f.)* motorcycle
motocicleta *(n., f.)* motorcycle
motor *(n., m.)* motor
mover *(v.)* to move
moverse *(v.)* to move
muchacha *(n., f.)* teenage girl
muchacho *(n., m.)* teenage boy
mucho *(adj.)* many
mudarse *(v.)* to move
mudo *(adj.)* mute
See also *quedarse mudo*
muerte *(n., f.)* death
muerto *(adj.)* dead
muerto *(part.)* dead
muestra *(n., f.)* sample
mujer *(n., f.)* woman
multitud *(n., f.)* multitude
mundial *(adj.)* world
mundo *(n., m.)* world
muñeca *(n., f.)* doll
municipio *(n., m.)* municipality
muriendo *(g.)* dying
muro *(n., m.)* wall
museo *(n., m.)* museum
música *(n., f.)* music
músico *(n., m.)* musician
musulmán *(adj.)* Muslim
muy *(adv.)* very

N

nacer *(v.)* to be born
nacido *(adj.)* born
nacimiento *(n., m.)* birth
nación *(n., f.)* nation
nacional *(adj.)* national
nada *(loc. adv.)* como si ~ like nothing
nada *(loc. adv.)* para ~ for nothing
nada *(pron. indef.)* nothing
nadar *(v.)* to swim
nadie *(pron. indef.)* nobody
naipes *(n., m.)* playing cards
naranja *(n., f.)* orange
naranjo *(n., m.)* orange tree
narcótico *(n., m.)* narcotic
nariz *(n., f.)* nose
natural *(adj., m./f.)* natural
naufragio *(n., m.)* shipwreck
náusea *(n., f.)* nausea
navaja *(n., f.)* pocketknife
navegar *(v.)* to navigate; to sail
Navidad *(n., f.)* Christmas
necesario *(adj.)* necessary
necesitado *(part.)* needed
necesitar *(v.)* to need
necio *(adj.)* irritating; bothersome
negar *(v.)* to deny
negocio *(n., m.)* business
negro *(adj.)* black
nervioso *(adj.)* nervous
nevada *(n., f.)* snowstorm
nevar *(v.)* to snow
nevera *(n., f.)* refrigerator
ni *(conj.)* neither
niebla *(n., f.)* fog
nieto *(n., m.)* grandchild
nieve *(n., f.)* snow
niña *(n., f.)* girl
niñez *(n., f.)* childhood
ningún *(indef. adj.)* no
ninguna *(indef. adj. & pron., f.)* none
ninguno *(indef. adj. & pron., m.)* none
niñito *(n., m.)* little boy
niño *(n., m.)* boy
nivel *(n., m.)* level
noble *(adj., m./f.)* noble; stoic; humane
noche *(n., f.)* night
nombre *(n., m.)* name
norma *(n., f.)* norm
normal *(adj., m./f.)* normal
normalmente *(adv.)* normally
norte *(n., m.)* north
nos *(pers. pron.)* us
nosotras *(pers. pron., f.)* we
nosotros *(pers. pron., m.)* we
nostalgia *(n., f.)* nostalgia
nota *(n., f.)* note
notar *(v.)* to note
noticia *(n., f.)* news
novela *(n., f.)* fiction
novelista *(n., n./f.)* novelist
novia *(n., f.)* girlfriend; bride
novio *(n., m.)* boyfriend; groom
novios *(n., m.)* bride and groom
nube *(n., f.)* cloud
nublado *(adj.)* cloudy
nuera *(n., f.)* daughter-in-law
nuestra *(poss. pron. & adj., f., sing.)* ours
nuestras *(poss. pron. & adj., f., pl.)* ours
nuestro *(poss. pron. & adj., m., sing.)* ours
nuestros *(poss. pron. & adj., m., pl.)* ours

nuevo *(adj.)* new
nuez *(n., f.)* nut
número *(n., m.)* number
nunca *(adv.)* never

O

¡Oh! *(interj.)* Oh!
oasis *(n., m.)* oasis
obedecer *(v.)* to obey
objeto *(n., m.)* object
obra *(n., f.)* work
obrero *(n., m.)* worker
obsequiar *(v.)* to give
observar *(v.)* to observe
obsoleto *(adj.)* obsolete
obstruir *(v.)* to obstruct; to block
obtener *(v.)* to obtain
obvio *(adj.)* obvious
occidental *(adj., inv.)* western
ocultarse *(v.)* to hide
ocupado *(adj.)* occupied
ocupar *(v.)* to occupy
ocurrido *(part.)* occurred
ocurrir *(v.)* to occur
odiar *(v.)* to hate
odioso *(adj.)* odious; hateful
odontólogo *(n., m.)* dentist
ofender *(v.)* to offend
oficial *(adj., m./f.)* official
oficial *(n., m./f.)* officer
oficina *(n., f.)* office
ofrecer *(v.)* to offer
oído *(part.)* heard
oír *(v.)* to hear
Ojalá *(interj.)* I hope that…
ojo *(n., m.)* eye
ola *(n., f.)* wave
oler *(v.)* to smell
oliva *(n., f.)* olive
olla *(n., f.)* pot
olvidadizo *(adj.)* forgetful
olvidado *(adj.)* forgotten
olvidado *(part.)* forgotten
olvidar *(v.)* to forget
onda *(n., f.)* wave
onza *(n., f.)* ounce
operación *(n., f.)* operation
opinar *(v.)* to have an opinion; to think; to believe
oponer *(v.)* to oppose
oportunidad *(n., f.)* opportunity
oprimir *(v.)* to oppress
oración *(n., f.)* prayer
orden *(n., f.)* order
orgánico *(adj.)* organic
organizar *(v.)* to organize
orgullo *(n., m.)* pride
orgulloso *(adj.)* proud
original *(adj., m./f.)* original
orilla *(n., f.)* riverbank
ornitólogo *(n., m.)* ornithologist
oro *(n., m.)* gold
orquesta *(n., f.)* orchestra
os *(pers. pron.)* you
oscurecer *(v.)* to get dark
oscuro *(adj.)* dark
osito *(n., m.)* teddy bear
oso *(n., m.)* bear
otoño *(n., m.)* autumn
otro *(adj.)* another
ovación *(n., f.)* ovation
oveja sheep
oveja *(n., f.)* sheep
oxígeno *(n., m.)* oxygen

P

paciencia *(n., f.)* patience
paciente *(n., m.)* patient
pacífico *(adj.)* peaceful
padre *(n., m.)* father
paella *(n., f.)* traditional Spanish rice dish
pagar *(v.)* to pay
página *(n., f.)* page
país *(n., m.)* country
paisaje *(n., m.)* landscape
pájaro *(n., m.)* bird
palabra *(n., f.)* word
pálido *(adj.)* pale
palo *(n., m.)* stick
paloma *(n., f.)* dove
palomitas de maíz popcorn
pan *(n., m.)* bread
panadería *(n., f.)* bakery
panadero *(n., m.)* baker
panameño *(adj.)* Panamanian
panecillo *(n., m.)* bun
panel solar *(n., m.)* solar panel
pantalón *(n., m.)* pant
pantanoso *(adj.)* marshy
pañuelo *(n., m.)* handkerchief
papa *(n., f.)* potato
papá *(n., m.)* dad
Papa *(n., m.)* Pope
papel *(n., m.)* paper
paquete *(n., m.)* package
par *(n., m.)* pair
para *(prep.)* for
paraguas *(n., m.)* umbrella
paramédico *(n., m.)* paramedic

parar *(v.)*	to stop
pararse *(v.)*	to stop; to stand up
parcela *(n., f.)*	parcel of land
parecer *(v.)*	to seem
parecerse *(v.)*	to be alike
pared *(n., f.)*	wall
parque *(n., m.)*	park
parqueadero *(n., m.)*	parking lot
párroco *(n., m.)*	clergyman
parte *(n., f.)*	part
participar *(v.)*	to participate
partida *(n., f.)*	start (race)
partido *(n., m.)*	party (political)
partido *(part.)*	left
partir *(v.)*	to leave
pasado *(adj.)*	past
pasado *(part.)*	passed
pasaje *(n., m.)*	ticket
pasando *(g.)*	passing
pasaporte *(n., m.)*	passport
pasar *(v.)*	to pass
paseando *(g.)*	wandering
pasear *(v.)*	to promenade
paseo *(n., m.)*	walkway; promenade
pasillo *(n., m.)*	hall; walkway
pasión *(n., f.)*	passion
paso *(n., m.)*	step
pastel *(n., m.)*	pie
pastelero *(n., m.)*	pastry cook
pastilla *(n., f.)*	pill
pastor *(n., m.)*	shepherd
pata *(n., f.)*	leg (animal or furniture)
patata *(n., f.)*	potato
patinar *(v.)*	to skate
patio *(n., m.)*	patio
patrón *(n., m.)*	boss
pavo *(n., m.)*	turkey
paz *(n., f.)*	peace
peatón *(n., m.)*	pedestrian
pecado *(n., m.)*	sin
pedido *(part.)*	asked
pedir *(v.)*	to ask
pegar *(v.)*	to stick
pegarse *(v.)*	to fight
peinado *(part.)*	combed
peinarse *(pron. v.)*	to comb
peine *(n., m.)*	comb
pelar *(v.)*	to peel
pelear *(v.)*	to fight
película *(n., f.)*	movie
peligro *(n., m.)*	danger
peligroso *(adj.)*	dangerous
pelo *(n., m.)*	hair
pelota *(n., f.)*	ball
peluquero *(n., m.)*	barber
pena *(n., f.)*	grief
pensado *(part.)*	thought
pensando *(g.)*	thinking
pensar *(v.)*	to think
pensionarse *(v.)*	to retire
peor *(adj. inv.)*	worse
pequeño *(adj.)*	small
pera *(n., f.)*	pear
perder *(v.)*	to lose
perderse *(v.)*	to get lost
pérdida *(n., f.)*	loss
perdido *(adj.)*	lost
perdido *(part.)*	lost
perdiendo *(g.)*	losing
perdiz *(n., f.)*	partridge
perdonar *(v.)*	to forgive
perezoso *(adj.)*	lazy
perfecto *(adj.)*	perfect
perfume *(n., m.)*	perfume
perico *(n., m.)*	parrot
periódico *(n., m.)*	newspaper
perla *(n., f.)*	pearl
permiso *(n., m.)*	permission
permitido *(part.)*	allowed
permitir *(v.)*	to permit; to allow
pero *(conj.)*	but
perpetuar *(v.)*	to perpetuate
perro *(n., m.)*	dog
perseguir *(v.)*	to pursue
persona *(n., f.)*	person
personalmente *(adv.)*	personally
pertinaz *(adj., m./f.)*	obstinate
pesadilla *(n., f.)*	nightmare
pesado *(adj.)*	heavy
pesar *(v.)* See *a pesar que*	to weigh
pescado *(n., m.)*	fish
pescar *(v.)*	to fish
peseta *(n., f.)*	old Spanish currency
peso *(n., m.)*	currency in some Latin American countries
peso *(n., m.)*	weight
pesquisa *(n., f.)*	investigation
petróleo *(n., m.)*	petroleum; oil
pez *(n., m.)*	fish
pianista *(n., m./f.)*	pianist
piano *(n., m.)*	piano
picar *(v.)*	to chop
pie *(n., m.)*	foot
piedad *(n., f.)*	pity
piedra *(n., f.)*	stone
piedrita *(n., f.)*	pebble
piel *(n., f.)*	skin
pierna *(n., f.)*	leg
piloto *(n., m./f.)*	pilot
pino *(n., m.)*	pine

pintado *(adj.)*	painted
pintar *(v.)*	to paint
pintor *(n., m.)*	painter
pintura *(n., f.)*	painting; paint
pisar *(v.)*	to step
piscina *(n., f.)*	pool
piso *(n., m.)*	apartment; floor
pista *(n., f.)*	clue
pistacho *(n., m.)*	pistachio
pizza *(n., f.)*	pizza
plan *(n., m.)*	plan
planear *(v.)*	to plan
planeta *(n., m.)*	planet
planta *(n., f.)*	plant; factory
plantar *(v.)*	to plant
plástico *(n., m.)*	plastic
plata *(n., f.)*	silver
plátano *(n., m.)*	plantain
platino *(n., m.)*	platinum
plato *(n., m.)*	dish
playa *(n., f.)*	beach
plaza *(n., f.)*	plaza
plazo *(n., m.)*	time limit
plomero *(n., m.)*	plumber
pluma *(n., f.)*	feather
población *(n., f.)*	population
poblar *(v.)*	to populate
pobre *(adj., m./f.)*	poor
poco *(adj.)*	little
podadora *(n., f.)*	lawn mower
poder *(v.)*	to be able
podido *(part.)*	been able
podrido *(part.)*	rotten
podrirse *(v.)*	to rot
poema *(n., m.)*	poem
poesía *(n., f.)*	poetry
poeta *(n., m./f.)*	poet
policía *(n., f.)*	police
policía *(n., m./f.)*	police officer
política *(n., f.)*	politics
político *(n., m.)*	politician
pollo *(n., m.)*	chicken
Polo Norte *(n., m.)*	North Pole
poner *(v.)*	to put; to place
ponerse *(v.)*	to become; to wear
poniendo *(g.)*	placing; putting
popular *(adj., m./f.)*	popular
popularización *(n., f.)*	popularization
por *(prep.)*	by
por qué *(adv. loc.)*	why
porque *(conj.)*	because
porqué *(n., m.)*	reason
portarse *(pron. v.)*	to behave oneself
portátil *(adj., m./f.)*	portable
portería *(n., f.)*	entrance
portero *(n., m.)*	doorman
portugués *(adj.)*	Portuguese
portugués *(n., m.)*	Portuguese language
poseer *(v.)*	to possess
posesionarse *(v.)*	to take possession
posibilidad *(n., f.)*	possibility
posible *(adj., m./f.)*	possible
posición *(n., f.)*	position
postal *(n., f.)*	postcard
poste *(n., m.)*	post
postre *(n., m.)*	dessert
practicar *(v.)*	to practice
prado *(n., m.)*	meadow; field
precio *(n., m.)*	price
precioso *(adj.)*	precious
precipitarse *(v.)*	to rush to do something
preciso *(adj.)*	exact
preferido *(adj.)*	preferred
preferir *(v.)*	to prefer
pregunta *(n., f.)*	question
preguntar *(v.)*	to ask
premiar *(v.)*	to reward
premio *(n., m.)*	prize
prender *(v.)*	to light
preocupado *(adj.)*	worried
preocupar *(v.)*	to worry
preocuparse *(v.)*	to get worried
preparación *(n., f.)*	preparation
preparado (part.)	prepared
preparar *(v.)*	to prepare
presentación *(n., f.)*	presentation
presentar *(v.)*	to present
presentarse *(v.)*	to show up; to introduce himself
presidencial *(adj., inv.)*	presidential
presidente *(n., m.)*	president
preso *(n., m.)*	prisoner
prestado *(adj.)*	loaned; lent
prestar *(v.)*	to lend
prestigio *(n., m.)*	prestige
presuponer *(v.)*	to presuppose; to assume
pretérito *(n., m.)*	past
prevaler *(v.)*	to prevail
prevenir *(v.)*	to prevent
prima *(n., f.)*	cousin
primate *(n., m.)*	primate
primavera *(n., f.)*	spring
primero *(adj.)*	first
primo *(n., m.)*	cousin
princesa *(n., f.)*	princess
principal *(adj., m./f.)*	main
príncipe *(n., m.)*	prince
principio *(n., m.)*	beginning; principle
prisa *(adv.)*	hurry
prisión *(n., f.)*	prison

prisionero *(n., m.)*	prisoner
privado *(adj.)*	private
probablemente *(adv.)*	probably
probado *(part.)*	tried; tested
probar *(v.)*	to try; to test
problema *(n., m.)*	problem
procesador *(n., m.)*	processor
procesión *(n., f.)*	procession
producción *(n., f.)*	production
producir *(v.)*	to produce
producirse *(v.)*	to happen
producto *(n., m.)*	product
profesión *(n., f.)*	profession
profesional *(n., m.)*	professional
profesor *(n., m.)*	professor; teacher
profundamente *(adv.)*	profoundly; deeply
profundidad *(n., f.)*	depth
programa *(n., m.)*	program
prohibido *(adj.)*	prohibited
prohibir *(v.)*	to prohibit
prolongar *(v.)*	to prolong
promesa *(n., f.)*	promise; pledge
prometedor *(adj.)*	promising
prometer *(v.)*	to promise
prometido *(adj.)*	promised
promocionar *(v.)*	to promote
promover *(v.)*	to promote
pronosticar *(v.)*	to prognosticate; to foretell
pronto *(adv.)*	fast; rapidly
propiedad *(n., f.)*	property
propina *(n., f.)*	tip
propio *(adj.)*	one's own
proponer *(v.)*	to propose
propuesta *(n., f.)*	proposal
proseguir *(v.)*	to continue
protector *(n., m.)*	protector
proteger *(v.)*	to protect
protesta *(n., f.)*	demonstration; rally
protestar *(v.)*	to protest
protocolo *(n., m.)*	protocol
proveer *(v.)*	to provide
próximo *(adj.)*	next; near
proyecto *(n., m.)*	project
prudencia *(n., f.)*	prudence; caution
prueba *(n., f.)*	test
psicólogo *(n., m.)*	psychologist
psiquiatra *(n., m./f.)*	psychiatrist
publicación *(n., f.)*	publication
publicado *(part.)*	published
publicar *(v.)*	to publish
publicidad *(n., f.)*	publicity; advertising
público *(n., m.)*	public
pueblo *(n., m.)*	town
puente *(n., m.)*	bridge
puerta *(n., f.)*	door
puerto *(n., m.)*	harbor
pues *(conj.)*	therefore
puesto que *(loc. conj.)*	since
punta *(n., f.)*	point; tip
punto *(n., m.)*	point
puntual *(adj., m./f.)*	punctual
pura	See *de pura*
puro *(adj.)*	pure

Q

que *(indef. pron.)*	that
qué *(interr. pron.)*	what
quedar *(v.)*	to remain
quedarse *(pron. v.)*	to stay
quedarse mudo *(idiom.)*	to be left speechless
quejarse *(v.)*	to complain
quemado (part.)	burned
quemarse *(v.)*	to get burned
querer *(v.)*	to want
querella *(n., f.)*	dispute
querido *(part.)*	wanted
queriendo *(g.)*	wanting
queso *(n., m.)*	cheese
quien *(indef. pron., sing.)*	who
quién *(interr. pron., sing.)*	who
quienes *(indef. pron., pl.)*	who
quiénes *(interr. pron., pl.)*	who
quieto *(adj., m.)*	quiet
química *(n., f.)*	chemistry
quizá(s) *(adv.)*	perhaps

R

rabia *(n., f.)*	rage; anger
radicar *(v.)*	to be rooted
radio *(n., f.)*	radio station
radio *(n., m.)*	radio set
raíz *(n., f.)*	root
rama *(n., f.)*	branch
rana *(n., f.)*	frog
rápidamente *(adv.)*	quickly
rapidez *(n., f.)*	rapidity
rápido *(adj.)*	quick
rasurarse *(v.)*	to shave
ratito *(n., m.)*	in a short while
rato *(n., m.)*	while
ratón *(n., m.)*	mouse
ratoncito *(n., m.)*	little mouse
raza *(n., f.)*	breed; race
razón *(n., f.)*	reason
razonable *(adj., m./f.)*	reasonable
razonar *(v.)*	to reason
reaccionar *(v.)*	to react
reactivo *(n., m.)*	reagent
real *(adj., m./f.)*	real

realidad *(n., f.)* reality
realizar *(v.)* to carry out, to do
realmente *(adv.)* really
reanudado *(part.)* resumed
rebelarse *(v.)* to rebel
rebelde *(n., inv.)* rebel; dissenter
recaer sobre *(v.)* to fall on
recesión *(n., f.)* recession
receta *(n., f.)* prescription; recipe
recibir *(v.)* to receive
recién *(adv.)* recent
recientemente *(adv.)* recently
recipiente *(n., m.)* recipient; container
recluir *(v.)* to imprison
recoger *(v.)* to collect
recogiendo *(g.)* collecting
recomendable *(adj., m./f.)* recommendable; advisable
recomendar *(v.)* to recommend
reconciliado *(part.)* reconciled
reconciliar *(v.)* to reconcile
reconfortante *(adj., m./f.)* comforting
reconocer *(v.)* to recognize
reconstruir *(v.)* to reconstruct
recordar *(v.)* to remember
recorrer *(v.)* to travel around
recorrido *(n., m.)* distance traveled; run
recostado *(adj.) estar ~* to be lying down
rector *(n., m.)* principal (school)
recuerdo *(n., m.)* memory
recuperar *(v.)* to recuperate; to recover
redactando *(g.)* editing; writing
redactor *(n., m.)* editor; journalist; writer
reducir *(v.)* to reduce
reemplazar *(v.)* to replace
reflector *(n., m.)* reflector
reflexionar *(v.)* to reflect; to think
refregar *(v.)* to scrub
refrescante *(adj., m./f.)* refreshing
refrigerador *(n., m.)* refrigerator
refugiarse *(v.)* to find refuge
regalar *(v.)* to give; to present
regalo *(n., m.)* gift
regar *(v.)* to water
región *(n., f.)* region
regresar *(v.)* to return
regularidad *(n., f.)* regularity
regularmente *(adv.)* regularly
rehacer *(v.)* to redo
reina *(n., f.)* queen
reír *(v.)* to laugh
relatividad *(n., f.)* relativity
releer *(v.)* to reread
reloj *(n., m.)* clock; watch
remedio *(n., m.)* remedy
remolacha *(n., f.)* beet
remover *(v.)* to remove
renta *(n., f.)* rent
renunciar *(v.)* to resign
reo *(n., m.)* prisoner; inmate
reparar *(v.)* to repair
reparto *(n., m.)* cast
repasar *(v.)* to review
repelente de insectos *(n., m.)* insect repellent
repente See *de repente*
repetir *(v.)* to repeat
reportaje *(n., m.)* report
reposo *(n., m.)* repose; tranquillity
reprender *(v.)* to scold
reputación *(n., f.)* reputation
requisito *(n., m.)* requirement
resbalarse *(v.)* to slip
rescatar *(v.)* to rescue
resentir *(v.)* to feel the effect; to suffer
reserva *(n., f.)* reservation
resguardarse *(v.)* to take shelter
resolver *(v.)* to solve
respetar *(v.)* to observe; to respect
resplandor *(n., m.)* brightness
responder *(v.)* to respond
respondido *(part.)* responded
responsabilidad *(n., f.)* responsibility
responsable *(adj., m./f.)* responsible
respuesta *(n., f.)* answer
restaurante *(n., m.)* restaurant
resto *(n., m.)* remainder
restringir *(v.)* to restrict
resumen *(n., m.)* summary
resumir *(v.)* to summarize
resurgir *(v.)* to resurge
retener *(v.)* to retain
retirado *(part.)* withdrawn
retirando *(g.)* withdrawing
retirar *(v.)* to retire; to withdraw
retirarse *(v.)* to leave; to go away
retorcer *(v.)* to twist
retornar *(v.)* to return
retraerse *(v.)* to isolate oneself
retroceder *(v.)* to back up; to go back
retrovisor *(n., m.)* rearview mirror
reumatismo *(n., m.)* rheumatism
reunido *(part.)* met
reuniendo *(g.)* gathering
reunión *(n., f.)* meeting
reunir *(v.)* to gather
reunirse *(v.)* to meet
revelador *(n., m.)* developer
revés, al *(loc. adv.)* the other way around
revisar *(v.)* to revise
revista *(n., f.)* magazine

revolución *(n., f.)*	revolution
revólver *(n., m.)*	revolver
revolver *(v.)*	to stir
revuelto *(adj.)*	scrambled; mixed-up
rey *(n., m.)*	king
rezar *(v.)*	to pray
riachuelo *(n., m.)*	brook; stream
rico *(adj.)*	wealthy; rich
riesgo *(n., m.)*	risk
rifa *(n., f.)*	lottery
riñón *(n., m.)*	kidney
río *(n., m.)*	river
riquísimo *(sup. adj.)*	extremely wealthy; very rich
risa *(n., f.)*	laughter
rival *(n., m.)*	rival
robar *(v.)*	to rob; to steal
rodaja *(n., f.)*	slice
rodeado *(adj.)*	surrounded
roer *(v.)*	to gnaw
rogar *(v.)*	to beg; to pray
rojo *(adj.)*	red
romano *(adj.)*	Roman
romántico *(adj.)*	romantic
romper *(v.)*	to break
romperse *(v.)*	to break
rompiendo *(g.)*	breaking
ropa *(n., f.)*	clothes
rostro *(n., m.)*	face
roto *(adj.)*	broken
rubio *(adj.)*	blond
rueda *(n., f.)*	wheel
ruido *(n., m.)*	noise
ruidosamente *(adv.)*	loudly
ruidoso *(adj.)*	noisy
rumbo *(n., m.)*	course
rumor *(n., m.)*	rumor
ruta *(n., f.)*	route

S

sábado *(n., m.)*	Saturday
saber *(v.)*	to know
sabido *(part.)*	known
sabiduría *(n., f.)*	wisdom
sacar *(v.)*	to remove
sacerdote *(n., m.)*	priest
sacrificio *(n., m.)*	sacrifice
sagrado *(adj.)*	sacred
sal *(n., f.)*	salt
sala *(n., f.)*	living room
salario *(n., m.)*	salary
salida *(n., f.)*	exit
salido *(part.)*	left
salir *(v.)*	to leave
salón *(n., m.)*	classroom
salsa *(n., f.)*	sauce
saltamontes *(n., m.)*	grasshopper
saltar *(v.)*	to jump
salud *(n., f.)*	health
saludado *(part.)*	greeted
saludar *(v.)*	to greet
salvadoreño *(adj.)*	Salvadorean
salvar *(v.)*	to save
salvo *(adv.)*	safe
san *(adj.)*	saint
sanar *(v.)*	to heal
sangre *(n., f.)*	blood
sano *(adj.)*	healthy
santiguarse *(v.)*	to cross oneself
santo *(adj.)*	saint
sapo *(n., m.)*	toad
sartén *(n., f.)*	frying pan
satisfacer *(v.)*	to satisfy
satisfecho *(adj.)*	satisfied
se *(pron.)*	itself
secar *(v.)*	to dry
seco *(adj.)*	dry
secretario *(n., m.)*	secretary
secreto *(n., m.)*	secret
sector *(n., m.)*	sector
secundaria *(n., f.)* la escuela ~	high school; secondary school
sed *(n., f.)*	thirst
seda *(n., f.)*	silk
seguir *(v.)*	to continue; to follow
según *(prep.)*	according to
seguro *(adj.)*	sure
selección *(n., f.)*	selection
seleccionado *(part.)*	selected
seleccionar *(v.)*	to select
sellar *(v.)*	to seal
selva *(n., f.)*	jungle
semáforo *(n., m.)*	signal; traffic light
semana *(n., f.)*	week
sembrar *(v.)*	to sow
semilla *(n., f.)*	seed
seña *(n., f.)*	sign
senador *(n., m.)*	senator
sencillez *(n., f.)*	simplicity
señor *(n., m.)*	Mr.; mister
señora *(n., f.)*	Mrs.; missus
señorita *(n., f.)*	Miss; young lady
sentar *(v.)*	to sit down
sentencia *(n., f.)*	sentence
sentido *(n., m.)*	sense
sentido *(part.)*	felt
sentir *(v.)*	to feel
sentirse *(v.)*	to feel
separado *(adj.)*	separated
separarse *(v.)*	to split up
septiembre *(n., m.)*	September
ser *(v.)*	to be

serenata *(n., f.)* serenade
serio *(adj.)* serious
serrote *(n., m.)* handsaw
servicio *(n., m.)* service
servido *(part.)* served
servir *(v.)* to serve
servirse de *(v.)* to use
seta *(n., f.)* mushroom
sí *(adv.)* yes
si *(conj.)* if
sí *(pers. pron.)* me
sicólogo *(n., m.)* psychologist
sido *(part.)* been
siembra *(n., f.)* sowing
siempre *(adv.)* always
siendo *(g.)* being
sierra *(n., f.)* mountain range; saw
siesta *(n., f.)* nap
siglo *(n., m.)* century
siguiente *(adj., m./f.)* following
silencio *(n., m.)* silence
silla *(n., f.)* chair
sillón *(n., m.)* armchair
similar *(adj.)* similar
simpático *(adj.)* nice; cute
simple *(adj., m./f.)* simple
simultáneamente *(adv.)* simultaneously
sin *(prep.)* without
sincero *(adj.)* sincere
sindicato *(n., m.)* union
sinfonía *(n., f.)* symphony
siniestra, a *(loc. adv.)* left side
sino *(conj.)* but
síntesis *(n., f.)* synthesis
síntoma *(n., m.)* symptom
sirviendo *(g.)* serving
sistema *(n., m.)* system
sitio *(n., m.)* place
situación *(n., f.)* situation
situar *(v.)* to situate
sobrar *(v.)* to exceed; to be left over
sobre *(n., m.)* envelope
sobre *(prep.)* on
sobresalir *(v.)* to excel
sobrevenir *(v.)* to happen unexpectedly
sobrina *(n., f.)* niece
sobrino *(n., m.)* nephew
social *(adj., m/f.)* social
sociedad *(n., f.)* society
socio *(n., f.)* partner; associate
socorrer *(v.)* to help
sofá *(n., m.)* sofa
sofreír *(v.)* to fry
sol *(n., m.)* sun
solar *(adj.)* solar
soldado *(n., m.)* soldier
soleado *(adj.)* sunny
solicitud *(n., f.)* request
solo *(adj.)* alone
sólo *(adv.)* only
soltar *(v.)* to release
soltero *(adj.)* single (man)
solución *(n., f.)* solution
sombrero *(n., m.)* hat
sonambulismo *(n., m.)* sleepwalking
sonando *(g.)* sounding; ringing
sonar *(n., m.)* sonar
soñar *(v.)* to dream
sonar *(v.)* to sound
sonido *(n., m.)* sound
sonora *(adj.)* onda~ sound wave
sonreír *(v.)* to smile
sonrisa *(n., f.)* smile
sopa *(n., f.)* soup
sopor *(n., m.)* torpor
sor *(n., f.)* sister (addressing a nun)
sorprender *(v.)* to surprise
sorprenderse *(v.)* to be surprised
sorprendido *(adj.)* surprised
sorpresa *(n., f.)* surprise
sosegar *(v.)* to calm
sospechoso *(n., m.)* suspicious
sostener *(v.)* to maintain
sótano *(n., m.)* basement
su *(pos. adj.)* its
suave *(adj., m./f.)* soft; smooth
suavidad *(n., f.)* softness; smoothness
subdesarrollado *(adj.)* underdeveloped
subido *(part.)* risen
subir *(v.)* to rise
subirse *(v.)* to climb up; to board
submarino *(adj.)* underwater
submarino *(n., m.)* submarine
suceder *(v.)* to happen
suceso *(n., m.)* event
sucio *(adj.)* dirty
sucursal *(n., f.)* branch office
sueco *(adj.)* Swedish
suegra *(n., f.)* mother-in-law
suegro *(n., m.)* father-in-law
suela *(n., f.)* sole
sueldo *(n., m.)* salary
suelo *(n., m.)* floor
sueño *(n., m.)* dream
suerte *(n., f.)* luck
suficiente *(adj., m./f.)* sufficient
sufrir *(v.)* to suffer
sugerir *(v.)* to suggest
suizo *(adj.)* Swiss
sumergir *(v.)* to submerge
superar *(v.)* to surpass; to transcend
superfluo *(adj.)* superfluous

supermercado *(n., m.)* supermarket
superstición *(n., f.)* superstition
suplicar *(v.)* to beg
suponer *(v.)* to suppose
sur *(n., m.)* south
sus *(pos. adj.)* their
suscripción *(n., f.)* subscription
sustituir *(v.)* to substitute
susto *(n., m.)* scare
sutil *(adj., m./f.)* subtle
suya *(poss. pron. & adj., f., sing.)* hers; yours
suyas *(poss. pron. & adj., f., pl.)* theirs; yours
suyo *(poss. pron. & adj., m., sing.)* his; yours
suyos *(poss. pron. & adj., m., pl.)* theirs; yours

T

tabaco *(n., m.)* tobacco
tablero *(n., m.)* blackboard
tacañísimo *(sup. adj.)* extremely tightwad
tacaño *(adj.)* tightwad
tal *(adj., m./f.)* such
taladro *(n., m.)* drill
talento *(n., m.)* talent
taller *(n., m.)* repair shop
tamal *(n., m.)* corn dish
también *(adv.)* also
tambor *(n., m.)* drum
tampoco *(adv.)* neither
tan *(adv.)* so
tango *(n., m.)* tango
tanque *(n., m.)* tank
tanto *(adj.)* so much
tanto *(adv.)* so much
tapar *(v.)* to cover
tapete *(n., m.)* rug
tapiz *(n., m.)* tapestry
tardar *(v.)* to delay
tarde *(adv.)* late
tarde *(n., f.)* afternoon
tarea *(n., f.)* task; homework
tarjeta *(n., f.)* card
tasa de interés *(n., f.)* interest rate
taxi *(n., m.)* taxi
taxista *(n., m./f.)* cabdriver
taza *(n., f.)* cup
té *(n., m.)* tea
te *(pers. pron.)* you
teatro *(n., m.)* theater
techo *(n., m.)* ceiling; roof
técnico *(n., m.)* technician
tele *(n., f.)* television
telefónico *(adj.)* telephonic
teléfono *(n., m.)* telephone
televisión *(n., f.)* television
televisor *(n., m.)* television set
tema *(n., m.)* topic
temer *(v.)* to fear
temible *(adj.)* fearsome
temperatura *(n., f.)* temperature
tempestad *(n., f.)* storm
temporada *(n., f.)* season
temprano *(adv.)* early
tender *(v.)* ~ la cama to make the bed
tener *(v.)* to have
tenido *(part.)* had
tenis *(n., m.)* tennis
tensión *(n., f.)* tension
tenue *(adj., m./f.)* tenuous; weak
teorema *(n., m.)* theorem
teoría *(n., f.)* theory
terminado *(part.)* finished
terminar *(v.)* to finish
término *(n., m.)* term
ternura *(n., f.)* tenderness
terremoto *(n., m.)* earthquake
terreno *(n., m.)* land; terrain
terrible *(adj., m./f.)* terrible
territorio *(n., m.)* territory
tertulia *(n., f.)* social gathering
tesis *(n., f.)* thesis
testigo *(n., m.)* witness
ti *(pers. pron.)* you
tía *(n., f.)* aunt
tiempo *(n., m.)* time
tienda *(n., f.)* store
tiernamente *(adv.)* tenderly
tierra *(n., f.)* earth; land
tigre *(n., m.)* tiger
timbrar *(v.)* to stamp
timidez *(n., f.)* shyness
tío *(n., m.)* uncle
típico *(adj.)* typical
tipo *(n., m.)* type
tirar *(v.)* to throw
tiritar *(v.)* to shiver
toalla *(n., f.)* towel
tocando *(g.)* playing (instrument)
tocar *(v.)* to play (instrument)
todavía *(adv.)* still
todo *(adj.)* all
tomado *(part.)* taken
tomarse *(v.)* to take; to drink
tomate *(n., m.)* tomato
tontería *(n., f.)* foolishness
tonto *(adj.)* silly
tormenta *(n., f.)* storm

tornando *(g.)*	becoming
toro *(n., m.)*	bull
torre *(n., f.)*	tower
torrencial *(adj., m./f.)*	torrential
torrencialmente *(adv.)*	tempestuously
torta *(n., f.)*	pastry; tart
tortilla *(n., f.)*	tortilla
tortuga *(n., f.)*	tortoise
tostada *(n., f.)*	toast
trabajador *(n., m.)*	worker
trabajando *(g.)*	working
trabajar *(v.)*	to work
trabajo *(n., m.)*	work
traer *(v.)*	to bring
tráfico *(n., m.)*	traffic
traje *(n., m.)*	suit
trampa *(n., f.)*	trap
tranquilizar *(v.)*	to calm down
tranquilo *(adj.)*	calm; tranquil
transbordador *(n., m.)*	shuttle
transcurso *(n., m.)*	course
transformarse *(v.)*	to convert; to turn into something
transitar *(v.)*	to transit
transmisión *(n., f.)*	transmission; broadcast
transparente *(adj., m./f.)*	transparent
tranvía *(n., m.)*	trolley
tras *(prep.)*	after
trasquilado *(adj.)*	sheared
trasto *(n., m.)*	stuff
tratado *(adj.)*	treated
tratar *(v.)*	to try; to treat
tratarse *(v.)* de	to be about
trato *(n., m.)*	deal
tren *(n., m.)*	train
trigo *(n., m.)*	wheat
triste *(adj., m./f.)*	sad
tristeza *(n., f.)*	sadness
tronco *(n., m.)*	trunk
tropa *(n., f.)*	troop
tropezado *(part.)*	tripped
tropezar *(v.)*	to trip
tropical *(adj., m./f.)*	tropical
trópico *(n., m.)*	tropics
truco *(n., m.)*	trick
trueno *(n., m.)*	thunder
tú *(pers. pron.)*	you
tu *(poss. adj.)*	your
tubería *(n., f.)*	plumbing
tumba *(n., f.)*	tomb
túnel *(n., m.)*	tunnel
turista *(n., m./f.)*	tourist
turístico *(adj.)* lugares ~	tourist places
turnarse *(v.)*	to take turns
tus *(poss. adj.)*	your
tuya *(poss. pron. & adj., f., sing.)*	yours; of yours
tuyas *(poss. pron. & adj., f., pl.)*	yours; of yours
tuyo *(poss. pron. & adj., m., sing.)*	yours; of yours
tuyos *(poss. pron. & adj., m., pl.)*	yours; of yours

U

ubicar *(v.)*	to locate
último *(adj.)*	last
un *(ind. art.)*	a
una *(ind. art.)*	a
unas *(ind. art., f.)*	some
únicamente *(adv.)*	only
único *(adj.)*	unique
unido *(adj.)*	united
universidad *(n., f.)*	university
unos *(ind. art., m.)*	some
urgencia *(n., f.)*	urgency
urgente *(adj., m./f.)*	urgent
urgentemente *(adv.)*	urgently
usado *(adj.)*	used
usado *(part.)*	used
usar *(v.)*	to use
uso *(n., m.)*	use; usage
usted *(pers. pron., sing.)*	you
ustedes *(pers. pron., pl.)*	you
útil *(adj.)*	useful
utilizando *(g.)*	using
utilizar *(v.)*	to use
uva *(n., f.)*	grape

V

¡Vale! *(interj.)*	OK!
vaca *(n., f.)*	cow
vacaciones *(n., f.)*	holidays
vacío *(adj.)*	empty
vacuna *(n., f.)*	vaccine
valentía *(n., f.)*	courage
valer *(v.)*	to be worth
valiente *(adj., m./f.)*	brave
valientísimo *(sup. adj.)*	extremely brave
valioso *(adj.)*	valuable
valor *(n., m.)*	value
vanidoso *(adj.)*	vain
vano *(adj.)*	vain
vapor *(n., m.)*	vapor
variado *(adj.)*	varied
variar *(v.)*	to vary
varios *(adj.)*	several
vaso *(n., m.)*	glass (cup)
vasto *(adj.)*	vast

vecino *(n., m.)* neighbor
vegetación *(n., f.)* vegetation
vela *(n., f.)* sail
velada *(n., f.)* party
velocidad *(n., f.)* speed; velocity
veloz *(adj., m./f.)* fast
venado *(n., m.)* deer
vencer *(v.)* to vanquish
vendaval *(n., m.)* gale
vendedor *(n., m.)* salesman
vendedora *(n., f.)* saleswoman
vender *(v.)* to sell
vendido *(adj.)* sold
venido *(part.)* come
venir *(v.)* to come
venta *(n., f.)* sale
ventana *(n., f.)* window
ver *(v.)* to see
verano *(n., m.)* summer
verbo *(n., m.)* verb
verdad *(n., f.)* truth
verdaderamente *(adv.)* truly
verde *(adj., m./f.)* green
verdura green (vegetable)
verdura *(n., f.)* vegetable
veredicto *(n., m.)* verdict
verídico *(adj.)* truthful
verse *(pron. v.)* to see oneself
versión *(n., f.)* version
verso *(n., m.)* verse
vespertino *(adj.)* vespertine; evening
vestido *(adj.)* dressed
vestido *(n., m.)* dress
vestir *(v.)* to dress
vestirse *(v.)* to dress oneself
veterinario *(n., m.)* veterinarian
vez *(n., f.)* time
vía *(n., f.)* way
viajado *(part.)* traveled
viajar *(v.)* to travel
viaje *(n., m.)* trip
vicepresidencia *(n., f.)* vice-presidency
víctima *(n., f.)* victim
vida *(n., f.)* life
vidrio *(n., m.)* glass
viejito *(n., m.)* elderly man (affectionate)
viejo *(adj.)* old
viendo *(g.)* seeing
viento *(n., m.)* wind
viernes *(n., m.)* Friday
vigilante *(n., m./f.)* security guard
vinagre *(n., m.)* vinegar
viniendo *(g.)* coming
vino *(n., m.)* wine
violencia *(n., f.)* violence
violonchelo *(n., m.)* violoncello
virgen *(n., f.)* virgin
virtud *(n., f.)* virtue
viruela *(n., f.)* smallpox
virus *(n., m.)* virus
visita *(n., f.)* visit
visitado *(part.)* visited
visitando *(g.)* visiting
visitante *(n., m.)* visitor
visitar *(v.)* to visit
vista *(n., f.)* view
visto *(part.)* seen
vitamina *(n., f.)* vitamin
viuda *(n., f.)* widow
víveres *(n., m.)* provisions
vivido *(part.)* lived
vividor *(n., m.)* freeloader
vivienda *(n., f.)* dwelling
viviendo *(g.)* living
vivir *(v.)* to live
vivo *(adj.)* alive
vocabulario *(n., m.)* vocabulary
volador *(adj.)* flying
volar *(v.)* to fly
volcán *(n., m.)* volcano
voleibol *(n., m.)* volleyball
volumen *(n., m.)* volume
voluntad *(n., f.)* will
volver *(v.)* to return
volverse *(v.)* to become
vosotras *(pers. pron., f., pl.)* you
vosotros *(pers. pron., m., pl.)* you
voto *(n., m.)* vote
voz *(n., f.)* voice
vuelta See also *dar la vuelta* turn
vuelto *(part.)* returned
vuestra *(poss. pron., f., sing.)* yours
vuestras *(poss. pron., f., pl.)* yours
vuestro *(poss. pron., m., sing.)* yours
vuestros *(poss. pron., m., pl.)* yours

Y

ya *(adv.)* already
yate *(n., m.)* yacht
yegua *(n., f.)* mare
yerno *(n., m.)* son-in-law
yo *(pers. pron.)* I

Z

zapato *(n., m.)* shoe
zarpado *(part.)* sailed
zarpar *(v.)* to sail
zoológico *(n., m.)* zoo
zurcir *(v.)* to darn